CLIFTON M. MILLER LIBRARY
Washington College
Chestertown, MD 21620

Presented By
U.S. Japanese
Cultural Center

A BURIED PAST

A BURIED PAST

AN ANNOTATED BIBLIOGRAPHY OF THE JAPANESE AMERICAN RESEARCH PROJECT COLLECTION

Compiled by

YUJI ICHIOKA
YASUO SAKATA
NOBUYA TSUCHIDA
ERI YASUHARA

*Research Associates
Asian American Studies Center
U.C.L.A.*

Compilers assisted by
Janice Roswell, Judith Roswell, & Lillemor Lindh

UNIVERSITY OF CALIFORNIA PRESS
BERKELEY, LOS ANGELES, LONDON

University of California Press
Berkeley and Los Angeles, California

University of California Press, Ltd.
London, England

Copyright © 1974, by
The Regents of the University of California

ISBN: 0-520-024541-5
Library of Congress Catalog Card Number: 73-83063

Printed in the United States of America

CONTENTS

ACKNOWLEDGMENTS 1

INTRODUCTION 3

GLOSSARY OF JAPANESE TERMS 17

I. JAPANESE GOVERNMENT ARCHIVAL DOCUMENTS, NOS. 1–78   19
    1. Foreign Ministry, 19
    2. Consulates, 34

II. BACKGROUND TO EMIGRATION, NOS. 79–148   36
    1. Origins and Causes, 36
    2. Guides to America, 42
    3. Emigration Journals, 46
    4. Other Journals and Magazines, 47

III. JAPANESE EXCLUSION MOVEMENT, NOS. 149–253   50
    1. General Works, 50
    2. Alien Land Laws, 58
    3. 1924 Immigration Act, 60
    4. U.S.-Japan Relations, 65

IV. GENERAL HISTORICAL WORKS, NOS. 254–324   69
    1. Overseas Japanese, 69
    2. Japanese in America, 71
    3. Regional and Local Histories, 74
    4. Histories by Prefectural Origins, 79

V. ECONOMICS, NOS. 325–351   83
    1. Published Works, 83
    2. Records of Organization, 85

VI. RELIGION, NOS. 352–453   88
    1. General Histories, 88
    2. Specific Church Histories, Albums, and Booklets, 90
    3. Church Records, 92
    4. Religious Periodicals and Church Bulletins, 93
    5. Other Published Works, 96

VII. SECOND GENERATION, NOS. 454–507 103
    1. Education, 103
        A. Japanese Language Schools, 104
        B. Textbooks, 108
        C. Study in Japan, 110
    2. Japanese American Citizens League, 111

VIII. SOCIO-CULTURAL MATERIALS, NOS. 508–537 112
    1. Published Works, 112
    2. Records of Organizations, 115

IX. JAPANESE ASSOCIATIONS, NOS. 538–568 117
    1. Published Works and Bulletins, 118
    2. Records of Japanese Associations, 119

X. LITERATURE AND POETRY, NOS. 569–620 124
    1. Fiction and Literary Essays, 124
    2. Poetry, 126

XI. NEWSPAPERS, PERIODICALS, YEARBOOKS, DIRECTORIES, AND
WHO'S WHOS, NOS. 621–778 132
    1. Newspapers, 132
    2. Published Newspaper Articles and Newspaper Clipping Files, 140
    3. Periodicals, 141
    4. Yearbooks and Special Publications, 145
    5. Directories, 147
    6. Who's Whos, 151

XII. AUTOBIOGRAPHIES AND BIOGRAPHIES, NOS. 779–838 . . . 153

XIII. PERSONAL PAPERS, NOS. 839–893 163

XIV. WORLD WAR II AND INTERNMENT, NOS. 894–956 173
    1. Assembly Center and Camp Newspapers, 173
    2. Other Published Works, 175
    3. Special Papers and Documents, 178

XV. PUBLISHED PHOTOGRAPHIC ALBUMS, NOS. 957–974 181

XVI. ORAL HISTORY TAPES, NOS. 975–1281 184

XVII. DISSERTATIONS AND THESES, NOS. 1282–1436 193

XVIII. MISCELLANEOUS, NOS. 1437–1462 205

INDEX 209

ACKNOWLEDGMENTS

This annotated bibliography has been compiled by four individuals with the financial support of the Asian American Studies Center. Excluding Yasuo Sakata, we have no past or present connections with the Japanese American Research Project other than having annotated the project collection, and this publication is not a part of the projected publication series of the project. In the course of compiling it, we have received assistance from a number of persons to whom we would like to express our sincere appreciation: David M. Farquhar, Associate Professor of History, for his initial counsel; Harry K. Honda, editor of the *Pacific Citizen*, for helpful information; Seizo Oka, Karl Yoneda, and Mr. and Mrs. Minoru Fujita for allowing us to tap their knowledge of personalities and documents; Miki Fujita for toiling through the summer of 1972 to type the first draft; and Philip Huang, the former acting director, and past and present members of the Asian American Studies Center for supporting our endeavor. Finally, we gratefully acknowledge the financial support of the Japanese American Research Project Committee of the Japanese American Citizens League for the preparation of the final manuscript copy. Although we have tried to avoid them, we no doubt have been guilty of errors, and we alone of course assume all responsibility for them.

Like other recent books on Japanese-Americans, this bibliography is an outgrowth of current interest in Japanese-Americans and other minorities. Our ignorance of the history of Japanese immigrants and their descendants is due not to a lack of historical sources, but to the failure of past and present researchers to study existing Japanese-language sources. We hope that this annotated bibliography will stimulate future in-depth studies of lasting value. At this juncture, the history of Japanese immigrants, in our considered opinion, remains essentially a buried past awaiting the serious student.

Asian American Studies Center
University of California at Los Angeles
April, 1973

YUJI ICHIOKA
YASUO SAKATA
NOBUYA TSUCHIDA
ERI YASUHARA

INTRODUCTION

In recent years an intense interest in the experience of minority groups has emerged, not only among minority groups themselves but also in segments of the larger society. The flood of new publications on and by minorities reflects this interest. Ideally it should entail a search for a meaningful historical past—the debunking of old distortions and myths, the uncovering of hitherto neglected or unknown facts, and the construction of a new interpretation of that past. Interest in Japanese-Americans is no exception to the general trend. Absorbed as they are in the question of their ethnic identity, Japanese-Americans too are looking at their past. Rather than reexamining their entire history, however, they, (and others) have tended to highlight the World War II internment ordeal. Reflecting this preoccupation, various books on Japanese-Americans—some of dubious value—have been published in the last several years.

Most of these books fall into two major categories. First, there are sociological works written within a specific theoretical framework. Depending heavily on secondary historical works, they do not break new ground in historical knowledge of the Japanese immigrants and their descendants but rather rearrange established facts into a modified interpretative order. The best example is the recent book by William Petersen, *Japanese Americans* (New York, 1971). Similar works are Harry L. Kitano, *Japanese Americans: The Evolution of a Subculture* (Englewood Cliffs, N.J., 1969); Stanford M. Lyman, *The Asian in the West* (Reno, 1970); and Ivan H. Light, *Ethnic Enterprise in America: Business and Welfare among Chinese, Japanese, and Blacks* (Berkeley and Los Angeles, 1972). Secondly, there are works specifically devoted to some aspect of the wartime internment experience—these are the most numerous and of very uneven quality. They are Edward H. Spicer et al., *Impounded People: Japanese-Americans in the Relocation Centers* (Tucson, 1969); Audrie Girdner and Anne Loftis, *The Great Betrayal* (New York, 1969); Anthony L. Lehman, *Birthright of Barbed Wire: The Santa Anita Assembly Center for the Japanese* (Los Angeles, 1970); Dillon S. Myer, *Uprooted Americans: The Japanese Americans and the*

War Relocation Authority during World War II (Tucson, 1971); Paul Bailey, *City in the Sun: The Japanese Concentration Camp at Poston, Arizona* (Los Angeles, 1971); and Roger Daniels, *Concentration Camps USA: Japanese Americans and World War II* (New York, 1971). Past studies of Japanese-Americans have overwhelmingly concentrated on what happened to them. For example, we know a great deal about the Japanese exclusion movement that predated the internment camps. But we know very little about how the Japanese immigrants, the excluded, felt and thought about being excluded. In this sense, the recent books on internment are an extension of past historiography. Once again books on what happened to the Japanese have rolled off the presses. That the internment experience deserves serious study is beyond dispute. But the history of the Japanese in America dates back to the 19th century, and if the current interest remains predominantly restricted to that experience it can lead only to a myopic view of Japanese-American history.

A few publications fit into neither of the foregoing categories. William K. Hosokawa, *Nisei: The Quiet Americans* (New York, 1969), is a popular personalized narrative about the leaders and activities of the Japanese American Citizens League, the national organization of the second generation. Dennis M. Ogawa, *From Japs to Japanese: The Evolution of Japanese-American Stereotypes* (Berkeley, 1971), is a brief, superficial treatment of the stereotypic images of Japanese-Americans. Out of all the recent books, only two have the merit of contributing to our historical knowledge of the Japanese before World War II: Hilary Conroy and T. Scott Miyakawa (eds.), *East across the Pacific* (Santa Barbara, 1972), a collection of historical and sociological essays on Japanese-Americans, and Akira Iriye, *Pacific Estrangement: Japanese and American Expansion, 1897–1911* (Cambridge, 1972), a study of Japanese and American ideas and attitudes relating to expansion into the Pacific.

A SURVEY OF THE HISTORICAL LITERATURE

A broad survey of the English-language secondary historical literature preceding these recent publications points to the need to shift our attention to the Japanese immigrants before World War II. Practically the entire corpus of the historical literature on Japanese-Americans (excluding those in Hawaii) is tied directly or indirectly to the past exclusion movement. Some works concentrate on the exclusion movement. Among these are such scholarly studies as Raymond L. Buell, "The Development of the Anti-Japanese Agitation in the United States,"

Political Science Quarterly, 37:4 (December, 1922) and 38:1 (March, 1923); Jacobus tenBroek et al., "Genesis," *Prejudice, War and the Constitution*, part I(Berkeley and Los Angeles, 1954); and Roger Daniels, *The Politics of Prejudice* (Berkeley and Los Angeles, 1962). These studies set out to explain the origins, causes, and development of the exclusion movement. Others restrict themselves to one aspect of the movement. For example, there are specialized studies of the California land tenure controversy, such as Thomas A. Bailey, "California, Japan, and the Alien Land Legislation of 1913," *Pacific Historical Review*, 1:1 (March, 1932); Spencer C. Olin, Jr., "European Immigrant and Oriental Alien: Acceptance and Rejection by the California Legislature of 1913," *Pacific Historical Review*, 35:3 (August, 1966); Paolo E. Coletta, " 'The Most Thankless Task': Bryan and the California Alien Land Legislation," *Pacific Historical Review*, 36:2 (May, 1967); and Dudley O. McGovney, "The Anti-Japanese Land Laws of California and Ten Other States," and Edwin E. Ferguson, "The California Alien Land Law and the 14th Amendment," *California Law Review*, 35:1 (March, 1947). Though perfectly valid studies, all of these—and others like them—tell us nothing about Japanese immigrants except that they were objects of the exclusion movement.

Another set of works adds an international relations context to the study of the exclusion movement. Perhaps the best example is Thomas A. Bailey, *Theodore Roosevelt and the Japanese-American Crises* (Stanford, 1934), in which the 1906 San Francisco school question is placed within the context of the U.S.-Japan relations. Examining additional sources, Raymond A. Esthus, *Theodore Roosevelt and Japan* (Seattle, 1966), and Charles E. Neu, *An Uncertain Friendship: Theodore Roosevelt and Japan, 1906–1909* (Cambridge, 1967), do the same thing for this and other topics. Other studies along this line are Raymond L. Buell, *Japanese Immigration* (Boston, 1924), and Eleanor Tupper and George E. McReynolds, *Japan in American Public Opinion* (New York, 1937). Diplomatic histories, such as A. Whitney Griswold, *The Far Eastern Policy of the United States* (New York, 1939), Hikomatsu Kamikawa (ed.), *Japanese-American Diplomatic Relations in the Meiji-Taisho Era* (Tokyo, 1958), and Akira Iriye, *Across the Pacific: An Inner History of American-East Asian Relations* (New York, 1967), also discuss the Japanese immigration question. These works examine the exclusion movement in order to explain the frictions between Japan and America. Thus, they too do not tell us much about Japanese immigrants, except that they had something to do with the discord between the two nations.

There are innumerable works written during and after the exclusion movement that take sides on the controversy. Whether they are for or against Japanese immigration, certain questions recur in them again and again: Are the Japanese assimilable? What happens when racial intermarriage (amalgamation, as it was called) occurs? Is the picture-bride practice moral or immoral, legal or illegal? What is the Japanese birthrate? What are the purposes of Japanese language schools, and what is their influence on the second generation? Should the Japanese be granted naturalization rights? Is there economic competition between Japanese and white laborers? If so, how does it affect the standard of living of both? Are the alien land laws constitutional? Do they violate the international treaty between Japan and America? Is the Gentlemen's Agreement of 1907–1908 satisfactory? If not, what kind of immigration restriction is necessary? The answers to these questions comprise the content of the works in this category.

A few white American writers defended the Japanese within this framework. For example, Sidney L. Gulick's first book, *The American Japanese Problem* (New York, 1914), is a refutation of charges advanced by the proponents of exclusion, and a proposal of both naturalization rights for the Japanese and nondiscriminatory immigration restrictions. *American Democracy and Asiatic Citizenship* (New York, 1918), his subsequent work, which includes the Chinese, elaborates on this theme. Harry A. Millis wrote from the same perspective in *The Japanese Problem in the United States* (New York, 1915), which was based on the United States Immigration Commission, *Reports of the Immigration Commission*, part 25 (Washington, D.C., 1911).

White American writers also wrote from the opposite viewpoint, of course. Apart from the countless anti-Japanese tracts, a good example is Montaville Flowers, *The Japanese Conquest of American Opinion* (New York, 1917), which attacks the views and proposals of Gulick, Millis, and Japanese such as Karl K. Kawakami. Still others conclude that no Japanese immigration problem exists. Manchester E. Boddy, *Japanese in America* (Los Angeles, 1921), finds that the Japanese question is a manufactured one with no basis in fact, and Jean Pajus's later study, *The Real Japanese California* (Berkeley, 1937), arrives at an identical conclusion.

To counter the exclusionists, the Japanese themselves wrote many books. The most prolific author was Karl K. Kawakami. In the section devoted to Japanese immigration in his earliest work, *American-Japanese Relations* (New York, 1912), he argues for naturalization rights. His second book, *Asia at the Door* (New York, 1914), responds to the charges of nonassimilability and economic competition, while recording the achievements of prominent Japanese and discussing the 1913 California Alien Land Law. His next work, *The Real Japanese Question* (New York, 1921), takes up where the second left off and comprehensively covers all the questions.

Many other books were written by the Japanese, but none compares in importance to Yamato Ichihashi, *Japanese in the United States* (Stanford, 1932), because it is still the accepted standard work on the Japanese immigrants. Starting as a pamphlet in 1913, it was submitted in an expanded form as a doctoral dissertation at Harvard University in 1914 and then published the following year under the title *Japanese Immigration: Its Status in California* (San Francisco, 1915). This early version was designed to present facts on the Japanese in California as a retort to the exclusionists, relying heavily on the *Reports of the Immigration Commission*, Gulick's *American Japanese Problem,* and Millis's *Japanese Problem in the United States*. The 1932 edition is expanded and updated in many ways, with new chapters on the character and causes of Japanese emigration and the second generation, but it still retains the original purpose. Like all the other works cited, it tells us more about the exclusion movement than about the Japanese immigrant and his society. While Ichihashi did use some Japanese-language sources, these were very restricted, which further limits the value of the book. But for all its shortcomings, it remains the standard work incorporated into general histories of American immigration. Maldwyn A. Jones, *American Immigration* (Chicago, 1960), and Carl Wittke, *We Who Built America*, rev. ed. (Cleveland, 1967), for example, both depend heavily on it for their treatment of Japanese immigration.

In addition to the above studies, there are more specialized ones related to the exclusion movement. Roderick D. McKenzie, *Oriental Exclusion* (Chicago, 1928), and Eliot G. Mears, *Resident Orientals on the Pacific Coast* (Chicago, 1928), analyze the effect on the Chinese and Japanese of the 1924 Immigration Act and regulations and judicial decisions under it. Jesse F. Steiner, *The Japanese Invasion* (Chicago, 1917), studies the Japanese immigration question in terms of the physical features and skin pigmentation of the Japanese. And Milton R. Konvitz, *The Alien and the Asiatic in American Law* (Ithaca, 1946), treats the Asian immigrants' relation to immigration laws, citizenship, and other legal questions.

In the 1930's a number of studies were produced on the second generation. Departing somewhat from the previous framework, they explore the "problems" of the Nisei,[1] seeking answers to questions connected with their adjustment and assimilation into American society. Stanford University produced four such works. Based on interviews with approximately 10 percent of the Japanese population in California, the first volume, by Edward K. Strong, *Vocational Aptitudes of Second-Generation Japanese in the United States* (Stanford, 1933), compares the second generation to whites in terms of psychological tests, delinquency, and ability to use the English language. The second, also by Strong, *Japanese in California* (Stanford, 1933), provides data on the birthplace, age, sex, size of family, birth and death, education, occupation, and religious affiliation of the Japanese. The third, by Reginald Bell, *Public School Education of Second-Generation Japanese in California* (Stanford, 1935), compares Japanese and white students in public schools. The last, by Strong, *The Second-Generation Japanese Problem* (Stanford, 1934), summarizes the first three. Two points should be noted about these studies: 1) they are based on interviews, not on research into new historical sources; and 2) they are an extension of preceding studies, for they simply reexamine the Japanese question emphasizing the problems of the second generation. William C. Smith, *Americans in Process: A Study of Our Citizens of Oriental Ancestry* (Ann Arbor, 1937) and Forrest E. La Violette, *Americans of Japanese Ancestry* (Toronto, 1946), likewise study the problems of the second generation.

The remaining secondary works indicate the paucity of the historical literature. Our knowledge of the origins and causes of Japanese emigration consists of a ten-page article by Yosaburo Yoshida, "Sources and Causes of Japanese Emigration," *Annals of the American Academy of Political and Social Science*, 34:2 (September, 1909), and "Causes of Japanese Immigration," chapter 6 in Ichihashi's book, both of which provide merely superficial generalizations. The most solid (yet again incom-

---

1. The terms *Issei* and *Nisei* refer to the immigrant generation and the American-born second generation respectively. *Kibei* denotes Nisei who were entirely or partially educated in Japan. For additional Japanese words employed in the bibliography, see the Glossary of Japanese Terms. Throughout the bibliography we have used *Japanese immigrants*, *Japanese-Americans*, and *Japanese in America* interchangeably. In discussing the 19th century, it is impossible to make the distinction between Japanese immigrants and other Japanese in America. Many *dekasegi-shosei*, for example, though they eventually returned to Japan, laid the foundations of Japanese immigrant society. For the 20th century, however, when the term *Japanese in America* is used, we do not have in mind Japanese diplomats, businessmen, students, and other transient individuals.

plete) study on this topic with reference to Japanese emigration to Hawaii is Hilary Conroy, *The Japanese Frontier in Hawaii, 1868–1898* (Berkeley and Los Angeles, 1953). Hardly anything has been written on the origins of Japanese immigrant society. Inasmuch as the overwhelming emphasis has been on the exclusion movement, which began at the turn of the century, it is not surprising to find this void. The exceptions are Henry Taketa, "1969, the Centennial Year," *Pacific Historian*, 13:1 (winter, 1969), a brief essay on the 1869 Wakamatsu Tea Colony; Robert E. Park, *The Immigrant Press and Its Control* (New York, 1922), which has a short treatment of the early Japanese immigrant press in San Francisco; and the United States Immigration Commission, *Reports of the Immigration Commission*, part 25 (Washington, D.C., 1911), which has already been cited. There are no serious studies of the early Christian institutions of Japanese immigrant society, of the Gospel Society founded in 1877 from which the others originated, of the first *dekasegi-shosei* who laid much of the foundation of immigrant society, or of the crucial transmigration of laborers from Hawaii to the continental United States. In short, the origins and development of Japanese immigrant society are unknown.

To see Japanese immigrants as live participants in history, biographies and autobiographies of eminent and ordinary Issei are required. But what exists? The answer is: Very little. Aside from Karl K. Kawakami, *Jokichi Takamine: A Record of His American Achievements* (New York, 1928), and Gustav Eckstein, *Noguchi* (New York, 1931), two biographies of eminent Issei scientists; Kiyoko T. Kurosawa, "Seito Saibara's Diary of Planting a Japanese Colony in Texas," *Hitotsubashi Journal of Social Studies*, 2:1 (August, 1964), a sketch of the founder of the Japanese rice colony outside Houston; Eleanor Hull, *Suddenly the Sun* (New York, 1957), a biography of Shizuko Takahashi; and Tohru Morita, "The Story of a Japanese Emigrant: The Life of Domoto Takanoshin," *The East*, 5 (March/April, 1969), there are no biographical studies of Issei. The only autobiographies that come to mind are Haru Matsui, *Restless Wave* (New York, 1940); Etsu Inagaki Sugimoto, *A Daughter of the Samurai* (New York, 1929); Toru Matsumoto and Marion Olive Lerrigo *A Brother Is a Stranger* (New York, 1947); and Taro Yashima, *The New Sun* (New York, 1943) and *Horizon Is Calling* (New York, 1947) (these last two are more an autobiography through drawings). The literature on the second generation is no better. Besides the frequently cited autobiography by Monica Sone, *Nisei Daughter* (Boston, 1953), there are some autobiographical sketches in

Fisk University, Social Science Institute, *Orientals and Their Cultural Adjustment* (Nashville, 1946), and Dorothy S. Thomas, *The Salvage* (Berkeley and Los Angeles, 1952). The most recent autobiographies are Daniel I. Okimoto, *American in Disguise* (New York, 1971), and Jim Yoshida, *The Two Worlds of Jim Yoshida* (New York, 1972). Biographical studies of Nisei simply do not exist, save for Ralph G. Martin, *Boy from Nebraska* (New York, 1946), an account of the life of Ben Kuroki and his World War II exploits.

A number of other works of uneven historical value complete this broad survey. The often cited reference to the Japanese Associations, the most important Issei political organization, is a superficial eight-page article by Michinari Fujita, "The Japanese Associations in America," *Sociology and Social Research*, 13:3 (January/February, 1929). The only study of the eta or pariah caste is Hiroshi Ito, "Japan's Outcastes in the United States," in George De Vos and Hiroshi Wagatsuma, *Japan's Invisible Race* (Berkeley and Los Angeles, 1966). Masakazu Iwata, "The Japanese Immigrants in California Agriculture," *Agricultural History*, 36:1 (January, 1962), is a historical essay on the Japanese contributions to California agriculture. Yuji Ichioka, "A Buried Past: Early Issei Socialists and the Japanese Community," *Amerasia Journal*, 1:2 (July, 1971), is a recent study of early Issei socialists and anarchists. As for local or regional studies, there are Frank S. Miyamoto, "Social Solidarity among the Japanese in Seattle," *University of Washington Publications in the Social Sciences*, 11:2 (December, 1939); his later essay, "The Japanese Minority in the Pacific Northwest," *Pacific Northwest Quarterly*, 54:4 (October, 1963); Marvin G. Pursinger, "The Japanese Settle in Oregon, 1880–1920," *Journal of the West*, 5:2 (April, 1966); and Marjorie R. Stearns, *A History of the Japanese People in Oregon* (Eugene, 1939), yet another example of the exclusion-oriented studies. John Modell, a new student of Japanese-American history, has written "Class or Ethnic Solidarity: The Japanese American Company Union," *Pacific Historical Review*, 38:2 (May, 1969), and "Tradition and Opportunity: The Japanese Immigrants in America," *Pacific Historical Review*, 40:2 (May, 1971), the latter almost exclusively relying on survey data. Roger Daniels, "Westerners from the East: Oriental Immigrants Reappraised," *Pacific Historical Review*, 35:4 (November, 1966), is a review of the historiography of Chinese and Japanese immigrants. The latest summary of historical and sociological studies of Japanese immigrants in America and other countries is John B. Cornell and Robert J. Smith, "Japanese Immigrants Abroad," *Rice University Studies*, 56:4

(fall, 1970). Ernest R. May and James C. Thomson, Jr. (eds.), *American-East Asian Relations: A Survey* (Cambridge, 1972), is a valuable review of the literature on American-East Asian relations, including the Japanese immigration question.

While not comprehensive, this broad survey should make evident that the history of Japanese immigrants remains to be written.[2] In the judgment of one historian, "although some studies of Asiatic emigration were made during the period of the immigration restriction controversy, we still lack adequate histories of Chinese, Japanese, and other Far Eastern emigration. Indeed this vast field of investigation is untouched."[3] The sparse literature that is unrelated to the exclusion movement is so limited that it only touches the surface. The real need is to refocus our attention on the Japanese immigrants themselves, which requires the examination of Japanese-language source materials. Except for Ichihashi, Conroy, Iriye, Ichioka, and Miyamoto, past and present researchers have ignored these materials. On the one hand, they have not been equipped to handle the language, and, on the other hand, they have adhered to the myth that no such sources exist. Marcus L. Hansen, the pioneer in European immigration history, long ago called attention to the necessity of studying immigrant language materials and the intimate connection between the emigrant nation and the immigrant land.[4] Yet his elementary maxim has not been heeded in the study of Japanese immigrants. To delve below the surface and uncover the history of Japanese immigrants, future studies must be based on Japanese-immigrant-language source materials.

THE JAPANESE AMERICAN RESEARCH PROJECT

This is an annotated bibliography of the Japanese-language source materials of the Japanese American Research Project Collection at the University of California at Los Angeles. The Japanese American Research Project was initiated in August, 1962 with a substantial grant from the Japanese American Citizens League. The initial grant was supplemented

---

2. For the socio-psychological studies, wartime internment literature, and other works, see the bibliographies of English-language materials cited below in footnote 5.

3. Carlton C. Qualey, "Prospects for Materials in Immigration Studies," in Henry S. Commager (ed.), *Immigration and American History* (Minneapolis: University of Minnesota Press, 1961), p. 132.

4. Marcus L. Hansen, "The History of American Immigration as a Field for Research," *American Historical Review*, 32:3 (April, 1927), pp. 500–518.

by one from the Carnegie Corporation in 1964, and a third grant was awarded to the project in 1966 by the National Institute of Mental Health. Through a special agreement with the Board of Regents of the University of California, the project was headquartered at the University of California at Los Angeles, first under the directorship of T. Scott Miyakawa and then under Robert A. Wilson, and the institution was designated as the official repository of all collected materials.

The project originally had three major objectives: 1) to engage in historical studies on Japanese immigrants and their descendants; 2) to conduct sociological research and surveys; and 3) to collect and preserve historical source materials. The project devoted itself almost exclusively to the second objective from the outset, however. The original staff felt that intensive interviews of a representative sampling of surviving Issei would not only yield a large body of data for sociological studies but also provide a wealth of historical information. From the beginning, therefore, the resources and time of the project were channeled in this direction. Subsequent to the 1966 National Institute of Mental Health grant, a newly constituted staff further expanded the sociological orientation by including the second and third generations. The project then became, for all intents and purposes, a three-generational sociological research study, with the third objective—the collection and preservation of historical sources—pushed into the background as an almost inappropriate appendage. .

Thus there was no endeavor to carry out a systematic collection of historical sources. The materials that were actually acquired were on the whole secondary by-products of the interviews conducted for the sociological study. Many Issei respondents who were interviewed generously donated materials. Members of local chapters of the Japanese American Citizens League also donated certain sources, and the late Joe Grant Masaoka, the project administrator from 1965 to 1970, personally gathered a wide variety of materials on his frequent field trips. A small percentage of the materials was acquired by specific design at the suggestion of Yasuo Sakata—for example, the microfilms of Japanese Foreign Ministry archival documents. In addition, microfilmed copies of certain published materials in the Japanese National Diet Library were purchased through the financial support of the Asian American Studies Center of the University of California at Los Angeles.

In spite of the low priority accorded to the collection of materials, the manner in which they were acquired, and the obvious gaps in the collection, the Japanese American Research Project Collection is without doubt the most significant body of materials on the history of Japanese immigrants and their descendants.

THE COLLECTION AND BIBLIOGRAPHY

The collection for the most part consists of primary and secondary sources in the Japanese language. In compiling the annotated bibliography, we have emphasized this portion of the collection. Since various bibliographies of English-language materials have been published, we have not listed the English works that are in the collection in order to avoid unnecessary duplication, except when, in our judgment, they were sufficiently rare and valuable to warrant inclusion.[5] The single exception to this guiding principle has been the inclusion of dissertations and theses. Approximately 1,000 photographs, unidentifiable materials, and miscellaneous memorabilia in the collection have not been included. Besides the collection materials, we have included Japanese-language sources directly related to Japanese immigrants and additional dissertations and theses of the Research Library of the University of California at Los Angeles. Most of these materials were recently acquired by Che-Hwei Lin, the Asian American bibliographer of the Research Library, with the financial support of the Asian American Studies Center.

The technical details of the bibliography are straightforward. All titles are in lower case letters, except the first letter and words that are normally capitalized in English, i.e., Nihonjin [Japanese]. Compounds like

5. Readers are referred to the following bibliographies of English-language materials: Edward N. Barnhart, *Japanese American Evacuation and Resettlement* (Berkeley: University of California, General Library, 1958); Orpha Cummings and Helen E. Hennefrund, *Bibliography on the Japanese in American Agriculture* (Washington, D. C.: U. S. Government Printing Office, 1943) (U.S.D.A. Biblio. Bul. no. 3); Isao Fujimoto et al., *Asians in America: A Selected Bibliography* (Davis: University of California, 1971) (Asian American Research Project, Working Pub. no. 5); Harry L. Kitano et al., *Asian Americans: An Annotated Bibliography* (Los Angeles: University of California, Asian American Studies Center, 1971); William W. Lum, *Asians in America: A Bibliography* (Davis: University of California, 1969); William W. Lum, *Asians in America: A Bibliography of Master's Theses and Dissertations* (Davis: University of California, 1970) (Asian American Research Project, Working Pub. no. 2); U.S. Library of Congress, General Reference and Bibliography Division, *Japanese in the United States: A Selected List of References* (Washington, D.C.: U.S. Government Printing Office, 1946); U.S. National Archives, *Preliminary Inventories, No. 77: Records of the War Relocation Authority* (Washington, D.C.: U.S. Government Printing Office, 1955); U.S. War Relocation Authority, *Bibliography of Japanese in American*, 3 vols. (Washington, D.C.: U.S. War Relocation Authority, 1942–1943); U.S. War Relocation Authority, *Bibliography on War Relocation Authority: Japanese and Japanese-Americans* (Washington, D.C.: U.S. War Relocation Authority, 1945).

Hoku-Bei [North America] are separated by hyphens and capitalized in titles. If they appear as a part of an organizational title or journal, they are rendered without hyphens with the second half in lower case letters, i.e., Hokubei. Unless well-known Issei romanized their names differently or when otherwise noted, the standard Hepburn system of romanization has been employed. Japanese names are rendered in the traditional Japanese order—the last name first—without commas. Nisei and Kibei names, however, have been placed in the Western order. A few symbols are used throughout the bibliography: an asterisk (*) indicates materials wholly or partially about the Japanese in Hawaii and/or materials authored or published in Hawaii; a plus sign (+) indicates materials of the Research Library of the University of California at Los Angeles that do *not* form a part of the Japanese American Research Project Collection; and the letters *M* and *X* indicate microfilmed and xeroxed materials respectively. English titles that appear on Japanese-language publications and commonly accepted English equivalents of Issei organizations, newspapers, and periodicals are indicated by quotation marks within brackets. All other English renditions of Japanese titles and organizations are our translations. There is a glossary of Japanese terms following the introduction. The bibliography itself has been divided into eighteen chapters by balancing two opposing principles: the natural categories inherent in the collection and the imposed categories into which materials could be placed. Headnotes introduce the major categories, providing a brief historical background and summary evaluation of the materials included.

There are other bibliographies of Japanese-language materials to which interested researchers can turn. William Magistretti, "A Bibliography of Historical Materials in the Japanese Language on the West Coast Japanese," *Pacific Historical Review*, 12:1 (March, 1943), is an incomplete listing of secondary sources. Cecil H. Uyehara, *Checklist of Archives in the Japanese Ministry of Foreign Affairs, Tokyo, Japan, 1868–1945* (Washington, D.C.: U.S. Library of Congress, 1954), includes a significant catalogue of Japanese Foreign Ministry documents held in the Library of Congress concerning Japanese immigrants. *Newspapers on Microfilm*, 6th ed. (Washington, D.C.: U.S. Library of Congress, 1967), contains a listing of Japanese-language newspapers published in the United States that are held in the Library of Congress and other institutions. Mitsugu Matsuda, *The Japanese in Hawaii, 1868–1967* (Honolulu: University of Hawaii, 1968) (Social Science Research Institute, Hawaii Series no. 1), is a useful annotated bibliography of both

Japanese- and English-language sources on the Japanese in Hawaii. General bibliographies published in Japan also contain valuable listings of materials relating to the Japanese emigration ideology, emigration policies, and the overseas Japanese. The following bibliographies provide helpful listings on these topics: Kôbe Kôtô Shôgyô Gakkô Shôgyô Kenkyūjo, *Keizai Hôritsu Bunken Mokuroku* (Tokyo and Osaka: Hôbunkan, 1927), and its sequel, *Keizai Hôritsu Bunken Mokuroku Dai-Nishū* (Tokyo and Osaka: Hôbunkan, 1931); Amano Keitarô, *Hôsei Keizai Shakai Ronbun Sôran* (Tokyo: Tôko Shoin, 1927), and its supplement, *Hôsei Keizai Shakai Ronbun Sôran Tsui-hen* (Tokyo: Tôko Shoin, 1928); and Honjô Eijirô, *Nihon Keizaishi Bunken*, 6 vols. (Tokyo: Nihon Hyôronsha, 1953–1969).

Glossary of Japanese Terms

Bakufu, the central government during the Tokugawa period; also referred to as the Shogunate.
biwa, a Japanese lute.
dekasegi, a term originally denoting the practice of individuals (usually householdheads) temporarily leaving their villages or home towns to seek employment in order to supplement their income during the Tokugawa period. During the Meiji period, this original meaning was extended to the practice of going abroad temporarily for the same purpose.
dekaseginin, a person who engages in the practice of dekasegi.
dekasegi-shosei, dekaseginin who also are students.
gannen-mono, the designation for the 150-odd Japanese who arrived in Hawaii in 1868; also refers to the 40 who arrived in Guam in the same year.
Gedatsu Kingō, a syncretic religion that combines elements of Buddhism and Shintoism.
genseki, place of birth.
Gun, county; an administrative unit below the Ken.
haiku, a 17-syllable verse form.
Hokkaidō, the northern island of Japan.
imin, emigrant or immigrant.
imin kaisha, emigration company.
Jōdo Shinshū, the Pure Land Sect of Buddhism.
Kaigai Kyōkai, Overseas Association.
kanshi, Chinese poetry.
Ken, Prefecture.
kendō, Japanese swordsmanship.
Kenjinkai, Prefectural Association.
Konkōkyō, a Shinto sect.
koseki tōhon, family registry.
Meiji, the reign title of the Meiji Emperor, 1868–1912.
Nihonjinkai, Japanese Association.

Seichō no Ie, a new religion that combines elements of Shintoism, Buddhism, and Christianity.
senryū, a witty, satirical verse form.
shigin, the chanting of kanshi.
shokumin, colonist.
Shōwa, the reign title of the Showa Emperor, 1926 to the present.
shūshin, moral education.
Taishō, the reign title of the Taisho Emperor, 1912–1926.
tanka, a 31-syllable verse form.
Tōhoku, the Northeast section of the main island of Honshu.
Tokugawa, the period in Japanese history from 1603–1868.
yobiyose, a family member summoned by a Japanese resident in America.

I.
Japanese Government Archival Documents

Note: The documents listed below constitute one of the richest parts of the collection. By special permission of and arrangement with the Japanese Foreign Ministry, the Japanese American Research Project acquired microfilms of Foreign Ministry archival documents on Japanese emigration to America from 1866 to 1926. (Some documents on Latin America and China are also included.) Portions of these documents have been published in Nihon Gaimushō, *Nihon Gaikō Monjo* [Japanese Diplomatic Documents], but by no means all. Most of the 95 reels have many appended reports and other documents that throw light on the internal development of Japanese immigrant society. The additional microfilms, no. 67, are copies of the U.S. Library of Congress holdings. The special numbers correspond to the Library of Congress classification scheme, and readers are referred to Cecil H. Uyehara, *Checklist of Archives in the Japanese Ministry of Foreign Affairs, Tokyo, 1868–1945* (Washington, D.C.: U.S. Library of Congress, 1954). All the documents are indispensable for the study of the origins and causes of emigration, the origins and evolution of governmental emigration policies, the origins and development of immigrant society, and the governmental responses to the exclusion movement.

1. FOREIGN MINISTRY

在米本邦人ノ状況並渡米者取締關係雜件

1. Reel no. 1: Zai-Bei hompōjin no jōkyō narabini to-Beisha torishimari kankei zakken, 1-2 [Documents on the Japanese residing in America and the control of Japanese going to America, 1-2]. Consular and Washington Legation reports and Foreign Ministry instructions on the problem of "undesirable" Japanese residing in America from May, 1888 to February, 1894. Includes the correspondence exchanged between the Foreign Ministry and Prefectural governments on the question of controlling the emigration of "undesirables."

北米合衆國ニ於テ本邦人渡航制限及排斥一件

2. Reel no. 2: Hoku-Bei Gasshūkoku ni oite hompōjin tokō seigen oyobi haiseki ikken, 1-2 [Documents on emigration restrictions and anti-Japanese incidents in the United States, 1-2].

I. Consular and Legation reports and Foreign Ministry instructions on immigration problems of <u>dekasegi</u> laborers and women at Pacific Coast ports after the enactment of the March, 1891 Immigration Law of the United States and the rise of anti-Japanese incidents from April, 1891 to December, 1893. Contains considerable documents of the Foreign Ministry and Prefectural governments relating to the control of <u>dekasegi</u> emigration.

II. Consular and Legation reports on <u>dekasegi</u> laborers and anti-Japanese incidents on the Pacific Coast from June, 1895 to May, 1900. Contains documents exchanged between the Foreign Ministry and Prefectural governments on the enforcement of restrictions on <u>dekasegi</u> emigration to the United States and Canada. Also includes documents relating to emigration companies and agents in Japan, their recruitment policies and practices, and Japanese labor contractors in America and their activities.

北米合衆國ニ於テ本邦人渡航制限及排斥一件

3. Reel no. 3: <u>Hoku-Bei Gasshūkoku ni oite hompōjin tokō seigen oyobi haiseki ikken, 3-5</u> [Documents on emigration restrictions and anti-Japanese incidents in the United States, 3-5].

   I.   A continuation of Reel no. 2, Section II, through August, 1900. Includes documents of the Foreign Ministry and Prefectural governments relating to the enforcement of a measure to suspend the issuance of passports to <u>dekaseginin</u> going to the continental United States and Canada for an indefinite period from August 2, 1900.

   II. Documents on the problems arising in Japan from the enforcement of restrictions and the formulation of a new emigration policy by the Japanese government from December, 1900 to December, 1904. Includes Consular and Legation reports on the continuation of immigration problems on the Pacific Coast, the transmigration of laborers from Hawaii to the continental United States, and anti-Japanese incidents.

   III. Consular and Legation reports on the full scale eruption of the exclusion movement from February, 1905 to February, 1907.

北米合衆國ニ於テ本邦人渡航制限及排斥一件

4. Reel no. 4: <u>Hoku-Bei Gasshūkoku ni oite hompōjin tokō seigen oyobi haiseki ikken, 6-8</u> [Documents on emigration restrictions and anti-Japanese incidents in the United States, 6-8]. A continuation of Reel no. 3, Section III, through August, 1907.

北米合衆國ニ於テ本邦人渡航制限及排斥一件

5.* Reel no. 5: <u>Hoku-Bei Gasshūkoku ni oite hompōjin tokō seigen oyobi haiseki ikken, 9-11</u> [Documents on emigration restrictions and anti-Japanese incidents in the United States, 9-11]. A continuation of Reel no. 4 through May, 1908. Includes documents relating to the enforcement of restrictions on the transmigration of the Japanese from Hawaii, Canada, and Mexico to the continental United States.

北米合衆國ニ於テ本邦人渡航制限及排斥一件

6. Reel no. 6: <u>Hoku-Bei Gasshūkoku ni oite hompōjin tokō seigen oyobi haiseki ikken, 12-14</u> [Documents on emigration restrictions and anti-Japanese incidents in the United States, 12-14].

   I.   A continuation of Reel no. 5 through November, 1908.

II. Documents relating to the Gentlemen's Agreement from October, 1907 to June, 1909. Includes the official notes and memoranda exchanged between the Japanese Foreign Minister and the United States Ambassador to Japan and the correspondence between the Foreign Ministry, the Japanese Embassy and Consulates, and the Prefectural governments on the implementation of the agreement.

III. Consular reports and Foreign Ministry instructions on the invitation extended by the Chambers of Commerce of Japan to American businessmen and industrialists to promote better understanding of the Japanese immigration question from June to November, 1908.

北米合衆國ニ於テ本邦人渡航制限及排斥一件

7. Reel no. 7: Hoku-Bei Gasshūkoku ni oite hompōjin tokō seigen oyobi haiseki
* ikken, 15-17 [Documents on emigration restrictions and anti-Japanese incidents in the United States, 15-17]. Consular and Embassy reports on the import, character, and outcome of anti-Japanese resolutions and bills introduced in the State Legislatures of California, Nevada, Oregon, Nebraska, Wisconsin, and Illinois and in the Territorial Legislature of Hawaii from February, 1909 to January, 1910.

8. Reel no. 8:

北米合衆國ニ於テ本邦人渡航制限及排斥一件

I. Hoku-Bei Gasshūkoku ni oite hompōjin tokō seigen oyobi haiseki ikken, 18-19 [Documents on emigration restrictions and anti-Japanese incidents in the United States, 18-19]. A continuation of Reel no. 7 through April, 1912.

米國アイダホ州ユニオン・パシフィック鐵道工事ニ從事セル本邦人勞働者放逐事件ノ爲珍田領事出張一件

II. Beikoku Aidaho-shū Yunion Pashifikku tetsudō kōji ni jūjiseru hompōjin rōdōsha hōchiku jiken no tame Chinda Ryōji shutchō ikken [Documents relating to the special investigation by Consul Chinda of San Francisco on the expulsion of Japanese railroad construction workers of the Union Pacific in Idaho]. Consular reports on anti-Japanese acts against Japanese railroad workers in Southern Idaho from July to September, 1892.

在外各地本邦居留民關係雜件

III. Zaigai kakuchi hompō kyoryūmin kankei zakken, 1 [Miscellaneous documents relating to overseas Japanese, 1]. Miscellaneous documents relating to associations established by Japanese residents in China from 1893 to 1914.

9. Reel no. 9:

在外各地本邦居留民關係雜件

I. Zaigai kakuchi hompō kyoryūmin kankei zakken, 2 [Miscellaneous documents relating to overseas Japanese, 2]. A continuation of Reel no. 8, Section III, through 1926.

海外移住出稼雜件

II. Kaigai ijū dekasegi zakken, 1-2 [Miscellaneous documents relating to overseas dekasegi emigration, 1-2]. Documents relating to the overseas dekasegi emigration to the United States, Canada, Mexico, Brazil, Australia, the Dutch East Indies, the Philippines, the

South Pacific Islands, and the maritime province of Russia from 1870 to 1893; and documents relating to the recruitment and emigration of <u>dekaseginin</u> under contract by Japanese emigration companies and agents from 1894 to 1898.

移民關係雜纂

10. Reel no. 10: <u>Imin kankei zassan, 3-4</u> [Miscellaneous documents relating to Japanese emigrants, 3-4]. Documents relating to the recruitment and emigration of <u>dekaseginin</u> under contract by Japanese emigration companies and agents and the Japanese government supervision of their activities from 1898 to 1903.

移民關係雜件

11. Reel no. 11: <u>Imin kankei zakken, 8</u> [Miscellaneous documents relating to Japanese emigrants, 8]. Miscellaneous documents relating to <u>dekasegi</u> emigration to Southeast Asia, South America, and China from 1909 to 1914.

12. Reel no. 12:

明治移民株式會社業務上ノ實況調査並同會社ヨリ「ヴィクトリア」及「ハワイ」等へ出稼人募集渡航一件

I. <u>Meiji Imin Kabushiki Kaisha gyōmujō no jikkyō chōsa narabini dō-kaisha yori Bikutoria oyobi Hawai tō e dekaseginin boshū tokō ikken</u> [Documents relating to investigations of the business practices of the Meiji Emigration Company and its recruitment and shipment of <u>dekaseginin</u> to Victoria, B.C., Hawaii, and other places]. Documents on the management, financial status, and fraudulent practices of the Meiji Emigration Company of Kobe which recruited and shipped <u>dekaseginin</u> from May, 1893 to March, 1898.

布哇移民米國渡航禁止一件

II. <u>Hawai imin Beikoku tokō kinshi ikken</u> [Documents relating to the prohibition against the transmigration of Japanese emigrants from Hawaii to the continental United States]. Consular reports on the transmigration of Japanese laborers from Hawaii to the continental United States, on restrictive measures to halt this practice, and the problems of enforcement from May, 1902 to February, 1912.

北米合衆國米作地ヘ日本人移住取締雜件

III. <u>Hoku-Bei Gasshūkoku beisakuchi e Nihonjin ijū torishimari zakken</u> [Miscellaneous documents relating to the control of Japanese emigration to the rice growing region of the United States]. Consular reports on the state of rice culture in Texas and other Southern States, the prospects for Japanese emigrants there, and the early Japanese rice farmers in Texas from September, 1902 to 1909.

13. Reel no. 13:

テキサス州農業組合員渡航出願雜件

I. <u>Tekisasu-shū nōgyō kumiaiin tokō shutsugan zakken</u> [Miscellaneous application documents for Texas by settled agriculturalists]. Documents relating to applications for passports by settled agriculturalists for Texas from 1903 to 1908.

本邦移民布哇渡航一件

II. <u>Hompō imin Hawai tokō ikken</u> [Documents on Japanese emigrants to Hawaii].

Documents on negotiations and revisions of the 1886 Labor Convention from 1886 to 1888.

14. Reel no. 14:
    *

    北米合衆國及加奈陀農業組合員渡航出願雜件
    I. Hoku-Bei Gasshūkoku oyobi Kanada nōgyō kumiaiin tokō shutsugan zakken [Miscellaneous application documents for the United States and Canada by settled agriculturalists]. Documents relating to applications for passports by settled agriculturalists from 1906 to 1914.

    北米合衆國本土・布哇・加奈陀渡航本邦人員表送付一件
    II. Hoku-Bei Gasshūkoku hondo, Hawai, Kanada tokō hompōjin'inhyō sōfu ikken [Statistical tables of Japanese arrivals in the continental United States, Hawaii, and Canada]. Documents on the monthly statistical exchange between the American Embassy in Tokyo and the Japanese Foreign Ministry on Japanese arrivals and departures in the continental United States, Hawaii, and Canada from 1908 to 1916.

15. Reel no. 15:
    *

    北米合衆國本土及布哇出入本邦人員表在本邦米國大使ヨリ送付一件
    I. Hoku-Bei Gasshūkoku hondo oyobi Hawai deiri hompōjin'inhyō zai-hompō Beikoku Taishi yori sōfu ikken [Statistical tables of Japanese arrivals and departures in the continental United States and Hawaii forwarded to the Foreign Ministry by the United States Ambassador in Japan]. Documents on the monthly statistical exchange between the American Embassy in Tokyo and the Japanese Foreign Ministry on Japanese arrivals and departures in the continental United States and Hawaii from March, 1908 to February, 1911.

    米國ニ於ケル排日問題一件
    II. Beikoku ni okeru hai-Nichi mondai ikken, 1-2 [Documents on the Japanese exclusion question in America, 1-2]. Consular and Embassy reports on anti-Japanese bills and incidents from January, 1911 to April, 1913. Includes the revision of the Japanese-American Treaty of Commerce of 1894, the planned Panama-Pacific Exposition, and the pending 1913 California Alien Land Law.

    米國ニ於ケル排日問題一件
16. Reel no. 16: Beikoku ni okeru hai-Nichi mondai ikken, 3-4 [Documents on the Japanese exclusion question in America, 3-4]. A continuation of Reel no. 15, Section II, on the 1913 California Alien Land Law through October, 1913.

    米國ニ於ケル排日問題一件
17. Reel no. 17: Beikoku ni okeru hai-Nichi mondai ikken, 5-7 [Documents on the Japanese exclusion question in America, 5-7].

    I. Documents of the drafts of the Japanese government's proposed Convention on landownership and other matters in response to the 1913 California Alien Land Law, reports exchanged between the Japanese Embassy and the Foreign Ministry, and the negotiations thereto with the American government from July, 1913 to April, 1914.

II. Reports exchanged between the San Francisco Consulate General, the Foreign Ministry, and the Finance Ministry relating to financial assistance to Japanese farmers and the lending policy of the Yokohama Specie Bank branches in San Francisco and Los Angeles. Also includes documents relating to the legal problem of the disposition of land acquired by individuals before the enactment of the 1913 California Alien Land Law who died after its effective date.

III. Documents on anti-Japanese bills and incidents in Washington, Arizona, Idaho, Florida, and Alaska from January, 1913 to February, 1914.

米國ニ於ケル排日問題一件
18. Reel no. 18: Beikoku ni okeru hai-Nichi mondai ikken, 8-10 [Documents on the
 * Japanese exclusion question in America, 8-10].

I. Documents on the legal opinions of selected American attorneys concerning the 1913 California Alien Land Law solicited by the San Francisco Consulate and the Japanese Embassy. Also includes documents on other laws pertaining to aliens.

II. A continuation of Reel no. 17, Section I, through October, 1914. Includes the Japanese government's decision to discontinue negotiations for a Commercial Convention to guarantee Japanese rights.

米國ニ於ケル排日問題一件
19. Reel no. 19: Beikoku ni okeru hai-Nichi mondai ikken, 11-13 [Documents on the Japanese exclusion question in America, 11-13].

I. Consular and Embassy reports on the 1914 California election campaign and its results, focusing on the possible renewal of anti-Japanese legislation and the effects it would have on Japan's planned participation in the Panama-Pacific Exposition of 1915. Also includes Consular reports on the election results in Washington and Oregon.

II. Documents on the proceedings of the informal conference held in Washington, D.C. between Ambassador Shidehara and Ambassador Morris from September, 1920 to January, 1921 prompted by the 1920 California Alien Land Law initiative.

米國ニ於ケル排日問題一件
20. Reel no. 20: Beikoku ni okeru hai-Nichi mondai ikken, 14-15 [Documents on the Japanese exclusion question in America, 14-15]. A continuation of Reel no. 19, Section II. Includes the official record of proceedings as well as appeals by Japanese Associations to the Japanese government not to consent to revisions in the Gentlemen's Agreement of 1907-08 which would prevent the wives, children, and other family members of those Japanese legally in America from joining them.

呼寄歸國並營業等諸証明書發給ニ關シ在米公館(晚香坡ヲ除ク)ヨリ
報告一件
21. Reel no. 21: Yobiyose kikoku narabini eigyo to sho-shomeisho hakkyu ni kanshi zai-Bei Kokan (Bankuba wo nozoku) yori hokoku ikken [Documents on Japanese Consular reports (excluding Vancouver) pertaining to the issuance of yobiyose, returnee, financial statement, and other certificates]. Consular reports on yobiyose and other certificates issued to specific individuals from 1911 to 1913. Includes some reports for Brazil.

在外日本人送金送達雜件
22. Reel no. 22: Zaigai Nihonjin sōkin sōtatsu zakken, 1-4 [Miscellaneous docu-

ments on overseas Japanese remissions and delivery, 1-4]. Documents on monetary remissions of overseas Japanese in Latin America from 1911 to 1918.

23. Reel no. 23:

  在外日本人送金送達雑件
  I. Zaigai Nihonjin sōkin sōtatsu zakken, 5 [Miscellaneous documents on overseas Japanese remissions and delivery, 5]. Documents on monetary remissions of overseas Japanese primarily in Brazil from 1918 to 1921.

  本邦移民關係(北米ノ部)
  II. Hompō imin kankei (Hoku-Bei no bu), 1 [Documents on Japanese emigrants (North America), 1]. Selected reports of the Portland, Seattle, and San Francisco Consulates on the Japanese under their jurisdiction for 1922-23 with an emphasis on agriculture.

  本邦移民關係
24. Reel no. 24: Hompō imin kankei, 2-3 [Documents on Japanese emigrants, 2-3]. Miscellaneous documents on individual remissions, deaths and the disposition of property, and other personal matters from 1915 to 1926.

  米國ニ於ケル排日問題雜件
25. Reel no. 25: Beikoku ni okeru hai-Nichi mondai zakken, 1-2 [Miscellaneous documents on the Japanese exclusion question in America, 1-2]. Consular and Embassy reports on the whole on the American newspaper coverage of the exclusion question and U.S.-Japan relations from June, 1919 to January, 1922.

  米國ニ於ケル排日問題雜件
26.* Reel no. 26: Beikoku ni okeru hai-Nichi mondai zakken, 3-5 [Miscellaneous documents on the Japanese exclusion question in America, 3-5]. Consular reports on miscellaneous aspects of the exclusion movement, with an emphasis on the American press, from January, 1923 to November, 1924.

  米國ニ於ケル排日問題雜件
27. Reel no. 27: Beikoku ni okeru hai-Nichi mondai zakken, 6-7 [Miscellaneous documents on the Japanese exclusion question in America, 6-7].

  I. Foreign Ministry documents on the domestic response to the 1913 California Alien Land Law from April to October, 1913. Also includes Consular reports on individuals who came to America to investigate the California question during the summer of 1913.

  II. Consular reports on the opinions of selected individuals, groups, and journals regarding the 1913 California Alien Land Law from April, 1913 to July, 1914.

  米國ニ於ケル排日問題雜件
28: Reel no. 28: Beikoku ni okeru hai-Nichi mondai zakken, 8 [Miscellaneous documents on the Japanese exclusion question in America, 8]. Consular and Embassy reports on anti-Japanese legislation and incidents in Nevada, New York, Washington, Michigan, Oregon, Idaho, Montana, Louisiana, and Arizona from January, 1915 to February, 1923. Also includes scattered reports for California.

25

29. Reel no. 29:

   I. 在外本邦人米本土ヘ轉航關係雜件
   Zaigai hompōjin Bei-hondo e tenkō kankei zakken [Miscellaneous documents on the transmigration of overseas Japanese to the continental United States]. Consular reports and documents on individual cases of transmigration from Hawaii to the continental United States from 1917 to 1923.

   II. 在外邦人送金調査表
   Zaigai hōjin sōkin chōsahyō, 1-4 [Statistical tables on overseas Japanese remissions, 1-4]. Statistical data by Prefectures and other administrative units on the monetary remissions of overseas Japanese for the years 1920-23, including Hawaii and the continental United States.

30. Reel no. 30:

   I. 在外邦人送金調査表
   Zaigai hōjin sōkin chōsahyō [Statistical tables on overseas Japanese remissions]. A continuation of Reel no. 29, Section II, for 1924.

   II. 米國ニ於ケル排日問題雜件
   Beikoku ni okeru hai-Nichi mondai zakken, 1 [Miscellaneous documents on the Japanese exclusion question in America, 1]. Consular and Embassy reports on the American newspaper coverage for the months of April and May, 1924 on the passage of the 1924 Immigration Act. Also includes scattered Consular reports on the same subject from Canada, Mexico, and other countries as well as on anti-Japanese incidents in America from 1922 to 1926.

31. 米國ニ於ケル排日問題雜件
Reel no. 31: Beikoku ni okeru hai-Nichi mondai zakken, 2-3 [Miscellaneous documents on the Japanese exclusion question in America, 2-3].

   I. Documents relating to Americans visiting Japan from 1922 to 1925 at the invitation of the Japanese government or at personal expense who were considered favorably disposed to the Japanese government's position on the immigration question. Covers their itinerary and activities in Japan.

   II. Documents relating to the unofficial protests in Japan against the passage of the 1924 Immigration Act during the month of April. Includes protest cablegrams, resolutions, and petitions submitted to the Foreign Ministry and the American government by religious bodies, civic groups, educational organizations, private individuals, and others. Also includes a compilation of the opinions of Americans and other foreigners residing in Japan.

32. 米國ニ於ケル排日問題雜件
Reel no. 32: Beikoku ni okeru hai-Nichi mondai zakken, 4-6 [Miscellaneous documents on the Japanese exclusion question in America, 4-6]. A continuation of Reel no. 31, Section II.

米國ニ於ケル排日問題雜件
33. Reel no. 33: Beikoku ni okeru hai-Nichi mondai zakken, 7-10 [Miscellaneous documents on the Japanese exclusion question in America, 7-10].

   I. A continuation of Reel no. 32 for the remainder of 1924 with a few additional items for 1925.

   II. Consular reports on the renewed agitation against land leasing and the entry of picture-brides in California for 1919 and on anti-Japanese incidents in California for 1920 and 1921.

米國ニ於ケル排日問題雜件
34. Reel no. 34: Beikoku ni okeru hai-Nichi mondai zakken, 11-12 [Miscellaneous documents on the Japanese exclusion question in America, 11-12]. Consular reports on Japanese exclusion in California from 1920 to early 1923, including the activities of American organizations and individuals, Christian-based for the most part, opposed to the exclusion movement and the Japanese educational campaign to counter it.

米國ニ於ケル排日問題雜件
35.* Reel no. 35: Beikoku ni okeru hai-Nichi mondai zakken, 13-15 [Miscellaneous documents on the Japanese exclusion question in America, 13-15].

   I. Consular reports on Japanese exclusion in California from 1923 to 1925. Includes documents on the Los Angeles Examiner, the California White Spot Association, and the American Legion as well as on anti-Japanese incidents in Southern California.

   II. Consular reports on anti-Japanese measures introduced and/or passed by the Hawaiian Territorial Legislature from September, 1919 to November, 1922.

米國ニ於ケル排日問題雜件
36.* Reel no. 36: Beikoku ni okeru hai-Nichi mondai zakken, 16-17 [Miscellaneous documents on the Japanese exclusion question in America, 16-17].

   I. A continuation of Reel no. 35, Section II, from 1923 to 1925.

   II. Embassy reports and documents on the 1924 Immigration Act from December, 1923 to June, 1924.

米國ニ於ケル排日問題雜件
37. Reel no. 37: Beikoku ni okeru hai-Nichi mondai zakken, 18-19 [Miscellaneous documents on the Japanese exclusion question in America, 18-19].

   I. A continuation of Reel no. 36, Section II, through July, 1924.

   II. Consular and Embassy reports on the protest activities of American organizations and individuals regarding the anti-Japanese features of the 1924 Immigration Act from January to September, 1924.

米國ニ於ケル排日問題雜件
38. Reel no. 38: Beikoku ni okeru hai-Nichi mondai zakken, 20-21 [Miscellaneous documents on the Japanese exclusion question in America, 20-21].

   I. Consular and Embassy reports on miscellaneous aspects of the exclusion movement from June, 1924 to July, 1925.

II. Consular and Embassy reports on the 1920 California Alien Land Law initiative from March to December, 1920.

米國ニ於ケル排日問題雜件
39. Reel no. 39: <u>Beikoku ni okeru hai-Nichi mondai zakken, 22-24</u> [Miscellaneous documents on the Japanese exclusion question in America, 22-24].

I. Consular reports on the 1921 Washington Alien Land Law and the United Northwestern Japanese Association's legal battles to contest it from June, 1921 to June, 1925. Includes legal briefs.

II. Consular and Embassy reports on naturalization cases from February, 1921 to May, 1925. Covers the Ozawa Takao, Yamashita and Charles Hio Kono, Satō Ichizō, and Toyota Hidemitsu cases and includes legal briefs.

米國ニ於ケル排日問題雜件
40. Reel no. 40: <u>Beikoku ni okeru hai-Nichi mondai zakken, 25-27</u> [Miscellaneous documents on the Japanese exclusion question in America, 25-27]. Consular and Embassy reports, including newspaper clippings, on the American newspaper coverage of the passage of the 1924 Immigration Act from May to July, 1924. Also includes similar reports which survey the response of the press of Canada and countries in Latin America, Europe, Asia, with extensive reporting of the Chinese press.

米國ニ於ケル排日問題雜件
41. Reel no. 41: <u>Beikoku ni okeru hai-Nichi mondai zakken, 28-31</u> [Miscellaneous documents on the Japanese exclusion question in America, 28-31].

I. A continuation of Reel no. 40 concentrating on the East Coast newspapers from February to July, 1924. Also includes Foreign Ministry reports and documents on the Japanese response to the passage of the 1924 Immigration Act.

II. Consular reports on Japanese exclusion in Washington from April, 1919 to July, 1923.

III. Embassy reports on the Joint Conference between the President and selected U.S. Senators and Congressmen regarding the 1924 Immigration Act.

米國ニ於ケル排日問題雜件
42. Reel no. 42: <u>Beikoku ni okeru hai-Nichi mondai zakken, 32-34</u> [Miscellaneous documents on the Japanese exclusion question in America, 32-34].

I. Consular and Embassy reports on a U.S. Department of Interior directive which prohibited the leasing of Yakima Indian Reservation land in Washington to aliens and the hiring of alien agricultural workers from March, 1922 to March, 1925.

II. Documents on miscellaneous legal cases related to the exclusion question from 1923 to 1925.

III. Consular and Embassy reports on the California State Legislature for 1921. Covers the 1921 Alien Poll Tax Law, the Terui Heikichi Case, and the 1921 Foreign Language School Law.

米國ニ於ケル排日問題雜件
43.* Reel no. 43: <u>Beikoku ni okeru hai-Nichi mondai zakken, 35-36</u> [Miscellaneous documents on the Japanese exclusion question in America, 35-36].

I. Consular reports and documents on the Japanese language school controversy in Hawaii from July, 1922 to September, 1923.

II. Consular reports on anti-Japanese bills introduced in the California State Legislature in 1923 and 1925.

44. Reel no. 44: 米國ニ於ケル排日問題雑件 Beikoku ni okeru hai-Nichi mondai zakken, 37-38 [Miscellaneous documents on the Japanese exclusion question in America, 37-38]. Embassy reports on U.S. Congressional activities on immigration restrictions and other related matters from 1919 to 1921.

45. Reel no. 45: 米國ニ於ケル排日問題雑件 Beikoku ni okeru hai-Nichi mondai zakken, 39-41 [Miscellaneous documents on the Japanese exclusion question in America, 39-41].

    I. A continuation of Reel no. 44 through April, 1923.

    II. A continuation of Reel no. 32 for the months of May, June, and July, 1924. Generally consists of Prefectural Governors' reports on the protests against the 1924 Immigration Act in their Prefectures.

46. Reel no. 46: 米國ニ於ケル排日問題雑件 Beikoku ni okeru hai-Nichi mondai zakken, 42-43 [Miscellaneous documents on the Japanese exclusion question in America, 42-43].

    I. Consular reports on the 1920 California election campaign, the Alien Land Law initiative, and the results of the election from August to December, 1920.

    II. Consular reports on Japanese exclusion in Oregon from 1919 to 1925. Contains documents on proposed and/or passed anti-Japanese and related legislation, including the 1923 Oregon Alien Land Law.

47. Reel no. 47: 米國ニ於ケル排日問題雑件 Beikoku ni okeru hai-Nichi mondai zakken, 44-45 [Miscellaneous documents on the Japanese exclusion question in America, 44-45]. Consular reports on alien land laws and related anti-Japanese legislation enacted in Colorado, Nebraska, Nevada, Texas, Utah, Louisiana, Idaho, Montana, Arizona, New Mexico, Missouri, Kansas, Wyoming, Florida, and Washington from 1919 to 1925.

48. Reel no. 48: 米國ニ於ケル排日問題雑件 Beikoku ni okeru hai-Nichi mondai zakken, 46-48 [Miscellaneous documents on the Japanese exclusion question in America, 46-48].

    I. Consular reports on the picture-bride controversy from March, 1919 to August, 1922. Covers the Japanese government's decision to cease issuing passports to picture-brides and the Japanese community opposition to it. Also includes reports submitted by Prefectural Governors on the number of passports issued to picture-brides from 1915 to 1919.

    II. Embassy reports and documents on various immigration bills which were introduced in Congress from February, 1923 to April, 1924.

49. Reel no. 49: 米國ニ於ケル排日問題雑件 Beikoku ni okeru hai-Nichi mondai zakken, 49-51 [Miscellaneous documents on the Japanese exclusion question in America, 49-51].

I. A continuation of Reel no. 48, Section II, from September to December, 1923.

II. Embassy reports and documents on proposed Constitutional amendments to deprive American-born children of parents ineligible for citizenship of their U.S. citizenship from December, 1923 to July, 1924.

III. Embassy reports and documents on deportation bills, proposed amendments to the 1924 Immigration Act, and other matters related to immigration from August, 1924 to January, 1925.

米國ニ於ケル排日問題雜件
50. Reel no. 50: Beikoku ni okeru hai-Nichi mondai zakken, 52-53 [Miscellaneous documents on the Japanese exclusion question in America, 52-53]. Consular and Embassy reports on the origins, development, and politics of the 1920 California Alien Land Law initiative from November, 1919 to October, 1920.

米國ニ於ケル排日問題雜件
51. Reel no. 51: Beikoku ni okeru hai-Nichi mondai zakken, 54-57 [Miscellaneous
 *   documents on the Japanese exclusion question in America, 54-57].

I. Embassy reports and documents on the U.S. Supreme Court decisions of November, 1923 on the alien land laws of California and Washington. Covers the Terrace and Nakatsuka, Porterfield and Mizuno, Frick and Satow, and O'Brien and Inouye Cases.

II. Foreign Ministry documents relating to the problem of transporting emigrants to Hawaii and the continental United States, especially yobiyose, before the effective date of the 1924 Immigration Act from May to June, 1924.

III. Consular reports on the origins and development of the Survey of Race Relations Research Project headed by Dr. Robert E. Park of the University of Chicago from 1923 to 1925.

IV. Consular reports and documents on legal questions with respect to the 1913 and 1920 California Alien Land Laws from March to December, 1920. Covers land titles placed in the name of Nisei children, the formation of corporations, the Japanese-American Treaty of Commerce of 1911, and other matters.

米國ニ於ケル排日問題雜件
52. Reel no. 52: Beikoku ni okeru hai-Nichi mondai zakken, 58-59. [Miscellaneous documents on the Japanese exclusion question in America, 58-59]. Consular reports on litigation relating to the 1913 and 1920 California Alien Land Laws from September, 1920 to July, 1923. Includes legal briefs as well as documents on the activities of the Japanese Association of America and the Central Japanese Association of Southern California.

米國ニ於ケル排日問題雜件
53. Reel no. 53: Beikoku ni okeru hai-Nichi mondai zakken, 60-61 [Miscellaneous documents on the Japanese exclusion question in America, 60-61].

I. Consular reports on the aftereffects of the U.S. Supreme Court decisions of November, 1923 on alien land laws from October, 1923 to December, 1924. Covers the Kataoka and Sakurai Guardianship Cases, the plans of State and County District Attorneys, and other topics. Includes extensive documents on the financial straits of Japanese farmers.

II. Consular reports on American organizations and individuals opposed to the 1920 California Alien Land Law initiative from March to December, 1920.

米國ニ於ケル排日問題雜件
54. Reel no. 54: Beikoku ni okeru hai-Nichi mondai zakken, 62-65 [Miscellaneous documents on the Japanese exclusion question in America, 62-65].
*

I. A continuation of Reel no. 53, Section II, covering Southern California, the Pacific Northwest, and the East Coast. Includes reports of Prefectural Governors on the Japanese reaction to the passage of the initiative for the months of December, 1920 and January, 1921.

II. Miscellaneous documents on the post-World War I Americanization campaign, especially in Hawaii.

III. Consular reports on the compilation of Documental History of Law Cases Affecting Japanese in the United States, 1916-1924, 2 vols. (San Francisco, 1925), and on additional land litigation from May, 1924 to 1925.

IV. Foreign Ministry documents on the reactions in Japan to proposed Constitutional amendments to deprive the American-born Nisei of their American citizenship and the 1924 Immigration Act from July, 1923 to February, 1925. Includes reports by Prefectural Governors.

米國ニ於ケル排日問題雜件
55. Reel no. 55: Beikoku ni okeru hai-Nichi mondai zakken, 66-68 [Miscellaneous documents on the Japanese exclusion question in America, 66-68].

I. A continuation of Reel no. 54, Section IV. Additional Foreign Ministry documents on the protests against the passage of the 1924 Immigration Act in Japan, including protests in the National Diet.

II. Consular and Embassy reports on the effects of the 1924 Immigration Act on the Japanese in America, with particular reference to the elimination of the "endorsement right" delegated to local Japanese Associations to implement the terms of the Gentlemen's Agreement of 1907-08 from June, 1924 to December, 1925.

III. Foreign Ministry and Consular reports on the problems of returnees to America with the passage of the 1924 Immigration Act from April, 1924 to June, 1925. Includes extensive reports by Prefectural Governors.

米國ニ於ケル排日問題雜件
56. Reel no. 56: Beikoku ni okeru hai-Nichi mondai zakken, 69-70 [Miscellaneous documents on the Japanese exclusion question in America, 69-70]. Consular and Embassy reports on the implementation, interpretation, and legal problems of the 1924 Immigration Act from April, 1924 to August, 1925.

57. Reel no. 57:
*
米國ニ於ケル排日問題雜件
I. Beikoku ni okeru hai-Nichi mondai zakken, 71-73 [Miscellaneous documents on the Japanese exclusion question in America, 71-73]. Consular and Embassy reports on proposals to amend the 1924 Immigration Act from September, 1924 to July, 1925; and miscellaneous San Francisco Consular reports from June, 1913 to November, 1914.

31

　　　　　本邦移民關係
　　II. Hompō imin kankei, 1 [Documents relating to Japanese emigrants, 1].
　　　　Consular reports and Foreign Ministry instructions on the Central
　　　　Japanese Association of Hawaii to supervise Japanese affairs and con-
　　　　trol the transmigration of laborers to the continental United States
　　　　from November, 1903 to April, 1906; and miscellaneous Consular reports
　　　　on individual monetary remissions and the disposition of the assets
　　　　of deceased and returned Japanese from December, 1924 to May, 1925.

　　　　　本邦移民關係
58. Reel no. 58: Hompō imin kankei, 2 [Documents relating to Japanese emigrants,
*   2]. A continuation of Reel no. 57, Section II, from January, 1922 to
　　　August, 1925 on monetary remissions and other personal matters.

59. Reel no. 59:

　　　　　航海人明細鑑
　　I. Kōkaijin meisaikan [Passport registry]. A registry of passports
　　　　issued from 1867 to 1872.

　　　　　航海人明細簿
　　II. Kōkaijin meisaibo [Passport registry]. A continuation of above
　　　　through 1875.

　　　　　海外行免狀改正考案
　　III. Kaigai-yuki menjō kaisei kōan [Draft for the revision of the passport
　　　　law]. An 1875 draft to amend the passport law.

　　　　　外國官廳ニ於テ本邦人雇入關係雜件・米國之部墨國之部
　　IV. Gaikoku kanchō ni oite hompōjin yatoiire kankei zakken: Beikoku no
　　　　bu, Bokkoku no bu [Miscellaneous documents relating to Japanese
　　　　employed through the Japanese government: America and Mexico].
　　　　Documents relating to specific individuals employed abroad in
　　　　America and Mexico through the Japanese government from 1901 to
　　　　1913.

　　　　　海外行免狀沿革次第並事務例則
　　V. Kaigai-yuki menjō enkaku shidai narabini jimu reisoku [History of
　　　　passport laws and regulations]. Documents on passport laws, regu-
　　　　lations, and their revisions from 1868 to 1878.

　　　　　幕府以來發給海外行免狀及海外旅券類集
　　VI. Bakufu irai hakkyū kaigai-yuki menjō oyobi kaigai ryoken ruishū [File
　　　　of passports issued by the Bakufu and Meiji government]. A sample
　　　　collection of the different types of passports issued by the Bakufu
　　　　and Meiji government from 1866 to 1887.

　　　　　海外行免狀發行一件
　　VII. Kaigai-yuki menjō hakkō ikken [Documents relating to the issuance of
　　　　passports]. Documents relating to the correspondence exchanged
　　　　between the Foreign Ministry and the Japanese Legations and Consu-
　　　　lates abroad on the issuance of passports and the Japanese abroad
　　　　from 1868 to 1877.

60. Reel no. 60:

　　　　　於開港場免狀相渡候航海人明細鑑
　　I. Kaikōjō ni oite menjō aiwatashisōrō kōkaijin meisaikan [Passport regis-

try of Prefectures with open ports]. The passport registries of Hokkaido, Niigata, Kanagawa, Hyogo, and Nagasaki from 1868 to 1874.

邦人被傭雑件
II. Hōjin hiyatoi zakken [Miscellaneous documents relating to Japanese employed by foreigners]. Documents on specific individuals hired by foreigners for the purpose of taking them abroad to work from 1869 to 1901.

61. Reel no. 61:

開港場ニ於テ印章附與海外行人銘表
I. Kaikōjō ni oite inshō fuyo kaigai-yuki jimmeihyō [Passport registry of Prefectures with open ports]. A continuation of Reel no. 60, Section I, for 1875.

舊政府之節免状申受之者姓名調
II. Kyū seifu no setsu menjō mōshiuke no mono seimei shirabe [Roster of passports issued by the Bakufu]. A roster of passports issued by the Bakufu from 1866 to 1868.

62. Reel no. 62:

開港場及各府縣海外旅券附與人名表
I. Kaikōjō oyobi kakufuken kaigai ryoken fuyo jimmeihyō [Passport registry of Municipalities, Prefectures, and open ports]. The passport registries of Municipalities, Prefectures, and open ports which list sailors and Japanese employed by foreigners from 1878 to 1879.

海外行免状表
II. Kaigai-yuki menjōhyō [Passport registry]. A continuation of Reel no. 61, Section I, from 1876 to 1878.

63. Reel no. 63:
*
海外行免状書類
I. Kaigai-yuki menjō shorui [Documents relating to the issuance of passports]. Miscellaneous documents of the Foreign Ministry and Prefectures with open ports relating to the issuance of passports from 1868 to 1874.

渡航者名簿
II. Tokōsha meibo [Dekaseginin roster]. Registries of dekaseginin going to foreign countries, including Hawaii and the continental United States, under the auspices of emigration companies and agents for 1897.

海外旅券規則並其取扱手續制定及改正一件
64. Reel no. 64: Kaigai ryoken kisoku narabini sono toriatsukai tetsuzuki seitei oyobi kaisei ikken [Documents relating to passport laws, regulations, and their revisions]. A compilation of documents relating to passport laws and regulations and their revisions from February, 1878 to June, 1909. Includes the various drafts of laws and regulations.

旅券法規及同法規取扱手續ニ關スル訓令指令並旅券下附手續取締雑件
65. Reel nos. 65-73: Ryoken hōki oyobi dō-hōki toriatsukai tetsuzuki ni kansuru

kunrei shirei narabini ryoken kafu tetsuzuki torishimari zakken, 1-15 [Miscellaneous documents relating to Foreign Ministry instructions and orders on passport laws and regulations and the control of the issuance of passports, 1-15]. Documents on Foreign Ministry instructions and orders on the issuance of passports to concerned governmental offices from March, 1878 to December, 1926.

66. 在外邦人死亡及遺産關係雜件
 * Reel nos. 74-95: Zaigai hōjin shibō oyobi isan kankei zakken, 1-68 [Miscellaneous documents relating to deceased overseas Japanese and their assets, 1-68]. Documents relating to overseas Japanese who died abroad and the disposition of their assets from 1916 to 1926. Reels nos. 74-75 contain documents on deceased sailors and nos. 75-95 on Japanese residents in foreign countries arranged alphabetically, including many who died in Hawaii and the continental United States.

67. [外務省]
 + [Gaimushō]. ["Documents"]. 8 reels.

    SP-1, SP-50, SP-258, SP-263, S 10.1.1.0-1.

68. [外務省]　[叙勲者名簿]
    [Gaimushō]. ["Jokunsha meibo" [Medal recipients]]. 1 folder, n.d. Tokyo.

    A list of Issei, Nisei, and other Americans who received medals from the Japanese government between 1947 and 1968.

69. [外務省]　アメリカ局　日米修好通商百年記念外務大臣表彰者名簿
    [Gaimushō]. Amerika-kyoku. "Nichi-Bei shūkō tsūshō hyakunen kinen Gaimu Daijin hyōshōsha meibo" [Commemoration of 100 years of Japanese-American commercial amity: The Foreign Minister's list of recipients]. 1 folder, 1960. Tokyo. X.

    A list of 2,499 Issei and Nisei who received commendations from the Japanese Foreign Minister to mark the 100th anniversary of the Japanese-American Treaty of Amity and Commerce.

2. CONSULATES

70. [羅府日本領事館]
    [Rafu Nihon Ryōjikan]. "Centennial award list." 1 folder, 1960. Los Angeles.

    A list of Issei and Nisei who received medals and commendations from the Japanese government in 1960 to mark the 100th anniversary of the Japanese-American Treaty of Amity and Commerce.

71. 羅府日本領事館
    Rafu Nihon Ryōjikan. "Registration cards." 62 boxes, 1920-1941. Los Angeles.

    Three sets of registration cards of Japanese subjects under the jurisdiction of the Japanese Consulate of Los Angeles. The first set has over 42,000 cards on individuals registered between 1920 and 1924; the second about 8,833 cards for the period 1925 to 1940; and the third 82 cards for 1941. Includes date and place of birth, social and marital status, occupation, householdhead and family relationship, date of arrival and port of entry, property holdings, and current address.

72. 羅府日本領事館　登録人名簿
    Rafu Nihon Ryōjikan. "Tōrokunin meibo" [Registry]. MSS. 4 vols., 1926. Los Angeles.

    A comprehensive registry of the Japanese subjects residing within the jurisdiction of the Japanese Consulate of Los Angeles as of 1925.

73. 羅府日本領事館　在外本邦實業團体調
    Rafu Nihon Ryōjikan. "Zaigai hompō jitsugyō dantai shirabe" [List of overseas Japanese economic organizations]. MSS. 1 binder, 1939. Los Angeles.

    A list of Japanese business and agricultural associations in Southern California compiled by the Japanese Consulate of Los Angeles in March, 1939.

74. 羅府日本領事館　在留證明發行記録
    Rafu Nihon Ryōjikan. "Zairyū shomei hakkō kiroku" [Record of certificates of residence]. MSS. 1 vol., 1920-1941. Los Angeles.

    The record of certificates of residence issued by the Japanese Consulate of Los Angeles from December, 1920 to October, 1941.

75. 沙港日本領事館　第四回國勢調査表
    Shakō Nihon Ryōjikan. "Dai-yonkai Kokusei Chōsahyō" [The 4th National Census]. MSS. 1 vol., 1935. Seattle.

    A report of the 4th census of the Japanese within the jurisdiction of the Japanese Consulate of Seattle as of September 1, 1935.

76. [沙港日本領事館]　日米修交百年記念表彰者リスト
    [Shakō Nihon Ryōjikan]. "Nichi-Bei shukō hyakunen kinen hyōshosha risuto" [List of recipients to mark the 100th anniversary of Japanese-American amity]. 1 folder, [1960]. Seattle.

    A similar list to no. 70 of the Japanese Consulate of Seattle.

77. 桑港日本領事館　耕作物並ニ畏加載　實状調査
    Sōkō Nihon Ryōjikan. "Kōsakubutsu narabini eikasū" [Crops and acreage]; "Jitsujo chosa" [Census]. MSS. 1 binder, 1922-1923, 1926. San Francisco.

    A 1922-1923 survey report on the Japanese farmers in Stanislaus and Merced Counties and a census report of the Japanese in the same two counties as of January, 1926 by the Japanese Consulate of San Francisco.

78. 桑港日本領事館　職業並ニ戸口調査表
    Sōkō Nihon Ryōjikan. "Shokugyō narabini kokō chosahyō" [Business and household census]. MSS. 1 binder, 1920-1928. San Francisco.

    The annual census records of the Japanese in Stanislaus and Merced Counties compiled by the Japanese Consulate of San Francisco from 1920 to 1928.

II.
Background to Emigration

Note: Like the materials in Chapter I, the publications listed below are important for the study of the origins and causes of emigration. Worthy of special note are the works on the ideology of expansionism and emigration, the specific guides to America, and the journals specializing in emigration news, which carried a sizable body of "American letters." Though the journal and magazine articles listed in Section 4 have not been individually annotated, they are also very useful.

1. ORIGINS AND CAUSES

79. 淺見登郎　　新日本の植民政策　　　　　　　　　　　外交時報
Asami Nobuo. "Shin Nihon no shokumin seisaku" [A colonial policy for a new Japan], Gaikō Jihō [Revue Diplomatique], 43:517 (Jun. 15, 1926), 60-71; 44:518 (Jul. 1, 1926), 39-55; 44:519 (Jul. 15, 1926), 60-73; and 44:520 (Aug. 1, 1926), 69-81. M.

An extended essay on Japanese emigration policies. Making the distinction between shokumin [colonist] and imin [emigrant], between those who emigrate to newly acquired Japanese territories such as Korea and Taiwan and those who emigrate to foreign countries, the author believes there should be different emigration policies in accord with this distinction. The past failure to make this differentiation has led to confused thinking.

80. 外務省　　海外出稼人契約書類集
* [Gaimushō. Kaigai dekaseginin keiyaku shoruishū [Memoranda of agreements relating to the overseas dekasegi of Japanese laborers]. Tokyo: Gaimushō, 1892]. 8 + 15 + 7 + 11 + 4 + 7 + 8 + 7 pp. M (imperfect copy).

A compilation of the memoranda of agreements for 1891 and 1892, in both Japanese and English, entered into between Robert W. Irwin, special agent of the Hawaiian Bureau of Immigration and the Japanese dekaseginin to Hawaii; between Nippon Yoshisa Imin Kaisha [Nippon Yoshisa Emigration Company] and Francois Lutscher, agent of the Société Anonyme le Nickle of Paris, to recruit laborers to work in a mine in New Caledonia; between Nippon Yoshisa Imin Kaisha and Burns, Philips & Co., Ltd. of New Wales and Queensland, Australia for dekaseginin destined for Queensland; and between Nippon Meiji

Imin Kaisha [Nippon Meiji Emigration Company] and Frank Apton, agent of a coal mining company in Victoria, British Columbia.

81. 日置益　日本人口処分問題と外交政策　　外交時報
    Hioki Eki. "Nihon jinkō shobun mondai to gaikō seisaku" [The handling of the Japanese population question and foreign policy], Gaikō Jihō [Revue Diplomatique], 40:474 (Sep. 1, 1924), 20-33. M.

    An article criticizing the idea of emigration to South America as a solution to Japan's population problem. The author argues that another exclusion movement similar to those which occurred in North America will develop in South America as soon as the number of Japanese increases there. Because of close geographical, cultural, and historical ties as well as political, economic, and military significance, he favors emigration to Hokkaido, Korea, Manchuria, Mongolia, and Siberia.

82. 移民問題研究會　移民問題研究會とその事業
    Imin Mondai Kenkyūkai. Imin Mondai Kenkyūkai to sono jigyō [The Emigration Problem Research Society and its work]. Tokyo: Imin Mondai Kenkyūkai, 1938. 12 pp.

    A booklet describing the purposes of the Imin Mondai Kenkyūkai [Emigration Problem Research Society]. Founded in 1936 with the support of the Foreign Ministry, its purposes were to undertake research on the problems of emigration and to recommend policy solutions. Headed by Hayashi Hisajirō, it published a journal entitled Kaigai Ijū [Overseas Migration] as well as other publications.

83. 井上雅二　排日の米國と迎日の南米　　外交時報
    Inoue Masaji. "Hai-Nichi no Beikoku to gei-Nichi no Nan-Bei" [Anti-Japanese America and receptive South America], Gaikō Jihō [Revue Diplomatique], 42:502 (Nov. 1, 1925), 27-39. M.

    An article on the desirability of emigration to South America. The author believes there is no racial prejudice in South America unlike North America, and hence does not anticipate any recurrence of the Japanese exclusion movement there. Moreover, South America has an abundance of natural resources with a small population, making it an ideal place for future Japanese emigration.

84. 井上方勝　海外渡航者ノ義ニ付上申
    Inoue Masakatsu. Kaigai tokosha no gi ni tsuki jōshin [Report on the significance of Japanese going abroad]. Kobe: Inoue Masakatsu, 1893. 22 pp. M.

    A brief report on the status of working abroad which specifically criticizes the difficulties of securing a passport and the malpractices of emigration companies. Submitted to the Hyogo Prefectural Governor.

85. 井上方勝　南洋の移民
    Inoue Masakatsu. Nanyō no imin [The South Pacific emigrants]. Kobe: Inoue Masakatsu, 1894. 10 pp. M.

    A brief report on a small group which went to North Borneo to work. Covers the group's experience and concludes that North Borneo is an ideal place to dekasegi.

86. 石射猪太郎　移民問題と人口問題　　外交時報
    Ishii Itaro. "Imin mondai to jinkō mondai" [The immigration and population

questions], <u>Gaikō Jihō</u> [Revue Diplomatique], 44:518 (Jul. 1, 1926), 87-92. M.

    An article with the thesis that emigration cannot solve Japan's over-population problem. The number of emigrants, even under ideal conditions, would not be large enough to make it a realistic solution.

87. 神川彦松　幣原外相の消極的移民政策を排す　外交時報
Kamikawa Hikomatsu. "Shidehara Gaisō no shōkyokuteki imin seisaku wo haisu" [Reject Foreign Minister Shidehara's conservative emigration policy], <u>Gaikō Jihō</u> [Revue Diplomatique], 44:527 (Nov. 15, 1926), 1-9. M.

    An article attacking the Wakatsuki Cabinet for its "conservative" emigration policy. Rather than internal migration, according to the author, the Foreign Minister should support overseas emigration.

88. 黒田謙一　日本植民思想史
Kuroda Ken'ichi. <u>Nihon shokumin shisōshi</u> [History of Japanese emigration thought]. Tokyo: Kōbundō Shobō, 1942. 3 + 6 + 251 pp. M.

    Divided into two parts, this book analyzes the changing ideas on emigration during Tokugawa and early Meiji times. The second half is especially important because the ideas formed the background to Japanese emigration to America. The author examines the shift of ideas in this period from an initial concentration on the question of the settlement of Hokkaido to that of emigration abroad.

89. 諸井六郎　移植民問題に對する新外交政策　外交時報
Moroi Rokurō. "Ishokumin mondai ni taisuru shin gaiko seisaku" [A new foreign policy on the colonist question], <u>Gaikō Jihō</u> [Revue Diplomatique], 43:515 (May 15, 1926), 10-18. M.

    An article on emigration and over-population. The author suggests that emigration policies must be related to the development of trade and commerce to solve Japan's pressing population problem. Emigrants must be carefully screened and their emigration strictly controlled, not only to minimize possible friction in immigrant countries, but also to insure a parallel development of trade and commerce. The author feels that South America is ideal.

90. 武藤山治　米國移住論
Mutō Sanji. <u>Beikoku ijūron</u> [On migration to America]. Tokyo: Maruzen Shokan, 1887. 9 + 144 pp., illus. M.

    Based upon the author's visit to the Pacific Coast in 1885, this book contains: 1) a general description of the Pacific Coast States, especially of California; 2) a discussion of the status of Chinese laborers; 3) a proposal to establish emigration companies, modeled somewhat on the Chinese Six Companies, to encourage and facilitate the emigration of Japanese laborers to the Pacific Coast because of the high labor demand. Such companies, the author argues, would be not only beneficial for Japanese laborers but also profitable.

91. 永田稠　海外發展と我國の教育
Nagata Shigeshi. <u>Kaigai hatten to waga kuni no kyoiku</u> [Overseas development and our national education]. Tokyo: Dobunkan, 1917. 4 + 10 + 239 pp., photos. M.

    A treatise highlighting the need to educate and train the Japanese people to emigrate abroad and what such an education would entail. Chapter

6, pp. 220-239, surveys the state of Japanese language schools abroad, including those in America.

92. 蜷川新　　日本移民論　　　　　　　　　　　　　　　　外交時報
    Nanigawa Shin. "Nihon iminron" [On Japanese emigration], Gaikō Jihō [Revue Diplomatique], 7:82 (Sep. 1904), 58-62. M.

    A general article on Japanese emigration policies which supports emigration, urges long-term thinking, and insists upon flexibility from country to country.

93. 日本移民協會　　第二最近移植民研究
    Nihon Imin Kyōkai. Dai-ni saikin ishokumin kenkyū [Recent studies on emigration: No. 2]. Tokyo: Tōyōsha, 1918. 4 + 278 pp., photos. M.

    A sequel to no. 95 which consists of talks presented in 1917.

94. 日本移民協會　　海外移住
    Nihon Imin Kyōkai. Kaigai ijū [Overseas migration]. Tokyo: Nihon Imin Kyōkai, 1923. [3] + 6 + 263 pp. M.

    A collection of talks presented by various individuals and sponsored by the Nihon Imin Kyōkai [Japan Emigration Association] in Tokyo in 1923. Touches upon contemporary emigration policies, the need to encourage permanent emigration, employment prospects, and the relationship of emigration to trade and finance. Most of the talks concern emigration to South America, especially Brazil.

95. 日本移民協會　　最近移植民研究
    Nihon Imin Kyōkai. Saikin ishokumin kenkyū [Recent studies on emigration]. Tokyo: Tōyōsha, 1917. 2 + 6 + 506 + app. 37 pp., photos. M.

    A collection of talks sponsored by the Nihon Imin Kyōkai [Japan Emigration Association] in the summer of 1916 on various aspects of Japanese emigration by different individuals--on "over-population" and emigration, the meaning and significance of emigration, emigration policies, and the conditions of immigrant lands. Two specific talks on North America, one by Uehara Etsujiro and the other by Suzuki Bunji, are included. Laws related to emigration are reproduced in the 37-page appendix.

96. 大河尋常高等小學校　　移民と教育
*   Ōgawa Jinjō Kōtō Shōgakkō. Imin to kyōiku [Emigration and education]. Hiroshima: Ōgawa Jinjō Kōtō Shōgakkō, 1918. [2] + 4 + 13 + 556 pp., maps. M.

    Compiled by the faculty of the Ogawa Higher Elementary School in Hiroshima, this volume surveys the immigrant countries to which the Japanese have emigrated and the Japanese in them. America, including Hawaii, is discussed on pp. 152-240. Based upon the prevalent idea of over-population, it advocates education which will adequately prepare the Japanese to emigrate to solve this problem. Concludes with an evaluation of the preparation required to emigrate abroad.

97. 大河平隆光　　日本移民論
    Ōkawahira Takamitsu. Nihon iminron [On overseas migration of the Japanese]. Tokyo: Tokyo Bunbudō, 1905. [2] + 6 + 8 + bibliog. 4 + 368 pp., tables, apps. M.

    A treatise on the desirability of promoting the overseas migration of dekaseginin under careful government auspices to provide relief for the impoverished agrarian population, to secure capital through monetary remissions of the dekaseginin, to create demand for Japanese exports abroad, and to seek sources of raw materials. South America is considered an ideal place for such migration.

98. 奥宮健之　北米移民論
    Okumiya Takeyuki. Hoku-Bei iminron [On Japanese emigration to North America]. Tokyo: Tōkyōdō, 1903. [3] + 83 + apps. 59 pp. M.

    A treatise critical of the emigration policy of the Japanese government, arguing that it restricts the emigration of those Japanese who would be acceptable to Americans. Recommends the immediate removal of restrictions and the adoption of a new policy to facilitate the emigration of "qualified" emigrants to America.

99. 関口野薔薇　日本移民問題の過去及び現在
    Sekiguchi Nobara. "Nihon imin mondai no kako oyobi genzai" [The past and present Japanese immigration question], The Japan Theo-Psychic Culture, 15:6 (Jun. 1963), 161-166.

    A brief essay on the Nihon Rikkōkai [Japan Self-Help Society] and its prewar activities.

100. 社會政策學會　移民問題
     Shakai Seisaku Gakkai. Imin mondai [Emigration problems]. Tokyo: Dōbunkan, 1910. 2 + 1 + 316 pp. X.

     The record of the third conference of the Shakai Seisaku Gakkai [Society on Social Policies] held on December 19-20, 1909 in Tokyo. The main topic for this conference was the various problems relating to emigration, including those touching upon emigration to America.

101.* 志賀重昂　南洋時事
     Shiga Shigetaka. Nanyō jiji [South Pacific affairs]. Tokyo: Maruzen Shōsha Shoten, 1887. 6 + 2 + 7 + 4 + 5 + 196 pp., map, tables. M.

     A report on the economic conditions and the state of Western colonial and commercial expansion in the South Pacific islands and Australia which the author visited aboard a Japanese naval training ship in 1886. Throughout the book, the author emphasizes the need for Japan to vigorously pursue a policy of commercial and colonial expansion in the South Pacific in order to ease her population pressure and to provide relief to the impoverished laboring class. Also includes a brief report on the dekaseginin to Hawaii who began migrating to the islands in 1885.

102. 島貫兵太夫　力行會とは何ぞや
     Shimanuki Hyōdayū. Rikkōkai to wa nanzo ya [What is the Self-Help Society?]. Tokyo: Keiseisha, 1911. 11 + 4 + 182 + 39 pp. M.

     An autobiography of Shimanuki Hyōdayū, the founder of the Nihon Rikkōkai [Japan Self-Help Society], interwoven with the history and activities of the organization. A Christian society founded in 1897, it rendered assistance to the poor youth from rural areas to either study abroad or emigrate on a permanent basis. Includes the Constitution and the regulations and by-laws governing the various sections of the organization.

103. 田村丙子　海外發展に關する勝田大藏大臣講演・全國中少農の分布及其經濟状態
     Tamura Heishi (ed.). Kaigai hatten ni kansuru Katsuda Ōkura Daijin kōen; Zen

koku chū-shōnō no bunpu oyobi sono keizai jōtai [Finance Minister Katsuda's speech on overseas development; the national distribution of medium and small farmers and their economic status]. Tokyo: Kaigai Kōgyō Kabushiki Kaisha, 1918. 47 + 33 pp. M.

Two unrelated items. The first is the text of a talk presented by Finance Minister Katsuda on August 6, 1918 before the Nihon Imin Kyōkai [Japan Emigration Association] on the relationship between emigration and foreign investment as well as on the need for preparatory education. The second surveys the economic status of medium and small farms, and concludes that the farmers in these categories are potential emigrants because of economic hardship.

104. 東郷實　日本植民論
Tōgō Minoru. Nihon shokuminron [On Japanese colonization]. Tokyo: Bunbudō, 1906. 7 + 8 + 388 pp., plates. M.

A treatise which calls for Japanese agriculturalists to become colonists in Korea, Manchuria, and Taiwan. Written after the Russo-Japanese War of 1904-05, the author argues that colonization is necessary to consolidate Japan's military victories.

105. 恒屋盛服　海外殖民論
* Tsuneya Moriyuki. Kaigai shokuminron [On overseas expansion of the Japanese]. Tokyo: Hakubunsha, 1891. Plates 3 + 2 + 2 + 6 + 345 pp., tables, map. M.

A treatise advising the Japanese government to pursue a vigorous policy of colonial and maritime expansion with the support of a strong naval force. The author believes that the colonial expansion of the Japanese will not only solve the population problem of Japan but also enable her to expand her maritime trade in competition with Western powers. As prospective places for the Japanese to establish colonies, he selects Mexico, Central and South America, the South Pacific, Southeast Asia, and Hawaii.

106. 内田定槌　大和民族の海外發展　外交時報
Uchida Sadatsuchi. "Yamato minzoku no kaigai hatten" [The overseas development of the Japanese people], Gaikō Jihō [Revue Diplomatique], 42:505 (Dec. 15, 1925), 35-39. M.

An article on education and emigration. Believing that Japanese unemployment and poverty can be solved by emigration, the author proposes reforms in the Japanese educational system, including the adoption of romanization and the study of appropriate foreign languages and of conditions in immigrant countries, to prepare prospective emigrants. South America is considered a desirable place to which to emigrate.

107. 山田筆三郎　大廣島縣創刊第十五周年
Yamada Fudesaburō. Dai-Hiroshima-ken: Sōkan dai-jūgoshūnen [Greater Hiroshima Prefecture: Special 15th anniversary issue]. Hiroshima: Hiroshima-ken Kaigai Kyōkai, 1930. 169 pp., photos.

A special 15th anniversary issue of the Dai-Hiroshima-ken published by the Hiroshima-ken Kaigai Kyōkai [Hiroshima Prefecture Overseas Association]. Founded in 1915 as the Hiroshima-ken Shokumin Kyōkai, this organization disseminated information about immigrant countries and facilitated emigration from Hiroshima Prefecture; it changed its name to the Hiroshima-ken Kaigai Kyōkai in October, 1918. Its official organ started as a quarterly entitled Hiroshima-ken Naigai Jihō in 1916, became a monthly in October, 1917, and then changed to the Dai-Hiroshima-ken in February, 1920. This special issue contains the history of the Hiroshima-ken Kaigai Kyōkai and information on immigrant countries, particularly Brazil.

108. 山本熊太郎　移民政策の萎微　　　　　　　　外交時報
Yamamoto Kumatarō. "Imin seisaku no ibi" [Wilting emigration policy], Gaikō Jihō [Revue Diplomatique], 45:535 (Mar. 15, 1927), 63-70. M.

An article critical of the Japanese government's lack of a clear, positive emigration policy. The author views emigration as a solution to Japan's population problem as well as a way to expand trade and commerce.

109. 山本美越乃　我国民の海外發展に關する史的概観　　外交時報
Yamamoto Miono. "Waga kokumin no kaigai hatten ni kansuru shiteki gaikan" [A historical outline of Japanese overseas development], Gaikō Jihō [Revue Diplomatique], 26:307 (Aug. 15, 1917), 59-68. M.

A general, interpretative essay on Japanese history. Being an island nation, Japan has had a continuous history of outward expansion, the author writes. Viewing this past history as an expression of "Japanese national character," he traces it through different periods down to Taisho times.

2. GUIDES TO AMERICA

110. 赤峰瀬一郎　米國今不審議
Akamine Seichirō. Beikoku ima fushingi [Mysterious America]. Tokyo: Jitsugakukai Eigakkō, 1887 (2nd printing). 3 + 7 + 148 pp., illus.

An early description of San Francisco and California in the 1880's. The author came to San Francisco in 1880 and remained for five years. Includes some observations of the few Japanese and the Fukuinkai [Gospel Society] in San Francisco during this period.

111. 秋廣秋郊　海外苦學案内
Akihiro Shūkō (ed.). Kaigai kugaku annai [How a poor student can go abroad]. Tokyo: Hakuhōdō, 1904. 4 + 2 + 5 + 184 pp. M.

Designed as a guide for poor students, this volume contains reprints of letters sent to the editor by self-supporting students in the United States, Hawaii, Canada, Germany, and France along with the advice and suggestions of the editor for prospective students who, too, desire to study abroad but lack the means.

112. 天野寅三郎　渡米羅針
Amano Torasaburō. To-Bei rashin [A compass to go to America]. Tokyo: Tōkyō Kōseisha, 1904. [5] + 52 pp. M.

A brief guide providing bits of useful information concerning where and how one applies for passports, how to dress and behave on the ship, how to answer the inquiries of United States Immigration inspectors, and how to find jobs after landing. Also includes information about the Tōkyō Kōseisha, a society which assisted prospective emigrants and was headed by the author.

113. 飯島榮太郎　　米國渡航案内
    Iijima Eitarō. Beikoku tokō annai [A guide to going to America]. Tokyo: Hakubunkan, 1902. [2] + 3 + 2 + 6 + 320 + app. 38 pp., plates, photos, map. M.

    A guide to America which provides general information as well as specific facts on the American educational system, matriculation requirements, and curricula, especially of colleges and universities. The appendix consists of a list of selected American colleges and universities.

114. 石田隈治郎　　來れ日本人
    Ishida Kumajirō. Kitare Nihonjin ["Come, Japanese!"]. Tokyo: Privately printed, 1887. 10 + 165 pp., plates, illus. M.

    A guide to America for prospective students which concentrates on California and the San Francisco area. Contains general information on emigration procedures, the passage across the Pacific, and American custom regulations; also has information on the American educational system, matriculation requirements, and possible courses of study.

115. 石塚猪男藏　　現今渡米案内
    Ishizuka Iozō. Genkon to-Bei annai [A current guide to America]. Osaka: Ishizuka Shoten, 1903. 4 + 4 + 154 + app. 38 pp. M.

    A general guide to emigration requirements, shipping companies, the Pacific Coast and Japanese immigrant society. Also includes a brief section on Mexico and the Japanese. The 38-page appendix consists of Japanese and American laws pertaining to immigration.

116. 片山潜　　新渡米
    Katayama Sen. Shin to-Bei [New guide to America]. Tokyo: Tobei Kyōkai, 1904. 3 + 3 + 3 + 8 + 104 + 13 pp. M.

    An updated version of no. 117 and no. 119.

117. 片山潜　　渡米案内
    Katayama Sen. To-Bei annai [Guide to America]. Tokyo: Rōdō Shimbunsha, 1901. 2 + 2 + 68 + app. 11 pp. M.

    A brief guide to America primarily for students and laborers. The author describes his own 13-year experience in America as a student and laborer from 1884 to 1896. Also has reprints of short notes from students studying in America. The appendix consists of basic English.

118. 片山潜　　渡米の秘訣
    Katayama Sen. To-Bei no hiketsu [Secrets on going to America]. Tokyo: Tobei Kyōkai, 1906 (?). 8 + 4 + 144 + app. 54 pp. M.

    An updated and expanded guide to America which has information on employment, the Texas Japanese rice colony, and a special section on women. The 54-page appendix consists of basic English.

119. 片山潜　　續渡米案内
    Katayama Sen. Tsuzuki to-Bei annai [Guide to America: A sequel]. Tokyo: Tobei Kyōkai, 1902. 4 + 87 pp. M.

    A sequel to no. 117. Contains additional information on American social customs, mode of living, and updated facts on employment and schools. Also has "American letters" from members of the Tobei Kyōkai [Association for the America-bound] organized by the author in 1902.

120. 河村鐵太郎　　　最近活動北米事業案内
Kawamura Tetsutarō. <u>Saikin katsudō Hoku-Bei jigyō annai</u> [Guide to current jobs in North America]. Tokyo: Hakubunkan, 1906. [6] + 2 + 14 + 340 pp., photos. M.

Based upon the author's 4-year personal experience in America, this book presents facts on labor conditions and wages by skilled versus unskilled, urban versus rural job categories and on the prospects for employment for Japanese workers.

121. 木村芳五郎　　井上胤文　　最近正確布哇渡航案内
*   Kimura Yoshigorō and Inoue Tanefumi. <u>Saikin seikaku Hawai tokō annai</u> [Current accurate guide to Hawaii]. Tokyo: Hakubunkan, 1904. 2 + 4 + 2 + 10 + 192 + app. 26 pp., maps, photos. M.

Divided into three parts, this guide provides: 1) general information on emigration requirements; 2) a description of the Japanese communities of Honolulu and Hilo; and 3) a section devoted to Hawaiian history and geography as well as the social, economic, and political conditions there. The 26-page appendix consists of Japanese and American laws pertaining to immigration.

122. 北澤寅之助　　成澤金兵衛　　新撰渡米案内
Kitazawa Toranosuke and Narizawa Kinpei. <u>Shinsen to-Bei annai</u> [New guide to America]. Tokyo: Naigai Shuppan Kyōkai, 1906. 3 + 140 + apps. 77 pp. M.

A brief guide to America for prospective workers and students. The authors feel that Japanese emigration to America should be for the purpose of establishing a "New Japan" on the Pacific Coast.

123. 島貫兵太夫　　最近渡米策
Shimanuki Hyōdayū. <u>Saikin to-Beisaku</u> [Current ways of going to America]. Tokyo: Nihon Rikkōkai, 1904. [4] + 170 + 4 pp. M.

A guide to America in a question-and-answer format published by the Nihon Rikkōkai [Japan Self-Help Society]. Compiles typical questions asked of the organization by persons wishing to go to America and its answers to them.

124. 島貫兵太夫　　新渡米法
Shimanuki Hyōdayū. <u>Shin to-Beihō</u> [New methods of going to America]. Tokyo: Hakubunkan, 1911. 10 + 7 + 262 pp., photos. M.

An updated and expanded version of no. 123 and no. 125.

125. 島貫兵太夫　　渡米案内
Shimanuki Hyōdayū. <u>To-Bei annai</u> [Guide to America]. Tokyo: Chūyōdō, 1901. 2 + 6 + 236 pp. M.

A guide to America mainly based upon the author's experience in America from November, 1897 to May, 1898. Includes selected diary entries.

126. 清水鶴三郎　　米國勞働便覽
Shimizu Tsuruzaburō. <u>Beikoku rōdō benran</u> [Labor handbook for America]. San Francisco: Shimizu Tsuruzaburō, 1903 (2nd printing). 2 + 2 + 5 + 352 pp., plates. M.

An extensive, practical English handbook designed for Japanese workers in America, with some information about employment opportunities.

127. 松庵生　　　　渡米の栞
Shōansei (pseud.). To-Bei no shiori [Guide to America]. Tokyo: Sasaki Kansuke, 1901. 7 + [2] + 156 pp. M.

A short guide on the preparation and emigration requirements necessary for going to America. Also provides a directory of Japanese organizations in San Francisco.

128. 富田源太郎　　大和田彌吉　　米国行独案内・一名桑港事情
Tomita Gentarō and Ōwada Yakichi. Beikoku-yuki hitori annai: Ichimei Sōkō jijō [How to go to America alone: Guide to San Francisco]. Yokohama: Kaiinsha, 1886. [6] + 2 + 3 + 2 + 90 + 76 + app. 24 pp. M.

A guide to America geared for students which is divided into two parts. The first is an abbreviated translation of an 1883 publication entitled Stranger's guide to San Francisco and vicinity which describes San Francisco and the Bay Area. The second discusses the pros and cons of going abroad, supplies information on lodging and food expenses and on schools, and depicts the small Japanese community in San Francisco.

129. 渡辺勘次郎　　海外出稼案内
Watanabe Kanjirō. Kaigai dekasegi annai [A guide to working abroad]. Tokyo: Naigai Shuppan Kyōkai, 1902. 6 + 2 + 4 + 108 + app. 27 pp. M.

A book on how to work abroad, mainly in America, which attacks the unscrupulous practices of emigration companies and suggests ways to avoid them. Published under the auspices of the Imin Hogo Kyōkai [Association to Protect Emigrants], an organization formed in 1902 to encourage emigration, to eliminate the malpractices of emigration companies, and to work for free, unrestricted emigration.

130. 渡辺四郎　　海外立身の手引
Watanabe Shirō. Kaigai risshin no tebiki [A guide to success abroad]. Tokyo: Unteisha, 1902. 3 + [2] + 62 + 73 pp. M.

A brief guide to America which contains information on passport requirements, ships, and employment possibilities in America, especially as domestic help. Also has laws and regulations pertaining to going and living in America. The bulk consists of a 73-page introduction to English conversation.

131. 山根吾一　　最近渡米案内
Yamane Goichi. Saikin to-Bei annai [Recent guide to America]. Tokyo: Tobei Zasshisha, 1906. 2 + 2 + 190 + 12 pp., photos. M.

A collection of miscellaneous essays on America intended as a guide. All the essays first appeared in the Tobei Zasshi (see no. 139). A 12-page section on English conversation is appended.

132. 吉村大次郎　　獨立自給北米遊學案内
Yoshimura Daijirō. Dokuritsu jikyū Hoku-Bei yūgaku annai [Guide to self-supporting, independent study in North America]. Osaka: Okashima Shoten, 1903. 12 + [2] + 3 + 180 pp., photos. M.

A guide to America for students which complements no. 133 by the same author. Discusses passport procedures, the passage, and arrival formalities and provides information on being a "school boy," matriculation problems, and the American educational system.

133. 吉村大次郎　　青年の渡米
Yoshimura Daijirō. Seinen no to-Bei [America-bound youth]. Tokyo: Chūyōdō Shoten, 1902. 173 pp. M.

A guide specifically designed for youth planning to study in America. Discusses the different educational purposes, passport procedures, the passage conditions, and disembarking formalities. Also has descriptions of the life of a "school boy" and of American schools from the grammar school level to colleges and universities.

134. 吉村大次郎　　渡米成業の手引
Yoshimura Daijirō. To-Bei seigyō no tebiki [A guide to further training in America]. Osaka: Okashima Shoten, 1903. 9 + [4] + 3 + 193 pp., photos. M.

A general guide to America for agriculturalists, artisans, educators, ministers, white collar workers, laborers, entertainers, and women. Includes a general description of the Japanese in America and a list of Japanese organizations.

3. EMIGRATION JOURNALS

135. 亜米利加
Amerika ["The America"]. v. 11:1, 2 (Jan. 1, Feb. 1, 1907); v. 11:5-v. 13:5 (May 1, 1907-May 1, 1909). Monthly. Tokyo. M (except v. 11:1, 2).

A continuation of the Tobei Zasshi (see no. 139). The title change begins with v. 11:1 (Jan. 1, 1907), but the content remains essentially the same as its predecessor.

136. 力行世界
Rikkō Sekai [The Self-Help World]. no. 340 (Apr. 1933). Monthly. Tokyo.

A monthly publication of the Nihon Rikkōkai [Japan Self-Help Society] which features articles on emigration primarily to South America.

137. 殖民協會報告
*
Shokumin Kyōkai Hōkoku [Report of the Colonial Association]. no. 1-5 (Apr.-Aug. 1893); no. 11 (Feb. 1894); no. 13-37 (Apr. 1894-May 1896); no. 39-50 (Jul. 1896-Jun. 1897); no. 52-86 (Aug. 1897-Mar. 1901). Monthly. Tokyo. M.

The official monthly organ of the Shokumin Kyōkai [Colonial Association] headed by Viscount Enomoto Takeaki, a former Minister of Foreign Affairs, based in Tokyo. A civilian organization, it was formally established in February, 1893 to seek and disseminate information about various conditions in foreign lands with the ultimate goal of discovering appropriate places for future Japanese colonies. Based on the whole upon Japanese Consular reports and reports of individuals dispatched by the organization to investigate designated areas, this monthly contains information on the geography, climate, and population; the political, economic, and social conditions; and the Japanese, if any, and the attitudes toward them of specific areas and countries, including North, Central, and South America, the Hawaiian Islands, the Philippines, the South Pacific, Australia, New Zealand, and Southeast Asia. From issue no. 69 (Aug. 1899), the title of the monthly changed to Shokumin Jihō [The Colonial News]. An important source for the early history of Japanese emigration to Hawaii and the continental United States.

138. 渡米新報
Tobei Shimpō [America-bound News]. v. 1:1-4 (May 1907-Aug. 1907); v. 2:1-4 (Sep. 1907-Dec. 1907); v. 6:1-12-v. 7:1-3 (Jan. 1908-Mar. 1909). Monthly. Tokyo. M.

The official organ of the Nihon Rikkōkai [Japan Self-Help Society], a Christian organization formed by Shimanuki Hyōdayū in 1897 to assist the poor youth from rural areas to either study abroad or emigrate. Contains informative articles on America, sketches of successful Japanese immigrants, regular correspondence from members in America and other countries, and a question-and-answer column on the procedures and problems of going to America. From v. 6:1 (Jan. 1908) this monthly continues the numbering of the Rikkō [Self-Help], another publication of the organization which was discontinued.

139. 渡米雑誌
Tobei Zasshi [America-bound Magazine]. v. 9:7-9, 12 (Jul. 3-Sep. 3, Dec. 3, 1905); v. 10:4-8, 10, 11 (Apr. 3-Aug. 3, Oct. 1, Nov. 1, 1906). Monthly. Tokyo.

The official organ of the Tobei Kyōkai [Association for the America-bound], an organization formed by Katayama Sen in 1902 in Tokyo to encourage the Japanese to go to America. It is a continuation of an earlier publication, the Rōdō Sekai [Labor World], the first labor journal, which had been launched in 1897 under the editorship of Katayama. Except for a short three week period in which the Rōdō Sekai became a daily under the title Naigai Shimpō [Domestic and Foreign News] in January, 1902, it continued until March, 1903 when its title changed to Shakaishugi [Socialism]. Katayama used the Rōdō Sekai and its successor as the official organ of the Tobei Kyōkai to disseminate information about America, combining such information with knowledge about socialism and labor problems. In January, 1905 the Shakaishugi changed to the Tobei Zasshi which then focused exclusively on the procedures to go to America and news about it. It carries many articles on America for prospective emigrants as well as "American letters" from members of the organization already in America.

4. OTHER JOURNALS AND MAGAZINES

140. 亜細亜
   * Ajiya [Asia]. M.

Fifty-three selected reports, mostly written by shosei in San Francisco, published in the Ajiya from July, 1891 to July, 1894. The reports range over such topics as the Japanese residents of San Francisco, early anti-Japanese incidents, and some articles on the origins and causes of Japanese emigration. A few articles on Japanese residents in Hawaii are included.

47

141. 實業之日本
Jitsugyō no Nihon [Jitsugyo no Nihon]. M.

   One hundred eight selected articles published in the Jitsugyō no Nihon from October, 1899 to May, 1913. Includes many "American letters" and reports by Japanese residents of America such as Ban Shinzaburō, Asakawa Kan'ichi, and Saibara Seitō and visitors such as Takahashi Sakuei and Katayama Sen on the Japanese in America and the Texas Japanese rice colony; biographical sketches of prominent individuals, including Ban Shinzaburō, Takamine Jōkichi, and Ushijima Kinji; and other articles which relate to the origins and causes of Japanese emigration. The contributors also include such notables as Ōkuma Shigenobu, Uchida Sadatsuchi, and Nitobe Inazō.

142. 國民の友
* Kokumin no Tomo ["The Nation's Friend"]. M.

   Sixty-six selected articles published in the Kokumin no Tomo from February, 1888 to June, 1898. Includes articles on the shosei and other early residents of San Francisco, emigration and overseas expansion, racial conflict and the immigration question, and U.S.-Japan relations. Asakawa Kan'ichi in America was a leading contributor.

143. 三田商業界
Mita Shōgyōkai [The Mita Commercial World]. M.

   Forty-five selected articles published in the Mita Shōgyōkai from February, 1907 to July, 1924 (the title of the journal changed to Jitsugyō no Sekai [The Jitsugyo World] from v. 5:1 (May, 1908)). Includes many articles on Japanese residents in America and the exclusion movement by such Issei as Yamaoka Ototaka, Hattori Ayao, Okuda Heiji, Fujioka Shirō, Ichihashi Yamato, and Sakai Shizuo; and also articles on the Japanese emigration policy and overseas expansion by Shibusawa Eiichi, Shimanuki Hyōdayū, Ōkura Kihachirō, and others.

144. 日本人
Nihonjin [The Japanese]. M.

   Ninety selected articles published in the Nihonjin from May, 1888 to November, 1913 (the title of the journal changed to Nihon oyobi Nihonjin [Japan and the Japanese] from no. 450 (January, 1907)). The articles range over the emigration and colonization questions, the exclusion movement, and U.S.-Japan relations. The contributors include Shiga Shigetaka, Miyake Yūjirō, Katayama Sen, Yoneda Minoru, Inada Shūnosuke, Fujioka Shirō, and others.

145. 太陽
* Taiyō ["The Sun"]. M.

   One hundred twenty-three articles and reports, a few in English, published in the Taiyō from June, 1895 to October, 1923. Ranging over the emigration and colonization questions, the dekaseginin in America, the American annexation of Hawaii, and the exclusion movement, they are authored by Kawakami Kiyoshi, Kawasaki Minotarō, Suehiro Shigeo, Yoneda Minoru, and others. Includes v. 14:3 (February, 1908), a special issue devoted to the racial conflict between the yellow and white races, and v. 16:15 (November, 1910), another special issue devoted to the overseas expansion of the Japanese people.

146. 東京經濟雜誌
* Tōkyō Keizai Zasshi ["The Tokyo Economist"]. M.

Two hundred seventeen selected articles and reports published in the Tōkyō Keizai Zasshi from February, 1884 to September, 1913 which relate to the origins and causes of Japanese emigration, the dekaseginin in America and other countries, and the exclusion movement. Includes articles by Abiko Kyūtarō and Takahashi Sakuei.

147. 東洋經濟新報
* Tōyō Keizai Shimpō ["The Oriental Economist"]. M.

Ninety selected articles published in the Tōyō Keizai Shimpō from October, 1897 to March, 1915 which relate to the origins and causes of Japanese emigration, the Japanese residents of Hawaii and the continental United States, British Columbia, and Mexico, and the exclusion movement, with a significant number of pieces on the Japanese rice colony in Texas. The contributors include Hanihara Masao, Ōkuma Shigenobu, Takekoshi Yosaburō, Katayama Sen, Hyūga Terutake, Ban Shinzaburō, and others.

148. 通商彙纂
* Tsūshō Isan [Reports of the Bureau of Commercial Affairs]. M.

Twenty-nine selected reports published in the semi-monthly, Tsūshō Isan, the official publication of the Bureau of Commercial Affairs, Ministry of Foreign Affairs, from November, 1904 to August, 1912. Mainly statistical reports compiled by the Foreign Ministry and Japanese Consulates on Japanese residents in America and Canada. Also includes reports on dekaseginin and emigration companies.

III.
Japanese Exclusion Movement

1. GENERAL WORKS

149. 有馬純清　米國の排日
 Arima Sumikiyo. Beikoku no hai-Nichi [Anti-Japanese America]. Tokyo: Keisei Shoten, 1922. 8 + 4 + 360 pp., plate. M.

   A collection of miscellaneous articles by the former publisher and editor of the Hokubei Jiji [The North American Times] in Seattle. The title is drawn from the first portion of the book which has articles on the Japanese exclusion movement. The rest of the volume contains articles on American institutions, American national character, Japanese national character, and other topics.

150. アリゾナ日本人會　北米合衆國アリゾナ州排日事件
 Arizona Nihonjinkai. Hoku-Bei Gasshūkoku Arizona-shū hai-Nichi jiken [The anti-Japanese incident in the State of Arizona, U.S.A.]. Phoenix: Arizona Nihonjinkai, 1934. [2] + 39 pp., photos. X.

   A brief account of the systematic attempt by Arizonans to expel the few Japanese from the Salt River Valley near Phoenix, Arizona in 1934.

151. 綾川武治　人種問題研究
 Ayakawa Takeji. Jinshu mondai kenkyū [Study of the race question]. Tokyo: Sōkyō Shoten, 1925. 4 + 19 + 107 + 586 pp., bibliog. M.

   A study of the race question which is divided into two parts. Part one provides a theoretical framework in terms of the general distinction between "white" and "colored." Part two analyzes the specific racial problems of America, Canada, Australia, and South Africa within this framework. The Chinese and Japanese exclusion movements in America are discussed on pp. 1-98.

152. 藤井新一　米國排日原因の諸相　　　　　　　　　　外交時報
 Fujii Shin'ichi. "Beikoku hai-Nichi gen'in no shosō" [The various causes of Japanese exclusion in America], Gaikō Jihō [Revue Diplomatique], 40:470 (Jul. 1, 1924), 83-100; 40:471 (Jul. 15, 1924), 69-88; and 40:472 (Aug. 1, 1924), 94-114. M.

   An extended article which analyzes the political, economic, and social causes of Japanese exclusion.

153. 藤岡繁朗　民族發展の先驅者
 Fujioka Shirō. Minzoku hatten no senkusha [Pioneers of Japanese development]. Tokyo: Dōbunsha, 1927. 5 + 12 + 637 pp., plates, apps.

A miscellaneous collection of newspaper articles first published in the Rafu Shimpō. The first part reprints articles on the exclusion movement, includes a chapter on the second generation, and concludes with a short discussion of Mexico and the Japanese there. Consisting of the remaining two-thirds of the book, the second half has the following appendices: 1) the author's Mexico travel notes; 2) reprints of newspaper articles from 1922 to 1926 on different topics; 3) translations of American laws and regulations relating to aliens; and 4) translations of Mexican laws and regulations relating to aliens.

154. 後藤武男　最近米國の眞相
Gotō Takeo. Saikin Beikoku no shinsō [Facts on present-day America]. Tokyo: Mita Shobō, 1922. M (imperfect copy).

A collection of re-edited newspaper articles on America from the 1919 Versailles Peace Conference to the Washington Conference on Arms Limitation of 1921-22. The JARP microfilm only includes those chapters on the racial question, the Japanese in America, and the exclusion movement: Chapter 18, pp. 338-359; Chapter 20, pp. 365-380; and Chapters 22-25, pp. 413-537.

155. 原田豊次郎　米國の排日問題に就て　外交時報
Harada Toyojirō. "Beikoku no hai-Nichi mondai ni tsuite" [On the Japanese exclusion question in America], Gaikō Jihō [Revue Diplomatique], 10:116 (Jul. 1, 1907), 75-78. M.

A general assessment of anti-Japanese incidents.

156. 原田豊次郎　桑港學校問題と日米條約　外交時報
Harada Toyojirō. "Sōkō gakkō mondai to Nichi-Bei Jōyaku" [The San Francisco school question and the Japanese-American Treaty], Gaikō Jihō [Revue Diplomatique], 10:113 (Apr. 1907), 37-45. M.

An article on the October, 1906 San Francisco school issue as a violation of the Japanese-American Treaty of 1894.

157. 平沼淑郎　亜細亜人移住は世界問題　外交時報
Hiranuma Yoshirō. "Ajiyajin ijū wa sekai mondai" [The migration of Asiatics is a global problem], Gaikō Jihō [Revue Diplomatique], 20:234 (Aug. 1, 1914), 12-19. M.

An article on the Asiatic exclusion movements in both America and Canada which discusses the fate of the Chinese, Japanese, and Indians in both countries.

158. 今村恵猛　重要なる教書及宣言
* Imamura Emyō (ed.). Jūyo naru kyōsho oyobi sengen ["Five appeals to American patriotism"]. Honolulu: Hompa Hongwanji Mission, 1917. [12] + 100 + 86 pp.

A collection of five historic American documents in both English and Japanese to inform the Japanese in Hawaii about American patriotism.

159. 稻畑勝太郎　加特力教徒と對米國　外交時報
Inabata Katsutarō. "Katorikkukyōto to tai-Beikoku" [Catholics and America], Gaikō Jihō [Revue Diplomatique], 42:495 (Jul. 15, 1925), 158-160. M.

A reprint of a memorial addressed to the Pope dated 2/17/25 submitted by Inabata Katsutarō, the head of the Osaka Chamber of Commerce, protesting the exclusion movement and soliciting his opinion and of the reply from the Holy See dated 4/30/25.

160. 稻原勝治　　米國の排日は人種戰爭也　　　　外交時報
    Inahara Katsuji. "Beikoku no hai-Nichi wa jinshu sensō nari" [Japanese exclusion in America is racial war], Gaikō Jihō [Revue Diplomatique], 39:467 (May 15, 1924), 31-47. M.

    An article which reviews the history of Chinese and Japanese exclusion as a fundamental problem of race.

161. 稻原勝治　　米國の人口及移民問題　　　　　外交時報
    Inahara Katsuji. "Beikoku no jinkō oyobi imin mondai" [The American population and immigration questions], Gaikō Jihō [Revue Diplomatique], 17:200 (Mar. 1, 1913), 47-56. M.

    An essay on the history of European immigration to America in the 19th and early 20th century. Discusses the nativist alarm with this new immigration and the problems of Americanization.

162. 石川安次郎　　日本人の米國歸化權　　　　　外交時報
    Ishikawa Yasujirō. "Nihonjin no Beikoku kikaken" [Japanese naturalization rights in America], Gaikō Jihō [Revue Diplomatique], 35:414 (Feb. 1, 1922), 6-23. M.

    An article on the question of naturalization rights for Japanese immigrants which reviews the history of the exclusion movement and the Ozawa Case pending before the U.S. Supreme Court.

163. 神川彦松　　バーネット移民法の成立　　　　外交時報
    Kamikawa Hikomatsu. "Bānetto iminhō no seiritsu" [Origins of the Burnett immigration bill], Gaikō Jihō [Revue Diplomatique], 25:302 (Jun. 1, 1917), 1-18. M.

    An article on the legislative history of immigration restriction bills in the U.S. Congress from 1911 to 1916, concentrating on the Burnett immigration bill.

164. 金井重雄　　人種差別撤廢問題
    Kanai Shigeo (ed.). Jinshu sabetsu teppai mondai [The problem of eliminating racial discrimination]. Tokyo: Nisshōkai, 1919. 56 pp. M.

    A collection of speeches presented by different individuals on 3/22/19 in Tokyo on the subject of racial discrimination and its elimination. These talks coincided with the Japanese government's abortive efforts to seek a racial equality clause in the League of Nations Covenant at the Paris Peace Conference. Among the speakers there were: Ebara Soroku, Kasai Shigeharu, Kamada Eikichi, Ōkuma Shigenobu, Merle Davis, Gilbert Bowles, Arthur D. Berry, and others.

165. 煙山專太郎　　米國加州知事ジョンソン氏　　外交時報
    Kemuyama Sentarō. "Beikoku Kashū Chiji Jonson-shi" [Governor Johnson of California], Gaikō Jihō [Revue Diplomatique], 17:205 (May 15, 1913), 118-123. M.

    A profile of Governor Hiram W. Johnson, depicting him as an irascible man who acts on feeling rather than reason.

166. 木村享　　米國の支那人排斥法　　　　　　　外交時報
    Kimura Akira. "Beikoku no Shinajin haisekihō" [The Chinese Exclusion Acts of America], Gaikō Jihō [Revue Diplomatique], 45:536 (Apr. 1, 1927), 96-105. M.

An analysis of the Chinese Exclusion Acts as violations of the Burlingame Treaty between Ch'ing China and the United States.

167. 小林政助　　米國と人種的差別の研究　　　　外交時報
Kobayashi Masasuke. Beikoku to jinshuteki sabetsu no kenkyū [Study of America and racial discrimination]. Tokyo: Bunsendō Shoten, 1919. 2 + 3 + 3 + 4 + 3 + 6 + 155 pp., map, charts, photos, bibliog. M.

An examination of racial discrimination in America in terms of psychological, social, economic, and political factors. Also analyzes the exclusion movement and American religious ideas. The author was the founder and head of the Japanese units of the Salvation Army in America.

168. 松枝保二　　米國排日の實相
Matsueda Yasuji. Beikoku hai-Nichi no jissō [Facts about Japanese exclusion in America]. Tokyo: Dai Nippon Yūbenkai, 1925. 19 + 3 + 306 pp. M.

A study of the exclusion movement from its inception down to the 1924 Immigration Act which emphasizes the political aspects of it, including the principal anti-Japanese politicians and newspapers.

169. 三並良　　文化問題としての日米問題　　　　外交時報
Minami Ryō. "Bunka mondai to shite no Nichi-Bei mondai" [The Japanese-American question as a cultural problem], Gaikō Jihō [Revue Diplomatique], 40:477 (Oct. 15, 1924), 82-91. M.

An article on the decline and influence of Christianity and Christian clergymen in America. Interprets this general state of affairs as an important background to Japanese exclusion.

170. 半澤玉城　　排日問題の教訓　　　　外交時報
Nakazawa Tamaki. "Hai-Nichi mondai no kyōkun" [The lessons of the Japanese exclusion question], Gaikō Jihō [Revue Diplomatique], 39:468 (Jun. 1, 1924), 1-9. M.

An article spelling out the negative lessions of the exclusion question--the meaninglessness of internationalism, the restricted meaning of justice and humanity, the dilemma of seeking peace, the bankrupt policies of the Japanese Foreign Ministry, and the limitations of parliamentary government.

171. 蜷川新　　所謂米人の公正とは何ぞ　　　　外交時報
Nanigawa Shin. "Iwayuru Beijin no kōsei to wa nanzo" [What is the so-called American fairness?], Gaikō Jihō [Revue Diplomatique], 36:429 (Sep. 15, 1922), 36-49. M.

An article which attacks the American concept of fair play by raising the examples of the treatment accorded to Black Americans, the exclusion of the yellow race, and the unequal terms of the Washington Conference of 1921-22.

172. 岡本剛　　排日問題と人種平等の論理　　　　外交時報
Okamoto Tsuyoshi. "Hai-Nichi mondai to jinshu byōdō no ronri" [The logic of the Japanese exclusion question and racial equality], Gaikō Jihō [Revue Diplomatique], 39:467 (May 15, 1924), 106-121; 39:469 (Jun. 15, 1924), 89-104; 40:470 (Jul. 1, 1924), 101-123; and 40:471 (Jul. 15, 1924), 88-112. M (except part II X).

An extended essay in four parts which reviews the exclusion of Chinese,

Japanese, and East Indians. The author concludes that Japan must appeal to America's sense of justice and fair play.

173. 大隈重信　　人種問題
Ōkuma Shigenobu. Jinshu mondai [The race question]. Tokyo: Waseda Daigaku Shuppanbu, 1919. 16 + 134 pp. M.

A short tract written after the Versailles Peace Conference of 1919 at which Japan failed to secure her demands for a racial equality clause in the League of Nations Covenant. While attacking racial discrimination based upon skin color, Ōkuma proposes to substitute a civilization measure (bummei hyōjun) with which to judge different races.

174. 奥村多喜衛　　排日豫防啓發運動
* Okumura Takie. Hai-Nichi yobō keihatsu undō [Educational campaign to prevent exclusion]. [Honolulu]: Privately printed, 1922 (?). 60 pp.

A booklet describing the Americanization campaign among the Japanese in Hawaii beginning in 1921. Led by the author himself, its aim was to encourage Issei to assimilate into American society and to raise their children as "good" American citizens, both goals being interpreted as fundamental solutions to the Japanese-American problem. Covers the first year of the campaign.

175. 奥村多喜衛　　布哇に於ける日米問題解決運動
* Okumura Takie. Hawai ni okeru Nichi-Bei mondai kaiketsu undō [Campaign to solve the Japanese-American problem in Hawaii]. Honolulu: Privately printed, 1928 (3rd edition). 111 pp.

An expanded version of above. Initially issued in 1925, it covers the first five-years of the Americanization campaign.

176. 奥村多喜衛　　布哇に於ける日米問題解決運動
* Okumura Takie. Hawai ni okeru Nichi-Bei mondai kaiketsu undō [Campaign to solve the Japanese-American problem in Hawaii]. Honolulu: Privately printed, 1934 (5th edition). [4] + 170 pp.

An expanded version of above which brings the narrative up through 1933. Includes the second generation.

177. 大山卯次郎　米國に於ける排日問題總勘定　　　　　外交時報
Ōyama Ujirō. "Beikoku ni okeru hai-Nichi mondai sō-kanjō" [A general assessment of the Japanese exclusion question in America], Gaikō Jihō [Revue Diplomatique], 45:535 (Mar. 15, 1927), 18-31. M.

The first half of this article reviews the history of the exclusion movement. The second half treats the growing problems of the second generation, and the author, a former Japanese Consul General in America, feels that the exclusion problem will now be in connection with the education, civil rights, and citizenship of this group.

178. 大山卯次郎　太平洋の彼岸
Ōyama Ujirō. Taiheiyo no higan [The Pacific Coast]. Tokyo: Hōchi Shimbunsha, 1925. [2] + 12 + 430 pp., illus.

A general history of the exclusion movement by a former Japanese Consul in Los Angeles (1915-1923) and in San Francisco (1923-1924). Chapters 1-2 cover the American political and educational system; Chapters 3-9 discuss the various aspects of the exclusion movement, beginning with an analysis of the earlier Chinese exclusion movement; and Chapters 10-20 treat more general topics--California geography, California mission history, and the California Indians.

179. Sailor's Union of the Pacific. "Minutes of meetings held at headquarters, San Francisco, California." Jan. 7, 1907-Dec. 27, 1910. San Francisco. M.

    The minutes of the Sailor's Union of the Pacific, one of the leading labor groups in favor of Japanese exclusion.

180. 島田軍吉　　獅子吼
*   Shimada Gunkichi. Shishikō [A lion's roar]. Honolulu: Privately printed, 1916. 176 pp.

    A collection of miscellaneous essays with one chapter on the exclusion movement, pp. 95-107.

181. 市民權獲得期成同志會　　日米問題に對する吾徒の主張
Shiminken Kakutoku Kisei Dōshikai. Nichi-Bei mondai ni taisuru wagato no shuchō [Our proposal for the Japanese-American problem]. [San Francisco]: Shiminken Kakutoku Kisei Dōshikai, 1913. 54 pp. X.

    A booklet which argues for naturalization rights for the Japanese. Issued by the Society for Promoting Japanese Naturalization Rights, an organization founded after the passage of the 1913 California Alien Land Law and based in San Francisco.

182. 鹽澤昌貞　　米國新移民法案に就て　　外交時報
Shiozawa Masatada. "Beikoku shin imin hōan ni tsuite" [New American immigration bills], Gaikō Jihō [Revue Diplomatique], 19:220 (Jan. 1, 1914), 28-42. M.

    An article which reviews past American immigration policies and the growth of the movement for restrictions, notes the discrimination against Asiatics contained in the new immigration bills, and calls for equal treatment of Asian and European immigration if restrictive measures are adopted.

183. 副島道正　　太平洋會議と移民問題　　外交時報
Soejima Michimasa. "Taiheiyō Kaigi to imin mondai" [The Pacific Conference and the immigration question], Gaikō Jihō [Revue Diplomatique], 52:597 (Oct. 15, 1929), 25-45. M.

    An article in retort to Herbert Croly, "Human potential in the politics of the Pacific," New Republic, no. 52 (Oct. 5, 1927), 164-172. To the allegation that, until Japan has addressed herself to the problem of overpopulation, she cannot insist upon immigration rights or preferential treatment of her exports, Soejima reviews the origin of the immigration question and the exclusion movement, the American view of the problem, and Japan's contrasting point of view.

184. 末廣重雄　　米國の排日問題と墨西哥　　外交時報
Suehiro Shigeo. "Beikoku no hai-Nichi mondai to Mekishiko" [The Japanese exclusion question in America and Mexico], Gaikō Jihō [Revue Diplomatique], 19:223 (Feb. 15, 1914), 11-36. M.

    An article which addresses itself to possible solutions to the Japanese exclusion movement caused, in the opinion of the author, by racial prejudice and fundamental cultural misunderstandings. To solve this problem, the author proposes a long-term educational campaign to change American public opinion and a plan to divert Japanese emigrants to Southern Mexico.

185. 末廣重雄　米國の排日に就いて　外交時報
Suehiro Shigeo. "Beikoku no hai-Nichi ni tsuite" [Japanese exclusion in America], Gaikō Jihō [Revue Diplomatique], 39:461 (Feb. 15, 1924), 19-33. M.

   A pessimistic analysis of the exclusion movement. The author feels that neither the American government nor the American public has the necessary understanding or desire.

186. 末廣重雄　米國最近の排日　外交時報
Suehiro Shigeo. "Beikoku saikin no hai-Nichi" [The current state of Japanese exclusion in America], Gaikō Jihō [Revue Diplomatique], 21:249 (Mar. 15, 1915), 11-25. M.

   An article on the temporary lull in anti-Japanese agitation because of the outbreak of World War I and anticipated opening of the Panama-Pacific Exposition of 1915. The author foresees renewed European immigration to the Western states in the postwar period, especially with the opening of the Panama Canal, creating additional problems of competition for Japanese immigrants. Warns of the resurgence of agitation and of the need for effective diplomacy and counter-measures.

187. 末廣重雄　北米の日本人
Suehiro Shigeo. Hoku-Bei no Nihonjin [The Japanese of North America]. Tokyo: Nishōdō, 1915. 2 + 2 + 5 + 276 pp. M.

   A study of the immigration question and U.S.-Japan relations. As a fundamental solution to the problems of the Japanese in America, the author proposes naturalization rights for them and an educational campaign to counter the exclusion movement. He also reviews the exclusion movement in Canada and includes a short section on the Japanese in Mexico.

188. 末廣重雄　公平無差別の待遇を要求せよ　外交時報
Suehiro Shigeo. "Kōhei musabetsu no taigū wo yōkyū seyo" [Demand fair, non-discriminatory treatment], Gaikō Jihō [Revue Diplomatique], 39:467 (May 15, 1924), 54-63. M.

   An article which reviews and counters all the past reasons raised in support of Japanese exclusion.

189. 鈴木半三郎　米國國民性の新研究
Suzuki Hansaburō. Beikoku kokuminsei no shin kenkyū [A new study of American national character]. Tokyo: Rakuyōdō, 1916. 8 + 11 + 4 + 400 pp., bibliog., photos.

   A study of the American people based for the most part upon Henry Van Dyke's The Spirit of America (1910) and Hugo Münsterberg's The Americans (1904) by the author who spent 8 years in America. Discusses the immigration question and the exclusion movement in Chapter 8 which is entitled "Jinshu mondai" [Racial problems], pp. 351-400.

190. 綱島住吉　排日問題と基督教徒
Tsunashima Kakichi. Hai-Nichi mondai to Kirisutokyōto ["Japanese problems in America"]. Tokyo: Keiseisha Shoten, 1916. 2 + 2 + 129 pp. M.

An examination of the exclusion question from a Christian perspective. The author came to America in 1914 representing Japanese Christians and appealed to the American Christian community to fight the injustices of the exclusion movement.

191. 若林平太郎　　　高田喜三樋　　加州日本人問題眞相
Wakabayashi Heitarō and Kōda Kisatsuchi. Kashū Nihonjin mondai shinsō [Facts about the Japanese problem in California]. San Francisco: Kashū Nihonjin Mondai Hakkōsho, 1911. 4 + 7 + 293 pp. M.

Divided into two parts, the first half consists of translations of key articles which appeared in the September, 1909 issue of the Annals of the American Academy of Political and Social Sciences devoted to the Chinese and Japanese, and the authors' analysis of the arguments advanced for and against Japanese exclusion. The second half consists of brief descriptions of the Japanese settlements in California and short biographical sketches of individuals in them.

192. 鷲津文三（尺鷹）　　在米日本人史観
* Washizu Bunzō (Shakuma). Zai-Bei Nihonjin shikan [A perspective on the history of the Japanese in America]. Los Angeles: Rafu Shimpōsha, 1930. 5 + 7 + name-index 19 + 295 + app. 82 pp., photos.

A work which covers the exclusion movement within the context of U.S.-Japan relations. Includes translations of articles by V.S. McClatchy and other exponents of exclusion as well as the author's essays on the 1913 California Alien Land Law, racial inequality, the psychology of exclusion, and other topics. The appendix is a catalogue of pioneers by occupational categories both in Hawaii and the mainland. The author was a long-time Issei newspaperman.

193. 渡辺已之次郎　　有色民族の大不平
Watanabe Minojirō. Yūshoku minzoku no daifuhei [The great dissatisfaction of colored peoples]. Osaka: Ōsaka Mainichi Shimbunsha, 1921. 3 + 9 + 403 pp. M.

An analysis of the racial situation throughout the world, especially the discrimination and segregation practiced by Great Britain and the United States which raise the specter of a racial war. According to the author, the solution to this problem depends on whether or not Great Britain and the United States understand and accept the legitimate aspirations and demands of the colored races. Both the Chinese and Japanese exclusion movements in America are discussed within this framework.

194. 八巻亮一　　日本人排斥條項を繞って　　　　　　外交時報
Yamaki Akikazu. "Nihonjin haiseki jōkō wo megutte" [On the conditions surrounding Japanese exclusion], Gaikō Jihō [Revue Diplomatique], 41:488 (Apr. 1, 1925), 108-116. M.

An article on the pro-Japan position of the Commission on Relations with Japan of the Federal Council of Churches of Christ in America contrasted with Valentine S. McClatchy's views. The author feels that American clergymen, if they hope to secure equal treatment for the Japanese, must show the falsity of two widespread ideas--that all Japanese have a lower standard of living than all Americans and that all Japanese are unassimilable.

195. 山中仲二　　奮闘の第一線
Yamanaka Chūji. Funtō no dai-issen [The frontline struggle]. Tokyo: Privately printed, 1925. 4 + 11 + 701 pp.

A collection of 150 newspaper editorials from 1911 to 1925 on the exclusion movement. The author was a newspaperman employed by the Nichibei Shimbun during this 14-year period.

196. 米田實　　米國の新移民政策　　　　　　　　　　　外交時報
Yoneda Minoru. "Beikoku no shin imin seisaku" [The new American immigration policy], Gaikō Jihō [Revue Diplomatique], 37:442 (Apr. 1, 1923), 133-142 and 37:444 (May 1, 1923), 47-58. M.

A running account and analysis of various new immigration bills before the U.S. Congress.

197. 米田實　　米國出生日本人の市民權　　　　　　　　外交時報
Yoneda Minoru. "Beikoku shussei Nihonjin no shiminken" [The citizenship rights of Japanese born in America], Gaikō Jihō [Revue Diplomatique], 31: 368 (Mar. 1, 1920), 25-34. M.

An article on the proposed Constitutional amendment to take away the citizenship of American-born Japanese and the prospects for its success.

198. 米田實　　排日問題再燃に就いて　　　　　　　　　外交時報
Yoneda Minoru. "Hai-Nichi mondai sainen ni tsuite" [The resurgence of the Japanese exclusion question], Gaikō Jihō [Revue Diplomatique], 30:353 (Jul. 15, 1919), 15-23. M.

An article on the resurgence of anti-Japanese agitation. Discusses the role of Senator James Phelan, the outcry for more stringent legislation, and warns of the future curtailment of picture-brides. Advises the Japanese in America to assimilate into American society.

2. ALIEN LAND LAWS

199. 千葉豊治　　排日問題梗概
Chiba Toyoji. Hai-Nichi mondai kōgai [Summary of the Japanese exclusion question]. San Francisco: Nichibeisha, 1913. [9] + 146 + app. 32 + bibliog. 3 pp. M.

A book designed to explain the 1913 California Alien Land Law and its background. Contains a short history of the exclusion movement, a summary of previously unsuccessful land law bills and the 1913 law itself, and a discussion of legal and other measures which the Japanese might take.

200. 稻原勝治　　排日問題の急轉直下　　　　　　　　　外交時報
Inahara Katsuji. "Hai-Nichi mondai no kyūten chokka" [The worsening Japanese exclusion question], Gaikō Jihō [Revue Diplomatique], 17:206 (Jun. 1, 1913), 78-83. M.

A narrative of events relating to Secretary of State William Jennings Bryan's abortive efforts to prevent the passage of the 1913 California Alien Land Law in Sacramento.

201. 稲原勝治　　排日土地法今後の問題　　　　外交時報
    Inahara Katsuji. "Hai-Nichi tochihō kongo no mondai" [The Alien Land Law
    and the problem hereafter], Gaikō Jihō [Revue Diplomatique], 17:206 (Jun.
    1, 1913), 26-33. M.

    An article critical of the government's proposal to contest the 1913
    California Alien Land Law through a test case in court.

202. 稲原勝治　　排日案愈々可決　　　　　　外交時報
    Inahara Katsuji. "Hai-Nichian iyoiyo kaketsu" [The final passage of the
    Japanese exclusion bill], Gaikō Jihō [Revue Diplomatique], 17:205 (May
    15, 1913), 82-87. M.

    A summary of the legislative history of the 1913 California Alien Land
    Law.

203. 稲原勝治　　加州排日問題經過　　　　　外交時報
    Inahara Katsuji. "Kashū hai-Nichi mondai keika" [The status of the Japanese
    exclusion question in California], Gaikō Jihō [Revue Diplomatique], 17:207
    (Jun. 15, 1913), 93-96. M.

    A narrative of events from May 19 to June 6 relating to the 1913 Califor-
    nia Alien Land Law.

204. 稲原勝治　　加州排日案の其後　　　　　外交時報
    Inahara Katsuji. "Kashū hai-Nichian no sono go" [Subsequent to the Japanese
    exclusion bill in California], Gaikō Jihō [Revue Diplomatique], 18:208
    (Jul. 1, 1913), 90-93. M.

    A continuation of above from June 6 to June 19.

205. 岩本英夫　　加州外國人土地法は北米合衆國憲法及び加州憲法に
    　　　　　　違反す　　　　　　　　　　外交時報
    Iwamoto Hideo. "Kashū Gaikokujin Tochihō wa Hoku-Bei Gasshūkoku Kempō oyobi
    Kashū Kempō ni ihansu" [The California Alien Land Laws violate the U.S.
    Federal Constitution and California State Constitution], Gaikō Jihō [Revue
    Diplomatique], 38:455 (Nov. 15, 1923), 43-64 and 38:456 (Dec. 1, 1923),
    77-95. M.

    An interpretative essay on the 1913 and 1920 California Alien Land Laws
    as violations of both the U.S. Federal and California State Constitutions.

206. 末廣重雄　　加州排日問題根本的解決策　　外交時報
    Suehiro Shigeo. "Kashū hai-Nichi mondai konponteki kaiketsusaku" [A basic
    measure to solve the California Japanese exclusion question], Gaikō Jihō
    [Revue Diplomatique], 17:204 (May 1, 1913), 7-14. M.

    An article which advocates naturalization rights for Japanese immigrants
    as the fundamental solution to the pending 1913 California Alien Land Law
    and other exclusion measures.

207. 米田實　　米國の排日運動撲滅策　　　　外交時報
    Yoneda Minoru. "Beikoku no hai-Nichi undō bokumetsusaku" [A policy to elim-
    inate the Japanese exclusion movement in America], Gaikō Jihō [Revue Di-
    plomatique], 17:204 (May 1, 1913), 14-23. M.

    An article which proposes three countermeasures to the pending California Alien Land Law: 1) a direct governmental appeal to the President of the United States; 2) an immediate test case to contest the legislation as a violation of the Japanese-American Treaty of 1911; and 3) to secure naturalization rights for the Japanese immigrants.

3. 1924 IMMIGRATION ACT

208. 赤名精一　　通俗米國移民法講話
   Akana Seiichi. Tsūzoku Beikoku iminhō kōwa [Popular lectures on American immigration laws]. Tokyo: Hakubundō, 1929. 2 + 16 + 389 pp., apps.

   A collection of ten lectures on the 1924 Immigration Act, analyzing what types of individuals are admissible to America. The appendices consist of the Act itself and its subsequent revisions.

209. 船越光之丞　　對米問題私觀　　　　　　　　　外交時報
   Funagoshi Mitsunojō. "Tai-Bei mondai shikan" [A private view of the American problem], Gaikō Jihō [Revue Diplomatique], 39:467 (May 15, 1924), 10-19. M.

   An article which interprets the 1924 Immigration Act as specifically directed against Japan and as basically motivated by racial prejudice. The author feels that it is a national insult, deriving from Japan's unequal relations with the United States.

210. 外務省　　一九二四年米國移民法制定及之ニ關スル日米交渉經過
   Gaimushō. Senkyūhyakunijūyonen Beikoku Iminhō seitei oyobi kore ni kansuru Nichi-Bei kōshō keika [The enactment of the 1924 Immigration Act and the course of Japanese-American negotiations]. Tokyo, 1924. 2 + 13 + 5 + 172 + 37 pp. X.

   A Japanese Foreign Ministry publication which compiles into one volume the communications between the Foreign Ministry and the Japanese Embassy on the 1924 Immigration Act and other proposed discriminatory legislation. Also contains Japanese translations of English materials relating to the Act and other proposed legislation and the Japanese government's formal protest notes.

211. 外務省　　一九二四年米國移民法制定及之ニ關スル日米交渉經過公文書英文附屬書
   Gaimushō. Senkyūhyakunijūyonen Beikoku Iminhō seitei oyobi kore ni kansuru Nichi-Bei kōshō keika kōbunsho Eibun fuzokusho [The enactment of the 1924 Immigration Act and the course of Japanese-American negotiations: Official documents and related English sources]. Tokyo, 1924. 268 pp. X.

   A supplement to above.

212. 臥龍學人　　一九二四年米國移民法と日米通商條約との關係　　外交時報
   Garyū Gakujin (pseud.). "Issenkyūhyakunijūyonen Beikoku Iminhō to Nichi-Bei Tsūshō Jōyaku to no kankei" [The relationship between the 1924 Immigration Act and the Japanese-American Treaty of Commerce], Gaikō Jihō [Revue Diplomatique], 44:526 (Nov. 1, 1926), 133-143. M.

   An article taking the position that the Japanese-American Treaty of 1911 cannot be used as a basis for protesting the 1924 Immigration Act.

Since the American government insists the regulation of immigration is strictly a domestic matter, the treaty violation argument is an exercise in abstract meaning without any effectiveness.

213. 林富平　　　外國旅券下附及査證手續・上巻 米國編
    Hayashi Tomihei. Gaikoku ryoken kafu oyobi sashō tetsuzuki, jōkan: Beikoku-hen [Passport and visa application procedures, vol. I: America]. Tokyo: Kaigai Tsūshinsha, 1929. [7] + 61 + 10 pp.

    An explanation of the passport and visa requirements for entry or reentry into America, especially in the light of the 1924 Immigration Act. The 10-page appendix consists of the Japanese regulations governing the issuance of passports.

214. 稲原勝治　　　排日第七週年を迎ふ　　　　　　外交時報
    Inahara Katsuji. "Hai-Nichi dai-shichishūnen wo mukau" [The beginning of the 7th year of Japanese exclusion], Gaikō Jihō [Revue Diplomatique], 55:614 (Jul. 1, 1930), 11-33. M.

    An extended review of the history of the exclusion movement and the 1924 Immigration Act. Notes the basic solution still lies with the granting of naturalization rights to the Japanese.

215. 稲原勝治　　　排日第四週年を迎ふ　　　　　　外交時報
    Inahara Katsuji. "Hai-Nichi dai-yonshūnen wo mukau" [The beginning of the 4th year of Japanese exclusion], Gaikō Jihō [Revue Diplomatique], 46:542 (Jul. 1, 1927), 1-18. M.

    An article noting the beginning of the 4th year of the 1924 Immigration Act.

216. 稲原勝治　　　排日移民法第八週年を迎ふ　　　外交時報
    Inahara Katsuji. "Hai-Nichi iminhō dai-hasshūnen wo mukau" [The beginning of the 8th year of the 1924 Immigration Act], Gaikō Jihō [Revue Diplomatique], 59:638 (Jul. 1, 1931), 24-45. M.

    A pessimistic analysis of the prospects for revisions of the 1924 Immigration Act to place the Japanese under the same quota system as Europeans.

217. 神崎驥一　　　對米移民問題は打切りか　　　　外交時報
    Kanzaki Kiichi. "Tai-Bei imin mondai wa uchikiri ka" [Is the American immigration question over?], Gaikō Jihō [Revue Diplomatique], 47:556 (Feb. 1, 1928), 74-84. M.

    An article on the second conference sponsored by the Institute of Pacific Relations held in Honolulu in July, 1927. The author, the one-time Secretary of the Japanese Association of America, laments the fact that the immigration issue was not discussed as it was during the first conference held in 1925.

218. 松原一雄　　　法律上より觀たる排日問題　　　外交時報
    Matsubara Kazuo. "Hōritsujō yori mitaru hai-Nichi mondai" [The Japanese exclusion question from a legal point of view], Gaikō Jihō [Revue Diplomatique], 39:468 (Jun. 1, 1924), 20-27. M.

    An examination of the 1924 Immigration Act from the perspective of existing international laws, the concept of national sovereignty, and the Japanese-American Treaty of 1911.

219. 守山森人　米國新移民法實施上の諸問題　　外交時報
Moriyama Morito. "Beikoku shin iminhō jisshijō no sho mondai" [Various enforcement problems of the new American immigration law], Gaikō Jihō [Revue Diplomatique], 40:477 (Oct. 15, 1924), 91-97. M.

　　An article on the problems of the legally admissible Japanese under the 1924 Immigration Act, especially businessmen and company employees and their wives.

220. 中島九郎　對米日支移民問題の解剖
Nakashima Kurō. Tai-Bei Nisshi imin mondai no kaibō [An examination of the Japanese and Chinese immigration question in America]. Tokyo: Ganshōdō Shoten, 1924. 3 + 4 + 207 pp. M.

　　A study of the 1924 Immigration Act. Divided into three parts, it first surveys the history of the Chinese and Japanese exclusion movements, then examines the origin, passage, and content of the 1924 Immigration Act, and concludes with the protests against it in Japan and the turn toward immigration to Brazil and renewed Pan-Asian thinking.

221. 半澤玉城　對米記念日　　外交時報
Nakazawa Tamaki. "Tai-Bei kinenbi" [An American anniversary], Gaikō Jihō [Revue Diplomatique], 44:518 (Jul. 1, 1926), 1-9. M.

　　An editorial noting the start of the third year of the 1924 Immigration Act which takes the occasion to criticize America and review the meaning of the exclusion movement.

222. 大島高精　對米政策を決定せよ　　外交時報
Ōshima Kōsei. "Tai-Bei seisaku wo kettei seyo" [Settle upon an American policy], Gaikō Jihō [Revue Diplomatique], 39:469 (Jun. 15, 1924), 43-64. M.

　　An article on the "imperialistic" ambition of America in Asia, calling for a united Asia under Japanese leadership to oppose it. Interprets the 1924 Immigration Act as an expression of American imperialism--while expanding in Asia, America has excluded all Asians which is a domestic manifestation of outward expansion.

223. 大山卯次郎　米國の移民政策及現行移民法の適用　　外交時報
Ōyama Ujirō. "Beikoku no imin seisaku oyobi genkō iminhō no tekiyō" [American immigration policy and the application of the current immigration law], Gaikō Jihō [Revue Diplomatique], 45:538 (May 1, 1927), 68-78. M.

　　An examination of the 1924 Immigration Act with reference to the Japanese in terms of the non-immigrant, non-quota immigrant, and quota immigrant categories.

224. 大山卯次郎　亞排日移民法第七周年　　外交時報
Ōyama Ujirō. "Chō hai-Nichi iminhō dai-shichishūnen" [The beginning of the 7th year of the 1924 Immigration Act], Gaikō Jihō [Revue Diplomatique], 55:614 (Jul. 1, 1930), 44-52. M.

　　An article interpreting the 1924 Immigration Act as an "insult" to American ideals, not to the Japanese people. The author believes that the prospects for revisions do not warrant optimism, for the old exclusionists will fight against them in Congress where the real battle will take place.

225. 大山卯次郎　排日移民法第十周年　　　　　外交時報
Ōyama Ujirō. "Hai-Nichi iminhō dai-jūshūnen" [The beginning of the 10th year of the 1924 Immigration Act], Gaikō Jihō [Revue Diplomatique], 67: 686 (Jul. 1, 1933), 1-6. M.

An updated assessment of the 1924 Immigration Act and the prospects for revisions.

226. 大山卯次郎　排日移民法第九周年　　　　　外交時報
Ōyama Ujirō. "Hai-Nichi iminhō dai-kyūshūnen" [The beginning of the 9th year of the 1924 Immigration Act], Gaikō Jihō [Revue Diplomatique], 63: 662 (Jul. 1, 1932), 1-13. M.

Same as above.

227. 大山卯次郎　排日移民法に就ての回顧　　　外交時報
Ōyama Ujirō. "Hai-Nichi iminhō ni tsuite no kaiko" [Looking back on the 1924 Immigration Act], Gaikō Jihō [Revue Diplomatique], 46:542 (Jul. 1, 1927), 41-50. M.

An article analyzing the politics which led up to the passage of the 1924 Immigration Act. The author feels there is nothing that can be done to remedy the law, except to wait for the day when Americans will realize the injustice contained in it.

228. 大山卯次郎　排日移民法の修正に就て　　　外交時報
Ōyama Ujirō. "Hai-Nichi iminhō no shūsei ni tsuite" [Revision of the 1924 Immigration Act], Gaikō Jihō [Revue Diplomatique], 54:613 (Jun. 15, 1930), 1-10. M.

An article on the revision of the 1924 Immigration Act. If the law was revised to place Japanese immigrants under the same quota system as European immigrants, Japan would reap no concrete benefits because no more than 100-odd immigrants would be admitted. Since the law embodies the assumption that the Japanese are an inferior people, such a change, though important, would remove only this basic insult to the Japanese, still leaving the problems of naturalization, existing alien land laws, and other civil rights issues.

229. 澁澤榮一　日米問題の解決と對支新方策　　外交時報
Shibusawa Eiichi. "Nichi-Bei mondai no kaiketsu to tai-Shi shin hōsaku" [The solution to the Japanese-American problem and a new China policy], Gaikō Jihō [Revue Diplomatique], 39:467 (May 15, 1924), 63-68. M.

The first part of this article responds to the 1924 Immigration Act. While hoping for its eventual repeal, the author proposes a Japanese-American Joint Commission to impartially investigate the status of the Japanese immigrants.

230. 副島道正　排日案を論じて亞州の民族に檄す　外交時報
Soejima Michimasa. "Hai-Nichian wo ronjite Ashū no minzoku ni gekisu" [The Japanese exclusion bill and an appeal to the peoples of Asia], Gaikō Jihō [Revue Diplomatique], 39:467 (May 15, 1924), 48-53. M.

An article which interprets the 1924 Immigration Act as a national insult. The author reports his past support for cooperation with America and Great Britain, but concludes that he can no longer do so, realizing Japan must assume the leadership in Asia against Western powers.

231. 末廣重雄　　排日案通過　　　　　　　　　　　外交時報
     Suehiro Shigeo. "Hai-Nichian tsūka" [The passage of the Japanese exclusion
        bill], Gaikō Jihō [Revue Diplomatique], 39:466 (May 1, 1924), 1-8. M.

     An article on the passage of the 1924 Immigration Act through the House
of Representatives, concentrating upon the House Immigration and Naturalization Committee's rejection of the recommendation of Secretary of State Hughes
to treat Japanese and European immigrants alike.

232. 鈴木三郎　　排日問題の眞相
     Suzuki Saburō. Hai-Nichi mondai no shinsō [Facts of the Japanese exclusion
        question]. Osaka: Ōsaka Mainichi Shimbunsha, 1924. 2 + 101 pp. M.

     A short work on the origins, passage, and content of the 1924 Immigra-
tion Act.

233. 東郷實　　北米移民法改正問題と日本将来の移民策　　外交時報
     Tōgō Minoru. "Hoku-Bei iminhō kaisei mondai to Nihon shōrai no iminsaku"
        [The North America immigration law revision question and Japan's future
        emigration policy], Gaikō Jihō [Revue Diplomatique], 55:614 (Jul. 1,
        1930), 1-10. M.

     An article pointing out that any amendment to the 1924 Immigration Act
will not increase Japanese emigration to America. The author admonishes
those who are rejoicing over prospects for changes and draws their attention
to the need for more studies on emigration to other areas to solve the problem of over-population.

234. 山中仲二　　排日移民法の改正楽観すべきか　　　　外交時報
     Yamanaka Chūji. "Hai-Nichi iminhō no kaisei rakkan subeki ka" [Should we be
        optimistic about revisions in the 1924 Immigration Act?], Gaikō Jihō
        [Revue Diplomatique], 55:614 (Jul. 1, 1930), 34-44. M.

     An article warning against undue optimism concerning possible revisions
in the 1924 Immigration Act. Since Americans do not understand Japanese
feelings regarding the law, there still remains an unbridgeable hiatus
between American public opinion, unchanged from the time of the passage of
the law, and Japanese sentiments.

235. 米田實　　米國移民政策の一面　　　　　　　　　　外交時報
     Yoneda Minoru. "Beikoku imin seisaku no ichimen" [One aspect of the Ameri-
        can immigration policy], Gaikō Jihō [Revue Diplomatique], 40:474 (Sep. 1,
        1924), 33-42. M.

     An article on the diplomatic aspect of the passage of the 1924 Immi-
gration Act, particularly the significance of Ambassador Hanihara's protest
note to Secretary of State Hughes dated 4/10/24.

236. 米田實　　排日的移民法に接して　　　　　　　　　外交時報
     Yoneda Minoru. "Hai-Nichiteki iminhō ni sesshite" [Latest news of the 1924
        Immigration Act], Gaikō Jihō [revue Diplomatique], 39:467 (May 15, 1924),
        19-30 and 39:468 (Jun. 1, 1924), 28-36. M.

     An analysis of the secondary reasons for the passage of the 1924 Immi-
gration Act such as Ambassador Hanihara's protest note to Secretary of State
Hughes and the political capital made by leading proponents of the law.

237. 米田實　　今後の移民問題　　　　　　　　　　　外交時報
Yoneda Minoru. "Kongo no imin mondai" [The immigration question hereafter], Gaikō Jihō [Revue Diplomatique], 40:471 (Jul. 15, 1924), 1-13. M.

　　Interpreting emigration as a solution to Japan's problem of overpopulation, this article examines the restrictive immigration policies of America, Canada, and Australia in the aftermath of the 1924 Immigration Act. Concludes that South America is the only place to which Japanese emigrants can go.

238. 米田實　　日米移民問題の解決如何　　　　　　　外交時報
Yoneda Minoru. "Nichi-Bei imin mondai no kaiketsu ikan" [How will the Japanese-American immigration question be solved?], Gaikō Jihō [Revue Diplomatique], 54:613 (Jun. 15, 1930), 35-47. M.

　　An article on the reported remarks made by Congressman Albert Johnson, the Chairman of the House Committee on Immigration and Naturalization, to the effect that he will support revisions in the 1924 Immigration Act which will place the Japanese under the same quota system as European immigrants.

239. 米田實　　日米移民の一問題　　　　　　　　　　外交時報
Yoneda Minoru. "Nichi-Bei imin no ichi mondai" [A problem in Japanese-American immigration], Gaikō Jihō [Revue Diplomatique], 58:632 (Apr. 1, 1931), 45-53. M.

　　An article on the nature of the 1924 Immigration Act quota system, its defects, and how it would operate for the Japanese if the law was revised.

240. 在沙港日本領事館　　七月一日より實施されたる新移民法と注意事項
Zai-Shakō Nihon Ryōjikan. Shichigatsu tsuitachi yori jisshi saretaru shin iminhō to chui jikō [The 1924 Immigration Act and its provisions effective July 1st]. Seattle, 1924. 32 pp.

　　An explanatory booklet on the 1924 Immigration Act published by the Japanese Consulate of Seattle.

4. U.S.-JAPAN RELATIONS

241. 赤松寛美　　軍人の見たる排日と對米策
Akamatsu Hiroyoshi. Gunjin no mitaru hai-Nichi to tai-Beisaku [A military man's views of Japanese exclusion and an American policy]. Tokyo: Nisshindō, 1924. 3 + 3 + 4 + 176 pp., plate. M.

　　A work written in response to the 1924 Immigration Act by an Army Colonel which interprets the exclusion movement as caused by racial prejudice and the United States as an expansionist power. The author foresees the possibility of a future conflict in the Pacific with the Philippines occupying the strategic region and calls for a build-up of more naval power.

242. 原勝郎　　　米國州權論　　　　　　　　　　　　　　　　外交時報
    Hara Katsurō. "Beikoku shūkenron" [American states' rights], Gaikō Jihō
    [Revue Diplomatique], 17:205 (May 15, 1913), 14-27. M.

    An article on the U.S. Constitution and the division of powers between
the federal and state governments. Argues that President Wilson and Secretary of State Bryan must choose between states' rights and treaty obligations
to maintain friendly relations with Japan.

243. 原田豊次郎　　米國觀
    Harada Toyojirō. Beikokukan [Perspectives on America]. Tokyo: Yūhōkan,
    1903. 2 + 2 + 7 + 140 + apps. 34 + 25 pp., map. M.

    A polemical work which interprets America as a political, economic,
and military expansionist power in the Pacific. The Chinese and Japanese
exclusion movements are covered within this context in Chapter 12, pp. 123-
140.

244. 長谷川新一郎　　在米邦人の觀たる米國と米國人
    Hasegawa Shin'ichirō. Zai-Bei hōjin no mitaru Beikoku to Beikokujin
    [America and Americans as seen by a Japanese in America]. Tokyo: Jitsu-
    gyō no Nihonsha, 1937. 4 + 5 + 456 + 7 pp., plate, photo. M.

    A work on American society and U.S.-Japan relations. A graduate of
U.S.C. and a long-time resident of Los Angeles, the Issei author analyzes
American political, religious, and educational institutions as well as
American racial attitudes and problems. He also writes about his participa-
tion in the Japan Society of Southern California and the organization's
activities to foster better U.S.-Japan relations.

245. 平元經堂　　　戰後の日本
    Hiramoto Mōdō (pseud.). Sengo no Nichi-Bei [Postwar Japan and America].
    Los Angeles: Hiramoto Shuppan Jimusho, 1918. 12 + 7 + 464 pp.

    A work on post-World War I U.S.-Japan relations. Emphasizes the need
for further Japanese economic development and the crucial importance of the
triangular relationship between Japan, America, and China. Chapter II, pp.
43-96, treats the exclusion movement.

246. 加藤文護　　最近の在米同胞
    Katō Bungo. Saikin no zai-Bei dōhō [The present condition of the Japanese
    in America]. Tokyo: Nihon Zusho Shuppan, 1921. 5 + 11 + 506 + app. 20
    pp., photos. M.

    A book divided into two parts. The first looks at the political and
military significance of the Pacific area, the importance and role of the
Hawaiian Islands, the American national character, the American economy, and
finally U.S.-Japan trade relations. The second half provides a summary of
the economic and social life of the Japanese, mainly in California, and
surveys the exclusion movement.

247. 川島伊佐美　　日米外交史
  + Kawashima Isami. Nichi-Bei gaikōshi [History of U.S.-Japan diplomatic
    relations]. San Francisco: Hatae Minoru, 1932. 7 + 11 + 887 + [2] pp.,
    plates + supplement 68 pp.

    A chronological history of the diplomatic relations between Japan and
America. The author, a long-time Issei newspaperman, places the exclusion
movement and Japanese immigrant society at the core of his chronology,

seeing them as the chief source of conflict between the two nations. The
years after the Sino-Japanese War of 1894-95 are stressed in his year-by-
year chronology which ends in 1930. The supplement covers the Manchurian
Incident of 1931 and the events which preceded it.

248. 北昤吉　　對米根本策私案　　　　　　　　　　　　　外交時報
Kita Reikichi. "Tai-Bei konponsaku shian" [A fundamental, personal proposal
  for an American policy], Gaikō Jihō [Revue Diplomatique], 39:469 (Jun. 15,
  1924), 64-74. M.

   An article suggesting that Japan must adopt a Japanese version of the
Monroe Doctrine in Asia to nurture its own power. Written in response to
the 1924 Immigration Act.

249. 國策研究會　　新國是の提唱
Kokusaku Kenkyūkai. Shin Kokuze no teishō [New national policy proposals].
  Tokyo: Kibōkaku, 1924. 6 + 3 + 5 + 339 pp. M.

   A collection of talks sponsored by the Kokusaku Kenkyūkai [Study Society
on National Policies] in May, 1924. Chapter II entitled "Gaikō sasshin"
[Reform of foreign relations], pp. 77-237, is related to Japanese-American
history. The talks in this Chapter are on U.S.-Japan relations, touching
upon such topics as the exclusion movement, racial prejudice, and the 1924
Immigration Act. They are by Soeda Juichi, Yamada Saburō, Soejima Michimasa, Shiba Teikichi, and Uehara Etsujirō.

250. 大石挨一　　日米問題實力解決策
Ōishi Kiichi. Nichi-Bei mondai jitsuryoku kaiketsusaku [Power solutions
  to Japanese-American problems]. Tokyo: Sankōdō, 1916. 12 + 4 + 7 +
  896 pp., photos.

   A work putting forth the view that only Japanese national strength--
military, economic, educational, social, and moral--will provide the key to
fundamental solutions to Japanese-American problems. Written with the
anti-Japanese movement in the immediate background, the author interprets
the exclusion movement in terms of racial prejudice. The author himself
was a 20-year resident of America.

251. 副島道正　　日米海軍力競爭と日米戰爭論　　　　　　外交時報
Soejima Michimasa. "Nichi-Bei kaigunryoku kyōsō to Nichi-Bei sensoron"
  [The Japanese-American naval armament race and a Japanese-American war],
  Gaikō Jihō [Revue Diplomatique], 33:396 (May 1, 1921), 1-12 and 33:397
  (May 15, 1921), 1-17. M.

   A general essay on American expansion into the Pacific and U.S. naval
policy which at the same time is highly critical of Japanese foreign policy.
Regarding the exclusion movement, the author feels it is a regional problem
localized in California, and so he does not consider it a possible cause for
war between the two nations.

252. 末廣重雄　　日米移民問題の解決如何　　　　　　　　外交時報
Suehiro Shigeo. "Nichi-Bei imin mondai no kaiketsu ikan" [How to solve the
  Japanese-American immigration question], Gaikō Jihō [Revue Diplomatique],
  35:419 (Apr. 15, 1922), 39-45. M.

   An article on the possibility and desirability of incorporating into a
new Japanese-American Treaty a proviso which would guarantee equal treatment
with regard to the ownership and leasing of land. The author feels such a
proviso, even if possible, should not be hastily considered, for it would
feed into the exclusion movement.

253. 高橋作衞　　日米之新關係
 * Takahashi Sakuei. Nichi-Bei no shin kankei [New U.S.-Japan relations]. Tokyo: Shimizu Shoten, 1910. 4 + 2 + 4 + 402 pp., apps. M.

　　A collection of essays on U.S.-Japan relations by a Professor of International Law at Tokyo University who visited America in 1908-09. Chapter V, "Imin mondai" [The immigration question], pp. 161-262, treats the exclusion movement and the Japanese immigrants. Four of the five appendices relate to Japanese-American history: a 1907 report on Vancouver and the Japanese; a 1910 report on the Japanese in Washington; a summary of the Japanese Texas rice colony; and a summary of conditions in Hawaii.

IV.
General Historical Works

Note: The secondary works listed below should dispel the myth that no such works exist. The most significant general history of Japanese emigration is no. 256, while no. 261 is an excellent study of emigration from Wakayama Prefecture. The best general history of the Japanese immigrants and their descendants on the continental United States is no. 275. The valuable regional histories are no. 280 for Hawaii, no. 290 and no. 293 for Southern California, no. 300 for the Pacific Northwest, no. 296 and no. 298 for the Rocky Mountain area, and no. 289 for New York. No. 272 and no. 291 provide very accurate chronological histories, and no. 264 and no. 283 are two postwar publications that are full of historical reminiscences. The Prefectural histories generally are akin to Who's Who publications.

1. OVERSEAS JAPANESE

254. 大日本文明協會　　日本人の海外發展
*   Dai Nihon Bummei Kyōkai. Nihonjin no kaigai hatten [History of the Japanese abroad]. Tokyo: Dai Nihon Bummei Kyōkai Jimusho, 1916. 9 + 3 + 8 + 446 pp. M.

    A survey of the overseas Japanese throughout the world designed to illustrate the "pioneering" aspect of the Japanese character. Discusses the geographical, social, and political factors, the status of economic and trade relations, and the Japanese population in specific countries and areas. Chapter 7, pp. 292-369, covers America, including the Hawaiian Islands, and Canada.

255. 移民問題研究會　　事變下・在外日本人の展望
*   Imin Mondai Kenkyūkai. Jihenka zaigai Nihonjin no tenbō [Prospects for overseas Japanese after the China Incident]. Tokyo: Imin Mondai Kenkyūkai, 1940. 4 + 252 pp. X.

    A collection of talks given by different individuals in October, 1939 on overseas Japanese under the sponsorship of the Imin Mondai Kenkyūkai [Emigration Problem Research Society]. Three talks are related to Japanese-American history: "Shin Tōa kensetsu to zaigai Nihonjin," pp. 1-31, by Shimomura Hiroshi which discusses the general relationship between the construction of a "New Asia" and the overseas Japanese; "Zai-Bei hōjin dai-nisei mondai no tenbō," pp. 121-163, by Fujimura Nobuo which treats the second-generation problem in America; and "Kaigai takushoku jigyō yonjūnen," pp. 225-252, by Nagata Shigeshi which provides a summary of Japanese emigration to Hawaii, North and South America, and Manchuria.

256. 入江寅次　邦人海外發展史
* Irie Toraji. Hōjin kaigai hattenshi [History of Japanese expansion abroad]. Tokyo: Ida Shoten, 1942. 2 + 2 + 538 + 546 + chronology 8 pp. M.

   A standard history of Japanese emigration to Hawaii, North and South America, Oceania, and Manchuria from 1868 through the 1930's with a strong prewar nationalistic bias which is an expanded version of an earlier work published in 1938. Organized chronologically, it is divided into two major parts. The first covers the period 1868 to 1907 and the second from 1908 to 1936. The author was a one-time member of the Japanese diplomatic corps.

257. 海外日系人連絡協會　　　第五回海外日系人大會報告書
Kaigai Nikkeijin Renraku Kyōkai. Dai-gokai Kaigai Nikkeijin Taikai hōkoku-sho [Report of the 5th Conference of Overseas Japanese]. Tokyo: Kaigai Nikkeijin Renraku Kyōkai, 1965. 88 pp., photos.

   A summary report of the 5th Conference of Overseas Japanese held in Tokyo in 1964. The conference was attended by Hideshima Shichisaburō, Kōda Keisaburō, and Katō Kisaburō of the United States.

258. 紀元二千六百年奉祝海外同胞東京大會本部
     紀元二千六百年奉祝海外同胞東京大會の全貌
Kigen Nisenroppyakunen Hōshuku Kaigai Dōhō Tōkyō Taikai Honbu. Kigen Nisen-roppyakunen Hōshuku Kaigai Dōhō Tōkyō Taikai no zenbō [The Overseas Japanese Tokyo Conference Commemorating the 2600th Anniversary of the Birth of Japan]. Tokyo: Kigen Nisenroppyakunen Hōshuku Kaigai Dōhō Tōkyō Taikai Honbu, 1940. 44 pp., photos.

   A pamphlet announcing the preparations and preliminary outline of the Overseas Japanese Tokyo Conference Commemorating the 2600th Anniversary of the Birth of Japan. Sponsored by the Japanese government, this conference was held in November, 1940.

259. 巻島徳寿　　　日本移民概史
* Makishima Tokuhisa (ed.). Nihon imin gaishi [Outline of Japanese emigration]. Tokyo: Kaigai Kōgyō Kabushiki Kaisha, 1937. 6 + 100 pp. M.

   A brief survey of Japanese emigration from Meiji times which includes a treatment of emigration to Hawaii, pp. 29-34, and North America, pp. 37-42. Authored by Hamano Hideo.

260. 永田稠　　信濃海外移住史
Nagata Shigeshi. Shinano kaigai ijūshi [History of overseas migration from Shinano]. Nagano: Shinano Kaigai Kyōkai, 1952. [4] + 6 + 324 pp., photos.

   A history of emigration from Nagano Prefecture, especially to Brazil and Manchuria, under the auspices of the Shinano Kaigai Kyōkai [Shinano Overseas Association] established in 1922 by the author. Chapter II, pp. 15-47, treats the emigration from this Prefecture to North America.

261. 和歌山県　　和歌山県移民史
* Wakayama-ken. Wakayama-ken iminshi [History of emigration from Wakayama Prefecture]. [Wakayama-shi]: Wakayama-ken, 1957. [3] + table of contents 17 + 1193 pp., photos, tables, maps, bibliog., chronologies, name-index.

An encyclopedic but scholarly history of emigration from Wakayama Prefecture from the 19th century to the post-World War II period. Provides a detailed analysis of the origins and causes by regions and villages. Includes a treatment of the overseas Japanese settlements of North, South, and Central America, Hawaii, Australia, Southeast Asia, and Manchuria, and contains a valuable bibliography. Compiled by Ikemura Heitarō, Shiozaki Keizō, and Mori Keizō.

262. 山下草園　奉祝紀元二千六百年と海外同胞
* Yamashita Sōen. Hōshuku Kigen Nisenroppyakunen to kaigai dōhō [Commemoration of the 2600th Anniversary of the Birth of Japan and the overseas Japanese]. Tokyo: Hōshuku Kigen Nisenroppyakunen to Kaigai Dōhō Kankōkai, 1941. 4 + 3 + 223 pp., plate, photos.

A description of events and participants in the ultra-nationalistic Overseas Japanese Tokyo Conference Commemorating the 2600th Anniversary of the Birth of Japan held in Tokyo in November, 1940, with an emphasis upon the Japanese from Hawaii.

2. JAPANESE IN AMERICA

263. 安部磯雄　北米之新日本
Abe Isoo. Hoku-Bei no shin Nihon [The new Japan of North America]. Tokyo: Hakubunkan, 1905. 3 + 4 + 216 pp., photos. M.

A general treatment of the Japanese in America by a Waseda University professor and a Christian socialist. He views the exclusion movement as rooted in racial prejudice, looks for more emigration from Japan, and anticipates that the Pacific Coast will become the meeting ground for the East and West. The statistical data on Japanese agriculture and businesses are derived from the Nichibei Nenkan [Japanese American Yearbook], no. 1, 1905.

264. 藤岡紫朗　歩みの跡
Fujioka Shirō. Ayumi no ato [Traces of a journey]. Los Angeles: Ayumi no Ato Kankō Kōenkai, 1957. Photos 16 + 18 + 16 + 701 pp., name-index.

A collection of newspaper articles which first appeared in the Rafu Shimpō. According to the author, he reedited them somewhat for this publication. Covering the Issei generation, the articles range over many subjects, but stress stories about different personalities and anecdotes about events and places from the beginning of Japanese immigration in the 19th century down to the post-World War II period. In addition, the articles encompass all Japanese settlements on the mainland, including Alaska, Canada, and Mexico. Because the writer himself was an Issei pioneer and a lifelong journalist who knew many of the people about whom he writes, this volume provides a wealth of historical information.

265. 加藤十四郎　在米同胞発展史
Katō Jūshirō. Zai-Bei dōhō hattenshi [History of the Japanese in America]. Tokyo: Hakubunkan, 1908. [2] + 4 + 239 pp., photos. M.

An early general work covering the Japanese population in America (excluding Hawaii but including Alaska) and Canada. Its emphasis is upon the

71

social, economic, and political development of Japanese communities, with particular attention paid to the Pacific Northwest region. Includes biographical sketches of the leading Japanese in specific geographical areas. The author was a former newspaperman with the vernacular press.

266. 加藤新一　アメリカ移民百年史
\+ Katō Shin'ichi. Amerika imin hyakunenshi [Hundred-year history of Japanese immigrants in America]. v. I-III. Tokyo: Jiji Tsūshinsha, 1965. v. I, 293 pp., photos; v. II, 287 pp., photos; v. III, 291 pp., photos.

   An abbreviated version of no. 267.

267. 加藤新一　米国日系人百年史
Katō Shin'ichi. Beikoku Nikkeijin hyakunenshi [Hundred-year history of the Japanese-American]. San Francisco: Shin Nichibei Shimbunsha, 1961. 23 + 1431 + Who's Who index 19 pp., photos, bibliog.

   A general history of the Japanese in America through 1960 which relies heavily upon no. 275 and no. 290. The author has simply extracted entire passages from these two works, dropping sentences and altering words here and there, to compile this history. The bulk consists of a Who's Who.

268. 永井松三　日米文化交渉史・第五巻移住編
+* Nagai Matsuzō (ed.). Nichi-Bei bunka kōshōshi, dai-gokan: Ijū-hen [A history of Japanese-American cultural relations, v. 5: Emigration]. Tokyo: Yōyōsha, 1955. 1 + 15 + 632 pp., photos, chronology, bibliog.

   A general history of the Japanese in the continental United States and Hawaii from the beginning of Japanese emigration in the 19th century until 1930 published as a part of a six-volume series on Japanese-American cultural relations. The first part covers the Japanese on the mainland and relies heavily upon no. 275; and the second is devoted to the Japanese in Hawaii. The editor was a former Japanese Consul in San Francisco.

269. 社会文庫　社会主義者・無政府主義者・人物研究史料(1)
\+ Shakai Bunko. Shakaishugisha museifushugisha: Jimbutsu kenkyū shiryō (1) [Socialists and anarchists: Historical sources on individuals (1)]. Tokyo: Kashiwa Shobō, 1964. 309 pp., plates, name-index.

   A part of an 8-volume series on the early socialist and anarchist movement in late Meiji times under the general editorship of Suzuki Mōsaburō. This volume reproduces the original koseki tōhon of confirmed or suspected socialists and anarchists, including those in America, and the investigative entries of their activities by the Japanese Ministry of Home Affairs.

270. 社会文庫　社会主義者・無政府主義者・人物研究史料(2)
\+ Shakai Bunko. Shakaishugisha museifushugisha: Jimbutsu kenkyū shiryō (2) [Socialists and anarchists: Historical sources on individuals (2)]. Tokyo: Kashiwa Shobō, 1966. [4] + 258 pp., photos.

   A sequel to above which has a section on America entitled "Zai-Bei Nihonjin shakaishugi undōshi wo tsukutta hitobito" [The people who made the history of the Japanese socialist movement in America], pp. 115-128. Also includes an interview with Iwata Sakutarō and brief essays by Nobeoka Tsunetarō and Karl Yoneda.

271. 社会文庫　在米社会主義者・無政府主義者沿革
\+ Shakai Bunko. Zai-Bei shakaishugisha museifushugisha enkaku [A history of

Japanese socialists and anarchists in America]. Tokyo: Kashiwa Shobō, 1964. 535 pp., plates.

A part of the above series which reproduces the secret reports compiled by the Japanese Ministry of Home Affairs on the activities of the Japanese socialists and anarchists in America from December, 1903 to June, 1911. Includes a short historical essay on them by Matsuo Shōichi.

272. 藤賀與一　日米關係在米國日本人發展史要
Tōga Yoichi (comp.). Nichi-Bei kankei zai-Beikoku Nihonjin hatten shiyō [A chronological history of U.S.-Japan relations and the Japanese in America]. Oakland: Beikoku Seisho Kyōkai Nihonjinbu, 1927. [8] + 390 pp., plate, map.

A year-by-year chronology of important events, with some interpretative notes, in the history of U.S.-Japan relations and the Japanese in America which starts in 1769 and ends in 1927. Since the compiler began this work as a history of the Japanese Christian churches in America, there are many entries on this subject.

273. 寅井順一　北米日本人總覽
Torai Jun'ichi. Hoku-Bei Nihonjin sōran [Compendium of the Japanese of North America]. Tokyo: Chūōdō Shobō, 1914. 2 + 2 + 12 + 386 pp., photos. M.

A general survey of the Japanese in Washington, Oregon, and California. Contains brief descriptions of each state and the specific regions within them in which the Japanese reside, summaries of the Japanese communities, and short biographical sketches of the leading figures in them, including many photographs.

274. 植村寅　北米之日本人
* Uemura Tora. Hoku-Bei no Nihonjin [Japanese of North America]. Tokyo: Naigai Shuppan Kyōkai, 1912. 6 + 10 + 2 + 2 + 2 + 366 + apps. 32 pp., photos. M.

An early comprehensive survey of the Japanese in North America. Includes chapters on American society; the historical background to emigration to North America; the Japanese communities of California, Washington, Oregon, and other states as well as British Columbia, Alaska, and Hawaii; the types of employment in which the Japanese are engaged and the income derived therefrom; the monetary remissions to Japan and their relationship to trade between Japan and America; the political and social status of the Japanese; the exclusion movement; and the Japanese government's emigration policy. The 32-page appendices consist of the treaties, laws, and regulations pertinent to the Japanese in America.

275. 在米日本人會　在米日本人史
Zaibei Nihonjinkai. Zai-Bei Nihonjinshi [History of the Japanese in America]. San Francisco: Zaibei Nihonjinkai, 1940. [10] + 20 + 7 + 1295 pp., plates, photos.

The standard comprehensive history of the Japanese in America published under the auspices of the Japanese Association of America. Divided into six major parts, it has the following: 1) an introductory survey of the history of the Japanese in America; 2) detailed topical histories of agriculture, commerce, fisheries, labor, religion, education, publications, sports, population and occupation, governmental offices and organizations, and others; 3) historical surveys of local Japanese communities by regions, including

Canada; 4) a history of the exclusion movement; 5) an outline of the second generation; and 6) a diplomatic history of U.S.-Japan relations. Though written before World War II, this volume has yet to be replaced by any newer work in English or Japanese.

3. REGIONAL AND LOCAL HISTORIES

276. 米國西北部聯絡日本人會　　米國西北部在留日本人發展略史
Beikoku Seihokubu Renraku Nihonjinkai. Beikoku Seihokubu zairyū Nihonjin hatten ryakushi [A brief history of the Japanese of the Pacific Northwest in America]. Seattle: Beikoku Seihokubu Renraku Nihonjinkai, 1921. 107 pp. M.

A historical survey of the Japanese of the Pacific Northwest published by the United Northwestern Japanese Association. Treats the exclusion movement, the Japanese government's emigration policies, the Japanese Associations, and the fight for naturalization rights and the litigation against anti-Japanese legislation. Includes some statistical data.

277. 藤井秀五郎　　大日本海外移住民史 第一編布哇
* Fujii Hidegorō. Dai Nihon kaigai ijūminshi: Dai-ippen Hawai [History of Japanese emigration abroad: Part I, Hawaii]. Osaka: Kaigai Chōsakai, 1937. 4 + [4] + 2 + 53 + 3 + 96 + 6 + 6 + 97 pp., map, plates, photos.

A general work on the Japanese of Hawaii which is divided into three main parts. Part I is on the origins of Japanese emigration to Hawaii; Part II discusses the development and current state of the Japanese communities; and Part III is a Who's Who.

278. 藤井秀五郎　　新布哇
* Fujii Hidegorō. Shin Hawai [New Hawaii]. Tokyo: Bunkensha, 1902 (rev. ed.). 6 + 6 + 28 + 698 pp., map, photos. M.

An encyclopedic history and description of Hawaii and the Japanese population written primarily for prospective new emigrants in Japan.

279. 福永虎治郎　　三輪治衷　　布哇郡嶋誌 第壹卷 加哇篇
* Fukunaga Torajirō and Miwa Haruie. Hawai Guntōshi dai-ikkan Kawai-hen [Gazetteer of the Hawaiian Islands: vol. I, Kauai]. Lihue: Kauai Shimpōsha, 1916. 2 + 2 + 5 + 426 pp., photos.

A history and general description of the island of Kauai. The Japanese population on the island is treated within this context. Includes a Who's Who in Kauai.

280. ハワイ日本人移民史刊行委員会　　ハワイ日本人移民史
* Hawai Nihonjin Iminshi Kankō Iinkai. Hawai Nihonjin iminshi ["A history of Japanese immigrants in Hawaii"]. Honolulu: Hawai Nikkeijin Rengō Kyōkai, 1964. xxxiii + photos 133 + 581 pp., chronologies.

A standard history of the Japanese in Hawaii from 1868 to the post-World War II period published by the United Japanese Society of Hawaii. Includes many chronologies and footnotes.

281. 北加日本人會　　北加日本人發展史
    Hokka Nihonjinkai. Hokka Nihonjin hattenshi [History of the Japanese of
    Northern California]. [Chico]: Hokka Nihonjinkai, 1922. [6] + 43 pp.
    M.

    A brief history of the Japanese in the Chico area, emphasizing the
Japanese Association of Chico.

282. 石岡彦一　　日本人事情
    Ishioka Hikokazu. Nihonjin jijō [The status of Japanese]. Tokyo: Ishioka
    Hikokazu, 1907. 8 + 4 + 2 + 70 + 574 + 75 pp., photos. M.

    One of the earliest works on the Japanese of the Pacific Northwest and
Canada. Provides a general description of Washington relative to the lum-
ber industry, agriculture, fisheries, mining, railroad, shipping, and educa-
tion as well as a concise summary of the Japanese throughout the Pacific
Northwest. The bulk of this volume consists of a 574-page Who's Who by
Prefectural origins. The remaining 75 pages are devoted to Canada and a
Who's Who in British Columbia.

283. 伊藤一男　北米百年桜
    Itō Kazuo. Hoku-Bei hyakunen sakura [Hundred-year old cherry blossoms in
    North America]. Seattle: Hokubei Hyakunen Sakura Jikkō Iinkai, 1969.
    1140 pp., photos, map, chronology, bibliog., index.

    A recent volume on the history of the Japanese in the Pacific North-
west, including those in British Columbia and Alaska. Based upon interviews
and personal accounts, it is essentially a social history of the Issei
viewed through their own eyes. Organized topically, it has vivid Issei
recollections of working in the railroads, lumber mills, mines, Alaskan
fisheries and canneries, and other subjects. Includes sections on Japanese
women, stowaways, and prostitutes.

284. 金井重雄　　伊藤晩松　　　北米之日本人
    Kanai Shigeo and Itō Banshō (pseud.). Hoku-Bei no Nihonjin [The Japanese
    of North America]. San Francisco: Kanai Tsūyaku Jimusho, 1909. [12] +
    510 pp., plates, photos.

    One of the earliest works on the Japanese in California (despite the
title, it is restricted to California). Descriptive in nature, it covers
all the major Japanese settlements, and includes short biographical
sketches of certain individuals in each settlement.

285. 柏村一介　　北米踏査大観
    Kashiwamura Kazusuke. Hoku-Bei tōsa taikan [A broad survey of North Ameri-
    ca]. v. I. Tokyo: Ryūbundō, 1911. 4 + 2 + 16 + 666 pp., photos.

    A comprehensive survey of Japanese settlements in California written
for readers in Japan. Based upon the author's personal on-the-spot survey
carried out from 1908-1910, it provides a descriptive survey of Japanese
settlements and short biographical sketches of certain individuals in them.

286. 川添善一　　移植樹の花開く
  * Kawazoe Zen'ichi. Ishokuju no hara hiraku [Blossoming flowers from trans-
    planted trees]. Honolulu: Ishokuju no Hana Hiraku Kankōkai, 1960. 23 +
    529 pp.

    A collection of newspaper articles on the history of the Japanese in
Hawaii from its inception to the present. The articles are about personali-

ties and events primarily based upon the author's research, interviews, and personal experiences. The author is a journalist with the Hawaii Times.

287. 丸山千曲　亞郡同胞大勢一覧
Maruyama Senkyoku (pseud.). Agun dōhō taisei ichiran ["Doings of the Japanese in Alameda County"]. Oakland: Shin Sekai Shimbun, 1908. [3] + 79 + 50 pp., map, photos. M.

An early work on the Japanese in Alameda County, principally in the cities of Oakland, Berkeley, and Alameda. Provides an outline of economic activities and short biographies of successful individuals. Includes some statistical data for 1907, a list of Japanese organizations and their members, and an address directory.

288. メリスビル地方日本人會　北加四郡日本人發展史
Merisubiru Chihō Nihonjinkai. Hokka yongun Nihonjin hattenshi ["History of the Japanese in the big four"]. Marysville: Merisubiru Chihō Nihonjinkai, 1932. 6 + 120 pp.

The only work on the Japanese in the four Northern California counties of Yuba, Sutter, Butte, and Colusa. Contains an outline of the various religious, social, and educational organizations as well as the Marysville Japanese Association.

289. 水谷渉三　紐育日本人發展史
Mizutani Shōzō. Nyūyōku Nihonjin hattenshi [History of the Japanese of New York City]. New York: Nyūyōku Nihonjinkai, 1921. 5 + 9 + 2 + 8 + 870 pp., plate, charts, photos.

An early work on the Japanese of New York City which focuses primarily upon U.S.-Japan trade relations. Beginning with a summary of the development of trade relations, it provides a detailed discussion of trade items and the shipping and banking institutions involved, a description of the various social, religious, and economic organizations, including the New York Japanese Association, within the Japanese community, and a history of the various diplomatic and economic missions dispatched from Japan to America.

290. 南加日系人商業会議所　南加州日本人七十年史
Nanka Nikkeijin Shōgyō Kaigisho. Nan Kashū Nihonjin shichijūnenshi ["Japanese in Southern California: A history of 70 years"]. Los Angeles: Nanka Nikkeijin Shōgyō Kaigisho, 1960. 34 + 756 + English preface xi + English summary 67 pp., photos, chronology, bibliog.

For reasons unknown, this volume was published to replace no. 293. Unlike its predecessor, this work spans a 70-year period from 1890 to 1959 and is edited by Katō Shin'ichi. Based for the most part upon preexisting secondary sources, it is organized differently with a greater emphasis upon the prewar period and the outlying Japanese communities.

291. 南加日系人商業會議所　南加州日本人史
Nanka Nikkeijin Shōgyō Kaigisho. Nan Kashū Nihonjinshi [History of the Japanese in Southern California]. Los Angeles: Nanka Nikkeijin Shōgyō Kaigisho, 1956. 370 pp., photos.

A chronological history of events relating to the Japanese in Southern California primarily from 1885 to 1918 drawn from the vernacular press, with explanatory notes. Compiled by Saigusa Jisaburō before World War II for the Southern California Japanese Historical Society in 1939, it was not published then. The Japanese Chamber of Commerce of Southern California issued it as the first of a two-volume series on the history of the Japanese in Southern California.

292. 南加日系人商業會議所　　南加州日本人史
Nanka Nikkeijin Shōgyō Kaigisho. "Nan Kashū Nihonjinshi" [History of the Japanese in Southern California]. MSS. 16 folders, n.d.

The original but incomplete manuscript of above which covers the period 1888 to 1915.

293. 南加日系人商業會議所　　南加州日本人史　後篇
Nanka Nikkeijin Shōgyō Kaigisho. Nan Kashū Nihonjinshi kōhen [History of the Japanese in Southern California: v. II]. Los Angeles: Nanka Nikkeijin Shōgyō Kaigisho, 1957. 10 + 13 + 773 + index 28 pp., photos, chronology.

A sequel to no. 291 edited by Ochi Dōjun covering the period 1919 to 1955. Unlike the first volume, this one provides a narrative history divided into three periods: 1) the prewar period from 1919 to the start of World War II; 2) the wartime period and internment; and 3) the postwar period and recovery. In treating the wartime internment, especially the conflicts within the camps, the editor discreetly mentions no names. The two volumes together form the standard history published in the postwar period on the Japanese in Southern California.

294. 大橋貫造　　北米加州スタクトン同胞史
Ōhashi Kanzō. Hoku-Bei Kashū Sutakuton dōhoshi [A history of the Japanese of Stockton, California]. Stockton: Su-shi Nihonjinkai, 1937. 9 + 6 + 391 pp., photos, map.

A descriptive digest of the Japanese in the Stockton area. The bulk of this work consists of a chronological history of the Stockton Japanese Association. Also includes economic and social organizations, religious institutions, and Japanese language schools.

296. 路機時報社　　山中部と日本人
Rokki Jihōsha. Sanchūbu to Nihonjin [The Rocky Mountain region and the Japanese]. Salt Lake City: Rokki Jihōsha, 1925. [18] + 591 pp., photos, maps.

A general history of the Japanese in Utah, Idaho, Wyoming, and Nevada compiled by the Rocky Mountain Times. Includes a treatment of the Japanese in railroad construction, mining, agriculture, and small businesses, and summaries of local Japanese Associations, agricultural organizations, churches, and other groups. Half of the volume consists of a Who's Who.

297. 坂久五郎　　サンタマリア平原日本人史
Saka Hisagorō. Santa Maria Heigen Nihonjinshi [A history of the Japanese in the Santa Maria Valley]. Guadalupe: Gadarūpu Nihonjinkai, 1936. 17 + [2] + 13 + 424 pp., plates, photos.

A local history of the Japanese in the Santa Maria Valley. Includes a general description of the valley, a summary of the exclusion movement, and a history of the Japanese in this area from 1900. Also includes a history of the Guadalupe Japanese Association and other economic, educational, religious, and social organizations. An extended Who's Who completes this work.

298. 鈴木六彦　　インターマウンテン同胞發達史
Suzuki Rokuhiko, et al. Intāmaunten dōhō hattatsushi ["The development of the intermountain Japanese colonies"]. Denver: Denba Shimpōsha, 1910. 7 + 3 + 619 + directory-index 16 pp., photos.

    The earliest work on the Japanese in the Rocky Mountain region. The product of four different writers, it covers the Japanese in Colorado, Utah, Wyoming, Nebraska, and Kansas. Contains invaluable data on population, wages, occupation, and agricultural costs and prices with reference to the Japanese. Biographical sketches, especially of labor contractors for railroads and mining companies, take up half the volume.

299. 武居熱血　　布哇一覧
* Takei Nekketsu. Hawai ichiran [A guide to Hawaii]. Honolulu: Motoshige Shinjudō, 1914. [208] pp., photos, maps.

    A guide to Hawaii comprised of detailed maps of Japanese settlements by island.

300. 竹内幸次郎　　米國西北部日本移民史
Takeuchi Kōjirō. Beikoku Seihokubu Nihon iminshi [History of Japanese immigrants in the Pacific Northwest of America]. Seattle: Taihoku Nippōsha, 1929. 2 + 2 + 2 + 4 + 22 + 1204 + name-index 15 pp., plates, photos. M.

    An early comprehensive history of the Japanese in Washington and Oregon published by the Taihoku Nippō [The Great Northern Daily News]. Concentrating heavily on the Seattle area, it covers the history of the Washington Japanese Association and the United Northwestern Japanese Association, the exclusion movement, the problems of naturalization and dual nationality, and includes chapters on all the major economic, social, cultural, and educational institutions. Also has summaries of the Japanese communities of Tacoma, Spokane, and other local areas. Concludes with 18 biographies of prominent leaders, statistical data on population, and an extended Who's Who.

301. 竹内幸助　　サンピドロ同胞發展録
Takeuchi Kōsuke. San Pidoro dōhō hattenroku [Record of the development of the Japanese in San Pedro]. Terminal Island: Takeuchi Kōsuke, 1937. [10] + 192 + app. 124 pp., photos. M.

    A descriptive digest of the Japanese fishing community of San Pedro up to 1936, consisting of summaries of the main social, religious, educational, and economic institutions. A 124-page Who's Who is appended.

302. タコマ日本人會　　タコマ紹介
Takoma Nihonjinkai. Takoma shōkai ["Port of Tacoma"]. Tacoma: Takoma Nihonjinkai, 1922. 5 + [4] + 3 + 134 pp., maps, photos. M.

    A brief guide to the city of Tacoma and its surrounding counties. The first part is devoted to a general description of the geography, climate, and economy of this area. The second provides a summary of Japanese communities in and around Tacoma.

303. タコマ週報社　　タコマ市及地方日本人史
Takoma Shūhōsha. Takoma-shi oyobi chihō Nihonjinshi [History of the Japanese in Tacoma and vicinity]. Tacoma: Takoma Shūhōsha, 1941. 265 pp., photos.

A general history of the Japanese in Tacoma and the surrounding communities of Fife, Sumner, Puyallup, Alderton, Orting, Olympia, and Shelton. Covers the educational and religious institutions, Japanese Associations and other socio-cultural organizations, the Nisei population, and finally anecdotes about people and events related by key pioneers.

304. 登森杢雄　　對岸の声
Tomori Mokuo. Taigan no koe ["Voice of Pacific Shore"]. Portland: Privately printed, 1969. 262 pp., photos.

A collection of miscellaneous articles devoted to the Issei pioneers of the Pacific Northwest and U.S.-Japan relations. Of particular interest are those articles on Yamaoka Ototaka, Takaki Shintarō, and other Issei figures of this area. The author came to America in 1924 and worked for the Oregon Japanese newspaper for many years.

305. 渡部七郎　　布哇歴史
* Watanabe Shichirō. Hawai rekishi [History of Hawaii]. Tokyo: Kōgakkai Kyōikubu, 1935. [6] + 8 + 462 + app. no. 1 118 + app. no. 2 220 pp., map, photos, illus.

A general history of the Hawaiian Islands and the Japanese community produced by a 15-year resident. Appendix no. 1 is a chronological description of Japanese language schools; appendix no. 2 is a Who's Who.

306. ヤキマ日本人會　　ヤキマ平原日本人史
Yakima Nihonjinkai. Yakima Heigen Nihonjinshi [History of the Japanese in the Yakima Valley]. Yakima: Yakima Nihonjinkai, 1935. 21 + 23 + chronology 8 + 399 + directory 27 pp., photos.

A local history with summaries of the Japanese Association, religious groups, Japanese language schools, the exclusion movement, agricultural activities, and other topics. Also has population statistics, an extended Who's Who, and a 27-page Nisei directory.

4. HISTORIES BY PREFECTURAL ORIGINS

307. 古川榮次　　南加州と鹿児島縣人
Furukawa Eiji. Nan Kashū to Kagoshima kenjin. [Southern California and the Japanese from Kagoshima Prefecture]. Tokyo: Nihon Keisatsu Shimbunsha, 1920. 2 + 5 + 2 + 1 + 3 + 26 + 468 + 8 pp., plate, photos. M.

A book designed to introduce the Japanese from Kagoshima Prefecture in Southern California and to assist prospective new emigrants in Japan. Provides detailed explanations of emigration procedures and American social customs. Most of the book consists of an extended Who's Who and an address directory.

308. 廣瀬半令　　在米甲州人奮闘五十年史
Hirose Shūrei. Zai-Bei Kōshūjin funtō gojūnenshi [History of the 50-year struggle of the Japanese from Koshu in America]. Los Angeles: Nanka Yamanashi Kaigai Kyōkai, 1934. 2 + 2 + 14 + 557 pp., plates, photos.

A work on the Japanese from Yamanashi Prefecture, especially in California. Presents a history of the Japanese from this Prefecture, including their contributions to Japanese language newspapers, financial institutions, the laundry business; five biographical sketches of leading pioneers; and an outline of the Yamanashi Prefectural Associations of Northern and Southern California. Concludes with an address directory and a Who's Who in America and Canada.

309. 廣田恒五郎　　在米福岡縣人と事業
Hirota Tsunegorō. Zai-Bei Fukuoka kenjin to jigyō [Japanese from Fukuoka Prefecture and their enterprises in America]. Los Angeles: Zaibei Fukuoka Kenjin to Jigyō Hensan Jimusho, 1936. 2 + 2 + 2 + 3 + 8 + name-index 16 + 160 + 508 + 77 pp., plates, photos.

An expanded version of no. 310 which includes Washington, Oregon, Wyoming, Colorado, Arizona, and Mexico as well as California. Includes a 508-page Who's Who and a 77-page directory.

310. 廣瀬恒五郎　　在米福岡縣人史
Hirota Tsunegorō. Zai-Bei Fukuoka kenjinshi [History of the Japanese from Fukuoka Prefecture in America]. Los Angeles: Zaibei Fukuoka Kenjinshi Hensan Jimusho, 1931. [1] + 3 + 4 + 7 + name-index 8 + 125 + 303 + apps. 122 + directory 89 pp., photos.

A chronological survey of the Japanese from Fukuoka Prefecture mainly restricted to California. Includes brief summaries of emigration from Fukuoka, the Nisei, various Prefectural organizations, and the outstanding pioneers like Ushijima Kinji and Ike Hyakumatsu; and a 303-page Who's Who. The appendices consist of a directory of Fukuoka Nisei in Japan from the mainland, Hawaii, and Canada; Constitutions of Prefectural organizations; the Southern California Fukuoka Book of the Deceased; a directory of Fukuoka Prefectural Associations; and a 89-page directory of Japanese from Fukuoka in America and Canada.

311. 開原榮　　加州廣島縣人發展史
Kaihara Sakae. Kashū Hiroshima kenjin hattenshi [History of the Japanese from Hiroshima Prefecture in California]. Sacramento: Yorozu Shoten, 1916. 6 + 4 + 622 + directory 68 pp., plates, photos.

The earliest work treating the Japanese from Hiroshima Prefecture in California which stresses agricultural activities. Provides statistics for the years 1912-1913 broken down into Gun origins, data on the distribution of those engaged in agricultural pursuits, and information on the various Prefectural organizations throughout the state. Concludes with a Who's Who in California.

312. 風早勝一　　南加州岡山縣人發展史
Kazahaya Katsu'ichi. Nan Kashū Okayama kenjin hattenshi [History of the Japanese from Okayama Prefecture in Southern California]. Los Angeles: Nan Kashū Okayama Kenjin Hattenshi Hensanjo, 1955. 11 + 21 + photos 40 + 470 pp., plates.

A history of the Okayama Prefectural Association and the Okayama Women's Society of Southern California. Includes an extended Who's Who and a list of the deceased.

313. 三重縣海外協会　　三重縣人北米發展史
Mie-ken Kaigai Kyōkai. Mie kenjin Hoku-Bei hattenshi [History of the Japanese from Mie Prefecture in North America]. Tsu-shi: Mie-ken Kaigai Kyōkai, 1966. 7 + [6] + 336 pp., photos.

A very brief history of emigration from Mie Prefecture, a summary history of the Mie Prefectural Association of Southern California and a membership roster as of 1940, and a list of Mie immigrants by year and by Gun origins. Concludes with an extended Who's Who.

314. 水谷萬嶽　　北米愛知縣人誌
Mizutani Bangaku. Hoku-Bei Aichi kenjinshi [Publication of the Japanese from Aichi Prefecture in North America]. Sacramento: Aichi Kenjinkai, 1920. [30] + 7 + 474 + apps. 159 pp., photos.

A history of the Japanese from Aichi Prefecture who generally settled in the Sacramento delta region. Presents a summary of emigration from Aichi to America beginning in 1889, detailed data on agricultural and business activities, and a history of the Aichi Prefectural Association. The three appendices are: a Who's Who, a Prefectural Association membership roster, and a Prefectural directory.

315. 中村正敏　　迎田勝馬　　在米の肥後人
Nakamura Masatoshi and Mukaeda Katsuma. Zai-Bei no Higojin [The Japanese from Higo in America]. Los Angeles: Nanka Kumamoto Kaigai Kyōkai, 1931. 2 + 4 + 6 + name-index 11 + 940 pp., plates, map, photos.

A history of the Japanese from Kumamoto Prefecture and the branches of the Kumamoto Overseas Association primarily in California. Includes an extended Who's Who.

316. 南加福井縣人會　　南加福井縣人五十年史
Nanka Fukui Kenjinkai. Nanka Fukui kenjin gojūnenshi [Fifty-year history of the Japanese from Fukui Prefecture in Southern California]. Los Angeles: Nanka Fukui Kenjinkai, 1953. 3 + 207 pp., photos.

A summary description of the past activities of the Japanese from Fukui Prefecture and their Prefectural Association in Southern California. Includes a list of the deceased and a directory.

317. 岡直樹　　北米の高知縣人
Oka Naoki. Hoku-Bei no Kōchi kenjin [Japanese from Kochi Prefecture in North America]. San Francisco: Oka Naoki, 1921. 4 + 3 + photos 62 + 425 pp.

A history of the Japanese from Kochi Prefecture in California and other states. Includes short essays on different topics and records of personal experiences by various individuals, a Who's Who, and a directory. Also provides information about conditions in America and the exclusion movement designed to inform readers in Japan.

318. 佐藤安治　　加州と福島縣人・南加篇
Satō Yasuji. Kashū to Fukushima kenjin: Nanka-hen [California and the Japanese from Fukushima Prefecture: Southern California]. Los Angeles: Kashū Fukushima Kenjin Hattenshi Hensanjo, 1929. 7 + 11 + 262 + 277 pp., photos. M.

A history of emigration from Fukushima to America, of the Fukushima Prefectural Association of Southern California, and of the Fukushima Overseas Association and its activities. Includes an extended Who's Who.

319. 妹尾萬郎　　奥州廣島縣人發展史
Senō Manrō. Ōshu Hiroshima kenjin hattenshi [History of the Japanese from Hiroshima Prefecture in Oregon]. Tokyo: Senō Manrō, 1916. 21 + 2 + 1 + 140 pp., photos. M.

A brief history of the Oregon Hiroshima Prefectural Association. Includes the organization's Constitution and by-laws and an extended Who's Who.

320. 竹田順一　在米廣島縣人史
Takeda Jun'ichi. Zai-Bei Hiroshima kenjinshi [History of the Japanese from Hiroshima Prefecture in America]. Los Angeles: Zaibei Hiroshima Kenjinshi Hakkōsho, 1929. 16 + 18 + 698 pp., photos, apps.

The standard history of the Japanese from Hiroshima Prefecture in California, Washington, and Oregon. Provides summaries of each state and locale, statistical data on population, birthrate, distribution, and monetary remissions, and histories of local Prefectural Associations and other institutions. Two-thirds of this volume consists of a Who's Who. Appendix I is a list of Hiroshima notables; appendix II is a directory.

321. 富本岩雄　在米和歌山縣人發展史
+ Tomimoto Iwao. Zai-Bei Wakayama kenjin hattenshi [History of the Japanese from Wakayama Prefecture in America]. Sacramento: Tomimoto Iwao, 1915. 2 + 2 + 3 + 2 + 8 + 2 + 2 + 2 + 7 + 1090 pp., photos.

A history of the Japanese from Wakayama Prefecture. Includes essays on race relations, specific individuals, and Mexico. Concludes with an extended Who's Who by Gun origins.

322. 露木惣藏　昭和聖代在米神奈川縣人
Tsuyuki Sōzō. Shōwa Seidai zai-Bei Kanagawa kenjin [Japanese from Kanagawa Prefecture in America in the Showa Era]. Kanagawa (?): Zaibei Kanagawa Kenjinsha, 1934. [1] + 11 + 8 + 246 + 3 pp., plates, photos. M.

An expanded version of no. 323 which includes Washington and Canada.

323. 露木惣藏　在米神奈川縣人
Tsuyuki Sōzō. Zai-Bei Kanagawa kenjin [Japanese from Kanagawa Prefecture in America]. Kanagawa (?): Zaibei Kanagawa Kenjinsha, 1915. 2 + 1 + 10 + 230 pp., photos. M.

A Who's Who of the Japanese from Kanagawa Prefecture in California by local area. Includes a very brief summary of the Kanagawa Prefectural Association.

324. 谷津利一郎　在米宮城縣人史
Yatsu Riichirō. Zai-Bei Miyagi kenjinshi [History of the Japanese from Miyagi Prefecture in America]. Los Angeles: Zaibei Miyagi Kenjinshi Hensan Jimusho, 1933. 11 + 7 + 11 + 351 pp., map, photos.

A history of the Japanese from Miyagi Prefecture. Contains a short background on emigration from this Prefecture, some population statistics, and a list of Japanese from Miyagi living in Southern California. Also includes brief histories of the Southern California Miyagi Prefectural Association and the Northern California Tohoku Association. Concludes with over 200 biographies and a directory.

V. Economics

1. PUBLISHED WORKS

325. 藤井整　農家の爲に
  Fujii Sei. Nōka no tame ni [For farmers]. Los Angeles: Komatsu Yoshimoto, 1924. 89 pp.

   A practical guide on how to manage farms in the light of the alien land laws.

326. 加州花卉市場株式會社　　　加州日本人花園業發展史
 + Kashū Kaki Ichiba Kabushiki Kaisha. Kashū Nihonjin kaengyō hattenshi [History of Japanese floriculture in California]. San Francisco: Kashū Kaki Ichiba Kabushiki Kaisha, 1929. 7 + 6 + 308 pp., photos.

   A history of Japanese floriculture in California published by the California Flower Market, Inc., an organization founded in 1912 to advance the welfare of Japanese growers.

327. 加州日本人中央農會　　　老農懇親會記念
  Kashū Nihonjin Chūō Nōkai. Rōnō konshinkai kinen [Conference of experienced farmers]. San Francisco: Kashū Nihonjin Chūō Nōkai, 1909. 166 pp. X.

   The proceedings of a conference of Japanese farmers held in Stockton in January, 1909 to exchange information and knowledge on matters relating to agriculture. Published by the Central Japanese Agricultural Association of California, an organization which emerged out of this conference.

328. 加州日本人靴工同盟會　　　加州日本人靴工同盟會會報
  Kashū Nihonjin Kutsukō Dōmeikai. Kashū Nihonjin Kutsukō Dōmeikai kaihō [Bulletin of the California Japanese Shoemakers League]. no. 1 (1909). San Francisco. 72 + 7 pp. X.

   The bulletin of the California Japanese Shoemakers League initially formed in 1893 and headquartered in San Francisco. A 7-page roster of its 300 members as of January, 1909 is appended.

329. 國際食糧農業協會　　　アメリカの米と稲作
  Kokusai Shokuryō Nōgyō Kyōkai. Amerika no kome to inasaku [American rice and rice culture]. Tokyo: Kokusai Shokuryō Nōgyō Kyōkai, 1954. [2] + 4 + 270 pp.

   Only the last section of this work concerns Japanese-American history. Contains a lecture by Saibara Kiyoaki and an open discussion with him concerning his 50-year experience of growing rice in Texas. Saibara Kiyoaki was the son of Saibara Seitō, one of the founders of the Japanese Texas rice colony outside of Houston in 1903.

330. 久保田鉄夫　　大日本農会北米支会創立三十周年記念
Kubota Tetsuo (ed.). Dai Nippon Nōkai Hoku-Bei shikai sōritsu sanjūshūnen kinen [Commemoration of the 30th anniversary of the founding of the North American branch of the Greater Japan Agricultural Society]. Tokyo: Dai Nippon Nōkai, 1960. [3] + 16 + 446 pp., plates, photos.

A volume dedicated to commemorate the 30th anniversary of the North American branch of the Greater Japan Agricultural Society. Divided into three sections, it provides the following: 1) essays on different aspects of the Japanese in agriculture in America by Issei; 2) a chronological history of the North American branch, centered in California, from its inception in 1930 in Southern California; and 3) biographical sketches of its members.

331. 村井狡　　在米日本人産業總覽
Murai Kō. Zai-Bei Nihonjin sangyō sōran [A compendium of Japanese agriculture in America]. Los Angeles: Beikoku Sangyō Nippōsha, 1940. 3 + 6 + 979 pp., plates, photos.

The only comprehensive survey of the Japanese in agriculture. Compiled under the direction of Murai Kō, the President of the Beikoku Sangyō Nippō of Los Angeles, its core consists of his newspaper articles. Includes detailed information on agricultural techniques, brief histories of Japanese agriculture by state and locale, and a Who's Who.

332. 南加花市場　　南加花市場發展史
Nanka Hana Ichiba. Nanka Hana Ichiba hattenshi [History of the Southern California Flower Market]. Los Angeles: Nanka Hana Ichiba, 1952. [10] + 220 + 163 pp., photos.

A history of the Southern California Flower Market which is divided into prewar and postwar periods. Initially formed in 1912 and incorporated as a non-profit organization in 1914, its purposes were to aid marketing, production, and knowledge of floriculture. Includes chronological excerpts from its official records and a listing of its officers over the years.

333. 農商務省商工局　　米國テキサス州に於ける米作に關する報告
Nō-Shōmushō Shōkōkyoku. Beikoku Tekisasu-shū ni okeru beisaku ni kansuru hōkoku [Report on rice culture in Texas]. Tokyo: Nō-Shōmushō Shōkōkyoku, 1905. 2 + 24 pp. M.

A brief report on rice culture in Texas and in particular on the beginning of the Japanese rice colony there by the Commerce and Industry Bureau, Ministry of Agriculture and Commerce.

334. 農商務省水產局　　海外に於ける本邦人の漁業狀況
* Nō-Shōmushō Suisankyoku. Kaigai ni okeru hompōjin no gyogyō jōkyō [State of the fishing industry of overseas Japanese]. Tokyo: Nō-Shōmushō Suisankyoku, 1918. 5 + 178 pp. M.

Japanese Consular reports on the fishing industry of overseas Japanese throughout the world generally submitted in 1917. Includes reports of the San Francisco, Los Angeles, and Honolulu Consulates. Compiled by the Fisheries Bureau, Ministry of Agriculture and Commerce.

335. 桑港美術雑貨商同盟會　　桑港美術雑貨商同盟會要覧
Sōkō Bijutsu Zakkashō Dōmeikai. Sōkō Bijutsu Zakkashō Dōmeikai yōran ["Japanese Art Goods Merchants' Association"]. San Francisco: Sōkō Bijutsu Zakkashō Dōmeikai, 1936. 71 pp.

    A chronological history of the Japanese Art Goods Merchants' Association of San Francisco founded in 1903.

336. ヨネダ・カール　在米日本人労働者の歴史
* Yoneda Kāru. Zai-Bei Nihonjin rōdōsha no rekishi [History of Japanese laborers in America]. Tokyo: Shin Nihon Shuppansha, 1967. 230 pp., plates.

    A history of Japanese laborers in America, including Hawaii. Written from the perspective of a workingman and leftist, it covers the Japanese workers in sugar plantations, mining, railroad construction, lumber mills, and agriculture; also touches upon Japanese socialists and communists. The author is a long-time member of the I.L.W.U. in San Francisco.

337. 吉村大次郎　　北米テキサス州の米作
Yoshimura Daijirō. Hoku-Bei Tekisasu-shū no beisaku ["The cultivation of rice and other crops in Texas"]. Osaka: Kaigai Kigyō Dōshikai, 1903. 8 + 206 pp., map, photos. M.

    An analysis of rice culture in Texas and the beginnings of the Japanese rice colony there.

338. 吉村大次郎　　テキサス州米作の實驗
Yoshimura Daijirō. Tekisasu-shū beisaku no jikken ["The agricultural industries in Texas; being a sequel to the cultivation of rice in Texas"]. Osaka: Kaigai Kigyō Dōshikai, 1905. [2] + 4 + 145 pp., map, photos. M.

    A sequel to above based upon the author's one-year experience in Texas in 1904 south of Houston.

2. RECORDS OF ORGANIZATIONS

339. Civic Unity Hostel. ["Account books"]. MSS. 7 books, 1945-1946. San Jose.

    The records of income and expenditures of the Civic Unity Hostel in San Jose, California from September, 1945 to August, 1946. Includes a guest book and a record of wages paid to the employees.

340. 南加中央産業組合　　市場報告書
Nanka Chūō Sangyō Kumiai. Shijō hōkokusho ["Annual market report"]. 1938. Annual. Los Angeles. (Japanese and English).

    The annual report of the Co-operative Farm Industry of Southern California on agricultural commodities.

341. 南加日本人商業會議所　　　　記録
Nanka Nihonjin Shōgyō Kaigisho. ["Kiroku" [Records]]. MSS. 3 vols. and 1 folder, 1917-1927. Los Angeles.

　　　The partial records of the Japanese Chamber of Commerce of Southern California. Originally founded as the Japanese Businessmen's Association of Los Angeles in October, 1905 and renamed in January, 1917 as the Japanese Chamber of Commerce of Southern California. The records consist of the following:
　　　"Kiroku" [Records], 3 vols., 1918-1927. Minutes and transactions.
　　　"Gigeihin tenrankai kifusha hōmeiroku oyobi gigeihin tenrankai shuppin mōshikomihikae" [Craft show: List of donors and list of exhibitors and their crafts], 1 folder, 1924.

342. 南加日本人食料品商組合　　　　記録
Nanka Nihonjin Shokuryōhinshō Kumiai. "Kiroku" [Record]. MSS. 1 vol., 1926-1927. Los Angeles.

　　　The minutes of the Japanese Grocers' Association of Southern California from October, 1926 to April, 1927, an organization established in October, 1926 within the Japanese Chamber of Commerce of Southern California to promote prosperity among Japanese grocers.

343. 南加聯合砂糖大根耕作者組合　　　　記録
Nanka Rengō Satōdaikon Kōsakusha Kumiai. "Kiroku" [Records]. MSS. 1 book, 1917. Los Angeles.

　　　The minutes of the Associated Sugar Beet Growers of Southern California from March to July, 1917.

344. 南格農業組合　　　　記録
Nankaku Nōgyō Kumiai. "Kiroku" [Record]. MSS. 1 vol., 1918-1937. Swink.

　　　The minutes of the Agricultural Union of Southern Colorado from January, 1921 to February, 1937. Includes the Constitutions of the Japanese Association of Southern Colorado organized in March, 1918 and of the Agricultural Union of Southern Colorado established after the former was dissolved in January, 1921.

345. 南格農業家聯合協議會　　　　記録及名簿
Nankaku Nōgyōka Rengō Kyōgikai. "Kiroku oyobi meibo" [Records and membership roster]. MSS. 1 vol., 1922-1927. Swink.

　　　The minutes of the United Farmers' Association of Southern Colorado from July, 1922 to March, 1927 on the price of fruits and the recruitment and wage scale of seasonal farm laborers. Also contains a membership roster and the Association's revised governing rules of December, 1922.

346. 奥殿中央農會　　　　記録
Okuden Chūō Nōkai. "Kiroku" [Records]. MSS. 1 box (11 folders) and 3 vols., 1921-1958. Ogden.

　　　The records of the Ogden Central Japanese Farmers Association from 1921 to 1958. Established in January, 1917 as the Okuden Chūō Nōgyō Kumiai [The Ogden Central Agricultural Association], it was renamed as the Okuden Chūō Nōkai in July, 1925. Includes the minutes, financial reports, correspondence, memberships, and other miscellaneous documents.

347. 奥殿中央農會　　奥殿中央農會會報
Okuden Chūō Nōkai. Okuden Chūō Nōkai kaihō [Annual report of the Ogden Central Japanese Farmers Association]. 1938, 1939, 1941, 1948-1952, 1956. Annual. Ogden.

The annual report of the Ogden Central Japanese Farmers Association.

348. 羅府日本人實業組合　　會員名簿
Rafu Nihonjin Jitsugyō Kumiai. "Kaiin meibo" [Membership roster]. MSS. 1 vol., 1908-1915. Los Angeles.

The record of monthly dues paid by the members of the Japanese Businessmen's Association of Los Angeles from January, 1908 to February, 1915. The Association was organized in October, 1905 and was the precursor of the Japanese Chamber of Commerce of Southern California.

349. 羅府時計商組合　　記錄
Rafu Tokeishō Kumiai. "Kiroku" [Records]. MSS. 1 vol., 1917-1927. Los Angeles.

The minutes of the Japanese Jewelers' Association of Los Angeles from April, 1917 to November, 1927. Established in March, 1917 to protect the interests of Japanese jewelers.

350. ターラック實業會　　記錄
Tārakku Jitsugyōkai. "Kiroku" [Records]. MSS. 1 vol., 1916-1921. Turlock.

Miscellaneous documents of the Japanese Farmers' Association of Turlock from February, 1916 to December, 1921. Established to protect the interests of Japanese cantaloupe growers, it was reconstituted as the Japanese Association of Stanislaus County in 1919. Includes the governing rules of the Farmers' Association, minutes, financial records, and a brief history of the Japanese in Turlock since 1907.

351. Turlock Farm Corporation. "Records." MSS. 2 vols. and 3 boxes, 1922-1933. Turlock.

Miscellaneous records of the Turlock Farm Corporation from August, 1922 to September, 1933, a corporation organized to cope with the California Alien Land Laws. Consists of financial and business records, copies of lease contracts between landowners and the corporation from March, 1929 to August, 1932, and other documents.

VI.
Religion

Note: The materials listed below are of uneven quality. The best source on the Fukuinkai [Gospel Society], the first Japanese organization in America, is no. 377. The best general history of the Christian churches is no. 359; no noteworthy general history of the Buddhist churches is included, except the works of Imamura Emyō for Hawaii, nos. 354–357. The collected writings of Kobayashi Masasuke, no. 410, and Ernest A. Sturge, no. 445, and the almost complete records of the Los Angeles Methodist Episcopal Church, no. 379, are valuable. The best periodical for the early history of the Christian churches of California is no. 398. For additional scattered church bulletins, see the Hoshimiya Family Papers, no. 849.

1. GENERAL HISTORIES

352. 福島熊藏　在米日本人宣教七十五年史
Fukushima Kumazō. Zai-Bei Nihonjin senkyō shichijūgonenshi [A 75-year history of Christian work among the Japanese in America]. Los Angeles: Nanka Kirisutokyō Remmei, 1952. 20 pp.

　　A brief summary of the Japanese Christian churches from the establishment of the Gospel Society in 1877 in San Francisco down to the post-World War II era.

353. 北加基督教會同盟　開教八十年史
Hokka Kirisuto Kyōkai Dōmei. Kaikyō hachijūnenshi [An 80-year history of the Japanese mission]. San Francisco: Hokka Kirisuto Kyōkai Dōmei, 1957. [4] + 96 pp., photos.

　　A booklet commemorating the 80th anniversary of the beginning of the Japanese Christian churches in America.

354. 今村惠猛　布哇本派本願寺開教三十年記念誌
* Imamura Emyō. Hawai Hompa Hongwanji kaikyō sanjūnen kinenshi ["A short history of the Hongwanji Buddhist Mission in Hawaii, 1897-1927"]. Honolulu: Hompa Hongwanji Mission, 1927. [14] + 59 + English summary 18 pp., photos.

　　A summary history of the Hongwanji Buddhist Mission in Hawaii to commemorate its 30th anniversary.

355. 今村惠猛　布哇開教誌要
* Imamura Emyō. Hawai kaikyō shiyō ["History of the Hongwanji Mission in

Hawaii"]. Honolulu: Hawaii Hompa Hongwanji Mission, 1918. 38 + 18 + 365 + English summary 28 pp., plates.

A general historical survey of the 20-year Hompa Hongwanji Buddhist Mission in Hawaii. Treats the opening of the mission headquarters and its activities and the many churches dispersed throughout the islands under it. The author was the head of the mission.

356. 今村恵猛　本派本願寺布哇開教三十五年記要
* Imamura Emyō. Hompa Hongwanji Hawai kaikyō sanjūgonen kiyō ["A short history of the Hongwanji Buddhist Mission in Hawaii"]. Honolulu: Hompa Hongwanji Mission, 1931. 16 + 2 + 89 + English summary 23 pp., photos.

An updated version of no. 354.

今村恵猛　本派本願寺布哇開教史
357. Imamura Emyō. Hompa Hongwanji Hawai kaikyōshi [A history of the Hompa
* Hongwanji Mission in Hawaii]. Honolulu: Hawaii Hompa Hongwanji Mission, 1918. 38 + 28 + 570 pp., plates, photos.

An expanded version of no. 355.

358. 村野孝顕　佛教海外傳道史
* Murano Kōken (ed.). Bukkyō kaigai dendōshi [A history of the Buddhist mission abroad]. Los Angeles: Hokubeizan Zenshūji, 1933. 17 + 6 + 333 + 62 pp., photos, plates.

Divided into two parts, the first half of this book is devoted to the activities of Rev. Isobe Hōsen, the head of the Hokubeizan Zenshuji Temple in Los Angeles, in Korea, Hawaii, and America. The second half provides a brief history of the Buddhist mission in America beginning with the Buddhist participation in the World's Parliament of Religion held in Chicago in 1893.

359. 南加日本人基督教教會聯盟　　　　　在米日本人基督教五十年史
* Nanka Nihonjin Kirisutokyō Kyōkai Remmei. Zai-Bei Nihonjin kirisutokyō gojūnenshi [A 50-year history of the Japanese Christian church in America]. Los Angeles: Nanka Nihonjin Kirisutokyō Kyōkai Remmei, 1932. 2 + 5 + 142 pp.

A brief but valuable history of the beginning and development of the Japanese Christian church in America. Covers all denominations and includes Hawaii.

360. 生長の家本部　米國に於ける神の足跡
* Seichō no Ie Honbu. Beikoku ni okeru Kami no sokuseki [God's imprints in America]. Tokyo: Kōmyō Shisō Fukyūkai, 1939. [5] + 206 pp., photos.

A record of the first mission, in the person of Kaminishi Masatarō, dispatched by the headquarters of the Seicho no Ie in Tokyo to America in 1938. Includes testaments by various individuals in North and South America and Hawaii.

361. 寺川抱光　北米開教沿革史
Terakawa Hōkō (ed.). Hoku-Bei kaikyō enkakushi [History of the North American Hongwanji Mission]. San Francisco: Hongwanji Hokubei Kaikyō Honbu, 1936. [2] + 4 + 4 + 588 pp., plate, photos.

A chronological history of the North American Hongwanji Mission. Provides a chronology of important events from 1898 to 1935, brief descriptive histories of each church under the mission, an outline of the Y.M.B.A. League of North America, and resolutions of ministerial conferences.

362. 藤賀與一　　北加基督教會便覽
Tōga Yoichi (ed.). Hokka Kirisuto kyōkai benran [Handbook of the Japanese Christian churches in Northern California]. San Francisco: Hokka Kirisuto Kyōkai Dōmei, 1936. 3 + 8 + 232 pp., photos.

　　A handbook with a chronological history of the Japanese churches and brief descriptions of the churches in Northern California.

2. SPECIFIC CHURCH HISTORIES, ALBUMS, AND BOOKLETS

363. Gardena Valley Young Buddhist Association. Shining wheel. Gardena: Gardena Buddhist Church, 1953. [104] pp., photos.

　　A photographic album of the Gardena Valley Young Buddhist Association.

364. 一世伝導部　　写眞が語る六十五年史
Issei Dendōbu. Shashin ga kataru rokujūgonenshi ["Sixty-five years in pictures"]. Spokane: Highland Park Methodist Church, 1967. 317 pp., photos.

　　A Japanese-English photographic history of the Highland Park Methodist Church in Spokane, Washington established in 1902 compiled by the Issei Commission on Evangelism.

365. 中村順三　　サンディゴ傳道二十年史
Nakamura Junzō. San Deigo dendō nijūnenshi [A 20-year history of the San Diego mission]. San Diego: First Japanese Congregational Church, 1927. 25 + 12 pp., photos.

　　An English-Japanese pamphlet essentially about the First Japanese Congregational Church of San Diego going back to 1907.

366. 中村順三　　ウヰンタースバーグ日本人基督教傳道館・二十年記念
　　　　　　　　オレンヂ郡日本人傳道史
Nakamura Junzō. Wintāsubāgu Nihonjin Kirisutokyō Dendōkan: Nijūnen kinen Orenji-gun Nihonjin dendōshi ["Japanese Presbyterian Mission of Wintersburg, California": Commemoration of the 20th anniversary of the Japanese mission of Orange County]. Wintersburg: Japanese Presbyterian Mission, 1924. 30 + English text 8 pp., photos.

　　An English-Japanese pamphlet to commemorate the 20th anniversary of the establishment of the Japanese Presbyterian Mission of Wintersburg, California in Orange County. Includes a list of all those baptized from 1904 in this mission.

367. 小見正博　　バークレー自由メソヂスト教會創立四十週年記念
Omi Masahiro. Bākurē Jiyu Mesojisuto Kyōkai sōritsu yonjūshūnen kinen [Fortieth anniversary of the Berkeley Free Methodist Church]. Berkeley:

Berkeley Free Methodist Church, 1956. [4] + 25 + English text 16 pp., photos.

A Japanese-English booklet issued to commemorate the 40th anniversary of the founding of the Berkeley Free Methodist Church in 1916.

368. San Jose Buddhist Church. <u>Golden Anniversary, 1949-1950</u>. San Jose: San Jose Buddhist Church, 1950 (?). 88 pp., photos.

A photographic album commemorating the 50th anniversary of the San Jose Buddhist Church.

369. Seattle Buddhist Church. <u>Seattle Betsuin, 1954</u>. Seattle: Seattle Buddhist Church, 1955 (?). [157] pp., photos.

A photographic album of the Seattle Betsuin with the short text in both Japanese and English.

370. シヤトル日本人メソヂスト教會　創立四拾五年記念號
Shiyatoru Nihonjin Mesojisuto Kyōkai. <u>Sōritsu yonjūgonen kinengō</u> ["Forty-fifth anniversary, 1904-1949"]. Seattle: Seattle Japanese Methodist Church, 1949. 8 + English text 7 pp., photos.

A Japanese-English pamphlet of the Seattle Japanese Methodist Church and its history.

371. 桑港佛教會　桑港佛教會開教三十年記念誌
Sōkō Bukkyōkai. <u>Sōkō Bukkyōkai kaikyō sanjūnen kinenshi</u> [A 30th anniversary publication of the San Francisco Buddhist Church]. San Francisco: Sōkō Bukkyōkai, 1930. [15] + 250 pp., plates, photos, apps.

A history of the San Francisco Buddhist Church established in 1899. Includes reminiscences of former ministers, including Rev. Nishijima Kakuryō, the first minister, and Honda Ryū who preceded him in 1898 to investigate the possibility of establishing missions. The five appendices are: a chronological list of ministers; the current Board of Directors; church rules and regulations; the 1929 Fiscal Report; and the Book of the Deceased.

372. タコマ日本人メソヂスト教會　創立五十周年記念
Takoma Nihonjin Mesojisuto Kyōkai. <u>Sōritsu gojūshūnen kinen</u> ["50th anniversary, 1907-1957"]. Tacoma: Tacoma Japanese Methodist Church, 1957. 36 pp., photos.

An English-Japanese booklet of the Tacoma Japanese Methodist Church and its history.

373. ワッソンビル ウェストビュウ長老教會　傳道開始六十年記念
Wassonbiru Uesutobyū Chōrō Kyōkai. <u>Dendō kaishi rokujūnen kinen</u> ["60th anniversary, 1898-1958"]. Watsonville: Westview Presbyterian Church, 1958. 31 + 21 pp., photos.

An English-Japanese booklet with a chronological history of the Watsonville Westview Presbyterian Church.

374. 和多田又治郎　山東三州佛教會五十年史
Watada Matajirō (ed.). <u>Santō Sanshū Bukkyōkai gojūnenshi</u> ["The Tri-State

Buddhist Church, 1916-1966"]. Denver: Tri-State Buddhist Church, 1968. 273 pp., photos.

A Japanese-English photographic album of the Tri-State Buddhist Church located in Denver, Colorado.

375. West Los Angeles Community Methodist Church. <u>30th anniversary dedication,</u> 1930-1960. Los Angeles: West Los Angeles Community Methodist Church, [1960]. [61] pp., photos.

An English-Japanese photographic album of the West Los Angeles Community Methodist Church.

376. 湯木庄次郎　羅府日本人美以教會四十年史
Yuki Shōjirō. <u>Rafu Nihonjin Mii Kyōkai yonjūnenshi</u> ["A 40 year history of the Los Angeles M.E. Church"]. Los Angeles: Rafu Nihonjin Mii Kyōkai, 1937. 2 + 186 pp., plate, photos.

A chronological history of the Los Angeles Methodist Episcopal Church established in 1896. Includes reminiscences of some of the early ministers of the church.

3. CHURCH RECORDS

377. 文倉平三郎　　　　　福音會沿革史料
[Fumikura Heisaburō (comp.)]. "Fukuinkai enkaku shiryō" [Gospel Society historical sources]. MSS. 1 box, 1935. X (except Part I, Section A).

A transcribed version in three parts of the official records of the Gospel Society from 1881 to 1897. A major primary source for the origins, activities, and membership of this Christian organization, the very first Japanese group organized in America in 1877 in San Francisco. Transcribed in 1935 from the original records by Fumikura Heisaburō, it includes his appended notes. Portions of it were serialized in the <u>Amerika Shimbun</u> from February, 1938 (see no. 621). The original transcribed version, except Part I, Section A, is in the hands of Seizō Oka of San Francisco.

378. 南加傳道團　　時局費寄附帳
Nanka Dendōdan. "Jikyokuhi kifuchō" [Emergency funds subscription list]. MSS. 1 vol., 1921. Los Angeles.

A record of contributions collected by the Japanese Church Federation of Southern California between April and June, 1921 for the purpose of conducting an Americanization campaign among the Japanese.

379. 羅府日本人美以教會　　記録
Rafu Nihonjin Mii Kyōkai. ["Kiroku" [Records]]. MSS. 47 vols., 4 boxes, 2 books, 6 notebooks, and 1 folder, 1897-1946. Los Angeles.

The almost complete records of the Los Angeles Japanese Methodist Episcopal Church from 1897 to 1946. The records consist of the following:

"Kaiin meibo" [Membership roster], 3 vols., 1897-1924, 1919, 1946.
"Kaiin kaiyū meibo" [List of church membership and friends], 1 folder, 1919.
"Kiroku" [Records], 3 vols. and 3 notebooks, 1899-1903, 1904-1906, 1909-1922, 1918-1920.
"Yakuinkai kiroku" [Records of the Board of Directors], 1 vol., 1932-1941.
"Kaishi: Yakuinkai kiroku, Shikikai kiroku" [Church records: Board of Directors and Four Seasons Society], 1 vol., 1922, 1926-1928.
"Kiroku oyobi shūkaihyō" [Records and services], 1 vol., 1920-1921.
"Nisshi" [Daily reports], 2 vols., 1907-1912, 1912-1918.
"Kaku shūkai kiroku" [Records of services], 1 notebook, 1933-1935.
"Kiroku (zatsu)" [Miscellaneous records], 2 boxes, 1916-1946.
"Fujinkai kiroku" [Women's Society records], 7 vols., 1916-1942.
"Fujikai kaikeibo" [Account book of the Women's Society], 1 vol., 1926-1937.
"Dendōbu kiroku" [Records of the Evangelical Section], 1 vol., 1930-1931.
"Sunday School record," 1 vol., 1908-1912.
"Hōmonroku" [Home visitation record], 2 books, 1919-1922.
"Kishukusha shishukusha meibo" [Boardinghouse registry], 1 vol., 1906-1922.
"Tsūchi, puroguramu, sono ta" [Notices, programs, etc.], 1 vol., 1924-1941.
"Seishūbo" [Services], 1 vol., 1910-1913.
"Kaikeibo" [Account book], 5 vols., and 2 notebooks, 1902-1939.
"Kaikei hōkoku" [Financial reports], 5 vols., 1913-1942.
"Kaikei kiroku (zatsu)" [Miscellaneous financial records], 5 vols., 1904-1942.
"Epōsu Dōmeikai kiroku" [Records of the Epworth League], 1 box, 1910-1919.
"Epōsu Dōmeikai Jizenbu kiroku" [Records of the Social Welfare Section of the Epworth League], 1 box, 1910-1916.
"Kyōkaidō kenchiku shikin boshū kiroku" [Records of contributions for the construction of a new church building], 2 vols., 1902-1906.
"Kifu kiroku" [Contribution records], 2 vols., 1904-1917.
"Kaidō kenchiku kifusha hōmeibo" [List of contributors], 1 vol., 1917.
"Kendōshiki kenkin kiroku" [Records of donations for the dedication ceremony], 1 vol., 1925-1927.
"Record of the Nisei Official Board," 1 vol., 1938-1942.
"Dendōkan kaitori kaikei" [Purchase account], 1 vol., 1920-1922.

4. RELIGIOUS PERIODICALS AND CHURCH BULLETINS

380. 米國護教

Beikoku Gokyō ["The Japanese American Christian Advocate"]. v. 14:6-v. 34:40 (Jul. 15, 1929-May 1964). Incomplete. Monthly. Berkeley. (Japanese and English).

Originally the official organ of the Pacific Japanese Methodist Episcopal Church and published under the auspices of the Superintendent of the Mission, Frank H. Smith, and edited by various individuals. Later changed to the Hokubei Mesojisuto ["The North American Methodist Advocate"] (exact date and issue unknown) and again in the postwar period to the Hokubei Mesojisuto ["The North American Methodist"] (exact date and issue unknown).

381. 米國高野山別院寺報
Beikoku Kōyasan Betsuin Jihō ["Koyasan News"]. v. 12:1 (Jan. 20, 1958). Monthly (?). Los Angeles. (Japanese and English).

　　　The newsletter of the Koyasan Buddhist Temple of Los Angeles.

382. 復活
Fukkatsu [Resurrection]. 1953-1965. Incomplete. Weekly. Chicago. Mimeo.

　　　The bulletin of the Chicago Japanese Congregational Church.

383. Japanese Methodist Episcopal Church Weekly News. 1938-1939. Incomplete. Weekly. Los Angeles. Mimeo.

384. イエスの友
Iesu no Tomo ["The Friend of Jesus"]. 1949-1961. Incomplete. Monthly. Los Angeles. Mimeo.

　　　The monthly publication of the Iesu no Tomo [The Friend of Jesus], a Christian organization formed under the influence of Kagawa Toyohiko.

385. The Japanese Student Bulletin. v. 5:4 (Jan. 1926). Monthly. New York.

　　　A monthly publication of the Japanese Students' Christian Association in North America.

386. 高原の星
Kōgen no Hoshi [Stars Over the Plateau]. no. 1, 2 (Feb. 1938, Dec. 1940). Irregular. Wapato. Mimeo.

　　　A mimeographed publication of the Wapato Japanese Methodist Church in Wapato, Washington.

387. 教壇
Kyōdan [Pulpit]. no. 1, 3 (Dec. 1948, Jan. 1950). Irregular. San Francisco.

　　　Japanese-English pamphlets irregularly issued by the headquarters of the Buddhist Churches of America on Buddhist topics.

388. 幻の翼
Maboroshi no Tsubasa ["Maboroshi no Tsubasa"]. no. 93, 94 (Apr., May 1954) no. 104 (Apr. 1955); no. 124-163 (Jan. 1957-Oct. 1962). Monthly. Los Angeles.

　　　A Christian monthly published and edited by Rev. Watanabe Sōsaburō.

389. The Methodist Voice. 1939-1942. Incomplete. Weekly. Los Angeles. Mimeo.

　　　The bulletin of the Los Angeles Japanese Methodist Church.

390. 南加福音時報
Nanka Fukuin Jihō ["The Southern California Gospel Herald"]. v. 5:1 (Apr. 10, 1935). Monthly. Los Angeles.

    The official organ of the Nanka Kirisutokyō Kyōkai Remmei [Japanese Church Federation of Southern California] edited by Kubota Kenzō.

391. Official Journal. 1923. Annual. Berkeley.

    The annual publication of the Pacific Japanese Methodist Episcopal Mission.

392. Official Journal. v. 1:1-4 (1940-1943); v. 7:1 (1964). Annual. Berkeley.

    The annual publication of the Pacific Japanese Provisional Annual Conference of the Methodist Church.

393. パサデナ日本人ユニオン教會週報
Pasadena Nihonjin Yunion Kyōkai Shūhō [Pasadena Japanese Union Church Weekly]. 1934-1936. Incomplete. Weekly. Pasadena. Mimeo.

394. 羅府メソヂスト
Rafu Mesojisuto [Los Angeles Methodist]. 1949-1966. Incomplete. Weekly. Los Angeles. Mimeo.

395. 羅府美以教會週報
Rafu Mii Kyōkai Shūhō [Los Angeles Japanese Methodist Episcopal Church Bulletin]. 1924-1942. Incomplete. Weekly. Los Angeles. Mimeo, except no. 34-156 (Feb. 28, 1932-Jul. 8, 1934).

396. 生命
Seimei ["The Life"]. 1949-1953. Incomplete. Weekly. Chicago. Mimeo.

    The bulletin of the Chicago Japanese Congregational Church.

397. 沙市日本人美以教會週報
Sha-shi Nihonjin Mii Kyōkai Shūhō [Seattle Japanese Methodist Episcopal Church Weekly]. 1926-1941. Incomplete. Weekly. Seattle.

398. 新天地
Shin Tenchi ["The Shin Ten Chi"]. v. 2:10-v. 3:6, 8-v. 5:1 (Nov. 1, 1911-Jun. 1, 1912, Aug. 1, 1912-Jan. 1, 1914). Monthly. San Francisco.

    Originally the official organ of the Hokka Kirisutokyōto Dōmei (Northern California Federation of Christians] established in January, 1910, this publication subsequently became the official organ of the Hokka Kirisutokyō Dendōdan [Japanese Interdenominational Board of Missions] organized in May, 1911 into which the former merged.

399. 天明
Temmei ["Daybreak"]. no. 69, 70, 73, 75 (Feb., Mar., Jun., Aug. 1950); no. 85, 91 (Jun., Dec. 1951); no. 97, 99, 100 (Jun., Aug., Sep. 1952). Monthly. Los Angeles. Mimeo.

    A Christian monthly published by Rev. Shiraishi Kiyoshi of the Baptist Church.

400. とも
*
    Tomo ["Friend"]. no. 100, 102 (Mar., May 1955); no. 120 (Dec. 1956); no. 132 (Dec. 1957). Monthly. Honolulu.

    A Christian monthly published by the Hawaii Evangelical Association.

401. 在米婦人新報
    Zaibei Fujin Shimpō ["Japanese Women's Herald in America"]. v. 28:3, 5 (Jul., Oct. 1929). Bi-monthly. Berkeley.

    A Christian women's bi-monthly published by Mrs. Takahashi Chinko and edited by Mrs. Wasa Rinko, featuring moral reform articles.

5. OTHER PUBLISHED WORKS

402. 米布研究會　　第二世と佛教
    Beifu Kenkyūkai. Dai-Nisei to Bukkyō [The Nisei and Buddhism]. Kyoto: Shinran Seijin Kenkyū Hakkōsho, 1935. [2] + 106 pp.

    A compilation of the opinions of Buddhist ministers in Japan, Canada, Hawaii, and the continental United States regarding the education of the Nisei and the future of the Jodo Shinshu Sect.

403. 遠藤礼子　恩寵を感謝しつつ医しの体験を語る
    Endō Reiko. Onchō wo kansha shitsutsu iyashi no taiken wo kataru [A story of a healing experience with gratitude for blessings]. Los Angeles: Privately printed, 1962. 79 pp.

    A testament of Christian belief and faith.

404. 福田美亮　　金光教の信心
    Fukuda Yoshiaki. Konkōkyō no shinjin [The Konkokyo faith]. San Francisco: Konkō Kyōtosha, 1957 (16th edition). 121 pp.

    An exposition of the Shinto Sect, Konkokyo, by the late head of the Konkokyo Mission in San Francisco.

405. ハイランドパーク・メソヂスト教會　北米の空に星は輝く
    Hairando Pāku Mesojisuto Kyōkai. Hoku-Bei no sora ni hoshi wa kagayaku [Stars shine in the North American sky]. Spokane: Highland Park Methodist Church, 1962. 20 + 380 pp., photos.

    A collection of testaments of Christian faith and belief by Issei members of the Highland Park Methodist Church in Spokane, Washington.

406. 布哇佛教青年會　　母國見學記念誌
*
    Hawai Bukkyō Seinenkai. Bokoku kengaku kinenshi ["Souvenir; mother country excursion, 1928"]. Honolulu: Y.M.B.A., 1929. 2 + 115 + English text 25 pp., photos.

    A record of a trip to Japan taken in 1928 by Nisei students under the auspices of the Young Men's Buddhist Association of Honolulu. Includes essays on Japan in both Japanese and English.

407. 第八回布哇佛教青年聯盟大會記録
 * Hawaii Y.B.A. Dai-Hakkai Hawai Bukkyō Seinen Remmei Taikai kiroku ["Report of the Eighth Territorial Y.B.A. Convention"]. Wailuku: Wailuku Y.B.A., 1937. 42 + 71 pp.

   A Japanese-English report of the Eighth Territorial Y.B.A. Convention held at the Wailuku Y.B.A. Auditorium, Wailuku, Maui, on August 19-23, 1937.

408. 北加基督教會同盟　　幻は消えず
 Hokka Kirisuto Kyōkai Dōmei. Maboroshi wa kiezu [An everlasting vision]. San Francisco: Hokka Kirisuto Kyōkai Dōmei, 1962. [9] + 315 pp., photos.

   A collection of Issei testaments of Christian belief and faith compiled and edited by Rev. Omi Masahiro.

409. 本派本願寺　　布哇佛教讀本
 * Hompa Hongwanji. Hawai Bukkyō tokuhon [Hawaii Buddhist reader]. Honolulu: Jikōen, 1939. 3 + 183 pp., photos, illus.

   A general Buddhist reader designed for the home which summarizes the history of Buddhism, its teachings and practices, and its particular condition in Hawaii.

410. 井深清庫　　日本民族の世界的膨脹・小林政助論文集
 Ibuka Seiko (ed.). Nihon minzoku no sekaiteki bōchō: Kobayashi Masasuke ronbunshū [The expansion of the Japanese throughout the world: The collected writings of Kobayashi Masasuke]. Tokyo: Keigansha, 1933. 21 + 29 + 922 pp.

   The collected writings of Major Kobayashi Masasuke, the leader of the Japanese units of the Salvation Army in America founded in July, 1919. This volume brings together his major publications written during his more than 30 years of Christian service to the Japanese community.

411. 飯島貫實　　生きた佛教
 Iijima Kanjitsu. Ikita Bukkyō [Living Buddhism]. Tokyo: Tōsei Shuppansha, 1955. iv + 374 pp., plate.

   An exposition of Buddhism by an Issei minister.

412. 今村惠猛　　米國の精神と宗教の自由
 * Imamura Emyō. Beikoku no seishin to shūkyō no jiyū [The American spirit and religious freedom]. Honolulu: Hawaii Hompa Hongwanji Mission, 1920. 6 + 90 pp.

   An interpretative essay defending the American Constitutional concept of religious freedom by the Bishop of the Hompa Hongwanji Mission of Hawaii.

413. 今村惠猛　　第一回汎太平洋佛教青年大會に寄す
 * Imamura Emyō. Dai-Ikkai Han-Taiheiyo Bukkyō Seinen Taikai ni yosu ["A message to the Delegates, First Pan-Pacific Y.M.B.A. Conference"]. Honolulu: Privately printed, 1930. 28 + 6 + English text 13 pp.

   An address by Bishop Imamura of the Hompa Hongwanji Mission of Hawaii before the First Pan-Pacific Y.M.B.A. Conference held in Honolulu from July 21-26, 1930.

414. 石川清　　福音と虚無
   Ishikawa Kiyoshi. Fukuin to kyomu [The gospel and nothingness]. Chicago: Ishikawa Kiyoshi, 1960. 11 + [7] + 754 pp.

   A collection of miscellaneous essays on Christianity by an Issei minister in Chicago.

415. 伊藤晩松　　不敬事件之真相
   Itō Banshō (pseud.). Fukei Jiken no shinsō [Facts about the Lèse-Majesté Incident]. Fresno: Shunjūsha, 1912. [10] + 200 pp., photos.

   A polemical indictment of Rev. Kitazawa Tetsuji, a Christian minister of the Japanese Methodist Episcopal Church in Fresno, for making "disrespectful" remarks about the Emperor's portrait in November, 1911.

416. 甲斐静七　　佛さまのお話
* Kai Shizuya. Hotoke-sama no ohanashi [Stories of the Buddha]. Honolulu: Kai Shizuya, 1917. 2 + 4 + 4 + 5 + 358 pp., illus.

   A children's Buddhist reader.

417. 川俣義一　　基督教の筋道
   Kawamata Giichi. Kirisutokyō no sujimichi [The logic of Christianity]. San Francisco: Hokka Kirisutokyō Dōmei, 1949. 4 + 172 pp.

   A collection of sermons by Rev. Kawamata Giichi.

418. 岸田英山　　解脱金剛とその教義
   Kishida Eizan. Gedatsu Kingō to sono kyōgi [Gedatsu Kingo and its teachings]. San Francisco: Beikoku Gedatsu Kyōkai, 1959. 3 + 1 + 2 + 3 + 6 + 200 pp., photos.

   An exposition of the Gedatsu Kingo faith by Bishop Kishida Eizan.

419. 小平尚道　　聖旨
   Kodaira Naomichi. Seishi [Providence]. Seattle: Seishi Kankōkai, 1950. 115 pp.

   A collection of sermons by Rev. Kodaira Naomichi.

420. 近藤長衛　　キリスト物語
   Kondō Chōyei. Kirisuto monogatari ["A story of Christ"]. Los Angeles: Kondō Shizuko, 1954 and 1956 (rev. ed.). 19 + 235 pp., maps, photos.

   A biographical story of Jesus Christ. The revised edition has a brief autobiographical sketch by the Issei author.

421. 近藤長衛　　日本の基督教教会の牧師教師に訴える
   Kondō Chōyei. Nihon no Kirisutokyō kyōkai no bokushi kyōshi ni uttaeru [An appeal to ministers and teachers of the Christian churches of Japan]. Los Angeles: Privately printed, 1960 (?). 20 pp.

   A short, personal protest, in a letter form, against the participation of Japanese Christians in the anti-Mutual Security Pact demonstrations of 1960 in Japan.

422. 小谷徳水　私の生活と信と
　* Kotani Tokusui. Watakushi no seikatsu to shin to [My life and faith]. Honolulu: Hawai Bukkyō Seinenkai, 1918. [4] + 160 pp.

　　　A personal discourse on Buddhism prompted by the author's illness and father's death.

423. 京極逸蔵　明るい仏教
　Kyōgoku Itsuzō. Akarui Bukkyō [Optimistic Buddhism]. Fresno: Maha Maya Society, 1954. [8] + 4 + 265 pp., photo.

　　　A treatise on Mahayana Buddhism by the late Rev. Kyōgoku Itsuzō (1887-1953), a native of Hiroshima who came to America in 1919 as a minister for the Nishi Hongwanji Sect.

424. 町田保　近代聖地の巡礼
　Machida Tamotsu. Kindai seichi no junrei ["A pilgrimage to modern Palestine"]. [Los Angeles]: Privately printed, 1962. [13] + 269 pp., photos.

　　　Impressions of a trip to Europe and the Middle East by an Issei Christian minister.

425. マキキ聖城教會　奥村牧師説教集
　* Makiki Seijō Kyōkai. Okumura Bokushi sekkyōshū [Collected sermons of Rev. Okumura]. Honolulu: Makiki Seijo Kyōkai, 1950 (?). 285 pp., photos, chronology.

　　　A collection of sermons by Rev. Okumura Takie of Hawaii. Includes a 2-page chronology of his life.

426. 松下巌　日用の糧
　Matsushita Iwao. Nichiyō no kate ["Our daily bread"]. Seattle: Matsushita Iwao, 1958. 10 + 95 pp.

　　　Christian proverbs and moral tales.

427. 三浦宗五郎　自由と眞理
　* Miura Sogorō. Jiyū to shinri [Liberty and truth]. Honolulu: Hayashi Benzo, 1908. 2 + 4 + 457 pp.

　　　Essays on Christianity to introduce non-believers to the religion.

428. 仲出川初子　わが生けるは
　Nakadegawa Hatsuko (ed.). Waga ikeru wa ["For me to live is Christ"]. Tokyo: Kirusuchansha, 1958. 151 + English text 58 pp., photos.

　　　A collection of tributes and eulogies to Rev. Clifford T. Nakadegawa and his wife who died in an automobile accident in April, 1953.

429. 中川善教　米布に使して
　* Nakagawa Zenkyō. Bei-Fu ni tsukai shite [On a mission to Hawaii and America]. Koyasan: Koyasan Shuppansha, 1954. 4 + 6 + 853 + 2 pp.

　　　A record of a mission dispatched by the Koyasan Temple from May to October, 1952 to Hawaii and the continental United States.

430. 西村正元　消えぬ燈火
　Nishimura Masamoto (ed.). Kienu tomoshibi [Eternal light]. Los Angeles:

Nishimura Masamoto, 1957. [3] + 69 pp.

A collection of Issei testaments of Christian belief and faith.

431. 西村正元　　新葉
Nishimura Masamoto. Wakaba [Young leaves]. Los Angeles: Rafu Jiyū Mesojisuto Kyōkai, 1953. 424 pp.

The correspondence of Rev. Nishimura Masamoto with the Los Angeles Free Methodist Church from 1944 to 1952.

432. 野崎霊海　　限りなき命
Nozaki Reikai. Kagiri naki inochi [A limitless life]. Tokyo: Jōdo Shūmusho, 1957. [10] + 11 + 488 pp., photos.

Radio talks on Buddhism presented by the author in Los Angeles.

433. 奥村多喜衞　　生甲斐ある生活
* Okumura Takie. Ikigai aru seikatsu [A life worth living]. Honolulu: Privately printed, 1930 (2nd printing). [1] + 7 + 9 + 361 pp.

A collection of Sunday talks akin to sermons by Rev. Okumura Takie. Originally published in 1927.

434. 奥村多喜衞　　人格構成の要素
* Okumura Takie. Jinkaku kōsei no yōso [The essential components of character]. Honolulu: Privately printed, 1925. [3] + 28 pp., photo.

A pamphlet on moral character based upon Christian principles.

435. 小見正博　　日本を親しく見たまま
Omi Masahiro. Nihon wo shitashiku mita mama [Personal views of Japan]. San Francisco: Hokka Kirisutokyō Kyōkai Dōmei, 1960. [15] + 154 pp., photos.

The record of an Issei Christian tour group which visited Japan in 1959-60 to attend the 100th Anniversary Commemoration of Christian Missions in Japan held in Tokyo from November 1-7.

436. 佐々木八重子　　讃美歌物語
Sasaki Yaeko (ed.). Sanbika monogatari [A story of hymns]. Tokyo: Shinkyō Shuppansha, 1954. 6 + 4 + 160 pp., photo.

The collected writings of Sasaki Suketsugu, the former choir director of the Seattle Japanese Methodist Episcopal Church, on Christian hymns posthumously published by his wife.

437. 関口野薔薇　　文芸と宗教
Sekiguchi Nobara. Bungei to shūkyō [Literature and religion]. Tokyo: Seishin Kagakusha, 1963. 447 pp., photos.

A collection of essays on various religious topics by an Issei writer who specialized in religion.

438. 関口野薔薇　　不老不死ハサヨガの行法
Sekiguchi Nobara. Furō fushi Hasa Yoga no gyōhō [Ageless and eternal: The Hatha Yoga method]. Osaka: Ningen Igakusha, 1955. [2] + 8 + 467 pp., photo.

A treatise on the methods of Hatha Yoga.

439.　関口野薔薇　　原始基督教神学
Sekiguchi Nobara. Genshi Kirisutokyo shingaku ["Theology of early Christianity"]. Shimizu: Nihon Shingaku Remmei, 1959. 8 + 239 pp., photo.

　　A treatise on the life of Jesus Christ.

440.　関口野薔薇　　科学と宗教
Sekiguchi Nobara. Kagaku to shūkyō [Science and religion]. Tokyo: Seishin Kagakusha, 1962. 452 pp., photos.

　　A collection of miscellaneous essays on religious topics.

441.　関口野薔薇　　日本神道神学
Sekiguchi Nobara. Nihon Shintō shingaku [The theology of Japanese Shinto]. Shimizu: Nihon Shingaku Remmei, 1955. 7 + 237 pp.

　　A discourse on Shintoism to disaffiliate it from Japanese militarism while highlighting its universal features.

442.　志垣武次郎　　唯一の救
Shigaki Bujirō. Yuiitsu no sukui ["The only salvation"]. Los Angeles: Privately printed, 1957. [2] + 61 pp.

　　A religious tract by a member of the Holiness Church.

443.　島田重雄　　岩上に神の宮なるまで
Shimada Shigeo. Ganjō ni kami no miya naru made [Until the new church was built]. Spokane: Privately printed, n.d. 54 pp. Mimeo.

　　An account of plans and contributions to construct the new Highland Park Methodist Church by Rev. Shimada Shigeo.

444.　末廣栄司　　基督に在る生活
Suehiro Eiji (ed.). Kirisuto ni aru seikatsu [A Christian life]. Los Angeles: Rafu Hōrinesu Kyōkai, 1959 (2nd printing). [8] + 147 pp.

　　A collection of religious essays by Rev. Kuzuhara Sada'ichi of the Los Angeles Holiness Church.

445.　ストウジ全集刊行會　　ストウジ全集
Sutōji Zenshū Kankōkai. Sutōji zenshū [The complete works of E.A. Sturge]. v. I-IV. Tokyo: Sutōji Zenshū Kankōkai, 1934-35. v. I, The Spirit of Japan, 1934, xx + 199 pp., photos, illus.; v. II, Genjitsu to sono kanata ni ["Living in two worlds"], 1935, 2 + [3] + 181 + 208 pp., photo; v. III, Sutōji den ["A life of E.A. Sturge"], 1935, 4 + 2 + 299 + chronology 16 + English summary 13 + 16 pp., photos; v. IV, Arrows from my quiver, 1935, iii + iv + 350 pp.

　　The complete works of Dr. Ernest A. Sturge (1856-1934) who played a major role in the development of Japanese Presbyterian churches on the Pacific Coast. From 1886 to 1934 he was the General Superintendent of the Japanese Presbyterian Churches and Mission of the Pacific Coast. Volume I is an anthology of his poems; volume II consists of religious essays in English and Japanese translation; volume III is his biography written by Miyazaki Kohachirō; and volume IV is a collection of his sermons.

446.　高橋理圓　　心の光に立つ
*　Takahashi Rien. Kokoro no hikari ni tatsu [A guide to enlightenment].

Honolulu: Sōtō Kyōkai, 1948. [7] + 141 pp.

A Buddhist booklet by a Honolulu Zen priest.

447. 高橋理圓　禪に根差して
Takahashi Rien. Zen ni nezashite [An introduction to Zen]. San Francisco: Nichibeizan Sōkōzenji, 1949. 119 pp.

An elementary manual on the discipline of Zen Buddhism.

448. 嵩原安綿　一貫の道
Takehara Yasutami. Ikkan no michi [A consistent philosophy]. Los Angeles: Privately printed, 1920. 13 + 68 pp.

A treatise on the inseparability of moral character and action based on Confucianism.

449. 嵩原安綿　國體の成就を前提とする大調和の世界
Takehara Yasutami. Kokutai no joju wo zentei to suru daichōwa no sekai [A harmonious world premised on the manifestation of the national polity]. Los Angeles: Privately printed, 1947. 165 pp.

A Shinto tract which formulates a basis for world peace.

450. 藤賀與一　北米教壇
Tōga Yoichi (ed.). Hoku-Bei kyōdan ["Japanese church pulpit in North America"]. v. I-II. Tokyo: Shinseidō, 1938. [4] + 3 + 4 + 367 + 15 pp., plate and [3] + 4 + 334 + 23 pp., plates.

A collection of sermons by Issei Christian ministers and leading laymen, including some in English.

451. Tsunoda Ryusaku. The essence of Japanese Buddhism. Honolulu: The Advertiser Press, 1914. 84 pp.
  *

An exposition of Buddhism.

452. 和田性海　米布を巡りて
  * Wada Seikai. Bei-Fu wo megurite [To Hawaii and America and back]. Koyasan: Kōyasan Shuppansha, 1953. 5 + 4 + 308 pp., photos.

An account of a trip to Hawaii and the continental United States taken in 1952 by a Koyasan priest which included visits to local temples.

453. 渡辺友一　黙示霊岳登山案内記
Watanabe Tomo'ichi. Mokushi reigaku tozan annaiki [An annotated guide to the Book of Revelation]. Los Angeles: Niisato Kan'ichi, 1953. 3 + 27 + 385 + apps. 71 pp., photos.

The Book of Revelation with explanatory notes. Also includes some tanka written while the author was interned during World War II.

VII.
Second Generation

1. EDUCATION

454. 青柳郁太郎　在外邦人第二世問題 第一輯
   * Aoyagi Ikutarō (ed.). Zaigai hōjin dai-nisei mondai dai-isshū [Problems of the second-generation overseas Japanese, no. 1]. Tokyo: Imin Mondai Kenkyūkai, 1940. 101 pp. X.

   A collection of essays on the educational problems of the second generation, especially in South and North America.

455. Hirohata, Paul T. (ed.). Orations and essays by the Japanese second generation of America. Los Angeles: The Los Angeles Japanese Daily News, 1932. iv + [4] + 118 pp.

   A collection of public school talks and essays by the second generation.

456. 松岡壽八　在米日本人第二世は何處へ行く　外交時報
   Matsuoka Toshiya. "Zai-Bei Nihonjin dai-nisei wa doko e iku" [Where is the second-generation Japanese in America going?], Gaiko Jihō [Revue Diplomatique], 61:650 (Jan. 1, 1932), 276-286. M.

   An essay on the problems of employment and marriage of the second generation.

457. 森重壽夫　廣島縣滞在米布出生者名簿
   * Morishige Toshio. Hiroshima-ken taizai Bei-Fu shusseisha meibo [Roster of American and Hawaiian-born Japanese residing in Hiroshima Prefecture]. Hiroshima: Hiroshima-ken Kaigai Kyōkai, 1932. 339 pp., photos.

   A roster of 11,317 American and Hawaiian-born Japanese living in Hiroshima Prefecture. Includes a list of eligible Nisei women and some information on the Hiroshima Prefecture Overseas Association and its various branches.

458. Nadeshiko. v. 1:1 (1929). Annual. Los Angeles.

   A graduation annual published by the Southern California Japanese College Students.

459. 日本米布協會　第二世と國籍問題・第二世叢書第三輯
   * Nihon Beifu Kyokai. Dai-Nisei to kokuseki mondai: Dai-Nisei Sosho dai-sanshu [The Nisei and the problem of nationality: Nisei Book Series no. 3]. Tokyo: Runbini Shuppansha, 1938. [3] + 3 + 52 pp., photo.

A booklet explaining Japanese Nationality Laws and their relationship to the Nisei issued by the Japan, America, Hawaii Society as part of its Nisei Book Series.

460. 新里貫一　在米の日本民族五百年の大計
Niisato Kan'ichi. Zai-Bei no Nihon minzoku gohyakunen no taikei [A 500-year plan for the Japanese in America]. Tokyo: Shimpōsha, 1940 (3rd printing). 12 + 85 pp., plate, photo.

A work on the problems of education, employment, and dual nationality of the second generation. Originally published in 1939.

461. 四至本八郎　日系市民を語る
Shishimoto Hachirō. Nikkei shimin wo kataru [Japanese-American citizens]. Tokyo: Shōkasha, 1934. 313 pp., photos. M.

Viewing the second generation as a bridge between Japan and America, this book presents the general and particular characteristics of the Nisei as seen by an Issei newspaperman. Includes a discussion of the Kibei and sketches of leading Nisei in various fields, and concludes with a personal statement about the author's hopes for and expectations of his son, Ichiro.

462.* 山田辰實　海外第二世問題
Yamada Tatsumi. Kaigai dai-nisei mondai [Problems of the overseas second generation]. Tokyo: Kibundō Shobō, 1936. 3 + 8 + 4 + 215 pp., plate, photo. M.

An analysis of the problems of the second generation in Hawaii, the continental United States, Canada, and Brazil. Examines the problems of education, marriage, family training, assimilation, and integration.

463.* 山下草園　日米をつなぐ者
Yamashita Soen. Nichi-Bei wo tsunagu mono [Those who link Japan and America]. Tokyo: Bunseisha, 1938. 8 + 483 pp., photos, bibliog.

A general critique of the problems of the second generation in Hawaii and the continental United States by an Issei journalist. Interpreting the Nisei as a bridge between Japan and America, it stresses how the second generation can make contributions to improve U.S.-Japan relations.

A. Japanese Language Schools

464.* マカワオ日本語學校新教師雇用問題ニ關シ照屋某ノ陰險陋劣行為ヲ排擊ス
[Anonymous]. Makawao Nihongo Gakkō shin kyōshi koyō mondai ni kanshi Akiya-bō no inken rōretsu kōi wo haigekisu [Denounce Mr. Akiya's base, deceitful actions on the problem of employing a new instructor for the Makawao Japanese Language School]. [Makawao], 1933. 26 pp. Mimeo.

A handwritten, mimeographed tract polemically attacking an Akiya who was involved in a controversy surrounding the hiring of a new teacher for the Makawao Japanese Language School on the island of Maui in 1933.

465.* 濃人鍬一　母國見學報告書
Atsuto Kuwa'ichi. Bokoku kengaku hōkokusho [Report of an excursion to Japan]. Tokyo: Atsuto Kuwa'ichi, 1938. 77 pp., plates, photos.

A summary report of a group of Japanese language school teachers and students which took an educational tour of Japan in 1937. The group originated in Hawaii.

466. Cortez Japanese Language School. "Account book." MSS. 1 book, 1939-1941. Cortez.

   The record of monthly tuitions paid by the students of the Cortez Japanese Language School from May, 1939 to December, 1941.

467. 遠藤幸四郎　見學旅行日誌記念帖
   Endō Kōshirō. Kengaku ryokō nisshi kinenchō [Souvenir album of an educational excursion]. Los Angeles: Nanka Nihongo Gakuen Kyōkai, 1939. 112 + English text 47 pp., photos.

   An English-Japanese souvenir album of a trip to Japan, Korea, Manchuria, and North China taken in 1939 by a group of Nisei under the auspices of the Southern California Japanese Language School Association.

468. 布哇中學校布哇高等女學校校友會　　　　校友會誌・卒業記念
* Hawai Chū Gakkō, Hawai Kōtō Jogakkō Kōyūkai. Kōyūkaishi: Sotsugyō kinen [Alumni Association publication: Graduation annual]. 1929 and 1935. Annual. Honolulu. Various paging, photos.

   The school annual of the Hawaii High School and Hawaii Girls' School.

469. 布哇教育會　　會報
* Hawai Kyōikukai. Kaihō [Bulletin]. no. 7 (1937). Annual. Honolulu.

   The annual bulletin of the Hawaii Education Association on its activities, its member schools, and Japanese language education.

470. 布哇教育會　　日語教育
* Hawai Kyōikukai. Nichigo kyōiku [Japanese language education]. no. 2, 4, 7 (1938, Apr. 1939, Jul. 1940). Irregular. Honolulu.

   A periodical on Japanese language education published by the Hawaii Education Association. Issue no. 7 (Jul. 1940) includes the Kaihō [Bulletin], no. 10 (Jul. 1940) of the Association.

471. 布哇教育會編纂部　　布哇日本語教育史
* Hawai Kyōikukai Hensanbu. Hawai Nihongo kyōikushi [History of Japanese language education in Hawaii]. Honolulu: Hawai Kyōikukai, 1937. 4 + 5 + 2 + 2 + 12 + 702 pp., photos.

   A history of the Hawaii Education Association and its central role in Japanese language education. Includes a detailed discussion of the Hawaii Territorial Government's efforts to regulate foreign language schools in the 1920's, and concludes with brief histories of the Association's branches.

472. ヒロ獨立中女學校　　ヒロ獨立中女學校新築記念誌
* Hiro Dokuritsu Chū Jogakkō. Hiro Dokuritsu Chū Jogakkō shinchiku kinenshi [Hilo Independent Girls' High School: New school building dedication publication]. Honolulu: Hawai Shōgyōsha, 1939. 63 pp., photos.

   A publication to commemorate the new school building of the Hilo Independent Girls' High School which has the graduation speeches for 1939, a roster of alumni, and a brief history of the school.

473. 北加日本語學園協會　　米國加州日本語學園沿革史
Hokka Nihongo Gakuen Kyōkai. Beikoku Kashū Nihongo gakuen enkakushi [History of Japanese language schools in California]. San Francisco: Hokka Nihongo Gakuen Kyōkai, 1930. 5 + 403 pp., photos, apps.

   A chronological history of Japanese language schools in Northern California and the Northern California Association of Japanese Language Schools. Includes short essays by different individuals on the second generation and the problems of Japanese language schools.

474. 近藤菊次郎　　復習問題及答案
 * Kondō Kikujirō (ed.). Fukushū mondai oyobi tōan ["Review questions and answers"]. Maui: Maui Kyōikukai, 1923. 135. pp.

   A handbook on American history and government for Japanese language school teachers to assist them to pass the certification examination required by the 1920 Territorial law regulating foreign language schools.

475. 馬哇教育會　　會員名簿
 * Maui Kyōikukai. "Kaiin meibo" [Membership roster]. MSS. 1 notebook, 1931. Wailuku.

   A membership roster as of July, 1931 of the Maui Education Association.

476. 南加教育會　　第二世の教育
   Nanka Kyōikukai. Dai-nisei no kyōiku [The education of the second generation]. Los Angeles: Nanka Kyōikukai, 1926. 80 + [50] pp.

   Short essays on the development of Japanese language schools, their educational philosophy and aims, and curricular and other problems. Includes a list of schools in Southern California complete with pupil-teacher statistics and budgetary data and a roster of supporters of the Southern California Educational Society.

477. 南加日本語學園協會　　第二世日本語作文集
   Nanka Nihongo Gakuen Kyōkai. Dai-Nisei Nihongo sakubunshū [Collection of Nisei compositions in Japanese]. Los Angeles: Nanka Nihongo Gakuen Kyōkai, 1939. 154 pp., photo.

   A collection of Japanese compositions by Nisei pupils of Japanese language schools in Southern California. The pupils range from 7 to 18 years old.

478. 日本語學園協同システム　　協同
   Nihongo Gakuen Kyōdō Shisutemu. Kyōdō [Cooperative]. No. 1, 2 (1952, 1959). Irregular. Los Angeles.

   A publication of the Japanese Language School Cooperative System, Inc. and its affiliated schools in Southern California on Japanese language education. Edited by Sugimachi Yaemitsu.

479. 大山卯次郎　米國に於ける日本語學校問題　　外交時報
 * Ōyama Ujirō. "Beikoku ni okeru Nihongo gakkō mondai" [The Japanese language school question in America], Gaikō Jihō [Revue Diplomatique], 46:545 (Aug. 15, 1927), 75-83. M.

   An article reviewing the various laws enacted to regulate foreign language schools in the 1920's in Hawaii and California and the successful legal battles against them. Also assesses the problems of teaching Japanese to the second generation.

480. 羅府上町第二学園　　　羅府上町第二学園史
    Rafu Uwa-Machi Dai-Ni Gakuen. Rafu Uwa-Machi Dai-Ni Gakuenshi [History of
    the Los Angeles Nippon Institute]. Los Angeles: Rafu Nippon Institute,
    1965 (?). 64 + [4] pp., photos.

    A chronological history of the Los Angeles Nippon Institute from
    1915 to 1965. Includes a membership directory.

481. 佐藤傳　　　米加に於ける第二世の教育
    Satō Tsutae. Bei-Ka ni okeru Dai-Nisei no kyōiku [The education of the
    Nisei in America and Canada]. Vancouver: Jikyōdō, 1932. 2 + 2 + 4 +
    14 + 452 pp., charts.

    A comprehensive treatment of Japanese language schools in America and
    Canada. Covers their beginning and development, their conflicting aims and
    philosophies, curriculum content, and administrative and management prob-
    lems. Also touches upon family education and the special characteristics
    of the Nisei.

482. 鈴木七郎　　　海外第二世の綴方集
  * Suzuki Shichirō (ed.). Kaigai Dai-Nisei no tsuzurikatashū [A collection of
    compositions by overseas Nisei]. Tokyo: Nihon Rikkōkai, 1938. 15 + 14
    + 337 pp., photos, app.

    A collection of Japanese compositions by Nisei in Canada, Hawaii, the
    continental United States, and South America. The compositions are divided
    into three levels: elementary, junior high, and high school. A short
    summary of Japanese language education in Canada is appended.

483. 玉本周陽　　　感想集
    Tamamoto Shūyō (ed.). Kansōshū [Impressions]. Marysville: Merisubiru
    Gakuen, 1937. 48 pp., photos.

    A collection of one-paragraph remarks by graduating students of the
    Marysville Japanese Language School in 1937.

484. 田辺三之丞　　布哇學生母國見學記念誌
  * Tanabe Sannojō. Hawai gakusei bokoku kengaku kinenshi [Souvenir album of
    the Hawaii student excursion of Japan]. Tokyo: Kibōsha, 1930. 3 + 9 +
    3 + 256 pp., photos.

    The record of a trip to Japan taken by 30 Japanese language school
    students from Hawaii in 1927.

485. ターラック日本語學園　　記録
    Tārakku Nihongo Gakuen. "Kiroku" [Records]. MSS. 1 box, 1930-1941.
    Turlock.

    Miscellaneous documents of the Turlock Japanese Language School from
    1930 to 1941: an account book from January, 1930 to January, 1938; minutes
    of the P.T.A. meetings of January, 1931; and six receipt books and monthly
    financial statements from April, 1934 to October, 1941.

486. ワイパフ學園校友會　　卒業記念校友會誌 1941
  * Waipafu Gakuen Kōyūkai. Sotsugyō kinen: Kōyūkaishi, 1941 [Graduation com-
    memoration: Alumni Association album, 1941]. Waipahu: Waipafu Gakuen
    Kōyūkai, 1941. 122 pp., photos.

    The 1941 school annual of the Waipahu Japanese Language School on the
    island of Oahu.

487. ワイルク學園　　卒業記念誌
 * Wairuku Gakuen. Sotsugyō kinenshi [Graduation annual]. 1931, 1939. Annual. Wailuku.

   Graduation annuals for the Wailuku Japanese Language School on the island of Maui.

488. 米田實　　在米日本人の一大問題　　外交時報
   Yoneda Minoru. "Zai-Bei Nihonjin no ichidai mondai" [A big problem among the Japanese in America], Gaikō Jihō [Revue Diplomatique], 26:312 (Nov. 1, 1917), 20-29. M.

   An article on the problem of securing qualified Japanese language school teachers in America. Cites the case of Inoue Kikuchi who had been hired as a teacher by the Japanese Association of Guadalupe, but who was denied entry into America because he was judged a "contract laborer."

B. Textbooks

489. 米國日本語研究會　　あたらしい日本語
   Beikoku Nihongo Kenkyūkai. Atarashii Nihongo [The new Japanese language]. 2nd and 5th year. Los Angeles: Beikoku Nihongo Kenkyūkai, 1963 (4th printing) and 1962 (4th printing). 52 pp., illus. and 46 pp., illus.

   A postwar Japanese language textbook series published in 1958 in Los Angeles.

490. 布哇教育會　　日本語讀本
 * Hawai Kyōikukai. Nihongo tokuhon [The Japanese language reader]. v. 5-6. Honolulu: Hawai Kyōikukai, 1929. 203 + 14 pp., illus. and 177 + 13 pp., illus.

   A Japanese language textbook series published by the Hawaii Education Association.

491. 布哇教育會　　日本語讀本・中等科用卷二
 * Hawai Kyōikukai. Nihongo tokuhon: Chūtōkayō kanni [The Japanese language reader: Intermediate series no. 2]. Honolulu: Hawai Kyōikukai, 1930. 188 + 50 pp., illus.

   An intermediate Japanese language textbook series published by the Hawaii Education Association.

492. 布哇教育會　　日本語讀本・高等課用
 * Hawai Kyōikukai. Nihongo tokuhon: Kōtōkayō [The Japanese language reader: Advanced series]. v. 1-2. Honolulu: Fushimi-no-miya Kinen Shōgakkai, 1921 and 1922. 320 pp., illus. and 330 pp., illus.

   An advanced Japanese language textbook series published by the Hawaii Education Association.

493. 布哇教育會　　修身書
 * Hawai Kyōikukai. Shūshinsho [Moral education text]. Honolulu: Hawai Kyōikukai, 1932. 172 pp.

   A manual for teachers on moral education.

494. 本派本願寺學務部　　中等日本語讀本
 * Hompa Hongwanji Gakumubu. Chūtō Nihongo tokuhon [Intermediate Japanese language reader]. v. 1-2. Honolulu: Hompa Hongwanji Gakumubu, 1925 and 1929 (rev. ed.). 120 pp., illus. and 145 pp., illus.

   An intermediate Japanese language textbook series published by the Hompa Hongwanji Mission.

495. 本願寺學務部　　日本語副讀本
 * Hongwanji Gakumubu. Nihongo fukutokuhon [The Japanese language supplementary reader]. v. 1-5. Honolulu: Hongwanji Gakumubu, 1928. Various paging, illus.

   A supplementary Japanese language textbook series published by the Hompa Hongwanji Mission.

496. 河村幽川　　アメリカ日本語讀本
   Kawamura Yūsen (ed.). Amerika Nihongo tokuhon [The American Japanese language reader]. San Francisco: Beikoku Nikkei Jidō Kyōiku Kenkyūkai, 1935. 241 + 8 pp.

   A collection of short stories and essays for intermediate and advanced students in Japanese language schools.

497. 中山天恃　　母のことば
   Nakayama Tenji. Haha no kotoba ["The mother's tongue"]. Los Angeles: Nakayama Tenji Shuppansha, 1924. [7] + 270 pp., photos, illus.

   A supplementary textbook for elementary Japanese.

498. 日本語學園編纂委員會　　日本語讀本
   Nihongo Gakuen Hensan Iinkai. Nihongo tokuhon [The Japanese language reader]. v. 1, 2, 4, 11, 13. San Francisco: Aoki Taiseidō, v. 1, 1930 (rev. ed.), 53 pp., illus.; v. 2, 1939 (rev. ed.), 51 pp., illus.; v. 4, 1928 (rev. ed.), 88 pp., illus.; v. 11, 1939 (rev. ed.), 102 pp., illus.; v. 13, 1931 (rev. ed., 4th printing), 106 pp., illus.

   The Japanese language school textbook series especially compiled for the second generation and officially approved by the California State Board of Education in August, 1923.

499. 杉町八重克　　日本語讀本
   Sugimachi Yaemitsu (ed.). Nihongo tokuhon [The Japanese language reader]. no. 10. Los Angeles: Rafu Dai-Ichi Gakuen and Pasadena Gakuen, n.d. 67 pp. Mimeo.

   A Japanese language reader published in Los Angeles.

C. Study in Japan

500. 内藤啓三　財団法人海外教育協会要覧
 Naitō Keizō. <u>Zaidan Hōjin Kaigai Kyōiku Kyōkai yōran</u> [Overseas Japanese Educational Association Foundation]. Kawasaki: Zaidan Hōjin Kaigai Kyōiku Kyōkai, 1940. 56 pp., photos.

   A booklet explaining the purposes of the Overseas Japanese Educational Association Foundation. Supported by both private and public funds, it was headed by Viscount Ishii Kikutarō and established in 1932 to educate the second generation from America and other countries. Includes a description of its affiliated school and dormitory.

501.* 日本米布協會　第二世と日本の學校・第二世叢書第六輯
 Nihon Beifu Kyōkai. <u>Dai-nisei to Nihon no gakkō: Dai-Nisei Sōsho dai-rokushū</u> [The second generation and Japanese schools: Nisei Book Series no. 6]. Tokyo: Runbini Shuppansha, 1938. 2 + 2 + 6 + 51 pp., plate.

   A guide to schools in Japan for the second generation, including those with special programs for the Nisei and their requirements.

502.* 日本米布協會　日本米布協會要覧
 Nihon Beifu Kyōkai. <u>Nihon Beifu Kyōkai yōran</u> [The Japan, America, Hawaii Society]. Tokyo: Nihon Beifu Kyōkai, 1937. 46 pp.

   A booklet on the Japan, America, Hawaii Society founded in 1932 to encourage Nisei from Hawaii, the continental United States, and Canada to study the Japanese language and culture in Japan. Includes information on the school and dormitory which it operated to fulfill this purpose.

503. 日本米布協會　日本留學の新しき方法・第二世叢書第九輯
 Nihon Beifu Kyōkai. <u>Nihon ryūgaku no atarashiki hōhō: Dai-Nisei Sōsho dai-kyūshū</u> [A new way to study in Japan: Nisei Book Series no. 9]. Tokyo: Runbini, 1938. 57 pp.

   A report on a group of Nisei students who went to Japan in 1937 to study Japanese for one year under the auspices of the Japan, America, Hawaii Society and with the cooperation of Rev. Tamai Yoshitaka of the Tri-State Buddhist Church in Denver.

504. Nisei Survey Committee. <u>The Nisei: A survey of their life in Japan</u>. Tokyo: Keisen Girls' School, 1939. vii + 55 + iv pp., photos.

   A survey of the educational, vocational, and social problems of 437 Nisei studying in the Tokyo-Yokohama area in 1939.

505.* 山下草園　日系市民の日本留學事情
 Yamashita Sōen. <u>Nikkei shimin no Nihon ryūgaku jijō</u> [The state of Japanese-Americans studying in Japan]. Tokyo: Bunseisha, 1935. 4 + 3 + 8 + 400 pp., apps., photos. M.

   A comprehensive examination of Nisei studying in Japan in the first half of the 1930's. Discusses their motives and goals, their daily school life, and their feelings and attitudes about Japan. Includes a matriculation guide to schools and dormitories as well as organizations which assist Nisei.

2. JAPANESE AMERICAN CITIZENS LEAGUE

506. Japanese American Citizens League. ["Records"]. 8 boxes, 1930-1970.

   Miscellaneous publications, records, and documents of the Japanese American Citizens League and its local chapters. The following items are included:
   Japanese American Citizens League Biennial National Convention, 1930, 1946-1966. Mimeo., except 1930.
   Minutes, Japanese American Citizens League, special emergency national conference, November 17-24, 1942. Salt Lake City, 1943. 120 pp. + supplements various paging. Mimeo.
   Masaoka, Mike, "Final report," April 22, 1944. X.
   Scattered issues of postwar publications.
   Documents relating to the Anti-Axis Committee, December 8, 1941-January 12, 1942, including minutes of meetings.
   Scattered reports of the Washington Office, ca. 1961-1964.
   Documents relating to the Endowment Fund Drive, 1953.
   92 completed questionnaires of Issei and Nisei in the Salt Lake City area, 1961.
   26 completed questionnaires of Issei in Utah County, Utah, n.d.
   Newspaper clipping files on internment, resettlement, and Nisei soldiers, ca. 1936-1947.
   Other miscellaneous memoranda, reports, programs, and announcements.

507. Japanese American Citizens League. Pocatello Chapter. "Records." MSS. 8 boxes and 4 vols., 1940-1956. Pocatello.

   Miscellaneous financial records, correspondence file from June, 1941 to December, 1958, and minutes of the Executive Board and Committees, 1946-1949.

VIII.
Socio-Cultural Materials

1. PUBLISHED WORKS

508. 赤堀最　　南加日本人野球史
   Akahori Masaru (comp.). <u>Nanka Nihonjin yakyūshi</u> [History of Japanese baseball in Southern California]. Los Angeles: Town Crier, n.d. [38] pp., photos, illus.

   A pictorial history of Japanese baseball in Southern California.

509. 後藤鎮平　　野球重百年祭記念・布哇邦人野球史
* Gotō Chinpei. <u>Yakyū ippyakunensai kinen: Hawai hōjin yakyūshi</u> ["Commemorations of baseball centennial: The Japanese baseballdom of Hawaii"]. Kaneohe: Hawai Hōjin Yakyūshi Shuppankai, 1940. 6 + 12 + 772 + English summary 7 + 29 pp., photos.

   A history of Japanese baseball in Hawaii.

510. 本派本願寺學務部　　話方と書翰文
* Hompa Hongwanji Gakumubu. <u>Hanashikata to shokanbun</u> [Speaking and writing]. Honolulu: Hompa Hongwanji Gakumubu, 1927 (rev. ed., 2nd printing). 93 + 98 pp.

   A manual on how to speak and write on formal and informal occasions.

511. 木山義喬　　漫畫四人書生
   Kiyama Yoshitaka. <u>Manga yonin shosei</u> [Cartoons of four students]. Oakland: Inhaku Dōshikai, 1931. 111 pp.

   Satirical cartoons on the Japanese through World War I, treating such topics as drinking and gambling, working as a school boy and farmhand, picture-brides, and others.

512. 開原榮　　故國に歸てから
   Kaihara Sakae. <u>Kokoku ni kaette kara</u> [After returning to my native country]. Sacramento: Yorozu Shoten, 1919. 6 + 195 pp.

   An account of a return trip to Japan taken from May, 1916 to February, 1917 by an Issei who first came to America in 1903. Includes impressions of changes in Japan, especially of Tokyo.

513. 松本一満　　　　泉
Matsumoto Kazumitsu. Izumi [Spring]. Los Angeles: Rafu Kinseikai, 1947. [8] + 14 + 70 + 98 pp., photos, illus. Mimeo.

Essays by members and supporters of the Kinseikai, a biwa and shigin study group in Southern California. Includes a membership roster and summaries of this group in the various internment camps during World War II.

514. 籾井一剣　　北米剣道大鑑
Momii Ikken. Hoku-Bei kendō taikan [A survey of kendo in North America]. San Francisco: Hokubei Butokukai, 1939. 14 + 6 + 28 + 1255 pp., plates, photos.

A history of the North American Butokukai established in 1929 to teach the second generation kendo. Written with a strong nationalistic bias, it includes a biography of its founder, Nakamura Tōkichi, and sketches of its officers and supporters, and an outline of local affiliates throughout California, Oregon, and Washington.

515. 村岡末蔵　　村岡式洋服裁方
Muraoka Suezō. Muraoka-shiki yōfuku saihō [The Muraoka style of Western tailoring]. Los Angeles: Beikoku Yōfuku Saidan Kenkyūjo, 1928. [4] + 179 pp., photo, illus.

A western clothing design manual complete with cutout patterns.

516. 名倉落陽　　　落陽孤雁
Nagura Rakuyō (pseud.). Rakuyō kogan [Solitary wild geese: Rakuyō]. San Francisco: Hinomoto Shōkai, 1912. 17 + 16 + 277 + 2 pp., plates, photo.

An Issei woman's views of the American home and American women. Includes selected entries from her diary written during her passage to America via Europe. The author was the wife of Ikeda Kandō, the publisher and editor of the Hokubei Hyōron in Oakland, California.

517. 中川頼覚　　日米作法の常識
Nakagawa Yoriaki. Nichi-Bei sahō no jōshiki ["Etiquette"]. Tokyo: Uedaya Shoten, 1937 (3rd printing). 3 + 2 + 3 + [2] + 3 + 16 + 398 + 4 pp., plates, photos, illus.

An etiquette manual written by a Seattle Japanese language school principal for the benefit of the second generation.

518. 南加小兒園　　南加小兒園小誌
Nanka Shōnien. Nanka Shōnien shōshi ["The Japanese Children's Home of Southern California"]. Los Angeles: Nanka Shōnien, 1939. 29 + English text 6 pp., photos.

A booklet on the Japanese Children's Home of Southern California established in February, 1914 which commemorates its 25th anniversary.

519. 成澤金兵衛　　米國物語
Narizawa Kinpei. Beikoku monogatari [American tales]. Tokyo: Taisanbō, 1918. 2 + 6 + 211 pp., photos.

Impressions of Japanese immigrant society based upon the author's 7-year sojourn in America from 1906 to 1913.

520. 新里貫一　　移民地哀話・家庭悲劇篇・第二世篇・失踪者篇
Niisato Kan'ichi. Iminchi aiwa [Sad tales in an immigrant land]. 3 vols. Tokyo: Shimpōsha, 1934-35. Katei higeki-hen [Family tragedies], 1934 (3rd printing), 12 + 4 + 2 + 181 pp., photos; Dai-nisei-hen [The second generation], 1934, 16 + 3 + 2 + 164 pp., photo, M.; Senkusha-hen [The pioneers], 1935, 8 + 15 + 2 + 163 pp., photos, M.

A 3-volume work portraying the hardships and tragedies of Japanese immigrants and their descendants. The first treats broken homes, the second touches upon Nisei delinquency and runaways, and the third depicts the problems of the Issei. The second has been translated by Eiji Tanabe and Carl Kondo under the title Nisei tragedy (Tokyo, 1937).

521. 田畑喜三郎　　在米者成功之友
Tabata Kisaburō. Zai-Beisha seikō no tomo [A companion to success for Japanese in America]. Tokyo: Shimizu Shoten, 1908. 18 + 10 + 172 + apps. 180 pp. M.

A homely guide for ordinary arrivals in America, containing advice on how to learn English, how to seek employment, how to avoid sickness and injuries, and information about educational prospects.

522. 徳島縣人會　　徳島縣人會々報
Tokushima Kenjinkai. Tokushima Kenjinkai kaihō [Bulletin of the Tokushima Prefectural Association]. Seattle: Tokushima Kenjinkai, 1915. 126 pp., photos.

The bulletin of the Tokushima Prefectural Association of Seattle established in 1902. Contains considerable information on the Japanese pioneers from this Prefecture in the Seattle area.

523. 角田柳作　　書齋學校社會
* Tsunoda Ryūsaku. Shosai gakkō shakai [Study, school, and society]. Honolulu: Hawai Benrisha, 1917. 2 + 2 + 291 pp., photo.

Essays on education, literature, and miscellaneous subjects by a former educator with the Hompa Hongwanji Mission.

524. 梅村重藏　　からだと健康
Umemura Jūzō. Karada to kenkō ["Look younger, live longer"]. Salt Lake City: Umemura Jūzō, 1966. [8] + 195 pp., illus.

A book on the secret of longevity by an Issei Christian.

525. 山下草園　　ウクレレの嘆き
* Yamashita Sōen. Ukurere no nageki [Sorrowful ukulele tunes]. Honolulu: Morishige Shosekiten, 1933. [6] + 490 pp., photo.

Stories about sensational crimes and sports in Hawaii, involving Japanese in some cases.

526. Yamauchi, Chester M. A report to the Board of Directors of the Japanese Children's Home. Los Angeles, 1952. 79 pp. Mimeo.

A survey of the desirability and feasibility of reestablishing the prewar Japanese Children's Home of Southern California.

2. RECORDS OF ORGANIZATIONS

527. 加州日本人慈惠會　　第二十四年度報告
    Kashū Nihonjin Jikeikai. "Dai-nijūyonendo hōkoku" [1924 report]. MSS. 1 folder, 1924-1925. San Francisco.

    The minutes of the Japanese Benevolent Society from August, 1924 to January, 1925. Includes a detailed 1924 financial report and the correspondence of the society from January to June, 1925.

528. コルーサ墓参會　記録
    Korūsa Bosankai. "Kiroku" [Records]. MSS. 1 vol., 1919, 1926-1949. Colusa.

    Brief reports of the Colusa Memorial Society and its annual visit to the Japanese cemetery from April, 1926 to May, 1949. Also includes the financial accounts of the Colusa Japanese Language School and a record of contributions.

529. 南加宮城縣人會　　會員名簿
    Nanka Miyagi Kenjinkai. "Kaiin meibo" [Membership roster]. MSS. 1 folder, 1967-1968. Los Angeles.

    The 1967 membership roster and financial report of the Miyagi Prefectural Association of Southern California and a few circulars sent to its members in 1968.

530. 南格修養會　　南格修養會記録
    Nankaku Shūyōkai. "Nankaku Shūyōkai kiroku" [Records of the Southern Colorado Character Building Society]. MSS. 1 vol., 1925-1939. Swink.

    The minutes and reports of the Southern Colorado Character Building Society from February, 1925 to August, 1939, an organization established in 1911 to improve the moral and intellectual culture of the Japanese in Southern Colorado.

531. 日本人養老院　　寄附者芳名
    Nihonjin Yōrōin. "Kifusha hōmei" [A list of contributors]. MSS. 1 vol., 1934-1941. Los Angeles.

    The record of contributions raised between May, 1931 and April, 1941 for the construction of the Yōrōin, a senior citizens' home, actually built in 1939 in Boyle Heights.

532. ポカテロ日本人青年會　　記録
    Pokatero Nihonjin Seinenkai. "Kiroku" [Records]. MSS. 3 vols., 1915-1919. Pocatello.

    The records of the Japanese Youth Association of Pocatello from February, 1915 to September, 1919. Established in February, 1915 as a fraternal body, it was redesignated as the Pokatero Nihonjin Aiyūkai and officially translated into English as the Japanese I.U. Association of Pocatello. Includes, minutes, membership rosters, financial reports and records.

533. 羅府禁酒會　　記錄
　　　Rafu Kinshukai. "Kiroku" [Records]. MSS. 1 vol., 1908-1910. Los
　　　Angeles.

　　　　　The minutes of the Prohibition Society of Los Angeles, founded by the
　　　Japanese Christian Church Federation of Southern California in February,
　　　1908, from its inception to February, 1910. Includes a membership roster
　　　and financial accounts.

534. ロスアンゼルス郡日本人人道會　　記錄
　　　Rosuanzerusu-gun Nihonjin Jindōkai. "Kiroku" [Records]. MSS. 1 vol.,
　　　1912-1916, 1922-1923. Los Angeles.

　　　　　The records of the Japanese Humane Society of Los Angeles County, a
　　　social welfare oriented organization founded in January, 1912, with reports
　　　of family squabbles from March, 1912 to January, 1916. Also includes the
　　　daily log of the Japanese Children's Home of Southern California from
　　　November, 1922 to June, 1923.

535. ターラック婦人會　　記錄
　　　Tārakku Fujinkai. "Kiroku" [Records]. MSS. 1 box, 1930-1942. Turlock.

　　　　　The incomplete records of the Turlock Women's Society. Minutes from
　　　January, 1940 to April, 1941; account books from February, 1940 to January,
　　　1942; and a roster of officers from December, 1938 to January, 1941, plus
　　　miscellaneous documents dating back to February, 1930.

536. ターラック社交倶樂部　　記錄
　　　Tārakku Shakō Kurabu. "Kiroku" [Records]. MSS. 4 vols. and 1 box, 1919-
　　　1941. Turlock.

　　　　　Miscellaneous financial records of the Turlock Social Club from 1919
　　　to 1941.

537. 德島縣人會　　記錄
　　　Tokushima Kenjinkai. "Kiroku" [Records]. MSS. 2 boxes (19 items), 1902-
　　　1948. Seattle.

　　　　　Miscellaneous records of the Tokushima Prefectural Association of
　　　Seattle from 1902 to May, 1948. Includes incomplete membership rosters,
　　　historical data collected by Akahori Masaru in 1941 for a projected but
　　　never published history of the organization, incomplete financial and
　　　other records, and some postwar documents on Nisei soldiers killed in
　　　action during World War II and newspaper clippings regarding fishing right
　　　and land litigation.

IX.
Japanese Associations

Note: The origins of the Japanese Associations date back to the founding of the Nihonjin Kyogikai [Japanese Deliberative Council] in San Francisco in May, 1900. Similar bodies were subsequently organized in the outlying Japanese communities. In 1906 the San Francisco organization, redesignated the Zaibei Nihonjin Rengō Kyōgikai [United Japanese Deliberative Council of America], became the central body to which newly formed local bodies affiliated. In 1908 the central body was again renamed the Zaibei Nihonjinkai [Japanese Association of America], and all local bodies were renamed Japanese Associations.

Eventually four major central Japanese Associations were established, to which all local bodies affiliated. These four were under the jurisdictions of the Seattle, Portland, San Francisco, and Los Angeles Japanese Consulates. In the Pacific Northwest, local bodies in Washington and Montana were linked to the Seihokubu Renraku Nihonjinkai [United Northwestern Japanese Association] located in Seattle. Local bodies in Oregon and Idaho were affiliated with the Ōshū Nihonjinkai [Japanese Association of Oregon] headquartered in Portland. The Japanese Association of America, the first and largest central body, originally embraced all the local bodies in California, Nevada, Utah, Colorado, and Arizona. In 1915, however, the Nanka Chūō Nihonjinkai [Central Japanese Association of Southern California] was inaugurated, and local bodies in Southern California, Southern Nevada, Arizona, and New Mexico became affiliated to it. All four central bodies (excluding the Southern California association in its first year) plus the Japanese Association of Canada together formed the Taiheiyō Engan Nihonjinkai Kyōgikai [Pacific Coast Japanese Association Deliberative Council], which convened annually from 1914 to 1929 to discuss common problems. New York City, Chicago, Washington, D.C., and Houston had independent Japanese Associations.

The richest materials are the complete records of the Walnut Grove Japanese Association, no. 553, and the almost complete ones of the Utah, Western Idaho, and Los Angeles Japanese Associations, no. 565, no. 560, and no. 557. The minutes of the annual meetings of the Pacific Coast Japanese Association Deliberative Council, no. 563, are also very valuable. All the records provide a wealth of historical information on the implementation of the Gentlemen's Agreement of 1907–1908 at the local level through the "endorsement right" system, the fight against the exclusion movement, the internal development of local communities, and other socio-economic data.

1. PUBLISHED WORKS AND BULLETINS

538. 米國西北部聯絡日本人會　　會務報告書
Beikoku Seihokubu Renraku Nihonjinkai. Kaimu hōkokusho [Transaction report]. Mar. 1, 1922 to Jul. 31, 1922. Semi-annual. Seattle. M.

   A transaction report of the United Northwestern Japanese Association of Seattle.

539. 米國西北部聯絡日本人會　　會務及會計報告書
Beikoku Seihokubu Renraku Nihonjinkai. Kaimu oyobi kaikei hōkokusho [Transaction and financial report]. Sep. 1, 1921 to Feb. 28, 1922. Semi-annual. Seattle. M.

   Same as above.

540. 藤岡紫朗　　米國中央日本人會史
+ Fujioka Shirō. Beikoku Chūō Nihonjinkaishi [A history of the Central Japanese Association of America]. Los Angeles: Beikoku Chūō Nihonjinkai, 1940. 12 + 445 pp., photos.

   A chronological history of the Central Japanese Association of Southern California and its affiliated locals from 1915 to 1940.

541. 山東日本人會　　在留日本人民勢調査報告
Santō Nihonjinkai. Zairyū Nihonjin minsei chōsa hōkoku [Report on the Japanese population in the Rocky Mountain region]. Denver: Santō Nihonjinkai, 1919. 20 pp.

   A statistical report on the Japanese population in Colorado primarily as of 1919.

542. 西部愛他保日本人會　　西部愛他保日本人會々報
Seibu Aidaho Nihonjinkai. Seibu Aidaho Nihonjinkai kaihō ["Annual report of Western Idaho Japanese Association"]. no. 7, 8 (1922, 1923). Annual. Boise.

543. シアトル日系人會　　十周年記念
Shiatoru Nikkeijinkai. Jūshūnen kinen [10th anniversary commemoration]. Shiatoru Nikkeijinkai, 1960. 153 pp., photos.

A chronological history of the Seattle Japanese Community Service founded in 1948 as the successor to the prewar Japanese Association.

544. ツラレ郡日本人會　　ツラレ郡日本人會々報
Tsurare-gun Nihonjinkai. Tsurare-gun Nihonjinkai kaihō [Bulletin of the Japanese Association of Tulare County]. no. 1 (Jan. 1922). Annual. Visalia. X.

545. 在米日本人聯合協議會　　在米日本人聯合協議會報告書
Zaibei Nihonjin Rengō Kyōgikai. Zaibei Nihonjin Rengō Kyōgikai hōkokusho [Report of the United Japanese Deliberative Council of America]. no. 1 (1907). San Francisco.

546. 在米日本人會　　州外視察報告
Zaibei Nihonjinkai. Shūgai shisatsu hōkoku [Report of observations of other states]. San Francisco: Zaibei Nihonjinkai, 1924. 34 pp.

A report on the geography, climate, economic conditions, and attitudes toward Japanese in the states of Florida and Georgia.

547. 在米日本人會　　出生届及國籍離脱の栞
Zaibei Nihonjinkai. Shussei todoki oyobi kokuseki ridatsu no shiori [Guide to registration of births and renunciation of Japanese nationality]. San Francisco: Zaibei Nihonjinkai, 1922. 12 + [8] pp.

An explanatory pamphlet of the 1916 amendment to the Japanese Nationality Law, regulating the registration of births and the renouncement of Japanese nationality.

548. 在米日本人會　　在米日本人會々報
Zaibei Nihonjinkai. Zaibei Nihonjinkai kaihō [Bulletin of the Japanese Association of America]. no. 1-3 (Jul. 1909, Jan., Jul. 1910). Semi-annual. San Francisco. X.

549. 在米日本人會　　在米日本人會會務報告及定期臨時代表者會議事録
Zaibei Nihonjinkai. Zaibei Nihonjinkai kaimu hōkoku oyobi teiki rinji daihyōshakai gijiroku [Transaction report and record of the regular and special delegate conferences of the Japanese Association of America]. 1931. Annual. San Francisco. Mimeo.

2. RECORDS OF JAPANESE ASSOCIATIONS

550. アイダホ州中央日本人會　　記録
Aidaho-shū Chuō Nihonjinkai. ["Kiroku" [Records]]. MSS. 2 folders and 4 boxes, 1919-1930. Pocatello.

The partial records of the Japanese Association of Central Idaho from 1919 to 1930. The records consist of the following:
"Kiroku" [Records], 1 box, 1919-1927. Financial and other records.
"Hasshinbun kobo" [Record of outgoing correspondence], 3 boxes (19 books), 1919-1930.
"Ei-nogyō chosahyo" [Questionnaires], 2 folders, 1922. Questionnaire

      files on the economic status of the Japanese under the jurisdiction of the Association as of 1922.
"Zairyū tōroku" [Registration cards], 114 cards, 1930.

551. アイダホ州日本人會聯合協議會 　　記録
Aidaho-shū Nihonjinkai Rengō Kyōgikai. "Kiroku" [Records]. MSS. 2 vols. and 1 box (3 items), 1917-1922. Pocatello.

    The incomplete records of the United Japanese Association of Idaho founded in 1913 to integrate all the local Associations of Idaho from 1917 to 1922. Includes a membership roster from 1917 to 1920, the incoming and outgoing correspondence file from January to March, 1919, and the correspondence of outgoing letters from January, 1921 to March, 1922.

552. 麦嶺日本人會 　　會計簿
Bakurei Nihonjinkai. "Kaikeibo" [Account book]. MSS. 1 notebook, 1925-1930. Berkeley.

    An account book of the Japanese Association of Berkeley from March, 1925 to December, 1930.

553. 河下日本人會 　　記録
Kawashimo Nihonjinkai. "Kiroku" [Records]. MSS. 7 vols., 1908-1942. Walnut Grove.

    The complete records of the Japanese Association of Walnut Grove from August, 1908 to February, 1942. First organized in August, 1908 as the Kawashimo Nōgyō Dōmeikai [Japanese Producers' Association of Walnut Grove], it was renamed as the Japanese Association of Walnut Grove in late 1909. The 7 volumes contain minutes of meetings, membership rosters, detailed financial reports, and the records of certificates issued.

554. 南加中央日本人會 　　記録
Nanka Chūō Nihonjinkai. ["Kiroku" [Records]]. MSS. 5 vols., 1915-1939. Los Angeles.

    The incomplete records of the Central Japanese Association of Southern California, organized as the central body for the local associations in Southern California, Southern Nevada, Arizona, and New Mexico in 1915 under the jurisdiction of the Japanese Consulate of Los Angeles. The records consist of the following:
    "Gijiroku" [Minutes of meetings], 1 vol., 1915-1934.
    "Nisshi" [Daily reports], 2 vols., 1930-1931, 1938-1939.
    "Shimbun kirinukichō" [Newspaper clippings], 1 vol., 1922.
    "San'indō shinsai gienkin ōbosha shimei" [List of contributors for
      the relief of victims of the San'indo Earthquake], 1 vol., 1927.

555. ポカテロ日本人會 　　記録
Pokatero Nihonjinkai. "Kiroku" [Records]. MSS. 1 box, 3 notebooks, 2 vols., 1917-1921. Pocatello.

    The incomplete records of the Japanese Association of Pocatello from its inception in 1917 to 1921. Includes a membership roster, financial records, incoming and outgoing correspondence file from April, 1920 to January, 1921, and other miscellaneous documents.

556. 羅府日本人協議會 　　會員名簿
Rafu Nihonjin Kyōgikai. "Kaiin meibo" [Membership roster]. MSS. 1 vol., 1905-1908. Los Angeles.

The record of monthly dues paid by the membership of the Japanese Deliberative Council of Los Angeles, the precursor of the Japanese Association of Los Angeles, from June, 1905 to December, 1908.

557. 羅府日本人會　　記錄
Rafu Nihonjinkai. ["Kiroku" [Records]]. MSS. 41 vols., 3 books, 1 folder, 1 box (7 folders), 1910-1941. Los Angeles.

The incomplete records of the Japanese Association of Los Angeles from 1910 to 1941. The records consist of the following:
"Kaihi boshū iinmei" [List of committee members to raise membership fees], 1 book, 1939-1940.
"Kaikeibo [Account books], 11 vols., 1910-1941.
"Kaihi boshū seisekihyō" [Membership due record], 1 folder, 1940.
"Kaiin meibo" [Membership roster], 6 vols., 1910-1921.
"Rafu Nihonjinkai kiroku" [Records of the Japanese Association of Los Angeles], 1 vol., 1919. Reports of the different Sections of the Association from April to December, 1919.
"Rafu Nihonjinkai kiroku" [Records of the Japanese Association of Los Angeles], 3 vols., 1917-1936. Minutes and transactions from January, 1917 to October, 1936.
"Kōgun imonbukuro" [Gift packages for the Imperial Army], 1 vol., 1940. A list of donors of gift packages for the Japanese Imperial Army from March to May, 1940.
"Renshū Kantai kangei kiroku suitōbo" [Records and expense accounts of the reception for the Imperial Training Squadron], 1 vol., 1922.
"Records of contributions," 1 vol., 1934-1937.
"Kyōshi shaon bansankai kankei shorui" [Records relating to the annual educators' banquet], 1 box (7 folders), 1935-1941.
"Kashū tochihō shūsei oyobi Ozawa jiken ni kansuru kifukin boshū kuiki oyobi iinhyō" [List of districts and committee members to raise contributions for the amendment of the California Alien Land Law and the Ozawa Case], 1 vol., 1919.
"Gosokui yōhaishiki hiyō kessan hōkoku" [Expense accounts for the celebration of the coronation of the Showa Emperor], 1 vol., 1928.
"Hikaiin oyobi kazoku tōrokubo" [Registry of non-members and their families], 1 vol., 1916.
"Shōmeibo" [Certificate record], 8 vols., 1909-1920.
"Shimbun kirinukichō" [Newspaper clippings], 5 vols., 1931, 1933, 1934, 1939, and 1939. Scrapbooks of newspaper clippings which are on the activities of the organization.
"Yachin Nesage Kisei Dōmeikai kiroku" [Records of the Tenant League]; "Chōhei yūyosha jimu, shōmei, todokede jimu" [Record of draft deferments and issuance of certificates], 1 vol., 1932-1937.
"Monthly statement," 2 books, 1936-1941.

558. 羅府日系人協議會　　書簡綴及び會計報告
Rafu Nikkeijin Kyōgikai. "Shokantsuzuri oyobi kaikei hōkoku" [Correspondence and financial reports]. MSS. 1 vol., 1948-1949. Los Angeles.

The outgoing correspondence files and circulars from April to November, 1948 and monthly financial reports from April, 1948 to January, 1949 of the Japanese American Community Council of Los Angeles, a postwar organization founded in September, 1947 as the successor to the prewar Japanese Association of Los Angeles.

559. 山中部日本人會　　記錄
Sanchūbu Nihonjinkai. "Kiroku" [Records]. MSS. 1 vol., 1934-1938. Ogden.

The partial records of the Intermountain Japanese Association from

January, 1934 to September, 1938. Includes the minutes of meetings, important news from Japan, and comprehensive annual reports with respect to the finance, membership, and activities of the Association.

560. 西部愛他保州日本人會　　記錄
Seibu Aidaho-shū Nihonjinkai. ["Kiroku" [Records]]. MSS. 9 vols. and 2 folders, 1909-1928. Boise.

The almost complete records of the Japanese Association of Western Idaho from 1909 to 1928. Officially established in August, 1910 and eventually merged with the Japanese Association of Central Idaho in 1935. The records consist of the following:
  "Nisshi" [Daily reports], 1 vol., 1909-1913. Minutes and transactions.
  "Nisshi kaikei" [Daily financial reports], 1 vol., 1909-1919. Financial reports from 1910 to 1917 and the minutes and financial records of the Nampa branch from November, 1909 to March, 1919.
  "Zairyū tōrokubo" [Registry of Japanese residents], 1 vol., 1910-1919.
  "Kaikeibo" [Ledger], 1 vol., 1914-1919.
  "Shōmeisho hakkō negai" [Applications for certificates], 2 vols., 1910-1920, 1921-1923.
  "Ta no Nihonjinkai yori juryō shita shinsho" [Letters, notices, and other documents from other Japanese Associations], 1 vol., 1921-1928.
  "Seishinbyōsha Aino Shigematsu-shi ni kansuru shoshin" [Correspondence concerning mental patient Aino Shigematsu], 1 folder, 1924-1926.
  "Juryō shita shotodoke" [Notifications received], 1 folder, 1926.
  "Zai-Pōtorando Teikoku Ryōjikan yori Seibu Aidaho-shū Nihonjinkai ni tsūtatsu no shorui" [Instructions issued by the Japanese Consulate of Portland to the Western Idaho Japanese Association], 2 vols., 1920-1928.

561. 新墨州日星協會　　記錄
Shin-Boku-shū Nissei Kyōkai. "Kiroku" [Records]. MSS. 1 vol., 1921-1927. Gallup.

The records of the Sun-Star Association of Gallup, New Mexico from June, 1921 to September, 1927, an Association founded in June, 1921 to cope with the 1921 New Mexico Alien Land Law. Includes minutes of meetings, a record of certificates issued, and other documents.

562. スタニスラウス日本人會　　記錄
Sutanisurausu Nihonjinkai. "Kiroku" [Records]. MSS. 1 box (6 folders), 1920-1928. Turlock.

The incomplete records of the Japanese Association of Stanislaus County from 1920 to 1928. Consists of various receipts, a small correspondence file for 1925, financial reports and minutes of the extraordinary meeting held in March, 1928 which led to the dissolution of the Association.

563. 太平洋沿岸日本人會協議會　　議事錄
Taiheiyō Engan Nihonjinkai Kyōgikai. "Gijiroku" [Minutes]. MSS. 1 vol., 1914-1928.

The minutes of all but one of the 16 annual meetings of the Pacific Coast Japanese Association Deliberative Council held from July, 1914 to August, 1928.

564. タコマ日本人會　　記錄
Takoma Nihonjinkai. "Kiroku" [Records]. MSS. 2 vols., 1908-1941. Tacoma.

The minutes of meetings, financial reports, budgets, and the Constitution of the Japanese Association of Tacoma from its inception in October, 1908 to December, 1941. Includes membership rosters, newspaper clippings, and incoming correspondence.

565. ユタ州日本人會　　記録
Yuta-shū Nihonjinkai. ["Kiroku" [Records]]. MSS. 48 vols. and 3 notebooks, 1908-1939. Salt Lake City.

The almost complete records of the Japanese Association of Utah from 1908 to 1939. Established first as the Enko-shi Nihonjinkai [Japanese Association of Salt Lake City] in January, 1908, it was renamed the Japanese Association of Utah in February, 1909. The records consist of the following:
"Shinsho kiroku" [Correspondence record], 3 vols., 1909-1922.
"Nisshi" [Daily reports], 18 vols., 1908-1917, 1922-1939.
"Shōmeishō daichō" [Certificate record], 3 vols., 1909-1922.
"Kaiin meibo" [Membership rosters], 8 vols., 1908-1925.
"Chōhei enki shōmeibo" [Draft deferment certificate record], 3 notebooks, 1911, 1921-1922.
"Kifusha hōmeibo" [List of contributors], 1 vol., 1910-1911.
"Nihonjin kyōdō bochi kaikeibo" [Japanese cemetery account book], 1 vol., 1911-1915.
"Kantō Daishinsai gienkin boshūchō" [Records of contributions for the victims of the Kanto Earthquake], 1 vol., 1923.
"Jikyoku shikin shūshi keisanbo" [Expense accounts of emergency funds], 2 vols., 1913-1914, 1921.
"Kaikeibo" [Account books], 11 vols., 1906-1925.

566. ワイルク日本人會　　記録
* Wairuku Nihonjinkai. "Kiroku" [Records]. MSS. 1 box and 2 vols., 1923-1935. Wailuku.

The incomplete membership rosters and miscellaneous documents of the Japanese Association of Wailuku from 1923 to 1935.

567. 華盛頓府日本人會　　記録
Washinton-fu Nihonjinkai. "Kiroku" [Records]. MSS. 3 vols., 1918-1941. Washington, D.C.

An account book of the Japanese Association of Washington, D.C. from its inception in February, 1918 to January, 1932; membership rosters from February, 1919 to February, 1930; and minutes and reports of the activities of the Association from February, 1918 to September, 1941.

568. 在米日本人會　　勘定帳
Zaibei Nihonjinkai. "Kanjōchō" [Account book]. MSS. 1 vol., 1915-1920. San Francisco.

A record of income from monthly dues and certificate fees of the Japanese Association of America from January, 1915 to August, 1920.

X.
Literature and Poetry

1. FICTION AND LITERARY ESSAYS

569. 保阪亀三郎(帰一) 吾輩の見たる亜米利加 下篇
Hozaka Kamesaburō (Kiichi). Wagahai no mitaru Amerika, gehen [America as I saw it, part 2]. Tokyo: Nichibei Shuppan Kyōkai, 1914. 439 pp., illus.

    A satirical work on Japanese immigrant society, the exclusion movement, and U.S.-Japan relations which is an adaptation of the famous Meiji novel by Natsume Sōseki, Wagahai wa neko de aru [I am a cat].

570. 時流
Jiryū [Current]. v. 1:5 (Sep. 1948). Monthly. Los Angeles.

    A general interest magazine of essays, fiction, and some poetry published from April, 1948 to July, 1950 by Takahashi Sozan and his wife, Kyoka.

571. 赫土
Kakudo [Shining Earth]. v. 1:1 (Mar. 1927). Irregular (?). Los Angeles.

    A magazine of prose and poetry published by the Kakudo Society of Los Angeles, a group formed in 1921 to promote the pictorial arts.

572. 鎚
* Kanashiki [The Anvil]. no. 1-3 (Feb., Apr., Oct. 1947). Irregular. Honolulu. Mimeo.

    A literary magazine edited and published by Ōi Tsunehide with essays and poetry as well as sections on flower arrangement, cooking, and the Japanese classics.

573. マグナ
Maguna [Magna]. v. 2:1 (Mar. 1916). Quarterly. Garfield.

    A literary journal of essays, fiction, and poetry published from the spring of 1915 by Japanese laborers employed by the Magna Copper Company refining plant of Utah.

574. NY文藝
N Y Bungei [The New York Bungei]. no. 7 (Dec. 1961). Annual. New York City.

    A magazine of fiction, essays, and some poetry edited by Akiya Ichiro and published since 1955 as the organ of the New York Bungei, a literary group.

575. 永原秀曉 (宵村)　夜に嘆く
Nagahara Hideaki (Shōson). Yoru ni nageku [Lament in the night]. Los Angeles: Sodosha, 1925. 110 pp.

　A novel with the hero as a petty thief and penniless bum. An example of the rarely mentioned Issei "failure."

576. 永田セツ子　松葉杖の老人
Nagata Setsuko (pseud.). Matsubazue no rōjin [An old man on crutches]. Fukuoka: Yuri Kakai, 1949. [3] + 108 pp.

　An anthology of essays and verses. Some essays are on the wartime internment experience. The author's real name is Kanehara Setsu.

577. 永田セツ子　我輩は犬である
Nagata Setsuko (pseud.). Wagahai wa inu de aru [I am a dog]. Fukuoka: Yuri Kakai Honbu, 1952. 276 pp.

　A novel of a Japanese-American family as seen through the eyes of a dog which is another adaptation of the famous Meiji novel by Natsume Soseki, Wagahai wa neko de aru [I am a cat].

578. 南加文芸
Nanka Bungei [Southern California Bungei]. no. 2 (Mar. 1966). Semi-annual. Los Angeles. Mimeo.

　A literary magazine of essays, fiction, and some poetry, first published in September, 1965 and currently still issued.

579.* 霜島武矢　信仰物語・悲しき人間譜 前篇
Shimojima Takeo. Shinkō monogatari: Kanashiki ningenfu, zenpen [A story of faith: A chronicle of a suffering man, part one]. Tokyo: Shimpōsha, 1938. 10 + 111 + 4 pp., photos.

　A novel portraying the conversion to Christianity of a young Japanese in California in the midst of great inner turmoil. Authored by a Christian missionary to Hawaii.

580. 鈴木書一郎 (無絃)　驚き入った母國の社會
Suzuki Kakuichirō (Mugen). Odorokiitta bokoku no shakai [The wonders of Japanese society]. Tokyo: Nimatsudo, 1923. 16 + 10 + 11 + 333 pp., photos.

　A satire of Japanese society through the medium of a wanderer who has just returned to his native land after many years abroad. Comparisons are often made with Japanese immigrant and American society.

581. 田中了々　クレブラの村
Tanaka Ryōryō. Kurebura no mura ["Tale of Culebra Village"]. Garland: Privately printed, 1965. [7] + 91 pp., photo.

　An idealized, fictional account of an agricultural commune attempted by the author in Colorado. Translated into English under the title Tale of Culebra Village (New York, 1967).

2. POETRY

582. 海老原直子　　歌集・オレンヂの沃野
   Ebihara Naoko. Kashū: Orenji no yokuya ["Japanese short poems: Fertile fields of oranges"]. [Tokyo]: Shinsei Shobō, 1961. 171 pp., photo.

   An anthology of tanka composed after the war by a long-time Issei resident of Los Angeles on various subjects.

583. 深野利一郎（春雨）　　春雨句集
   Fukano Riichirō (Shun'u). Shun'u kushū [Collection of haiku by Shun'u]. Seattle (?): Privately printed, 1962. 164 pp., photos, illus.

   A book of verses by Fukano Riichirō (1886-1961) compiled posthumously by his wife. Some 130 of her own verses are included as well as memorial verses and eulogies by friends.

584. 萩尾岩雄（芋作）　　移民のうた
   Hagio Iwao (Imosaku). Imin no uta [An immigrant's song]. Matsuyama: Daikōsha, 1961. [10] + 90 pp., photo.

   A slim volume of simple but moving free-style verses by an Issei farmer commemorating his Golden Wedding Anniversary and 58 years in America.

585. 北米川柳
   Hokubei Senryu [The North American Senryu]. v. 5:12 (Dec. 1950). Monthly. Seattle.

   The monthly organ of the Hokubei Senryū Ginsha [North American Senryu Society] of Seattle edited by Ichikawa Nuisaburō (Dogū). Began in 1946.

586. 本田新次郎（華芳）　　北米川柳
   Honda Shinjirō (Kahō, ed.). Hoku-Bei senryu [North American senryu]. Seattle: Hokubei Senryū Gosenkai, 1935. 4 + 361 pp., photos.

   An anthology of senryu to commemorate the fiftieth meeting of the Hokubei Senryū Gosenkai [North American Senryu Mutual Selection Society] of Seattle founded in 1929.

587. 岩田立枝　　歌集・白薔薇
   Iwata Tatsue. Kashū: Shirobara [White roses: A collection of tanka]. Montebello: Privately printed, 1969. 185 pp.

   An anthology of tanka dedicated to Issei pioneer women by an Issei Christian woman. Includes a short fictional piece, "Issei no tsuma" [An Issei wife], and an English postscript by her son, Masakazu Iwata.

588. 華陽會　　歌集華陽
   Kayōkai. Kashū kayō [An anthology of Kayo tanka]. Seattle: Kayōkai, 1927. [7] + 167 + [7] pp.

   An anthology of tanka commemorating the first anniversary of the Kayōkai [Kayo Tanka Society] of Seattle. Some 580 poems are presented by its members.

589. 華陽會　郡山參泉遺詠
Kayōkai. Kōriyama Sansen iei [Posthumous poems of Kōriyama Sansen]. Seattle: Kayōkai, n.d. [11] pp.

A booklet issued in memory of Kōriyama Tadashi (Sansen) with tanka by the deceased as well as by members of the Seattle Kayo Tanka Society.

590. 松田淑子　　黄なる顔・松田淑子歌集
* Matsuda Yoshiko. Kinaru kao: Matsuda Yoshiko kashū [Yellow face: A collection of tanka by Matsuda Yoshiko]. Tokyo: Shiratama Shobō, 1962. [6] + 156 pp.

An anthology of tanka by an Issei native of Kochi Prefecture and a resident of Hawaii. Composed in the 1950's and 1960's, they are about her life on the islands.

591. 松本登美子　　松本元之助（緑葉）　　歌集・ミシガン湖畔
Matsumoto Tomiko and Matsumoto Gennosuke (Rokuyō). Kashū: Mishigan kohan [By the shores of Lake Michigan: A collection of tanka]. [Tokyo]: Shinsei Shobō, 1960. 158 + 140 + [3] pp., photos.

An anthology of tanka by Matsumoto Tomiko and her husband, Gennosuke, on internment, postwar life in Chicago, their family, and other subjects.

592. 三枝松康雄（城南）　　虹帖
Miematsu Yasuo (Jōnan, ed.). Kōchō [Book of rainbows]. San Francisco: Privately printed, 1952. 74 pp., photo.

An anthology of congratulatory haiku sent to Miematsu Yasuo on the occasion of his 70th birthday.

593. 森田理一（玉兎）　　玉兎句集
Morita Riichi (Gyokuto). Gyokuto kushū [Collection of haiku by Gyokuto]. Allston: Privately printed, 1953. [2] + 302 + [1] pp., photos.

An anthology mostly of senryu composed between 1932 and 1952. A 50-page section of free-form haiku is included. Compiled to mark the author's 61st birthday and his 40-year residence in America.

594. 森田理一（玉兎）　　木槿・森田玉兎・周廿句集
Morita Riichi (Gyokuto). Mukuge: Morita Gyokuto, Shūjo kushū [Rose of Sharon: A collection of short verses by Morita Gyokuto and Shūjo]. Los Angeles: Privately printed, 1962. 294 pp., photos.

An anthology of senryu composed by Morita Riichi in Boston in 1953. Includes haiku written by his wife in Seattle dating back to 1935.

595. 永井元　　永井美い子詩文
Nagai Gen (ed.). Nagai Eiko shibun [Poems and other writings of Nagai Eiko]. San Francisco: Privately printed, 1929. 14 + 33 + 1346 + 29 pp., index, photos.

The collected writings of Nagai Eiko (1866-1928) compiled by her husband. A native of Chiba Prefecture, she came to America in 1902. This collection brings together her literary writings, miscellaneous essays, and "poetic diary," and the three major headings into which it is divided are introduced by biographical essays by her husband.

596. 永見伊都子　歌集・忍冬の花
    Nagami Itoko. Kashū: Suikazura no hana [Honeysuckles: A collection of tanka]. Kure: Nyoran Sanbō, 1955. 6 + 146 pp., photos.

    An anthology of 300 tanka arranged chronologically from 1927 to 1954 on the poet's 30 years in America.

597. 中村梅夫　朶雲
    Nakamura Baifu (pseud., ed.). Daun [Writings]. Denver: Cororado Ginsha, 1947. 58 pp., photos.

    An anthology of haiku, senryu, tanka, and other verse forms by Issei members of the Colorado Haiku Society.

598. 南詠會　歌集・南光
    Nan'eikai. Kashu: Nankō [Southern light: A collection of tanka]. Los Angeles: Nan'eikai, 1934. [2] + 300 + [6] pp., photo, illus.

    An anthology of tanka of the Nan'eikai of Los Angeles to mark its 10th anniversary.

599. みちのひびき
  * Nixon, Lucille M. and Tana, Tomoe (tr.). Michi no hibiki ["Sounds from the unknown: A collection of Japanese-American tanka"]. Denver: Alan Swallow, 1964. xxii + 133 pp.

    English translations of selected tanka with the original Japanese and romanized versions. Includes tanka from throughout the United States, including Hawaii.

600. 岡里忠(早志)　霧の隙・俳句鈔第一輯
    Oka Satotada (Sōshi, ed.). Kiri no sukima: Haikushō, dai-isshū [A glimpse through the fog: A first collection of haiku]. San Francisco: Privately printed, 1924. 79 pp.

    An anthology of free-style haiku composed between 1920 and 1924 by members of the Kiri no Sukima Haiku Circle of San Francisco.

601. レモン帖
    Remonchō [The Lemon Book]. Dec. 1916; Jan., Apr., Jun., Jul., Oct., Nov., Dec. (?) 1917; Feb. (?), Aug. (?) 1918; Jan., Apr., undated issue, 1919. Monthly. Upland.

    Published and edited by Jikihara Toshihei as the organ of the Remon Shisha [Lemon Poetry Society]. A magazine of free-style haiku, with some essays, fiction, and other verse forms, which began around 1915.

602. 佐藤駒吉　アビブの月・在米キリスト教信仰歌集
    Sato Komakichi (ed.). Abibu no tsuki: Zai-Bei Kirisutokyō shinkō kashū [The month of Abib: A collection of Christian religious tanka by Japanese in America]. Hayward: Privately printed, 1951. 21 + 94 + [6] pp.

    An anthology of haiku and some kanshi and tanka by Issei Christians as testaments of Christian faith and belief.

603. 川柳つばめ
    Senryū Tsubame [Swallow]. no. 62, 63 (Aug., Sep. 1952); Jan. 1953; v. 21 (Jan. 1965). Monthly. Los Angeles.

The postwar organ of the Tsubame Ginsha [Swallow Senryu Society] of Los Angeles edited by Kunitsugu Shirō. First published in January, 1940, discontinued during the war years, and then resumed publication in 1946.

604. 島晨吉郎　　　童帳
Shima Shinkichirō. Reichō [Notebook of spiritual verses]. [Los Angeles]: Privately printed, 1958. [4] + 118 pp.

An anthology of religious tanka by an Issei Christian.

605. 島晨吉郎　　　天聲人語
Shima Shinkichirō. Tensei jingo [The voice of heaven, words of man]. [Los Angeles]: Privately printed, 1948 (?). 148 pp.

Same as above.

606. 下山英太郎　　句集・沙漠の旅より
Shimoyama Eitarō. Kushū: Sabaku no tabi yori [From a desert journey: A collection of haiku]. Morioka: Privately printed, 1922. 51 pp.

A small pamphlet of some 250 free-style haiku composed between November, 1916 and May, 1918 by a former resident of Southern California.

607. 下山英太郎　　下山英太郎句集
Shimoyama Eitarō. Shimoyama Eitarō kushū [Shimoyama Eitarō haiku collection]. Los Angeles (?): Privately printed, 1917. 78 pp., photo.

A slim volume of free-style haiku composed from 1914 to 1916 in Southern California.

608. シヤトル短歌會　歌集・レニヤの雪
Shiyatoru Tankakai. Kashū: Renia no yuki [The snows of Mt. Rainier: A collection of tanka]. Tokyo: Chōonsha, 1956. 280 pp., photos.

An anthology of tanka by Issei and Kibei living in Washington and Canada. A photograph and short biography accompany each poet's tanka.

609. 相賀誠　　　渓芳歌集
* Sōga Makoto (ed.). Keihō kashū [A collection of tanka by Keihō]. [Honolulu]: Privately printed, 1957. 10 + 252 pp., photo.

An anthology of 900 tanka arranged in reverse chronological order beginning in 1957 and dating back to 1919 by Sōga Yasutarō (Keihō, 1873-1957). Sōga was a long-time newspaperman in Honolulu associated with the Hawaii Times and its predecessor.

610. たちばな
Tachibana [Orange Tree]. v. 1:2 (Oct. 1926); v. 20:3 (Jul. 1953); v. 23:1, 2 (Jan., Apr. 1956); v. 32:4 (Oct. 1965); v. 33:1, 2 (Jan., Apr. 1966). Quarterly. Los Angeles.

A quarterly of the Tachibana Ginsha [Tachibana Haiku Society] of Los Angeles founded in 1922. Formerly a bi-monthly, the magazine has been a continuous publication since 1930 with the exception of the war years.

611. たちばな吟社　北米句集
Tachibana Ginsha. Hoku-Bei kushu [North American haiku collection]. Los Angeles: Tachibana Ginsha, 1934. [4] + 677 pp., photos.

An anthology of over 11,000 haiku arranged by subject matter into five seasonal categories: the New Year, spring, summer, autumn, and winter. Includes short essays on different topics by members of the Tachibana Haiku Society of Los Angeles.

612. 高橋京香　故山
Takahashi Kyōka. Kozan [Home village]. Kamakura: Sōunsha, 1962. [2] + 8 + 145 pp., photos.

An anthology of 100 free-style haiku. The poet has also included a portion of her husband's diary as well as recollections about his 50 years in America. He was a newspaperman, and together they published a short-lived monthly, Jiryū, in Los Angeles after World War II (see no. 570).

613. 外川明　詩と随想集・蜜蜂のうた
Togawa Akira. Shi to zuisōshū: Mitsubachi no uta [Songs of the honeybee: A collection of poems and essays]. Tokyo: Aporonsha, 1962. 433 pp., photos.

An anthology primarily of free-form poetry interspersed with 20 short essays. Short biographical introductions to each of the 8 major sections recount the author's major activities at different stages in his life. The author, the son of an early Issei, was born in Japan in 1904 and came to the U.S. with his father who had made his first trip 18 years earlier.

614. 東津久仁短歌會　歌集・移植林
Totsukuni Tankakai. Kashū: Ishokurin [Transplanted grove: A collection of tanka]. San Francisco: Totsukuni Tankakai, 1958 (Totsukuni Book no. 2). 339 + English text 58 pp., photos.

An anthology of tanka on a variety of subjects by members of the Totsukuni Tanka Society of San Francisco. Includes the romanized and translated versions of 52 verses, biographical information on members, and a brief history of the society.

615. 常石芝音　北米ホトトギス入選句集
Tsuneishi Shisei (pseud., ed.). Hoku-Bei Hototogisu nyūsen kushū [Collection of haiku from North America published in the Hototogisu]. Hollywood: Tachibana Ginsha, 1951. [4] + 364 + [2] pp.

An anthology of haiku submitted by Japanese immigrants and published in the Hototogisu, a major haiku magazine in Japan, from 1916 to 1943.

616. 保田白帆子　北米ホトトギス入選第二句集
Yasuda Hakuhanshi (pseud., ed.). Hoku-Bei Hototogisu nyūsen, dai-ni kushū [Second collection of haiku from North America published in the Hototogisu]. Los Angeles: Tachibana Ginsha, 1958. 4 + 361 pp.

A sequel to above which reprints Issei haiku published in the Hototogisu from 1947 to 1957.

617. 保田白帆子　北米玉藻入選句集
Yasuda Hakuhanshi (pseud., ed.). Hoku-Bei Tamamo nyūsen kushū [Collection of haiku from North America published in the Tamamo]. Los Angeles: Tachibana Ginsha, 1959. 7 + 412 pp.

An anthology of haiku by members of the Tachibana Haiku Society of Los Angeles published in the Tamamo, a haiku magazine in Japan, from May, 1948 to May, 1958.

618. 安井松乃　　歌集・椰子の蔭
*   Yasui Matsuno. Kashū: Yashi no kage [The shade of the coconut tree: A
    collection of tanka]. Hiroshima: Shinjusha, 1951 (Shinju Book Series no.
    15). 151 pp., photos.

    An anthology of 350 tanka by the third wife of Yasui Satosuke (see
    below) composed between 1934 and 1950. A long-time resident of Maui and a
    Japanese language school teacher.

619. 安井里助（昭宗）　　歌集・銀劍草
*   Yasui Satosuke (Shōsō). Kashū: Ginkensō [Silversword: A collection of
    tanka]. Nagoya: Tanka Zasshi Henshūbu, 1950. 11 + [3] + 200 pp.,
    photos, illus., chronology.

    An anthology of 500-odd tanka by Yasui Satosuke (Shōsō, 1882-1950),
    the publisher and editor of the Maui Shimbun before World War II. Composed
    mainly in the 1940's, there are many poems on World War II and his two sons
    in the 442nd Regimental Combat Team. Includes some short essays.

620. 遊佐敬三（半僕）　　半僕全集
    Yūsa Keizō (Hanboku). Hanboku zenshū [The complete works of Hanboku].
    Santa Maria: Privately printed, 1940. 46 + 66 + 75 + 31 + 532 pp.,
    photos.

    Assorted haiku, tanka, senryu, essays, anecdotes, and "jokes" composed
    by Yusa Keizō, most of which are preceded by headnotes explaining the
    circumstances of composition. In addition, there are sections on: 1)
    the activities and membership of various organizations supporting the Japa-
    nese government in the late 1930's; 2) eulogies in memory of Aratani
    Setsuo; and 3) Issei poetry published in the New Year's edition of
    the immigrant press from 1907 to 1940.

XI.
Newspapers, Periodicals, Yearbooks, Directories, and Who's Whos

Note: Though far from complete, the newspapers listed below comprise the best single collection of Japanese-immigrant-language newspapers published in America. The first known newspaper dates back to 1886. Called the *Shinonome* [Dawn], it was a short-lived, mimeographed publication issued in San Francisco, which was quickly followed by many different publications. Scattered issues of a few of them are included. The most important newspapers are no. 628 and no. 629 for Hawaii, no. 666 for Seattle, no. 650 and no. 662 for San Francisco, no. 638 and no. 656 for Southern California, no. 637, no. 640, and no. 660 for the Rocky Mountain area, and no. 646 for New York City. The English sections of the major newspapers generally began as a significant feature in the early 1930's. The periodical collection is very sketchy; the most valuable yearbook is no. 711. In the annotation of the newspapers and periodicals, we have relied upon Ebihara Hachirō, *Kaigai Hōji Shimbun Zasshishi* [A History of Overseas Japanese Newspapers and Periodicals] (Tokyo: Gakuji Shoin, 1936), and Zaibei Nihonjinkai, *Zai-Bei Nihonjinshi* (see no. 275). Where these two have contradictory information, we have consulted the local and regional histories listed in Chapter IV.

1. NEWSPAPERS

621. アメリカ新聞
Amerika Shimbun ["The America Shimbun"]. v. 1:1-v. 3:82 (Aug. 3, 1929- May 27, 1939). Weekly. San Francisco.

A weekly news tabloid published and edited by Oka Shigeki. Temporarily suspended publication from February, 1931 to January, 1938 save for one issue. Resumed publication with v. 3:1 (Feb. 12, 1938) and ceased with 3:82 (May 27, 1939) when it merged with the Ōfu Nippō (see no. 653). In addition to current affairs, it carries valuable historical information.

622. アメリカ新聞

Amerika Shimbun ["America Shinbun"]. v. 3:1, 2 (May 29, 1957, Nov. 12, 1958). Irregular. San Francisco. (Japanese and English).

A revived postwar version of above which specializes in feature articles on the history of Japanese immigrants.

623. 米國實業時報

Beikoku Jitsugyō Jihō ["The American Industrial Times"]. no. 1 (Dec. 25, 1930). Weekly. Oakland.

A short-lived weekly specializing in agricultural, business, and industrial news. Published and edited by Shō Tatai.

624. 米國産業日報

Beikoku Sangyō Nippō ["The Sangyo Nippo"]. no. 22-1635 (Nov. 27, 1936-Mar. 21, 1942. Daily. Los Angeles. M. (Japanese and English).

Originally published as the Kashu Nōsan Shuhō ["California Farm News"] as the official weekly organ of the Nanka Nōkai Remmei [Southern California Farm Federation] which changed to a daily under the title, Nanka Sangyo Nippo ["The Japanese Industrial Daily"], also known as ["Southern California Japanese Daily"]. From August 5, 1938 it was renamed as the Beikoku Sangyō Nippō under the publisher, Murai Ko. A newspaper which specialized in agricultural and industrial news and which was one of the three Japanese dailies published in Southern California before World War II.

625. 中加時報
+

Chuka Jihō ["The Japanese Times of Central Cal."]. Jul. 1940-Feb. 1942. Weekly. Fresno. M.

A local weekly newspaper established in 1906 by Doi Uchizo which circulated primarily in the Fresno area. Published and edited by different individuals during the life of the paper until its demise in February, 1942.

626. 中央時報

Chuo Jiho ["The Central Times"]. no. 3, 4 (Jan. 1, 15, 1931). Weekly. San Francisco.

A short-lived weekly published by Izutsu Shiro.

627. 同胞

Doho ["Doho"]. no. 13-128 (Feb. 20, 1938-May 4, 1942). Semi-monthly. Los Angeles. M. (Japanese and English).

A leftist journal published and edited by Fujii Shuji.

628. 布哇報知
+*

Hawai Hōchi ["The Hawaii Hochi"]. Jan. 1942-Dec. 1958. Daily. Honolulu. M. (Japanese and English).

One of the two major Japanese newspapers continuously published in Honolulu. A major primary source for the Japanese communities of Hawaii along with the Hawai Taimusu (see no. 629). Established in December, 1912 by Makino Kinzaburō.

629. 布哇タイムス
+* Hawai Taimusu ["The Hawaii Times"]. Jan. 1936-Apr. 1969. Daily. Honolulu. M. (Japanese and English).

    The oldest, continuous Japanese newspaper published in Honolulu. Established on October 15, 1895 as the Yamato, renamed the Yamato Shimbun in August, 1896, and known primarily as the Nippu Jiji ["The Nippu Jiji"] from November 3, 1906 to November 1, 1942. From November 2, 1942 it was renamed the Hawai Taimusu.

630. 北米新報
+ Hokubei Shimpō ["The Hokubei Shimpo"]. Dec. 15, 1945-Dec. 27, 1962. Weekly. New York City. M (1945-1959, incomplete). (Japanese and English).

    A post-World War II weekly tabloid established on November 15, 1945 in New York City and published by the Japanese-American News Corp. Ceased publication on December 27, 1962 and was continued by the Nyūyōku Nichibei (see no. 652).

631. ホクシン
Hokushin ["The Hoku Shin"]. v. 12:4-12 (Feb. 9-Apr. 12, 1924); v. 14:11 (Apr. 3, 1926). Weekly. San Francisco.

    Established in 1913 and published and edited by Soejima Hachiro as the successor to an earlier publication entitled Kokumin Shimbun. From v. 14:11 (Apr. 3, 1926) it was published and edited by Ōsawa Eizō.

632. ほのるる新聞
+* Honoruru Shimbun ["The Honolulu News"]. Mar. 3, 1903. Daily. Honolulu. M.

    One of the early Japanese dailies of Honolulu established in December, 1899 by Kimura Yoshigorō. Ceased publication around 1916 or 1917.

633. JACL Reporter. v. 2:10, v. 3:1 (Oct. 1946, Jan. 1947). Monthly. Salt Lake City.

    A monthly publication of the National Headquarters of the Japanese American Citizens League published from January, 1945 to December, 1950. Edited by Mas Horiuchi with an emphasis on the activities of the National Headquarters.

634. ジャパンヘラルド
+ Japan Herarudo ["The Daily Japan Herald"]. Apr. 19, 1897. Daily. San Francisco. M.

    A lithograph daily established in April, 1897 by Okada Isaburo and others. From June, 1897 it was published under the title Soko Nihon Shimbun ["S.F. Japan Herald"] which became one of the two predecessors of the Nichibei Shimbun.

635. Japanese American Courier. v. 1:1-v. 15:745 (Jan. 1, 1928-Apr. 24, 1942). Weekly. Seattle.

    A second-generation English weekly published and edited by James Y. Sakamoto.

636. 階級戰
Kaikyūsen ["The Class Struggle"]. no. 12 (May 5, 1927). Monthly. San Francisco.

A monthly communist publication established and edited by Kenmochi Sada'ichi in June, 1926. From no. 19 (Mar. 5, 1928) the title changed to the Zaibei Rōdō Shimbun ["The Japanese Worker in America"] as the official publication of the Zaibei Nihonjin Rōdō Kyōkai [The Japanese Worker's Association of America]. From no. 35 (Jan. 10, 1930) it became a semi-monthly under the new title, Rōdō Shimbun ["The Rodo Shimbun"], as the official publication of the Japanese section of the American Communist Party (see Yoneda Papers, no. 893).

637. 格州時事
Kakushū Jiji ["The Colorado Times"]. no. 1-10042 (Feb. 7, 1918-Feb. 10, 1969). Tri-weekly. Denver. (Japanese and English).

In 1918 the Kororado Shimbun and Santō Jiji (see no. 640 and no. 660) merged to form the Kakushū Jiji. Published continuously until February 10, 1969 after which it was absorbed by the Nichibei Jiji (see no. 648). Frequency varied with time. A major primary source for the Japanese communities east of the Rocky Mountains.

638. 加州每日新聞
+ Kashū Mainichi Shimbun ["Japan California Daily News"]. Nov. 5, 1931-Dec. 28, 1968. Daily. Los Angeles. M. (Japanese and English).

One of the three major Japanese daily newspapers of Southern California published during the 1930's. Established on November 5, 1931 and published by Fujii Sei. Discontinued publication during the war years but resumed publication on August 11, 1947.

639. 金門日報
+ Kinmon Nippō ["The Golden Gate News"]. Jan. 17, 30, 1894. Daily. San Francisco. M.

A lithograph daily published from about February, 1893 to July, 1895 by Nagai Hajime and others in San Francisco.

640. コロラド新聞
Kororado Shimbun ["The Colorado Shimbun"]. no. 1-1539 (Feb. 25, 1911-Dec. 20, 1917). Daily. Denver.

The second Japanese language daily published in Denver. Succeeded by the Kakushū Jiji in 1918 (see no. 637).

641. 組合時報
Kumiai Jihō ["The Union Times"]. v. 1:1-2 (Oct. 10-Dec. 10, 1931). Bi-monthly. San Francisco.

The official publication of the Press Workers Union which was organized as a result of the strike by the Nichibei Shimbun employees in 1931. Contains considerable information about the strike from the point of view of the striking workers.

642. 協友時事
Kyoyu Jiji ["The Kyoyu Times"]. no. 78, 82 (Jun. 7, Jul. 31, 1919). Semi-weekly. Salt Lake City.

The official organ of the Rōdō Kyōyūkai [Japanese Labor Fraternity] established in January, 1918 by Japanese laborers in the Salt Lake City area to fight the labor contractor system.

643. 馬哇新聞
* Maui Shimbun ["The Maui Shimbun"]. no. 1-26268 (Jan. 1, 1915-Nov. 28, 1941). Semi-weekly. Wailuku. (Japanese and English).

A semi-weekly established on January 1, 1915 by Kaneko Tetsugo in Wailuku, Maui. Published and edited by Yasui Satosuke from 1920.

644. 南沿岸時報
+ Minami Engan Jihō ["The Southern Coast Herald"]. Jul.-Nov. 1941. Weekly. San Pedro. M.

Established first as the San Pidoro Taimusu [The San Pedro Times] in 1915, it changed its title to the Minami Engan Jihō in 1927 under the publisher, Hiraga Shigemasa. A local newspaper which circulated primarily in the Japanese fishing community of Terminal Island and East San Pedro of Southern California. Published until the outbreak of World War II.

645. 南加時報
Nanka Jiho ["The Nanka Jiho"]. 1934-1941. Weekly. Los Angeles. M (1940-1941).

A current affairs weekly published and edited by Yamada Sakuji of Los Angeles. Began publication around 1922 and ceased with the outbreak of World War II.

646. 日米時報
+ Nichibei Jihō ["The Japanese American Commercial News"]. Oct. 18, 1902-Nov. 29, 1941. Weekly. New York City. M.

Originally established on December 18, 1900 by Hoshi Hajime and Fukutomi Masatoshi as the Nichibei Shūhō ["The Japanese American Commercial Weekly"]. Changed to the Nichibei Jihō in 1920 under Maedagawa Kōichirō.

647. 日米時事
Nichibei Jiji ["The Nichibei Jiji"]. no. 449 (Oct. 29, 1931). Weekly. Los Angeles.

A weekly newspaper published and edited by Ishizaki Senmatsu. Began publication in 1922.

648. 日米時事
Nichibei Jiji ["Nichi Bei Times"]. Nov. 1957-Dec. 1961. Daily. San Francisco. M. (Japanese and English).

One of the two major Japanese newspapers established in the post-World War II period in San Francisco as the lineal descendant of the prewar Nichibei Shimbun (see no. 650). Established on May 18, 1946 and edited by Asano Shichinosuke. Currently still published.

649. 日米毎日
Nichibei Mainichi ["Japanese American Daily News"]. no. 1-354 (Feb. 18, 1966-Jun. 23, 1967). Daily. Los Angeles. (Japanese and English).

A successor to the Shin Nichibei (see no. 661). Published jointly by

Bruce Kaji and Yamada Akiyoshi. From no. 340 (Apr. 7, 1967), it became a semi-weekly tabloid published solely by the latter. Ceased publication in July, 1967.

650. 日米新聞
+ Nichibei Shimbun ["Japanese American News"]. Oct. 25, 1903; May 22, Jul. 4, 10, 11, 13, 19, 1905; Jun. 15, 1918; 1919-Oct. 1930; Mar.-Dec. 1931; Feb. 1932-May 3, 1942. Daily. San Francisco. M. (Japanese and English).

The second oldest, continuous newspaper published in San Francisco. Established on April 3, 1899 by Abiko Kyūtarō, published by him until his death in 1936 and continued by his wife until the outbreak of World War II. A major primary source.

651. The Nikkei Shimin. v. 1:1 (Oct. 15, 1929). Semi-monthly. San Francisco.

The official publication of the New American Citizens League of San Francisco founded on October 19, 1928, a Nisei organization which preceded the establishment of the Japanese American Citizens League. Succeeded by the Pacific Citizen (see no. 654).

652. ニューヨーク日米
+ Nyūyōku Nichibei ["The New York Nichibei"]. Jan. 1, 1963 to date. Weekly. New York City. (Japanese and English).

A weekly tabloid which is a continuation of the Hokubei Shimpō (see no. 630) from January 1, 1963. Currently still published.

653. 櫻府日報
Ōfu Nippō ["Sacramento Daily News"]. no. 348-3422 (May 20, 1909-Jun. 30, 1919); no. 3577-4795 (Jan. 1, 1920-Dec. 27, 1923); no. 9803-9840 (Jun. 16-Jul. 25, 1939); no. 9968 (Jan. 1, 1940); no. 10167, 10266 (Jan. 1, Apr. 28, 1941). Daily. Sacramento.

The oldest, continuous newspaper published in Sacramento. Established in 1907 by Mizutani Bangaku. From 1923 to 1939 it was published by Takeda Hisatarō and Oki Kenji. From May, 1939 until the beginning of World War II it was published by Oka Shigeki. A major primary source for the Japanese communities in the Sacramento area.

654. Pacific Citizen. v. 12:146, 148 (Oct., Dec. 1940); v. 13:149, 152-154,
+ 156, 157, 159 (Jan., Apr.-Jun., Aug., Sep., Nov. 1941); v. 14:161, 162 (Jan., Feb. 1942); v. 15:1 (Jun. 4, 1942) to date. Weekly. Los Angeles.

The official weekly organ of the Japanese American Citizens League. From 1931 the The Nikkei Shimin (see no. 651) changed to the Pacific Citizen and was published as a monthly tabloid until June 4, 1942 when it became a weekly. Before World War II it was issued first in Seattle and then later in San Francisco. From 1942 to 1953 it was issued in Salt Lake City and subsequently in Los Angeles where it is still published.

655. 羅府日米
+ Rafu Nichibei ["Los Angeles Japanese American"]. Oct.-Nov. 1930. Daily. Los Angeles. M.

137

The Los Angeles edition of the Nichibei Shimbun (see no. 650) published by Abiko Kyūtarō from 1922 to 1931.

656. 羅府新報
+ Rafu Shimpō ["The L.A. Japanese Daily News"]. Jul. 1914-Mar. 1942; Jan. 1946 to date. Daily. Los Angeles. M (through 1969). (Japanese and English).

　　　The oldest, continuous Japanese daily in Southern California established in April, 1904. Temporarily suspended publication during World War II and resumed publication on January 1, 1946.

657. 労働
Rōdō ["Labour"]. v. 13:167, 171 (Mar. 10, May 10, 1932); v. 18:298 (Oct. 10, 1937). Semi-monthly. Seattle.

　　　A labor publication published and edited by Miyata Kazue. Began publication in 1920.

658. 労働の力
Rōdō no Chikara ["The Workers' Power"]. v. 1:1 (Jun. 30, 1923). Monthly. New York City.

　　　The official publication of the Nihonjin Rōdō Kyōkai [Japanese Labour Association] of New York City. Edited by Nishimura Yoshio.

659. ロッキー新報
+ Rokkī Shimpō ["The Rocky Shimpo"]. Apr. 22, 1941-Mar. 1944; Jan. 1, 1945-Jun. 6, 1951. Tri-weekly. Denver. M (1941-1944). (Japanese and English).

　　　A local tri-weekly published in Denver and edited by Toda Shirō. Began publication in 1933 and ceased on June 6, 1951.

660. 山東時事
Santō Jiji ["The Santo Times"]. no. 1369-1609 (Mar. 3, 1917-Jan. 26, 1918). Daily. Denver.

　　　The successor to the first Japanese language newspaper, Denba Shimpō [The Denver Shimpo], published in Denver. The title changed in 1917 under the editorship of Nakagawa Kakutarō. Succeeded by the Kakushū Jiji (see no. 637).

661. 新日米
Shin Nichibei ["The New Japanese American News"]. no. 1-5089 (Apr. 5, 1947-Feb. 17, 1966). Daily. Los Angeles. (Japanese and English).

　　　One of the three major Japanese newspapers published in the postwar period in Southern California. Began as a weekly on April 5, 1947 published by Momii Ikken, gradually expanded into a semi-weekly and tri-weekly, until it became a daily from August 1, 1950. From September, 1953 it was published by the New Japanese American News Co., with Saburō Kido as its President. Ceased publication with no. 5089 (Feb. 17, 1966) and was continued by the Nichibei Mainichi (see no. 649).

662. 新世界新聞
+ Shin Sekai Shimbun ["The New World Daily"]. Nov. 4, 5, 1896; Feb. 10, Mar.

11, 1897; 1899-1900; Mar. 1908-Dec. 1941. Daily. San Francisco. M. (Japanese and English).

The first typeset and the oldest continuous Japanese newspaper published in San Francisco. Established on May 25, 1894 by Soejima Hachirō. From September, 1932 to June, 1935 it was entitled Shin Sekai Nichinichi Shimbun and from June 20, 1935 to the outbreak of World War II it was known as the Shin Sekai Asahi Shimbun ["The New World-Sun"]. A major primary source.

663. 桑港時事
+   Sōkō Jiji ["San Francisco Times"]. May 12, Nov. 13-15, 17, 19, 24, 1896; Jan. 5, Feb. 17, Mar. 6, 9, Apr. 15, 22, 23, 29, 1897. Daily. San Francisco. M.

A continuation of no. 664 under a new title (exact month and year of change unknown). Ceased publication sometime after April, 1897.

664. 桑港新報
+   Sōkō Shimpō ["The San Francisco"]. Jun. 16-21, 1893; Jan. 18, 1894. Daily. San Francisco. M.

A lithograph daily established as the Sōkō Shimbun [The San Francisco News] in December, 1892 by Yamato Masao, Watari Tokuji, and others. Changed to the Sōkō Shimpō on May 26, 1893. A publication of former participants in the early liberal movement in Japan living in political exile in San Francisco.

665. 桑港週報
  Sōkō Shūhō ["The San Francisco Weekly"]. v. 14:38, 40, 42-45 (Oct. 9, 23, Nov. 6-27, 1926); v. 15:1-3 (Jan. 1-15, 1927); v. 17:133, 134, 137, 140 (Aug. 24, 31, Sep. 21, Oct. 12, 1929); v. 18:160 (Mar. 15, 1930); v. 19: 220 (May 23, 1931); v. 20:250 (Jan. 1, 1932). Weekly. San Francisco.

A continuation of no. 631 from 1926. Published by Ōsawa Eizō and edited by different individuals, and continued by Nippon to Amerika (see no. 694).

666. 大北日報
+   Taihoku Nippō ["The Great Northern Daily News"]. Jan. 1911-Dec. 1937. Daily. Seattle. (Japanese and English).

One of the two major Japanese newspapers of Seattle published before World War II. Established on January 1, 1910 by Takeuchi Kōjirō and others and published continuously until the beginning of the war. A major primary source.

667. 大衆
  Taishū ["The Taishu"]. v. 21:389 (Oct. 31, 1940); v. 22:428 (Sep. 11, 1941). Weekly. Seattle.

A continuation of no. 657 under a new title.

668. 田鶴時報
  Takoma Jihō ["The Tacoma Japanese Times"]. no. 1569 (Apr. 7, 1932). Weekly. Tacoma.

A local weekly established in May, 1914 by Ōtsuka Shun'ichi. First

139

entitled the Takoma Shūhō [The Tacoma Weekly] which was renamed as the Takoma Jihō in December, 1915. In 1920 it temporarily became a daily; in 1921 it reverted to a weekly under the different title of Jiyū [Liberty], only to be redesignated as the Takoma Jihō in May, 1922. From 1926 to 1934 it was published and edited by Niimura Yasuhiko. Ceased publication in February, 1934.

669. Town Crier. no. 1282-2837 (Jan. 1, 1950-Dec. 31, 1954); no. 3634-4542 (Jan. 2, 1957-Dec. 16, 1959). Daily. Los Angeles. Mimeo.

    A mimeographed one-page Japanese news sheet issued by Akahori Masaru in Los Angeles. Established on July 1, 1946.

670. ユタ日報
+   Yuta Nippō ["The Utah Nippo"]. Jul. 2, 1943 to date. Tri-weekly. Salt Lake City. (Japanese and English).

    The oldest, continuous Japanese newspaper published in Salt Lake City. Established on November 3, 1914 and currently still issued.

2. PUBLISHED NEWSPAPER ARTICLES AND NEWSPAPER CLIPPING FILES

671. 安曇穗明　　　　旅心禮讚
Azumi Suimei (pseud.). Tabigokoro raisan [In praise of peregrination]. San Francisco: Taiheiyō Shobō, 1926. [12] + 256 pp.

    A collection of miscellaneous essays first published in the Nichibei Shimbun in 1924-1925. The author is the publisher and editor of Nippon to Amerika (see no. 694).

672. 藤井整　　米國に住む日本人の叫び
+   Fujii Sei. Beikoku ni sumu Nihonjin no sakebi [The cry of a Japanese living in America]. Los Angeles: Kashū Mainichi Shimbunsha, 1940. 2 + 16 + 420 pp.

    A collection of newspaper articles first published in the Kashū Mainichi Shimbun after the 1937 China Incident on Japanese-American relations, the immigrant community, and American society. The author was the publisher of the newspaper.

673. 藤井整　　N.R.A.の米國
Fujii Sei. N.R.A. no Beikoku [America under the N.R.A.]. Los Angeles: Kashu Mainichi Shimbunsha, 1934. 13 + 486 + 5 pp.

    A collection of miscellaneous newspaper articles first published in the Kashū Mainichi Shimbun in 1933. Edited by Aritomi Toranosuke, they cover President Roosevelt and his New Deal policies, international relations and the League of Nations, Japanese immigrant society; and other topics.

674. 池田貫道　　北米評論切抜
Ikeda Kandō. "Hokubei Hyōron kirinuki" [North American Review clippings].

140

Undated clippings from the Hokubei Hyōron on religion and education (see no. 685).

675.* 勝沼富造　　甘蔗のしぼり滓
   Katsunuma Tomizō. Kansho no shiborikasu [Refuse of processed sugar canes]. Honolulu: Katsunuma Kinen Shuppan Kōenkai, 1924. [6] + 310 pp., photos.

   A collection of miscellaneous essays on the Japanese in Hawaii which first appeared in the Nippu Jiji in 1922.

676. 松下巖　　猫のあくび
   Matsushita Iwao. Neko no akubi [A cat's yawn]. Tokyo: Ichihashi Shobō, 1955. 4 + 8 + 283 pp., photos.

   A collection of miscellaneous essays which first appeared in the Hokubei Hōchi from 1949-1954. Authored by a former Japanese language instructor at the University of Washington, they cover the wartime internment experience, American history and institutions, and other topics.

677. 岡村喜之　　三階の窓から
   Okamura Yoshiyuki. Sangai no mado kara [From the third floor window]. Pasadena: Tōkyōdō Shoten, 1929. 8 + 249 pp.

   A collection of miscellaneous newspaper articles which first appeared in the Rafu Nichibei Shimbun from 1922 to 1928.

678.* 相賀安太郎　　日満を覗く
   Sōga Yasutarō. Nichi-Man wo nozoku [A look at Japan and Manchuria]. Honolulu: Nippu Jijisha, 1935. [12] + 367 pp.

   A collection of newspaper articles which first appeared in the Nippu Jiji based on the author's trip to Japan and Manchuria from the fall of 1934 to the spring of 1935. The author was the editor of the newspaper.

679. 山本麻子　　心のかげ
   Yamamoto Asako (pseud.). Kokoro no kage [Shadow of the heart]. Tokyo: Meiji Shoin, 1939. 5 + 8 + 418 pp., photo.

   A collection of miscellaneous newspaper articles which first appeared in the Kashū Mainichi Shimbun in the 1930's. Some tanka are included. The author's real name is Aoki Hisa.

3. PERIODICALS

680. アメリカ畫報
   Amerika Gahō ["The American Graphic"]. v. 1:2, 6 (Jan. 1, Mar. 1, 1950). Semi-monthly. Los Angeles.

   A pictorial published by Matsumoto Honkō in Los Angeles.

681. 麥領學窓
Bakurei Gakusō ["Berkeley Lyceum"]. no. 8 (1917). Annual. Berkeley.

   The official publication of the Japanese Student Club of the University of California at Berkeley. The first number was issued in 1907. Includes essays on science and art and news of the activities of the club.

682. ガーデナーの友
Gādenā no Tomo ["Turf and Garden"]. no. 47, 53 (Mar., Sep. 1941); May, Aug., 1947; v. 10:12 (Dec. 1965). Monthly. Los Angeles. (Japanese and English).

   The official publication of the Nanka Teiengyō Remmei [Southern California Gardeners Federation] founded in 1937. Began publication in that year and was issued until December, 1941. Scattered issues were published in 1947, but it did not resume official and continuous publication until May, 1956.

683. 藝備人
Geibijin ["The Gei-Bi-Jin"]. no. 162 (Jan. 1928). Monthly. Los Angeles.

   The monthly publication of the Hiroshima Prefectural Association of Southern California. Began publication in January, 1912.

684. 五大州
Godaishū ["The Godaishu"]. no. 60 (Dec. 1, 1968). Monthly. Los Angeles.

   A monthly devoted to Japanese immigrants from Okinawa and their descendants published by Kaneshiro Takeo.

685. 北米評論
Hokubei Hyōron [North American Review]. v. 3:106 (Oct. 11, 1929). Weekly. Oakland.

   A current affairs weekly published and edited by Ikeda Kandō. Began publication in 1926 and continued until the start of World War II.

686. 實業月報
Jitsugyō Geppō ["The Japanese Industrial Report"]. no. 1-3 (Nov. 5, Dec. 5, 1916, Jan. 5, 1917). Monthly. Los Angeles.

   A monthly report published by the Japanese Businessmen's Association of Southern California.

687. 實業の布哇
* Jitsugyō no Hawai ["The Jitsugyo no Hawaii"]. v. 22:5 (May 1933). Monthly. Honolulu.

   A monthly specializing in economic news and the Japanese from Okinawa in Hawaii. Founded in 1911 and published and edited by Tōyama Tetsuo.

688. 加州花卉市場月報
Kashū Kaki Ichiba Geppō [California Flower Market Monthly]. no. 5 (Aug. 5, 1929). Monthly. San Francisco.

   A monthly on floriculture published by the California Flower Market.

689. 南加学窓
Nanka Gakusō ["Japanese El Rodeo"]. 1919. Annual. Los Angeles. (Japanese and English).

An annual published by the Japanese Student Association of the University of Southern California.

690. 南加日商だより
Nanka Nisshō-dayori ["Chamber of Commerce News"]. v. 1:1 (Jul. 15, 1963). Irregular. Los Angeles. (Japanese and English).

A postwar publication of the Japanese Chamber of Commerce of Southern California.

691. 南加商報
Nanka Shōhō ["Nanka Merchant's Bulletin"]. v. 14:9 (Sep. 20, 1939); v. 15: 1, 2, 6 (Jan. 20, Feb. 20, Jun. 30, 1940); v. 16:8, 9 (Aug. 30, Sep. 30, 1941). Monthly. Los Angeles. (Japanese and English).

The monthly publication of the Southern California Japanese Retail Grocers and Merchants' Association.

692. 日米評論
Nichibei Hyōron ["The Japanese American Review"]. v. 21:439 (Sep. 30, 1928); v. 27:489 (Feb. 27, 1935). Monthly. Seattle.

The longest, continuous monthly of the Pacific Northwest on current affairs, established in 1908 by Katayama Kageo.

693. 日米時代
Nichibei Jidai ["The Nichibei Jidai"]. v. 8:9, v. 9:2 (Sep. 1, 1954, Feb. 1, 1955). Monthly. Tokyo.

A postwar monthly newsletter published by Ozawa Takeo on U.S.-Japan relations and Japanese-American society from 1947. Features articles by individuals who returned to Japan prior to World War II but who re-established contacts with Japanese-American society after the war years. Absorbed by the Nippon to Amerika in 1956 (see no. 694).

694. 日本とアメリカ
Nippon to Amerika ["Nippon & America"]. v. 8:9 (Sep. 1938); v. 11:2 (Feb. 1941); v. 10:10 (Dec. 1956); v. 11:5, 6, 8, 9 (May, Jun., Aug., Sep. 1957); v. 15:1, 3, 5, 11 (Jan., Mar., May, Dec. 1961); v. 17:2, 9, 10 (Feb., Sep., Oct. 1963); v. 18:6, 10 (Jun., Dec. 1964); v. 19:1, 2, 5-7, 9, 10 (Jan., Feb., May-Jul./Aug., Oct., Nov. 1965); v. 20:2, 5, 9 (Feb., May, Sep./Oct. 1966); v. 21:1, 9 (Jan., Sep. 1967). Monthly. San Francisco.

A continuation of the Sōkō Shūhō (see no. 665) from 1934. A monthly on U.S.-Japan relations and Japanese-American society edited by Azumi Suimei. Ceased publication with v. 11:2 (Feb. 1941) and resumed publication in December, 1956 by absorbing no. 693 and continuing its numbering.

695. ろすあんぜるす
Rosuanzerusu ["Los Angeles Monthly"]. v. 1:6 (Jun. 1940). Monthly. Los Angeles.

A short-lived current affairs monthly with some fiction published and edited by Sasaki Shūichi (Sasabune).

696. ロスアンゼルス日本貿易懇話会会誌
Rosuanzerusu Nihon Bōeki Konwakai Kaishi ["Japan Traders' Club of Los Angeles"]. no. 1, 3, 5 (1962, 1963, 1965). Irregular. Los Angeles.

The publication of the Japan Traders' Club of Los Angeles on U.S.-Japan economic relations.

697. Scene. v. 2:3, 9 (Jul. 1950, Jan. 1951); v. 3:10, 11 (Feb., Mar. 1952); v. 4:5, 7 (Sep., Nov. 1952); v. 5:3, 4, 6, 13-17 (Jul., Aug., Oct. 1953, Aug.-Dec. 1954); v. 6:1-3, 5-8 (Jan.-Mar., May-Aug. 1955). Monthly. Chicago.

A Nisei monthly edited first by Togo Tanaka and then by Masamori Kojima on Japan, U.S.-Japan relations, and Japanese-Americans. The early issues have a Japanese language section. Began publication in 1949 and ceased with v. 6:8 (Aug. 1955).

698. 商業時報
* Shōgyō Jihō ["The Commercial Times"]. v. 13:5 (May 1933); v. 19:4 (Apr. 1939); v. 20:3, 12 (Mar., Dec. 1940); v. 21:5, 10, 11 (May, Oct., Nov. 1941); v. 22:12 (Dec. 1946). Monthly. Honolulu.

A monthly journal on political, social, economic, and cultural events in and outside of Hawaii published since August, 1921 (temporarily ceased publication from December, 1941 to November, 1946). Published and edited by Tsuchiya Seiichi.

699. 商業會議所月報
Shōgyō Kaigisho Geppō ["Chamber of Commerce Monthly Report"]. no. 1-45, 58 (Feb. 15, 1917-Dec. 25, 1922, May 10, 1924). Monthly. Los Angeles.

The monthly report of the Japanese Chamber of Commerce of Southern California. From issue no. 19 the publication is entitled Nanka Nihonjin Shōgyō Kaigisho Geppō ["The Monthly Report of Japanese Chamber of Commerce of So. California"].

700. 週間日米
Shūkan Nichibei ["The Japanese American Weekly"]. v. 1:1 (Jul. 6, 1929). Weekly. San Francisco.

A weekly publication specializing in articles on the family, education, and the second generation. Began as a weekly supplement to the Nichibei Shimbun in 1928, but became an independent publication with v. 1:1 (Jul. 6, 1929).

701. 在米婦人の友
Zaibei Fujin no Tomo [Women's Companion in America]. v. 11:1 (Jan. 1928). Monthly. Los Angeles.

A women's monthly published and edited by Aratani Ukitarō and Ishikawa Misao. Began publication in May 1918.

4. YEARBOOKS AND SPECIAL PUBLICATIONS

702. 布哇報知　日本語學校勝訴十周年記年誌
* Hawai Hōchi. Nihongo gakkō shōso jūshūnen kinenshi ["Tenth anniversary of the victory of the Japanese language school litigation"]. Honolulu: Hawai Hōchi, 1937. 554 + 5 pp., photos.

    A special 10th anniversary publication commemorating the U.S. Supreme Court decision of February 21, 1927 nullifying Territorial laws regulating foreign language schools. Includes an extended review of the litigation and commemoration events.

703. 布哇報知社　布哇の日本語學校ニ關スル試訴及附帶事件
* Hawai Hōchisha. Hawai no Nihongo gakkō ni kansuru shiso oyobi futai jiken [Japanese language school test case and related events in Hawaii]. Honolulu: Hawai Hōchisha, [1927]. 133 pp., photos.

    An earlier version of above which discusses the origins of the laws, the decision to oppose them in court, the internal community opposition to this decision, and the litigation process.

704. 布哇報知社　布哇日本人年鑑
* Hawai Shimpōsha. Hawai Nihonjin nenkan ["Hawaiian-Japanese annual"]. no. 10, 18, 19 (1912, 1922, 1924). Annual. Honolulu.

    Content varies from issue to issue. In general, each annual contains summaries of the major political and social events in Japan, America, and the world at large as well as Hawaii. A Japanese directory by island is appended which indicates occupation and Prefectural origin.

705. 布哇タイムス社　布哇タイムス創刊六十周年記念号
* Hawai Taimususha. Hawai Taimusu sōkan rokujūshūnen kinengō ["The Hawaii Times 60th anniversary, 1895-1955"]. Honolulu: Hawai Taimusu, 1955. Various paging.

    A special 60th anniversary publication of the Hawaii Times which contains many articles on the history of the Japanese in Hawaii, reminiscences, and biographical sketches.

706. 北米時事社　北米年鑑
Hokubei Jijisha. Hokubei nenkan ["The North American Times year book"]. no. 1, 2 (1910, 1911) and 1936. Annual. Seattle. no. 1, 2 M (imperfect copy).

    Three Hokubei Jiji annuals. The JARP Collection includes microfilms of only Chapter 4, pp. 1-96, of no. 1 on the history of Japanese immigrants; and Chapter 3, pp. 165-260, of no. 2, likewise on Japanese immigrants, and the appended 76-page Seattle directory.

707. 北米毎日新聞社　北米毎日新聞創刊十周年記念号
Hokubei Mainichi Shimbunsha. Hokubei Mainichi Shimbun sōkan jūshūnen kinengō ["Hokubei Mainichi 10th anniversary edition"]. San Francisco: Hokubei Mainichi Shimbunsha, 1960. 197 pp., photos.

    A special 10th anniversary publication commemorating the establishment of the Hokubei Mainichi of San Francisco. Includes some information on the background and history of the newspaper.

708. 實業之布哇　實業之布哇創刊三十周年記念號
 *   Jitsugyō no Hawai. Jitsugyō no Hawai sōkan sanjūshūnen kinengō ["The Jitsu-
      gyo no Hawaii: 30th anniversary edition"]. Honolulu: Jitsugyō no
      Hawai, 1941. 237 + English text 61 pp., photos.

      A special 30th anniversary publication of the Jitsugyō no Hawai, fea-
      turing articles on the worsening relations between Japan and the United
      States and the Japanese population in Hawaii.

709. 日米時事社　移民歸化混合法成立記念號
      Nichibei Jijisha. Imin kika kongōhō seiritsu kinengō ["Equality in citizen-
      ship and naturalization commemoration supplement"]. San Francisco:
      Nichibei Jijisha, 1952. 96 + English text 6 pp., photos.

      A special publication commemorating the passage of the Walter-McCarran
      Immigration and Naturalization Act of 1952.

710. 日米時事社　日米時事十周年記念号
      Nichibei Jijisha. Nichibei Jiji jūshūnen kinengō ["Special tenth anniversa-
      ry supplement of Nichi Bei Times"]. San Francisco: Nichibei Jijisha,
      1956. 64 + English text 8 pp., photos.

      A special publication to mark the 10th anniversary of the Nichibei Jiji,
      one of two postwar Japanese newspapers of San Francisco. Includes articles
      on the history of the newspaper and the postwar Japanese communities of
      Northern California.

711. 日米新聞社　日米年鑑
      Nichibei Shimbunsha. Nichibei nenkan [Japanese American yearbook]. no. 1,
      4, 6-12 (1905, 1908, 1910-1918). Annual. San Francisco. no. 1 X.

      The yearbook of the Nichibei Shimbun. Includes sections on U.S.-Japan
      diplomatic and trade relations, the Japanese communities of the continental
      United States with important statistical data, Japanese and American laws
      and regulations pertinent to Japanese immigrants, and special features. The
      early issues are particularly valuable as historical sources.

712. 日布時事社　布哇年鑑
 *   Nippu Jijisha. Hawai nenkan ["Hawaiian Japanese annual & directory"].
      1932-1933, 1937-1938. Annual. Honolulu.

      Format and content same as no. 704.

713. 櫻府日報社　櫻面都平原・日本人大勢一覽
      Ōfu Nippōsha. Sakuramento Heigen: Nihonjin taisei ichiran [The Sacramento
      Valley: An overview of the Japanese]. no. 2, 4 (1909, 1912). Annual.
      Sacramento. Various paging, photos. no. 2 M.

      An annual published by the Ōfu Nippō. No. 2 has valuable statistical
      and other information on Japanese farmers and laborers and a Who's Who and
      directory; no. 4 consists of biographical sketches and photographs of fifty
      individuals.

714. San Francisco Japanese Chamber of Commerce. Japanese-American trade year
     book. 1918. Annual. San Francisco. A32 + 568 pp., photos, charts.

      A yearbook devoted to U.S.-Japan trade relations.

715. 新世界新聞社　　巴奈馬太平洋萬國大博覽會・第一
Shin Sekai Shimbunsha. Panama Taiheiyō Bankoku Dai-Hakurankai: Dai-ichi ["Panama Pacific International Exposition: No. 1"]. San Francisco: Shin Sekai Shimbunsha, 1912. 2 + 6 + 2 + 377 + directory 204 + English summary 62 pp., plates, maps, photos.

A special publication of the Shin Sekai Shimbun to mark the projected opening of the 1915 Panama Pacific International Exposition.

716. 商業時報社　　布哇在留民御即位大禮奉祝記念帖
* Shōgyō Jihōsha. Hawai zairyūmin gosokui tairei hōshuku kinenchō [Commemoration publication to mark the coronation of the Showa Emperor of the Japanese in Hawaii]. Honolulu: Shōgyō Jihōsha, 1928. 92 pp., photos.

A special publication on the celebration of the Japanese in Hawaii to mark the formal accession of the Showa Emperor.

5. DIRECTORIES

717. Blaine Memorial Methodist Church. Membership directory. 1959-1960. Irregular. Seattle.

718. Buddhist Churches of America. 1964 directory. 1964. Irregular. San Francisco. 46 pp.

719. 中北加廣島縣人會聯盟協會　　中北加廣島縣人會聯盟協會々員名簿
Chū-Hokka Hiroshima Kenjinkai Remmei Kyōkai. Chū-Hokka Hiroshima Kenjinkai Remmei Kyōkai kaiin meibo [Membership roster of the Federated Hiroshima Prefectural Association of Northern and Central California]. 1935. Irregular. San Francisco. 104 pp., photo.

720. 江國甚三　　沙港岡山倶樂部人名簿
Ekuni Jinzō (comp.). Shakō Okayama Kurabu jimmeibo ["Seattle Okayama Club members list"]. 1959-1961. Irregular. Seattle.

721. 福井縣人會　　福井系人住所錄
[Fukui Kenjinkai]. Fukui-keijin jūshoroku [Fukui Prefectural directory]. 1962. Irregular. Los Angeles. [9] pp.

722. ハーバー日系人会　　ハーバー日系人住所錄
Hābā Nikkeijinkai. Hābā Nikkeijin jūshoroku ["Harbor: The Japanese directory"]. 1952, 1960. Irregular. Long Beach. Various paging.

723. Hanasono Photo Studio. Colorado Nihonjin denwacho and business directory. 1946. Irregular. Denver. 160 pp.

724. 廣島縣人会　　廣島縣人会会員名簿
Hiroshima Kenjinkai. Hiroshima Kenjinkai kaiin meibo ["Hiroshima Kenjinkai: Members list"]. 1960. Irregular. Seattle. [36] pp.

725. 北米報知社　　西北部日本人電話帖
Hokubei Hōchisha. Seihokubu Nihonjin denwachō ["The Northwest Japanese American directory"]. 1956. Irregular. Seattle.

　　　北米毎日新聞社　　　　北米毎日年鑑
726. Hokubei Mainichi Shimbunsha. Hokubei Mainichi nenkan, 1964 ["Hokubei Mainichi year book, 1964"]. 1964. Annual. San Francisco. 1131 pp.

　　　北米沖縄クラブ　　全米沖縄系人名住所錄
727. Hokubei Okinawa Kurabu. Zen-Bei Okinawa-kei jimmei jūshoroku [Okinawan directory of America]. 1955, 1958, 1961. Irregular. Los Angeles. Various paging.

　　　北米新報社　　紐育便覽
728. Hokubei Shimpōsha. Nyūyōku benran ["New York Japanese American directory"]. 1948-1949, 1956, 1963-1964. Irregular. New York. Various paging.

　　　　The 1948-1949 issue has a pictorial and written history of Japanese-Americans on the East Coast immediately after World War II.

　　　北米大陸生長の家連絡部　　　生長の家誌友名簿
729. Hokubei Tairiku Seichō no Ie Renrakubu. Seichō no Ie shiyū meibo [Seicho no Ie directory]. 1958. Irregular. [Los Angeles]. 45 pp.

730. JACL. Philadelphia Chapter. Greater Philadelphia area Japanese American residents directory. 1964. Irregular. Philadelphia. 17 pp.

731. JACL. Seattle Chapter. Greater Seattle Japanese telephone directory. 1965. Irregular. Seattle. 31 pp.

732. Japanese Community Council of West Los Angeles. W.L.A. Japanese community directory. 1958. Irregular. Los Angeles. 58 + 62 pp., photos.

733. The Japanese Student's Christian Association in North America. The direc-
*   tory of Japanese students in North America and Hawaii. 1929-1930, 1930-1931, 1934-1935, 1935-1936. Annual. New York City. Various paging.

　　　加州毎日新聞社　　加毎年鑑
734. Kashū Mainichi Shimbunsha. Kamai nenkan ["Year book and directory, 1939-1940"]. Annual. Los Angeles. 28 + 615 pp., photos.

　　　近藤菊次郎　　分類布哇日本人事業家年鑑
735. Kondō Kikujirō. Bunrui Hawai Nihonjin jigyōka nenkan ["Classified Japanese
*   business directory of Territory of Hawaii in English & Japanese, 1940-1941"]. Honolulu: Jigyōka Nenkansha, 1940. 381 pp.

736. Koyasan Buddhist Temple. Telephone directory. 1957, 1959, 1965. Irregular. Los Angeles. Various paging.

737. Los Angeles Japanese Baptist Church. Address list of members and friends. no. 7 (n.d.). Irregular. Los Angeles. 30 pp.

738.　　　　　　南加日本人電話帳
   Nakajima, H. Nanka Nihonjin denwachō ["The tel. & business directory of
   So. Calif."]. no. 34, 37 county and city editions (Mar. 1955, Jan. and
   Nov. 1963). Irregular. Los Angeles. Various paging.

739. 南加福岡縣人会　　　　福岡縣人と其家族
   Nanka Fukuoka Kenjinkai. Fukuoka Kenjin to sono kazoku ["Directory: Fukuoka Kenjinkai"]. 1949, 1955, 1963. Irregular. Los Angeles. Various
   paging.

740. 南加福島縣人会　　　　南加福島縣人住所錄
   Nanka Fukushima Kenjinkai. Nanka Fukushima Kenjin jūshoroku [Southern
   California Fukushima Prefectural Association directory]. 1958, 1962.
   Irregular. Los Angeles. Various paging.

741. 南加廣島縣人会　　　　南加廣島縣人住所錄
   Nanka Hiroshima Kenjinkai. Nanka Hiroshima Kenjin jūshoroku [Southern California Hiroshima Prefectural Association directory]. 1955, 1963. Irregular. Los Angeles. Various paging.

742. 南加熊本縣人会　　　　南加熊本縣人住所錄
   Nanka Kumamoto Kenjinkai. Nanka Kumamoto Kenjin jūshoroku ["Directory:
   Nanka Kumamoto Kenjinkai"]. 1963, 1965. Irregular. Los Angeles.
   Various paging.

743. 南加長野縣人会　　　　南加長野縣人住所錄
   Nanka Nagano Kenjinkai. Nanka Nagano Kenjin jūshoroku [Southern California
   Nagano Prefectural Association directory]. 1956, 1959, 1963. Irregular.
   Los Angeles. Various paging.

744. 南加日系人商業会議所　　南加日系人商業会議所年鑑
   Nanka Nikkeijin Shōgyō Kaigisho. Nanka Nikkeijin Shōgyō Kaigisho nenkan
   [Japanese Chamber of Commerce of Southern California annual]. 1961,
   1965. Annual. Los Angeles. Various paging.

745. 南加岡山系俱樂部　　　　米國太平洋沿岸岡山系人住所錄
   Nanka Okayama-kei Kurabu. Beikoku Taiheiyō Engan Okayama-keijin jūshoroku
   ["Directory: Okayama Kenjin, Pacific area, U.S.A."]. 1964. Irregular.
   Los Angeles. 145 pp., photos.

746. 南加パイオニヤ倶樂部　　會員名簿
   Nanka Paionia Kurabu. Kaiin meibo [Membership roster]. Los Angeles, 1941.
   13 pp.

747. 南加佐賀縣人会　　　　南加佐賀縣人会名簿
   Nanka Saga Kenjinkai. Nanka Saga Kenjinkai meibo [Southern California Saga
   Prefectural Association membership roster]. 1962. Irregular. Los
   Angeles. [8] pp.

748. 南加靜岡俱樂部　　　　南加靜岡縣人名簿
   Nanka Shizuoka Kurabu. Nanka Shizuoka Kenjin meibo ["Directory of Shizuoka-
   ken people in Southern California"]. no. 4, 5 (1961, 1966). Irregular.
   Los Angeles. Various paging, photos.

749. 南加山梨縣人会　　　　南加山梨縣人会住所錄
   Nanka Yamanashi Kenjinkai. Nanka Yamanashi Kenjinkai jūshoroku ["Directory
   of Nanka Yamanashi Kenjinkai"]. 1957. Irregular. Pasadena. 43 + 19
   pp., photo.

750. 南加山梨俱樂部　　　南加山梨俱樂部住所錄
Nanka Yamanashi Kurabu. Nanka Yamanashi Kurabu jūshoroku ["Directory of Nanka Yamanashi Club"]. 1961. Irregular. Pasadena. 68 pp., photos.

751. 日米新聞社　　　日米住所錄
Nichibei Shimbunsha. Nichibei jūshoroku ["The Japanese American directory"]. 1915, 1926, 1941. Annual. San Francisco. Various paging.

752. 日本人社　　　日本人名錄
Nipponjinsha. Nihon jimmeiroku ["The Japanese address book, 1938"]. New York: Nipponjinsha, 1938. 48 pp.

753. 西羅府日系人協議会　　　西羅府日系人住所錄
Nishi Rafu Nikkeijin Kyōgikai. Nishi Rafu Nikkeijin jūshoroku ["W.L.A. Japanese community directory"]. 1958. Annual. Los Angeles. 58 + 62 pp., photos.

754. Northern California Japanese Chamber of Commerce. Directory. 1964. Irregular. San Francisco. [48] pp.

755. Oishi, H. Japanese telephone directory: Seattle and vicinity. 1938, 1939. Annual. [Seattle]. Various paging.

756. 近江クラブ　　大老閧國百年記念・會員名簿
Ōmi Kurabu. Tairō kaikoku hyakunen kinen: Kaiin meibo [The 100th anniversary of the opening of Japan and Ii Naosuke: "Ohmi Club 1960 member list"]. 1960. Irregular. Seattle.

757. パサデナ日系人会　　　巴市日系人電話及住所錄
Pasadena Nikkeijinkai. Pa-shi Nikkeijin denwa oyobi jūshoroku ["The Japanese directory of Pasadena."]. 1956. Irregular. Pasadena. 14 + 112 pp., photos.

758. Pasadena Union Presbyterian Church. 1960 church directory. 1960. Annual. Pasadena. 25 pp.

759. 羅府日系人ホテル・アパート組合　　　羅府ホテル業便覧
Rafu Nikkeijin Hoteru Apāto Kumiai. Rafu hoterugyō benran ["Hotelmen's handbook"]. 1958, 1962. Irregular. Los Angeles. Various paging.

760. ロッキー時報社　　山東諸州日系人電話住所錄
Rokkī Jihōsha. Santō shoshū Nikkeijin denwa jūshoroku ["The Japanese-American telephone & address directory in the Eastern Rockies"]. 1961. Annual. Denver. 200 pp.

761. San Fernando Valley Japanese American Community Center. Annual and directory. 1961-1962, 1964-1965. Annual. Pacoima. Various paging.

762. Seattle Japanese Hotel & Apartment Association. Member's list. 1962. Irregular. Seattle.

763. 新日米新聞社　　　全米日系人住所錄
Shin Nichibei Shimbunsha. Zen-Bei Nikkeijin jūshoroku ["New Japanese

American News year book"]. 1949, 1952, 1955, 1959, 1966. Irregular. Los Angeles. Various paging, photos.

764. 新世界　　新世界アドレスブック
Shin Sekai. Shin Sekai adoresu bukku [The New World address book]. 1923, 1927. Annual. San Francisco. Various paging.

765. 新世界朝日　　新世界朝日年鑑
Shin Sekai Asahi. Shin Sekai Asahi nenkan ["1941 New World-Sun year book"]. 1941. Annual. San Francisco. 646 + Al-18 pp.

766. 鳥取クラブ　　鳥取縣人住所錄
Tottori Kurabu. Tottori Kenjin jūshoroku ["Tottori Club directory"]. 1962. Irregular. [Los Angeles]. 32 pp.

767. Town Crier. L.A. Japanese telephone directory. 1946. Irregular. Los Angeles. 22 pp.

768. The Utah Nippo. New Year's edition; Japanese-American address and telephone directory. 1962, 1967. Annual. Salt Lake City. Various paging.

769. West Los Angeles Community Methodist Church. Membership directory. n.d. Irregular. Los Angeles. [16] pp.

6. WHO'S WHOS

770. 北米報知新聞社　　北米報知南加百人物
Hokubei Hōchi Shimbunsha. Hokubei Hōchi Nanka hyaku jimbutsu [The North American Herald Southern California Who's Who]. Los Angeles: Hokubei Hōchi Shimbunsha, 1922. Al2 + B52 pp., photos.

771. 格州時事　　在米日系人興信録
Kakushū Jiji. Zai-Bei Nikkeijin kōshinroku ["Japanese American Who's Who"]. Denver: Kakushū Jiji, 1959. 345 + 112 pp., photos.

A Japanese-English Who's Who of the Japanese east of the Rocky Mountains. Also includes short essays on the history of the Japanese and a chronology of events from 1942 to 1956. The English section reprints an M.A. thesis by Fumio Ozawa entitled "Japanese in Colorado, 1900-1910" (Denver University, 1954).

772. 松田元介　　御大典記念・防長人士發展鑑
* Matsuda Motosuke. Gotaiten kinen: Bōchō jinshi hattenkan [The accession of the Showa Emperor: A Bocho Who's Who]. Yamaguchi: Santobō, 1932. [14] + 500 + 54 + 229 pp., plates, photos.

A Yamaguchi Prefecture Who's Who which has a section on the Japanese in Hawaii and the continental United States.

773. 松本本光　　加州人物大観・南加の巻
Matsumoto Honkō. Kashū jimbutsu taikan: Nanka no kan [Who's Who in California: Southern California]. Los Angeles: Shōwa Jihōsha, 1929. 6 + 9 + 492 pp., photos.

    A Who's Who in Southern California with extensive biographical information and photographs of close to 400 individuals.

774. 日米新聞社　　在米日本人人名辞典
Nichibei Shimbunsha. Zai-Bei Nihonjin jimmei jiten ["Japanese Who's Who in America"]. San Francisco: Nichibei Shimbunsha, 1922. [2] + 740 pp., plates, index.

    A Who's Who in America with some entries for Canada and Mexico. Organized alphabetically, it provides the following data : genseki, address, date of birth, year of arrival, occupational information, and marital status.

775. 阪本登美男　　ハワイ人物新地図
* Sakamoto Tomio. Hawai jimbutsu shin chizu [A new Who's Who in Hawaii]. Honolulu: Privately printed, n.d. [2] + 127 pp., photos.

776. 新世界新聞社　　在米日本人鑑
Shin Sekai Shimbunsha. Zai-Bei Nihonjinkan [Japanese Who's Who in America]. San Francisco: Shin Sekai Shimbunsha, 1922. 190 pp.

777. 鈴木胖三郎　　二世年鑑
* Suzuki Bansaburō. Nisei nenkan ["Nisei directory and Who's Who, 1939-1940"]. Honolulu: Nenkan Hensankai, 1939. 2 + 76 + 557 pp., photos.

    A Nisei Who's Who and directory. Includes a list of Japanese organizations, descriptions of conditions in Hawaii, and an autobiographical essay by Saigusa Jisaburō, an Issei pioneer and one-time resident of Southern California, in Japanese and English.

778. 戸田申三　　南加之日本人
Toda Shinzō. Nanka no Nihonjin [The Japanese of Southern California]. Tokyo: Hakubunkan, 1919. 4 + 4 + 3 + 16 + 560 pp.

    A Who's Who in Southern California with detailed biographical information organized by Prefectures.

XII.
Autobiographies and Biographies

Note: The autobiographies and biographies listed below provide accounts with which to capture and reconstruct the personal nature of the Japanese immigrant experience. Instead of remaining a nameless mass victimized by racial oppression and exclusion, the Japanese immigrants can be brought to life through these works. Autobiographical accounts of internment life during World War II have been included in this chapter. For additional materials, see Chapters XIII and XVI.

779. 安部清蔵　實生活途上の基督
 Abe Seizō. Jisseikatsu tojō no Kirisuto [Toward Christ in everyday life]. Tokyo: Keiseisha, 1931. 4 + 4 + 504 pp.

   An autobiography of an Issei graduate of Doshisha University who came to America in 1919.

780. 赤木悌二　渡米五十年の足跡
+ Akagi Teiji. To-Bei gojūnen no ashiato [Reflections upon 50 years in America]. Los Angeles: Privately printed, 1966. 346 pp., photos.

   An autobiography of a native of Okayama Prefecture who landed in America in 1907. Since the author is a follower of the Seicho no Ie faith, it is religious in nature. Includes the wartime internment and postwar periods.

781. アナハイムフリーメソヂスト教会　故岡本市兵衛牧師記念証詞集・苦難の僕
 Anahaimu Furī Mesojisuto Kyōkai. Ko-Okamoto Ichibei Bokushi kinen shōshishū: Kunan no shimobe ["In memoriam: Rev. Ernest I. Okamoto, suffering servant"]. Anaheim: Anaheim Japanese Free Methodist Church, 1966. 23 + English text [5] pp.

   A collection of tributes to the life and work of Rev. Okamoto Ichibei.

782. Arai, Kyoko. Holy dreams. [Houston]: Privately printed, 1960. 28 pp., photos.

   An abbreviated English translation of no. 783.

153

783. 新居姜子　　聖夢
Arai Kyōko. Seimu ["Holy dream"]. Houston: Privately printed, 1960. 77 pp., photos.

　　　An autobiography of a Christian Issei and long-time resident of Texas.

784. 有賀千代吉　　加納先生
Ariga Chiyokichi. Kanō Sensei [Rector Kanō]. Tokyo: Sei Mikaeru Shuppansha, 1951. 2 + 2 + 4 + 101 pp., photos.

　　　A biography of Kanō Hisanori, an Issei pioneer in Nebraska. A native of Tokyo, he arrived in America in 1916. A graduate of the University of Nebraska, he was long active as a farmer, civic leader, and rector in the Protestant Episcopal Church.

785. 淺野七之助　　在米四十年
Asano Shichinosuke. Zai-Bei yonjūnen [Forty-years in America]. Tokyo: Yūki Shobō, 1962. 294 pp., photos.

　　　An autobiography of an Issei newspaperman. A native of Iwate Prefecture, he came to America in 1918 and worked primarily for the Nichibei Shimbun before the war and the Nichibei Jiji after.

786. Five Pacific Coast Regional Committees and The Institute of Social and Religious Research. A Survey of Race Relations on the Pacific Coast. 1924-1925. 6 reels.

　　　Selected microfilmed documents of the Survey of Race Relations Research Project headed by Dr. Robert E. Park and deposited in the Hoover Institute Library, Stanford University. Reel no. 1 consists of selected papers, addresses, minutes, and statistical data; reels no. 2-6 contain autobiographical and biographical sketches of Issei and Nisei in Washington and California.

787. 藤岡紫朗　　光夫
Fujioka Shirō. Teruo [Teruo]. Los Angeles: Privately printed, 1951. 52 pp., photos.

　　　A short privately issued booklet dedicated to the memory of the author's fourth son, Teruo (1925-1944), who died in battle in Southern France fighting with the 442nd Combat Team.

788. 福田眞子　　忘れな草
Fukuda Masako. Wasurenagusa [Forget-me-not]. San Francisco: Konkōkyō San Furanshisuko Kyōkai, 1960. [8] + 189 pp., photos.

　　　Eulogies and messages of condolence in memory of the late Bishop Fukuda Yoshiaki (1898-1957) of the Konkokyo Mission.

789. 福田美亮　　抑留生活六年
Fukuda Yoshiaki. Yokuryū seikatsu rokunen [Six-years of internment life]. San Francisco: Konkōkyō San Furanshisuko Kyōkai, 1957. [8] + 135 pp.

　　　An autobiographical account of the author's internment experience. Includes his petition of protest addressed to President Roosevelt. The author was the late Bishop of the Konkokyo Mission.

790. 古屋孫次郎　　日本の使命と基督教
Furuya Magojirō. Nihon no shimei to Kirisutokyō [Christianity and Japan's mission]. Tokyo: Fujiya Shobō, 1939 (2nd printing). 2 + 4 + 6 + 370 pp., photo.

An autobiography of an Issei who first came to America in 1900, who graduated from the Chicago Theological Seminary in 1908, and who was active as a minister in Los Angeles until 1919. At the same time, it is a treatise on Christianity which attempts to harmonize Christian universalism and the particular ultra-nationalism of the 1930's.

791. 池田宣政　　偉人傳文庫・牛島謹爾
Ikeda Nobumasa. Ijinden Bunko: Ushijima Kinji [Great Men Biographical Series: Ushijima Kinji]. Tokyo: Dai Nihon Yubenkai, 1941. 4 + 6 + 344 + chronology 5 pp., illus., map, photos.

A biography of the well known Issei pioneer, Ushijima Kinji (1864-1926), designed especially for young readers. Known in English as George Shima, the Potato King, the subject was a native of the city of Kurume in Fukuoka Prefecture who came to America in 1888. His successful life as a potato grower and community leader is held up as an example to be emulated.

792. 猪野正義　　巨人西原清東
Ino Masayoshi. Kyojin Saibara Seito [Saibara Seitō, The giant]. Tosa: Saibara Seitō Sensei Shōtokuhi Kensetsu Kiseikai, 1964. 168 pp., photos.

A profile of the life of Saibara Seitō (1861-1939), one of the founders of the Japanese rice colony outside of Houston, Texas. A native of Kochi Prefecture and a former member of the Japanese Diet, he came to America in 1902 and studied at the Hartford Seminary before undertaking his pioneer work in rice culture in 1903.

793. 石田天海　　奇術五十年
Ishida Tenkai. Kijutsu gojunen [50-years as a magician]. Tokyo: Asahi Shimbunsha, 1961. 193 pp., photos.

An autobiography of an Issei magician.

794. 岩永友記　　友情の花籠
Iwanaga Tomoki (ed.). Yujo no hanakago [Flower basket of friendship]. Tokyo: Shimpōsha, 1934. 5 + 137 pp., photos.

Short tributes to Major Kobayashi Masasuke, the founder and leader of the Japanese units of the Salvation Army. Includes an autobiographical essay.

795. Japanese American Research Project. "Survey questionnaire files." 55 boxes, 1965-1966.

Files of the completed 73-page questionnaire schedules of the Japanese American Research Project of 1047 Issei on the continental United States who arrived prior to 1924.

796. 賀数著次　　日米開戦当時のイヌ物語
* Kakazu Hashiji. Nichi-Bei kaisen toji no inu monogatari [The story of a "traitor" during the outbreak of World War II]. Kona: Privately printed, 1960. [4] + 99 pp.

An autobiographical account of the author's anti-war stand during the late 1930's and the Japanese community. Also includes his opinions on the occupation and postwar status of Okinawa.

797. 上出雅孝　桑山仙蔵翁物語
Kamide Masataka. Kuwayama Senzō-ō monogatari [The story of Kuwayama Senzō]. Kyoto: Tankō Shinsha, 1963. [4] + 331 pp., photos.

A biography of Kuwayama Senzō, a native of Nagaoka, Niigata Prefecture. Arriving in America in 1901, he lived continuously in New York City, working in the retail merchandising and restaurant businesses.

798. 金城武男　沖縄移民の父・當山久三
* Kaneshiro Takeo (ed.). Okinawa imin no chichi: Tōyama Kyūzō [The father of Okinawan immigrants: Tōyama Kyūzō]. Los Angeles: Privately printed, 1959. 6 + 71 + English text 33 pp., photos.

A collection of tributes in memory of Tōyama Kyūzō (1868-1910), a native of Okinawa who was the pioneer of Okinawan immigrants to Hawaii and the continental United States.

799. 加納久憲　在米生活四十五年
Kanō Hisanori. Zai-Bei seikatsu yonjūgonen [Forty-five years of life in America]. [Tokyo]: Naigai Jōsei Chōsakai, 1962 (?). 58 pp., photos.

A brief autobiography of Kanō Hisanori (see no. 784).

800. 笠井博翁夜話刊行委員会　笠井博翁夜話
Kasai Hiroshi-ō Yawa Kankō Iinkai. Kasai Hiroshi-ō yawa [Fireside chats with Kasai Hiroshi]. Yokohama: Kasai Hiroshi-ō Yawa Kankō Iinkai, 1955. 58 pp., photos.

The opinions of Kasai Hiroshi, a native of Yamanashi Prefecture and a long-time resident of the Rocky Mountain region, on diverse topics. Includes an autobiographical sketch.

801. 樫谷純郎　恩寵の跡
Kashitani Junrō (ed.). Onchō no ato [After grace]. Los Angeles: Taiheiyō Engan Nikkeijin Furī Mesojisuto Nenkai, 1961 (2nd printing). 6 + 3 + 202 pp., photos.

Personal tributes and recollections by fellow ministers, friends, and laymen dedicated to Rev. Shigekawa Yoshimasa, a native of Ehime Prefecture who came to America in 1904. Includes a short autobiography.

802. 河田拳　放浪十年
Kawada Ken. Hōrō jūnen [Ten years of wandering]. Santa Barbara: Dokuritsu Kyōkai Shuppanbu, 1914. 4 + 311 pp., photos. X.

A collection of miscellaneous essays which are autobiographical in nature and religious in content by an Issei Christian minister. Includes selected diary entries from 1905 to 1911.

803. 河井義貞　明光の歩み
Kawai Yoshisada. Myōkō no ayumi [Light's journey]. Mitsugi: Kurenaisha, 1961. [4] + 22 + 159 pp., photos.

A religious autobiography of an Issei Christian and native of Hiroshima Prefecture.

804. 河上清　　祖國日本に訴う
Kawakami Kiyoshi. Sokoku Nihon ni uttau [An appeal to my native land: Japan]. Tokyo: Jiji Tsūshinsha, 1966. 334 pp.

　　A reprint of an earlier work published in 1949 under the title Bei-Sō tatakawaba: Sokoku Nihon ni uttau. Though essentially a work on postwar international relations, it includes a brief autobiographical chapter in which the author, a well known Issei journalist, reminisces about his motives for coming to America in 1901, discusses his early political philosophy, and finally touches upon Katayama Sen's activities in America during his last stay.

805. 形影生　　米國苦學實記
Keieisei (pseud.). Beikoku kugaku jikki [An authentic account of a working student in America]. Tokyo: Naigai Shuppan Kyōkai, 1911. 3 + 6 + 227 pp. M.

　　Written in a light vein, stressing unusual and humorous incidents, this autobiographical account narrates the author's experience as a school boy, dishwasher, kitchen helper, and cook, mainly in the San Francisco area.

806. 菊地賢治　　相墨久治氏の憶出
Kikuchi Kenji (ed.). Aizumi Hisaharu-shi no omoide [In memory of Aizumi Hisaharu]. Hollywood: Privately printed, 1967. [2] + 30 pp. Mimeo.

　　Short tributes by friends and relatives in memory of Aizumi Hisaharu (1886-1967), a native of Niigata Prefecture and a long-time resident of San Diego.

807. 北河慶次郎　　八十年の生涯と恩寵の數々
Kitagawa Keijirō. Hachijūnen no shōgai to onchō no kazukazu [An 80-year lifetime and its many blessings]. Kyoto: Hie Shobō, 1965. 236 pp., photos.

　　A religious autobiography of an Issei who came to America in 1902 and graduated from the Stanford University Medical School in 1919.

808. コイデ・ジョー　　ある在米日本人の記録
Koide Jō. Aru zai-Bei Nihonjin no kiroku [Record of a Japanese in America]. v. I-II. Tokyo: Yūshindō, 1967 and 1970. 261 pp. and 3 + 10 + 366 pp., plates.

　　An autobiography of an Issei leftist, a native of Tokyo and a graduate of Aoyama Gakuin. The first volume covers the period prior to World War II and includes his years in the Soviet Union; the second treats his wartime internment experience and his service to the American government from 1944.

809. 柑本雄二郎　　あたまのTV
Kojimoto Yūjirō. Atama no TV [A mental TV]. Gardena: Privately printed, 1964. 110 pp., plate.

　　Random autobiographical thoughts of an Issei native of Wakayama Prefecture.

810. 古庄豊　　井上角五郎君略傳
Kojō Yutaka. Inoue Kakugorō-kun ryakuden [Summary of the life of Inoue Kakugorō]. Tokyo: Inoue Kakugorō-kun Kōrō Hyōshōkai, 1919. [2] + [2] + chronology 12 + 212 + 4 pp., photos. M.

A biography of Inoue Kakugoro. Under the influence of Fukuzawa Yukichi, Inoue came to America in 1887 with 30 Hiroshima brethren with the intent of establishing a permanent Japanese colony. Though it lasted for less than a year, his pioneering attempt was an early significant episode.

811. 久布白落實　　父と良人
Kubushiro Ochimi. Chichi to otto [Father and husband]. Tokyo: Tokyo Shimin Kyōkai, 1936. [2] + 13 + 509 pp., photos.

Two interrelated biographies, one of the author's father, Rev. Okubo Shinjiro (1855-1914), and another of her husband, Rev. Kubushiro Naokatsu (1879-1921). Her father was an active Christian leader and minister from 1904 to 1914 in Northern California, while her husband was a minister for a short spell in Seattle.

812. 牧野金三郎伝編纂委員會　　牧野金三郎伝
* Makino Kinzaburo Den Hensan Iinkai. Makino Kinzaburo den ["Life of Kinzaburo Makino"]. Honolulu: Makino Michiye, 1967 (2nd printing). 143 + 160 pp., photos.

A Japanese-English biography of Frederick Kinzaburo Makino (1877-1953), the founder, publisher, and editor of the Hawaii Hochi and an active leader of the Japanese community.

813. 松田午三郎　　松田静子
Matsuda Umasaburo. Matsuda Shizuko [Matsuda Shizuko]. San Francisco: Nichibei Shimbunsha, 1924. 4 + 4 + 12 + 2 + 688 + 260 + 31 pp., photos.

A biography of the author's wife, Shizuko (1879-1922), dedicated to her memory. A native of Akita Prefecture, she married the author in 1906 and came with him to America in that same year. Includes letters and messages of condolence.

814. 三苫藤七　　三苫芳江　　在米六十年の回想
Mitoma Toshichi and Mitoma Yoshie. Zai-Bei rokujūnen no kaisō ["Recollections of 60 years in America"]. Tokyo: Kirisuto Shimbunsha, 1970. [4] + 255 pp., photos.

An autobiography of Mitoma Tōshichi, a native of Fukuoka Prefecture who came to America in 1907. Includes selected diary entries.

815. 中河頼覺　　曄子
Nakagawa Yoriaki. Akiko [Akiko]. Seattle: Privately printed, 1933. 11 + 13 + 6 + 265 + English text 33 pp., photos.

An informal biography of Nakagawa Akiko (1922-1933) by her father. English eulogies by her friends and teachers are included.

816. 日本神學
Nihon Shingaku ["The Japanese Shinto Theology"]. v. 19:12 (Dec. 1967).

A special issue of the Nihon Shingaku devoted to the life and memory of Sekiguchi Nobara (1888-1967), the noted Issei writer on religious subjects. A native of Niigata Prefecture, he was a long-time resident of Southern California.

817. 新里貫一　　鷲のごとく
Niisato Kan'ichi. Washi no gotoku [Like an eagle]. Los Angeles. Niisato Kan'ichi, 1955. 122 pp., photos.

An autobiographical sequel to no. 818.

818. 新里貫一　　闇に閃く聲なき聲
 Niisato Kan'ichi. Yami ni hirameku koe naki koe [Silent voices lighting the darkness]. Tokyo: Shimpōsha, 1934. 4 + 5 + 175 pp., photos.

   An autobiography of a devout Issei Christian. A long-time resident of Southern California, the author became blind in 1921. This account concentrates upon this and other tragic events which struck him, his Christian interpretation of them, and his firm resolve to work on behalf of the Japanese Christian churches.

819. 櫻府隠士　　在米成功の日本人
 Ōfu Inshi (pseud.). Zai-Bei seikō no Nihonjin [Successful Japanese in America]. Tokyo: Hōbunkan, 1904. 2 + 2 + 14 + 228 pp. M.

   Biographical sketches of successful Japanese, including Nakazawa Kanae of Santa Rosa; Ushijima Kinji, the Potato King of Stockton; Yoshiike Hiroshi, a horticulturist of Oakland; Ban Shinzaburō, a labor contractor of Portland; Inose Inosuke of Los Angeles; and Noda Otojirō of Watsonville. Also includes profiles of individuals who established the Japanese community of Florin.

820. 翁久允(六溪)　　金色の園　　高志人
 Ōkina Hisamitsu (Rokkei). "Konjiki no sono" [The golden garden], no. 6, 20, 26, Kōshijin, 23:8 (Aug. 1958), 3-13; 25:1 (Jan. 1960), 3-12; 25:9 (Sep. 1960), 3-17.

   The incomplete serialized autobiography of Ōkina Hisamitsu. Includes his life in America for about a quarter of a century as a journalist and literary figure in California and Washington.

821. 奥村多喜衛　　恩寵七十年
* Okumura Takie. Onchō shichijūnen [70 years of grace]. Honolulu: Privately printed, 1935. 124 pp., photos.

   An autobiography of Okumura Takie (1865-1951), a prominent Issei Christian minister. A native of Kochi Prefecture and a graduate of Doshisha, he arrived in Hawaii in 1894. As the founder and minister of the Makiki Church, he played a leading role in the Japanese community.

822. 奥村多喜衛　　信仰五十年
* Okumura Takie. Shinkō gojūnen [50-years of belief]. Honolulu: Privately printed, 1938. 52 pp., photo, chronology.

   An autobiographical sequel to above which covers the author's conversion to Christianity in 1888 while still in Japan, his decision to become a minister, and his life as a minister in Hawaii.

823. 大谷尚文　　白雲に希望は輝く
 Ōtani Naofumi. Hakuun ni kibō wa kagayaku [Hope shines upon a white cloud]. Minneapolis: Nikkeijin Gōdō Kirisuto Kyōkai, 1964. 5 + 244 pp., photo.

   An autobiography of an Issei Christian minister.

824. 佐々木脩一(ささぶね)　　ハリウッドの畸人・田中柊林
 Sasaki Shūichi (Sasabune). Hariuddo no kijin: Tanaka Shūrin [Hollywood's eccentric: Tanaka Shūrin]. Los Angeles: Taishūsha, 1938. 4 + 6 + 441 pp., photos.

   An informal biography of the Southern California poet, Tanaka Masaharu

(Shūrin), who was associated with the Tachibana Haiku Society of Los Angeles. Includes reminiscences by his friends and son as well as haiku and kanshi by Tanaka himself.

825. 佐々木修一（ささぶね）　抑留所生活記
Sasaki Shūichi (Sasabune). <u>Yokuryūjo seikatsuki</u> [A chronicle of internment life]. Los Angeles: Rafu Shoten, 1950. 559 pp., app., photos, illus.

An autobiographical account of the wartime internment experience by an Issei who was first interned at Fort Missoula, Montana and then at Amache, Colorado.

826. 佐々木修一（ささぶね）　あめりか生活
Sasaki Shūichi (Sasabune). <u>Amerika seikatsu</u> [Life in America]. Los Angeles: Taishūsha, 1937. 496 pp., photos.

Random autobiographical essays on people whom the Issei author met and events which occurred during his life in America. Includes four short fictional pieces and some verses.

827. 関口野薔微　アメリカで活躍した35人の日本人
Sekiguchi Nobara. <u>Amerika de katsuyaku shita sanjūgonin no Nihonjin</u> [Thirty-five Japanese who were active in America]. Tokyo: Uritani Yukihiro, 1967. 164 pp.

Biographical sketches of 35 Issei and Nisei in America.

828. 志垣武次郎　病床の慰安
Shigaki Bujirō. <u>Byōshō no ian</u> [A solace to sickness]. Los Angeles: Shigaki Bujirō, 1956. [2] + 119 pp.

A religious autobiography of an Issei Christian, a native of Kumamoto Prefecture and a member of the Japanese Holiness Church.

829. 白川咲　故白川長一郎昇天一周年記念誌
Shirakawa Saku (ed.). <u>Ko-Shirakawa Chōichirō shōten isshūnen kinenshi</u> [Booklet commemorating the first anniversary of the death of the late Shirakawa Chōichirō]. Los Angeles: Shirakawa Saku, 1953. 48 pp., photo.

A Christian booklet marking the first anniversary of the death of Shirakawa Chōichirō (1878-1952), a native of Aichi Prefecture and a former long-time resident of Los Angeles.

830. 相賀安太郎　鐵柵生活
* Soga Yasutarō. <u>Tessaku seikatsu</u> ["Life behind the barbwires"]. Honolulu: Hawaii Times, 1948. [12] + 390 + app. 20 pp., photos.

An autobiographical account of internment life by the former editor of the <u>Hawaii Times</u>. The 20-page appendix consists of a roster of Japanese from Hawaii who were interned.

831. 須々木榮　圖入回顧五十年
Susuki Sakae. <u>Zuiri kaiko gojūnen</u> ["My 50 years in America"]. Hollywood: W.M. Hawley, 1959. [3] + 224 pp., illus.

An autobiography of a native of Okayama Prefecture who came to America in 1898. A long-time resident of Los Angeles, the author studied medicine at the University of Southern California and later in Berlin. Includes 133 sketches by the author who was commonly known by his Anglicized name, Dr. Peter M. Suski.

832. 高橋理可　　江藤為治翁小傳
Takahashi Ayaka. Etō Tameji-ō shōden [Short biography of Etō Tameji]. Los Angeles: Privately printed, 1956. 28 pp., photo. Mimeo.

A brief, handwritten biography of Etō Tameji, a native of Kumamoto Prefecture who came to America in 1902 after two years in Hawaii. A pioneer in the San Luis Obispo area, he was a floriculturist, founder of the Co-operative Farm Industry of Southern California, and active in many other capacities in the Japanese community of Southern California.

833. 東ヶ崎菊松　　主に導かるるまま
Tōgasaki Kikumatsu. Shu ni michibikaruru mama [The Lord as my guide]. Tokyo: Inochi no Kotobasha, 1958. 19 pp., photo.

An autobiographical booklet of a pioneer Issei Christian.

833.1. 冨本岩雄　　無名白書
Tomimoto Iwao. Mumei hakusho [Anonymous white paper]. Tokyo: Kokusai Heiwa Sangyōkai, 1954. xxvi + 297 pp., photos.

Biographical sketches of John Aiso, Hiroshi Miyamura, Ben Kuroki, and Mike Masaoka; interviews with Fujioka Shirō and Mike Masaoka; and profiles of 300-odd Issei and Nisei. Includes brief essays on the exclusion movement, internment, and the second generation.

834. 冨本岩雄　　唐変木
Tomimoto Iwao. Tōhenboku [Blockhead]. Tokyo: Kokusai Heiwa Sangyōkai, 1961. 14 + 282 + 14 + 44 + 56 + 246 pp., photos.

Divided into three sections, this volume includes: 1) essays on U.S.-Japan relations, emphasizing the postwar period; 2) biographies of former Admiral Nomura Kichisaburo and Sasamori Junzō, the former Secretary of the Central Japanese Association of Southern California, and sketches of 45 Issei or other Japanese who have had connections with the Japanese immigrant community; and 3) an autobiographical account of the author's life in America during the first quarter of this century. Since he was a newspaperman during his American sojourn, he relates many interesting anecdotes about the immigrant press and the people involved with it.

835. 鶴谷次郎吉　　風波を越えて八十年
Tsurutani Jirōkichi. Fuha wo koete hachijūnen [Weathering the storm for 80 years]. Kobe: Hyōgo Kenritsu Awaji Nōgyō Kōto Gakkō, 1963. [2] + 8 + 282 pp., photos.

Selected letters addressed to the students of the Awaji Agricultural High School written by an Issei native of the island of Awaji in Hyogo Prefecture who came to America in 1901, relating the author's life and experiences in America.

836. 山本麻子　　茨ある白道
Yamamoto Asako (pseud.). Ibara aru hakudo [Hardships in a barren land]. n.p.: Privately printed, 1952. 5 + 264 pp.

A diary of the wartime internment experience of a former Japanese language teacher and contributor to the Kashū Mainichi. The diarist's real name is Aoki Hisa.

837. 山室武甫　在米同胞先覺小林政助伝
Yamamuro Buho. Zai-Bei dōhō senkaku Kobayashi Masasuke den [Seer among the Japanese in America: The life of Kobayashi Masasuke]. Tokyo: Yamamuro Gunpei Senshū Kankōkai, 1963. [8] + 378 pp., photos.

A biography of Major Kobayashi Masasuke, an early Issei pioneer who arrived in America in 1902 and who established Japanese units of the Salvation Army beginning in 1919. Includes reprints of his sermons and lectures and reminiscences of his friends and associates.

838. 横山源之助　海外活動之日本人
* Yokoyama Gennosuke. Kaigai katsudo no Nihonjin [Active Japanese abroad]. Tokyo: Shōkadō, 1906. 2 + 2 + 12 + 245 pp. M.

A book relating the story of the Japanese throughout the world through biographical sketches of selected individuals. Chapter I, pp. 1-20, covers the continental United States and provides profiles of Akabane Chūemon, Chinda Sutemi, and Abiko Kyutarō; Chapter VI, pp. 146-161, is on Hawaii and Japanese laborers.

XIII.
Personal Papers

Note: The major personal papers are no. 840, no. 849, and no. 857. The others vary in size and significance; many contain autobiographical and biographical materials. When biographical data are known and are appropriate, they are supplied preceding the annotations. For additional personal papers relating to the wartime internment, see Chapter XIV.

839. ABIKO PAPERS, 1968. 1 folder.

   A 15-page biography of Abiko Kyutaro by his son, Yasuo William Abiko.

840. AKAHORI FAMILY PAPERS, ca. 1908-1965. 40 boxes and 2 oversize scrapbooks.

   Akahori Masaru (赤堀最, 1884-   ). Journalist, businessman, and author. A native of Tokushima Prefecture who arrived in 1904. Secretary, Sacramento Valley Japanese Association and Placer County Japanese Association, and the Sacramento reporter, Nichibei Shimbun, from 1908 to about 1915; English editor, Japanese Chamber of Commerce, San Francisco, 1916-1917; reporter, Hokubei Hochi, Los Angeles, 1917-1919; reporter, Yomiuri Shimbun, Tokyo, 1919-1922; legal counsellor, Los Angeles, 1924-1933; editor, Taihoku Nippo, Seattle, 1934-1941; internee, Ft. Missoula, Montana, Lordsburg and Santa Fe, New Mexico, and Crystal Lake, Texas, 1941-1945; publisher, Town Crier, Los Angeles, postwar period. Pen names: Bennosuke (辨之助) and Oishi Hyoroku (大石兵六); also known in English as Ben M. Akahori. Christian; married, one daughter. Wife, Akahori Kiku (赤堀菊, nee Ishizuka (石塚), 1900-1961). A native of Kanagawa Prefecture who arrived in 1921. Formerly, Hosaka (穂坂) by first marriage. Divorced, 1928, and remarried, 1935.
   Family papers: 49 diary books and 7 notebooks, 1910-1965; extensive autobiographical materials; family correspondence file; 5 large scrapbooks and files of newspaper clippings of articles by Akahori, ca. 1910-1965; internment camp correspondence and papers, 1941-1946. Business records and papers: files of legal counselling office, 1924-1933; materials and documents relating to the Town Crier, 1946-1965; materials for projected but never published Who's Who publications; and other miscellaneous financial and legal papers.

841. ASHIZAWA PAPERS, ca. 1900-1965. 1 box.

   Ashizawa Riichi (芦澤雁一, 1882-   ). Photographer-merchant, San Francisco. A native of Yamanashi Prefecture who arrived in 1899.

Twenty-five photographs from about 1898 to 1916 and two manuscripts of his autobiography.

842. CHINO PAPERS, 1921-1964. 1 folder and 2 oversize scrapbooks.

Chino Tsuneji (茅野恒司, 1881-1964). Farmer, Southern California. A native of Nagano Prefecture who arrived in 1905. Prominent in agricultural and other community organizations, and active in the legal battles against the 1913 and 1920 California Alien Land Laws. Biographical sketches and two scrapbooks of newspaper clippings about him.

843. FUJII PAPERS, n.d. 1 folder.

Fujii Yoshito (藤井美人). Biography unknown. A Japanese manuscript on the Japanese hotel and apartment businesses of Seattle from the early 1890's to 1932, and biographical sketches of his father and older brother.

844. FUJIOKA PAPERS, ca. 1954-1959. 1 box.

Fujioka Shirō (藤岡紫朗, 1878-1957). Journalist, author, and community leader, Southern California. A native of Aomori Prefecture who arrived in 1897. Associated with the immigrant press in New York City, Seattle, and Los Angeles. Active as the one-time Secretary of the Central Japanese Association of Southern California. Historical sources, the partial manuscript, and newspaper clippings regarding the publication of Ayumi no ato (see no. 264).

845. HACHIMONJI PAPERS, 1918-1955. 1 box and 2 oversize scrapbooks.

Hachimonji Kumezō (八文字粂蔵, 1888-1956). Merchant-agricultural specialist, Southern California. A native of Miyagi Prefecture. Graduate, Tōhoku Gakuin. Arrived in 1918. Graduate, Columbia University, B.S. Owner, Valley Seed Company, El Monte, California, before World War II. Known as K. Hatchmonji. Memoirs, diary, newspaper clippings, letters, and scrapbooks.

846. HANAYA PAPERS, n.d. 1 folder.

Hanaya Koan (花谷小庵). Hawaii-born Nisei and itinerant railroad laborer in Idaho, Montana, Nevada, and Utah. An incomplete autobiographical account in Japanese of his experiences as a railroad laborer in the early 1900's.

847. HIBI PAPERS, 1893-1952. 1 box, 1 oversize scrapbook, 1 portfolio, and 42 paintings.

Hibi Matsusaburō (比日松三郎, 1886-1947). Artist. A native of Shiga Prefecture. Studied, Hosei University, Kyoto, 1905. Arrived in 1906. Attended California School of Fine Arts, San Francisco, 1919-1930. Taught art and Japanese. Resident Director, Topaz Relocation Center Art School, 1942-1945. Popularly known as George M. Hibi. 62 letters to his older brother in Japan from 1906 to 1931, elementary and middle school records, internment camp scrapbook, prints, sketches, and 42 oil paintings from 1942-1945, exhibition catalogues, and other miscellaneous papers.

848. HIDEKAWA PAPERS, 1961. 1 folder.

    Hidekawa Motohiko (秀川元彦). Biographical sketches of members of the Okayama Prefectural Association of San Francisco and a list of its officers before World War II.

849. HOSHIMIYA FAMILY PAPERS, 1901-1968. 14 boxes.

    Hoshimiya Tosuke (星宮外介, 1886-1970?). Japanese language school principal and teacher, Southern California. A native of Miyagi Prefecture. Graduate, Tōhoku Gakuin. Arrived in 1906. Principal of schools in Brawley, Moneta, Torrance, El Segundo, and Los Angeles before World War II. Interned at Lordsburg, New Mexico and Granada, Colorado. Japanese language instructor, University of Michigan, 1945-1946. Continued as a Japanese language school teacher after the war; also Secretary, Pasadena Japanese Community Center. Devout and active Christian. Wife, Hoshimiya Sadayo (星宮貞代, nee Nagai (永井), 1890-1968). A native of Miyagi Prefecture. Also a Japanese language school teacher. Arrived in 1914. Married, 1915; three children.
    Personal correspondence from the early 1930's to 1968, Japanese language school instructional materials, scattered and incomplete Japanese Christian church bulletins, income tax files from 1949 to 1964, detailed records of personal property during World War II, and miscellaneous records of naturalization, the Japanese Hospital of Los Angeles, and the Pasadena Japanese Community Center.

850. IWASAKI PAPERS, 1899-1945. 4 boxes.

    Iwasaki Yasukichi (岩崎安吉, 1876-   ). Farmer, Hillsboro, Oregon. A native of Shiga Prefecture. Arrived first in Vancouver, B.C. in 1899 and entered America in 1901. Briefly worked as a railroad worker in Missoula, Montana, a cannery worker in Anacortes, Washington, and a hotel manager in Tacoma. In 1904 he farmed in Auburn, moved to Sumner in 1906, and then settled down in Hillsboro in 1913. Interned at Minidoka, Idaho. 29 diary books from 1899-1900 and 1917-1945 and 2 handwritten autobiographical sketches.

851. JIKIHARA PAPERS, ca. 1906-1929. 6 boxes.

    Jikihara Toshihei (直原敏平, 1869-1929). Farmer, inventor, hermit-poet, Southern California. A native of Okayama (arrival year unknown). Resident of Upland. Publisher and editor of Remonchō (see no. 601). Business-farming records; diaries, 1909-1929; numerous autobiographical manuscripts; personal correspondence, 1916-1929; and other incidental papers.

852. KAGIWADA BROTHERS PAPERS, 1919-1947. 12 boxes and 1 oversize account book.

    Kagiwada Eiho (鍵和田榮保, 1895-   ). Insurance agent, Los Angeles. A native of Kanagawa Prefecture who arrived in 1914. Agent, Sun Life Assurance Company of Canada. Known as Frank E. Kagiwada. Brother, Kagiwada Yoshifusa (鍵和田芳房, 1898-   ). Partner in the insurance business. Known as Harry Y. Kagiwada. Approximately 500 folders of Canada Sun Life Japanese policyholders, 1924-1941; business records and other miscellaneous papers.

853. KANEHARA PAPERS, 1950-1963. 6 folders.

      Kanehara, Setsu (1916-   ). Poet and author. Kibei, born in Oakland, California. Graduate, girl's middle school, Miyazaki Prefecture. Returned to America in 1936. Pen name, Nagata Setsuko (永田セツ子). Letters from Issei poets and writers.

854. KANEKO PAPERS, ca. 1908-1954. 1 scrapbook.

      Kaneko Yosaburō (金子與三郎 , 1881-   ). Merchant, Utah. A native of Tokyo who arrived in 1904. A long-time resident of Ogden, Utah and active community leader. Newspaper clippings and personal mementoes of his life and family.

855.* KANO PAPERS, n.d. 1 folder.

      Kano, Toshiyuki (1914-   ). Hawaii-born Kibei. Former military intelligence officer in the Japanese military. Brief English recollections of his reactions to Japan's attack on Pearl Harbor and his experiences during World War II.

856. KASAI BROTHERS PAPERS, 1956-1963. 1 scrapbook and 1 folder.

      Kasai Kenji (笠井健治 , 1893-   ). Security broker, San Francisco. A native of Yamanashi Prefecture who arrived in 1915. Former head, Kasai Security Co., San Francisco, before World War II. Postwar President, Nikko-Kasai Security Co., and President, Japanese Chamber of Commerce of Northern California. Kasai Juji (笠井重治 , ca. 1877-   ). Journalist, orator, politician, and older brother. Arrived in 1903 at the age of 14. Graduate, University of Chicago, B.A., and Harvard University, M.A. Postwar President, Japan-American Cultural Society, Tokyo. An unpublished autobiography of Kasai Kenji together with the biography of his older brother, and a scrapbook of Kasai Jūji.

857. KASAI FAMILY PAPERS, 1904-1965. 7 boxes and 2 oversize scrapbooks.

      Kasai Yoshihiko (笠井喜彦 , 1890-   ). Insurance agent, Salt Lake City. A native of Yamanashi Prefecture who arrived in 1904. Agent, New York Life Insurance Co. Officer, Japanese Association of Utah; active member, JACL. Interned. Known as Henry Y. Kasai. Alice Kasai (ca. 1915-   ). Wife and Nisei. Married around 1937. Chairman, Nisei Victory Committee, Salt Lake City, 1944-1945. Active member, JACL.
      Autobiographical sketches and other biographical data, 1904-1965; personal correspondence, 1925-1965; financial and business records, 1913-1966; wartime internment papers; Nisei Victory Committee documents, including approximately 250 letters from Nisei soldiers, 1944-1947; and other papers.

858. KAWABE PAPERS, 1966. 1 folder.

      Kawabe Sotaro (川部惣太郎). A brief, handwritten essay on the history of the Japanese in Alaska.

859. KAWAKAMI FAMILY PAPERS, ca. 1906-1944. 1 folder and 1 scrapbook.

Kawakami Kiyoshi (河上清 , 1873-1949). Journalist, political commentator, and author. A native of Yamagata Prefecture who arrived in 1901. Kawakami, Clarke H. (1909-   ). Nisei, son. Former correspondent, Domei News Agency. Correspondence relating to the father's brief detention from December, 1941 to February, 1942, copies of 16 magazine and newspaper articles, and other incidental papers. Also 1 scrapbook of Clarke H. Kawakami of newspaper clippings and personal mementoes.

860. KAWAMURA PAPERS, n.d. 1 folder.

Kawamura Masahei (河村政平). Japanese language school principal and teacher, Isleton, California. Pen name, Yūsen (幽川). Xeroxed copies of 4 Japanese manuscripts on the early history of the Japanese.

861. KIKUCHI PAPERS, 1968. 1 folder.

Kikuchi, Miya S. (1902-   ). Nisei, born in Kauai, Hawaii. Graduate, University of California, B.A., 1930. Editor, English Section, Nichibei Shimbun. An autobiographical account of her visits to Japan and the prominent Japanese with whom she came into contact.

862. KIYOHARA PAPERS, 1896-1964. 2 boxes.

Kiyohara Danzō (清原団蔵 , 1881-1964). Businessman, Southern California. A native of Kumamoto Prefecture who arrived in 1894 when he was 14 years old. Attended public schools in Oakland and the University of California. Active in business ventures, including oil drilling in Texas and Southern California. Member of many Japanese-American organizations. English diaries, 1906-1908; correspondence relating to the Japanese-American Fraternity of Los Angeles, 1913-1914; the Japanese American League of Los Angeles, 1915-1917; the Japan Society of Los Angeles, ca. 1923-1926; and the Japan American Society of Los Angeles, 1913-1937; and other papers, including 2 photo albums.

863. KODAMA PAPERS, ca. 1967. 2 folders.

Kodama Hosoe (児玉細江 , nee Yoshikawa (吉川), 1895-   ). Teacher, flower arrangement and tea ceremony. A native of Yamaguchi Prefecture who arrived in 1919. Married to Kodama Kinsuke (児玉金助 , 1887-   ). A long-time resident of Seattle. A scrapbook containing an autobiography in Japanese, newspaper clippings, and photos.

864. KOGA PAPERS, 1903-1936. 1 folder.

Koga Gentarō (古賀源太郎 , 1883-   ). Farmer, Utah. A native of Saga Prefecture who arrived in 1903. Farm contracts, landing records, tax files, and other miscellaneous papers.

865. MARUMOTO PAPERS, ca. 1968. 1 folder.
    *

Marumoto, Masaji. Associate Justice, Supreme Court, Hawaii. Xeroxed copies of documents relating to the gannen-mono deposited in the Archives of Hawaii. Correspondence exchanged between Eugene M. Van Reed and the Foreign Ministries of the Hawaiian Monarchy and Japan, 1865-1869, the minutes of the Hawaiian Board of Immigration, 1868-1870, and the related diplomatic correspondence of the American and British Legations in Japan, 1868-1871.

866. MASAOKA PAPERS, 1942-1970. 9 boxes.

Masaoka, Joe Grant (1909-1970). Nisei, born in Fresno, California and raised in Salt Lake City. Regional Director, JACL, Public Relations Consultant, and Japanese American Research Project Administrator. Documents on the Sue Ishida alien land law escheat case, 1927-1966; correspondence and allied documents relating to George and Tom Oishi's claims against the Redevelopment Agency, City of Richmond, California, 1961-1964; legal briefs of cases involving Japanese-Americans, 1942-1961; and papers on the Japanese American Research Project and miscellaneous items.

867. MATSUMOTO PAPERS, 1941. 1 folder.

A valuable carbon copy of an English report on the economic history of Japanese immigrants in California from the early 1900's to 1940. Prepared by Tsuyoshi Matsumoto for the Central Japanese Association of Southern California.

868. MIHARA PAPERS, n.d. 1 binder.

Mihara Tokinobu (三原時信, 1897-   ). Newspaperman, Japanese language school teacher, author, San Francisco. A native of Ehime Prefecture. Graduate, Waseda University, B.A., 1920. Arrived in 1920. Became blind while interned at Heart Mountain. An autobiographical English manuscript entitled "Guided by my white cane."

869. MIKURIYA PAPERS, 1964-1965. 2 folders.

Mikuriya Tadafumi (三厨タダフミ, 1899-   ). Civil Engineer, East Coast. A native of Saga Prefecture. Graduate, Kumamoto Engineering College. Arrived in 1923. Graduate, University of Pennsylvania, B.S., 1926, and M.S., 1927. Business correspondence and a 50-page autobiographical manuscript in English.

870. MIYAGISHIMA PAPERS, 1960. 1 folder.

Miyagishima Nonkibō (宮城島吞気坊). A valuable Japanese manuscript on the socio-economic history of the Japanese in the Rocky Mountain region dating back to 1884. The author is unknown (Nonkibō is a pen name).

871. MURAKAMI PAPERS, 1929-1941. 1 box.

Murakami Noboru (村上昇, 1889-1958). Businessman, Los Angeles. A native of Hiroshima Prefecture who arrived in 1907. Secretary, Japanese Hotel and Apartment Association of Southern California. 9 diary books, 1929, 1933-1938, and 1940-1941; and a few letters, ca. 1936-1941.

872. NIIMURA PAPERS, 1922-1965. 1 folder.

   Niimura Eiichi (新村英一). Dancer-choreographer, New York City. A native of Nagano Prefecture who arrived in 1922. From 1932 he performed in the major theaters of America, Europe, Asia, and Africa. Director, "61," Ballet Arts School of Carnegie Hall. Popularly known as Yeichi Nimura. Concert press releases, a chronological table of concert tours and productions from 1937-1965, and magazine articles about Niimura and reviews of his performances.

873. NISHIMURA PAPERS, ca. 1919-1947. 1 box.

   Nishimura Yoshio (西村義雄 , 1875-1947). Laborer, socialist, and newspaperman. A native of Nara Prefecture. Arrived around 1906. Editor, Kyōyū Jiji (see no. 642) and Rōdō no Chikara (see no. 658). Reporter, Ōfu Nippō (see no. 653), 1939-1941. Pen name, Kantaishi (関太子). Letters, including some from Katayama Sen in Moscow, ca. 1928-1931, newspaper clippings of articles by Nishimura, and other miscellany.

874. NISHIOKA PAPERS, 1953-1961. 3 folders.

   Nishioka Ryōichi (西岡良一 , 1887-   ). Sales clerk and bookkeeper, Southern California. A native of Hiroshima Prefecture who arrived in 1906. Graduate, University of California, M.S. Zoology, ca. 1924. 39 letters from relatives in Japan.

875. OBATA PAPERS, 1965. 1 folder and 1 large painting.

   Obata Chiura (小圃千浦 , 1884-   ). Artist. Professor Emeritus of Art, University of California, Berkeley. A native of Iwate Prefecture who arrived in 1903. Biographical sketches in English and Japanese.

876. OI PAPERS, 1906-1966. 1 box and 1 oversize scrapbook.

   Ōi Matsunosuke (大井松之助 , 1885-   ). Jeweler-merchant, Southern California. A native of Kochi Prefecture who arrived in 1906. Active as an officer of various Japanese Associations. Founding member of the postwar Japanese Chamber of Commerce of Southern California. Three autobiographical manuscripts, internment scrapbook and papers, documents on the postwar Japanese Chamber of Commerce of Southern California, and other miscellany.

877. OKA PAPERS, ca. 1914-1957. 2 boxes.

   Oka Shigeki (岡繁樹 , 1878-1959). Mover, printer, newspaper publisher, socialist, and author. A native of Kochi Prefecture. Employed by the Yorozu Chōhō before arriving in 1902. Operated the Kinmon Press in San Francisco and published the Amerika Shimbun (see no. 621 and no. 622) and Ōfu Nippō (see no. 653). Interned at Heart Mountain but released to work for the U.S. government in India. 1 diary book, 1914; sources and manuscripts for a projected biography of Abiko Kyūtarō; Japanese newspaper clippings, and other miscellaneous personal papers.

878. PACKARD PAPERS, ca. 1921-1962. 1 folder.

   Packard, Mrs. Everett T. (1867-1968). A native of Charlemont, Massachusetts and a long-time resident of Fox Island near Tacoma, Washington.

Established friendly relations with the Japanese of Tacoma and Seattle. Newspaper clippings, photos, and papers.

879. SHIBUYA PAPERS, 1959-1960. 1 folder.

   Shibuya Kinkichi (澁谷欽吉, 1885-   ). Businessman, Utah and Southern California. A native of Fukushima Prefecture who arrived in 1920. Miscellaneous business and personal correspondence.

880. SHIGENO PAPERS, n.d. 1 folder.

   Shigeno Kinzuchi (繁野金槌, 1881-   ). Farmer, Moses Lake, Washington. Arrived in 1905. An autobiographical manuscript.

881. SHIGETOME PAPERS, 1965. 1 folder.

   Shigetome Tomejirō (重留留次郎, 1887-   ). Restaurateur, Los Angeles. A native of Kagoshima Prefecture who arrived in 1906. A 20-page autobiography.

882. SHIMA PAPERS, 1894-1965. 3 boxes.

   Shima Shinkichirō (島展吉郎, 1877-   ). Cactus nurseryman, Southern California. A native of Fukuoka Prefecture who arrived in 1894. Poet and devout Christian. Materials, notes, and drafts of Reichō and Tensei jingo (see no. 604 and no. 605); 1 diary book, wartime internment papers, and other miscellany.

883. SHIMIZU PAPERS, 1964. 1 folder.

   Shimizu Tōru (清水透). A summary history of the Jordan Dōshikai of Utah in English and Japanese. Originally established as a farmers' association in 1919.

884. SUSUKI PAPERS, ca. 1941-1961. 2 boxes and 1 oversize folder.

   Susuki Sakae (須ヶ木榮, 1875-1961). M.D., linguist, and author. A native of Okayama Prefecture who arrived in 1898. Photographer until 1913. Graduate, U.S.C. Medical School, 1917; additional studies at Berlin University. Practiced medicine in Southern California. Catholic. Commonly known as Dr. Peter M. Suski. Papers on his interest in Far Eastern studies, an English manuscript version of Zuiri kaiko gojūnen (see no. 831), and newspaper clippings.

885. SUTO PAPERS, ca. 1905-1964. 2 boxes and 1 oversize package.

   Sutō Kōtarō (須藤幸太郎, ca. 1883-1963). Nurseryman, Miami, Florida. A native of Kanagawa Prefecture who arrived in 1900. Miami resident since 1917. Personal correspondence, miscellaneous business records, English newspaper clippings, and photos.

886. TAGUCHI PAPERS, 1909-1935. 2 boxes.

Taguchi Kichimatsu (田口吉松 , 1881-   ). Merchant, Rocky Ford, Colorado. A native of Yamaguchi Prefecture who arrived in Hawaii in 1900 and transmigrated to the mainland in 1904. Colorado resident from about 1908. Miscellaneous business records and account books.

887. TAKAHASHI PAPERS, ca. 1940-1955. 1 scrapbook.

Takahashi Chiyokichi (高橋千代吉 , ca. 1870-   ). Tailor and bonsai grower, Berkeley. A native of Hiroshima Prefecture who arrived in 1896. A scrapbook of photos, newspaper clippings, and mementoes.

888. TOYOTA FAMILY PAPERS, ca. 1905-1965. 2 boxes.

Toyota Seitarō (豊田静太郎 , 1885-1959). Labor contractor, McGill, Nevada. A native of Hiroshima Prefecture who arrived in 1905. Operated the Japanese labor camp, Nevada Consolidated Copper Corporation, Ruth and McGill, Nevada, 1912-1941. Interned during World War II. Also known as Fred S. Toyota. Wife, Toyota Kame (豊田カメ , nee Tetsumura (鐵村), 1894-   ). A native of Hiroshima Prefecture who arrived in 1917. 4 children. Biographical materials on the entire family, internment camp correspondence, documents relating to Toyota Kame's efforts to seek restitution for losses incurred during her husband's internment, and other papers.

889. TSUDA PAPERS, ca. 1939-1962. 5 folders and 3 scrapbooks.

Tsuda Yasaburō (津田彌三郎). Christian minister. A native of Yamaguchi Prefecture. Served in Japanese Methodist churches in California and Washington. A brief essay on the Florin Japanese Methodist Church, copies of sermons, letters of commendation, and three scrapbooks of newspaper clippings.

890. YAMAGUCHI PAPERS, n.d. 1 folder.

Yamaguchi Tadashi (山口正 , 1887-   ). Businessman-importer, Seattle. A native of Fukui Prefecture who arrived in 1906. Former active member of the Japanese Associations of Bellingham, Tacoma, and Seattle. A brief autobiographical essay.

891. YAMASHITA PAPERS, 1943-1962. 1 scrapbook.

Yamashita Kihei (山下喜平 , 1885-   ). A native of Hiroshima who arrived in 1906. A long-time resident of Salinas, California. Personal mementoes of his life.

892. YASUI FAMILY PAPERS, ca. 1908-1945. 6 boxes and 1 oversize package.
*

Yasui Satosuke (安井里助 , 1881-1949). Journalist and Japanese language school teacher, Wailuku, Maui. A native of Hiroshima Prefecture. Graduate, Hiroshima Normal School. Arrived in Hawaii in 1907. Publisher, Maui Shimbun, 1920-1941 (see no. 643). Pen name, Shōsō (昭宗). Active in community affairs. Yasui Matsuno (安井松乃). Wife, Japanese language school teacher, and poet. Diary, 1910-1934 and 1939-41; Maui Shimbun Company log, 1925-1930; poems, letters, and memorabilia.

893. YONEDA PAPERS, ca. 1928-1970. 1 box.

Yoneda, Kāru (米田カール, 1906-   ). Longshoreman, communist, and author. Kibei, born in Glendale, California. Went to Japan in 1913 and returned to America in 1926. Active as a labor organizer, editor, and political activist in Southern and Northern California and Alaska. Interned at Manzanar and served in U.S. armed forces. Commonly known as Karl Yoneda; alias Karl Hama. Incomplete issues of leftist newspapers and periodicals published in the 1930's, including the Sōkō Taimusu, Zaibei Rōdō Shimbun, Rōdō Shimbun, and Dōhō; political pamphlets and leaflets; and miscellaneous personal papers on his activities, speeches, and articles.

XIV.
World War II
and Internment

Note: Japanese-Americans underwent their bitterest experience in the World War II internment. Many studies have been produced on this topic, treating the constitutional question, the responsible pressure groups, the War Relocation Authority, the organization and management of specific internment camps, and other facets. Few, if any, examine the experience from the Issei perspective. The mimeographed newspapers and other publications listed below offer this perspective. Autobiographical accounts of internment life are included in Chapter XII. The special numbers of no. 954 correspond to the classification scheme of the evacuation and resettlement documents deposited in the Bancroft Library of the University of California, Berkeley, and readers are referred to Edward N. Barnhart, *Japanese American Evacuation and Resettlement* (Berkeley: University of California, General Library, 1958).

1. ASSEMBLY CENTER AND CAMP NEWSPAPERS

894. Communiqué. no. 1-27, 29-41 (Oct. 23, 1942-Jan. 15, 19-Feb. 26, 1943). Tri-weekly. Denson. Mimeo.

895. Crystal City Times. v. 1:4-6 (Nov. 13-27, 1944); v. 2:32 (Aug. 13, 1945); v. 3:1, 3 (Jan. 2, 21, 1946). Weekly. Crystal City. Mimeo.

896. デンソン時報
 Denson Jihō ["Denson Jiho"]. no. 1-12, 14-24, 28, 30 (Dec. 8, 1942-Jan. 15, 22-Feb. 26, Mar. 12, 19, 1943). Tri-weekly. Denson. Mimeo.

897. Denson Tribune. v. 1:4, 6 (Mar. 12, 19, 1943). Tri-weekly. Denson. Mimeo.

898. **Desert Sentinel.** v. 1:4, 5, 15 (Nov. 30, Dec. 24, 1942, Jun. 21, 1943); v. 2:2 (Oct. 8, 1943); Oct. 22, Nov. 5, Dec. 22, 1943, Jan. 14, 24, 1944. Bi-weekly. Rivers. Mimeo.

899. **Gila News Courier.** v. 1:1, 2, 8, 9 (Sep. 12, 16, Oct. 7, 10, 1942); v. 2:4, supplement 3-5, 74, 76 (Jan. 9, Feb. 11-Mar. 27, Jun. 22, 26, 1943); v. 3: 4, 6, 9, 13 (Aug. 31, Sep. 4, 11, 21, 1943). Tri-weekly. Rivers. Mimeo.

900. **Granada Pioneer.** v. 1:1-v. 3:91 (Oct. 28, 1942-Sep. 15, 1945). Incomplete. Tri-weekly. Amache. Mimeo.

901. **Heart Mountain Sentinel.** v. 2:1, 10, 28 (Jan. 1, Mar. 6, Jul. 10, 1943); v. 3:33A, 42 (Aug. 12, Oct. 14, 1944); v. 4:22 (May 26, 1945); supplement no. 260, 261, 286, 353, 359 (Dec. 18, 19, 1944, Mar. 15, Oct. 9, 23, 1945). Weekly. Heart Mountain. (English and Japanese).

902. 比羅時報
 Hira Jihō ["Gila News Courier"]. no. 1-135 (Oct. 7, 1942-Sep. 11, 1943). Incomplete. Tri-weekly. Rivers. Mimeo.

903. 自治會時報
 Jichikai Jihō [Jichikai Times]. no. 1-455 (Jul. 9, 1943-Apr. 11, 1946). Incomplete. Daily. Crystal City. Mimeo.

904. **Manzanar Free Press.** v. 1:1-v. 2:1 (Apr. 11-Jul. 22, 1942). Incomplete. Tri-weekly. Manzanar. Mimeo.

905. **The Mercedian.** no. 1-20 (Jun. 9-Aug. 21, 1942); Souvenir edition, Aug. 29, 1942. Semi-weekly. Merced. Mimeo.

906. **The Minidoka Irrigator.** v. 3:2-6, 11-20 (Mar. 6-Apr. 3, May 8-Jul. 10, 1943). Weekly. Hunt. Mimeo.

907. パイオニア
 Paionia [The Pioneer]. v. 1:6-v. 3:85 (Oct. 30, 1942-Sep. 1, 1945); special editions, Sep. 5, 20, 1945. Incomplete. Tri-weekly. Amache. Mimeo.

908. **Rohwer Outpost.** v. 1:1-v. 7:5 (Oct. 24, 1942-Jul. 21, 1945). Semi-weekly. Rohwer. Mimeo.

909. **Rohwer Relocator.** v. 1:1-28 (May 5-Nov. 9, 1945). Incomplete. Irregular. Rohwer. Mimeo.

910. 朗和時報
 Rōwa Jihō ["Rohwer News"]. v. 1:1-4, v. 2:4-v. 7:37 (Dec. 12, 1942-Jan. 6, 1943, Jan. 13, 1943-Nov. 14, 1945). Tri-weekly. Rohwer. Mimeo.

911. ローズバーグ時報
 Rōzubāgu Jihō [The Lordsburg Times]. no. 1-247 (Aug. 26, 1942-Jun. 11, 1943). Incomplete. Daily. Lordsburg. Mimeo.

912. Santa Anita Pacemaker. Apr. 1-Oct. 7, 1942. Semi-weekly. Santa Anita.
  +   Mimeo. M.

913. サンタフェ時報
     Santa Fe Jihō [The Santa Fe Times]. no. 1-200 (Jul. 1, 1943-Feb. 24, 1944).
       Incomplete. Daily. Santa Fe. Mimeo.

914. Tanforan Totalizer. no. 1-19 (May 15-Sep. 12, 1942). Weekly. Tanforan.
       Mimeo.

915. 轉住時報
     Tenjū Jihō ["Relocation News"]. no. 3-23 (Jun. 2-Sep. 28, 1945). Incomplete.
       Irregular. Topaz. Mimeo. (Japanese and English).

916. トパーズ時報
     Topāzu Jihō ["Topaz Times News Daily"]. v. 1:1-v. 12:5 (Oct. 29, 1942-
       Aug. 31, 1945). Incomplete. Irregular. Topaz. Mimeo. (Japanese and
       English).

2. OTHER PUBLISHED WORKS

917. 赤堀最   ローズバーグ時報の内容と時報同人の消息・新約聖書概論
     Akahori Masaru (ed.). Rōzubāgu Jihō no naiyō to Jihō dōjin no shōsoku;
       Shinyaku Seisho gairon ["The Lordsburg Times and its staff"; "Life of
       Saint Paul"]. Lordsburg, 1943. 12 + 16 pp. Mimeo.

       Two unrelated items. The first is about the Lordsburg internment camp
     newspaper written by Kasai Kenji, and the second consists of lectures on
     the life of St. Paul by Rev. Kamae Takashi.

918. Downing, Ferne (ed.). Cactus blossoms. Pasadena, 1945. [22] pp., illus.
       Mimeo.

       English poems by Nisei students of Butte High School, Gila, Arizona.

919. 藤島泰輔   忠誠登録
     Fujishima Taisuke. Chūsei tōroku [Loyalty registration]. Tokyo: Yomiuri
       Shimbunsha, 1967. 292 pp., bibliog.

       A journalistic account of wartime internment.

920. グラナダ吟社   グラナダ吟社俳句集
     [Guranada Ginsha]. Guranada Ginsha haikushū [Granada Haiku Society collec-
       tion]. Amache, 1945. 106 pp., illus. Mimeo.

       An anthology of haiku written in 1944-1945 by members of the Granada
     Haiku Society to commemorate the closing of internment camps.

921. ハートマウンテン文藝
     Hāto Maunten Bungei ["Heart Mountain essay and poetry booklet"]. Dec. (?)
       1943; Mar., Jul., Sep. 1944. Monthly. Heart Mountain. Mimeo.

A monthly magazine of prose and poetry published at Heart Mountain from about December, 1943.

922. ハート山センチネル社　ハート山人名録
Hātosan Senchinerusha. Hātosan jimmeiroku [Heart Mountain internee roster]. Heart Mountain, 1945. A-D + 74 pp. Mimeo.

923. 服部尚之　徳山實太郎遺稿集・心影
[Hattori Takayuki (ed.)]. Tokuyama Jitsutarō ikōshū: Shin'ei [Shadow of the heart: A collection of posthumous senryu by Tokuyama Jitsutarō]. [Los Angeles]: Privately printed, 1963. 50 pp., illus. Ditto.

An anthology of senryu composed during internment by Tokuyama Jitsutarō (1889-1962).

924. 池田貫道　戦時下日系人と米國の實状
Ikeda Kandō. Senjika Nikkeijin to Beikoku no jitsujō [Japanese-Americans during the war and the real conditions of America]. v. I-III. Oakland: Daireikyō Kenkyūjo. v. I, [12] + 336 + 56 pp., 1950; v. II, [11] + 374 pp., 1951; v. III, [4] + 276 pp., photo, 1952.

A 3-volume work on World War II. Volume one covers the author's views of religion and his internment; volume two analyzes U.S. government press release policies, the use of the atomic bomb, and his criticisms of its use; and volume three discusses the triangular relationship of Great Britain, America, and the Soviet Union.

925. 鎌江孝　ローズバーグ日本人收容所人名録
Kamae Takashi (comp.). Rōzubāgu Nihonjin shūyōjo jimmeiroku [Roster of Japanese internees at Lordsburg]. Lordsburg, 1943. 35 pp. Mimeo.

926. 基督教會週報
Kirisuto Kyōkai Shūhō ["Crystal City Japanese Christian Church Weekly Bulletin"]. no. 2-95 (May 5, 1944-Feb. 8, 1946). Incomplete. Weekly. Crystal City. Mimeo.

927. 松本本光　復興線上に躍る歸還同胞
Matsumoto Honkō. Fukkō senjō ni odoru kikan dōhō [Japanese returnees on the road to recovery]. Los Angeles: Rafu Shoten, 1949. [7] + photos 120 + 336 pp.

A work on the internment camp experience of the Japanese from Los Angeles. Divided essentially into 4 sections, it covers the beginning of the war, forced internment, internment life, and the return to Los Angeles and economic recovery. Includes 400-odd biographies presented as examples of Japanese-Americans who have reestablished themselves.

928. もはべ
Mohabe [Mojave]. no. 4-31 (Jun. 1943-Sep. 1945). Incomplete. Monthly. Poston. Mimeo.

A literary monthly published from about March, 1943 to September, 1945 at Poston.

929. 永見伊都子　銀杏樹・永見伊都子詩文抄
Nagami Itoko. Ichōju: Nagami Itoko shibunshō [Gingko: Selected writings of Nagami Itoko]. Kure: Kyūrei Shobō, 1966. 156 pp., photo.

An anthology of free-style poetry composed during the war years from 1942 to 1944. Includes some tanka and random essays.

930. 中村梅夫　　　断腸百韻
Nakamura Baifu (pseud., ed.). Dancho hyakuin [One hundred poems of sorrow]. Denver: Privately printed, 1952. 54 pp., photo, illus.

An anthology of haiku by Tanaka Masaharu (Shūrin) composed in 1946 lamenting the conditions of his defeated homeland and his own situation as an internee.

931. Noguchi, Ayako. Vignette: A pictorial record of life in the Fresno Assembly Center. Fresno, 1942. 79 pp., illus. Mimeo.

932. The Outpost. The pen. Rohwer, 1943. 82 pp., illus. Mimeo.

An English booklet highlighting the first year of internment at Rohwer, Arkansas.

933. ポピイ
Popii [Poppies]. Oct., Dec. 1944/Jan. 1945-Jun., Aug. 1945. Monthly. Topaz. Mimeo.

A haiku monthly of the Poppy Haiku Club at Topaz, Utah.

934. ポピイ之會　　ポピイ句集
Popii no Kai. Popii kushū [Poppies: A haiku collection]. Topaz, 1945. 49 pp., illus. Mimeo.

An anthology of free-style haiku by members of the Poppy Haiku Club at Topaz, Utah.

935. ポストン文藝
Posuton Bungei ["Poston Poetry"]. Mar. 1943; Sep. 1945. Monthly (?). Poston. Mimeo.

A prose and poetry magazine published by the Poston Poetry Club until September, 1945. The last issue includes a section of memoirs on life at Poston.

936. 朗和時報　朗和之一年
Rōwa Jihō. Rōwa no ichinen [One year at Rohwer]. Rohwer, 1943. 66 pp. Mimeo.

A booklet on the first year of internment at Rohwer, Arkansas.

937. 坂本きじゆ　　木村毅　　第四四二部隊
Sakamoto Kiju and Kimura Ki. Dai-Yon'Yon'Ni Butai [The 442nd Regimental Combat Team]. Tokyo: Ōbunsha, 1949. 223 pp., photos.

A journalistic account of the exploits of the 442nd Regimental Combat Team.

938. サンタフェ時報社　サンタフェ日本人収容所人名録
Santa Fe Jihōsha. Santa Fe Nihonjin shūyōjo jimmeiroku [Roster of Japanese internees at Santa Fe]. Santa Fe, 1943. 50 pp. Mimeo.

939. サンタフェ基督教會　　會員教友名簿
Santa Fe Kirisuto Kyōkai. Kaiin kyōyū meibo [Roster of church membersnip and friends]. Santa Fe, 1943. 20 pp. Mimeo.

940. 左右木舞城　　慰霊句集
[Sauki] Ijō (pseud., ed.). Irei kushū [Book of memorial verses]. Salt Lake City: Privately printed, 1945. 74 pp.

   A collection of haiku, mostly by internees, in memory of Nisei soldiers killed in action in Europe.

941. テキサス詩社　　流れ星
Tekisasu Shisha. Nagareboshi [Shooting stars]. Crystal City, 1945. [4] + 96 pp. Mimeo.

   A volume of tanka by members of the Texas Poetry Club at Crystal City.

942. トパーズ消費組合　　トパーズ消費組合二週年記年誌
Topāzu Shōhi Kumiai. Topāzu Shōhi Kumiai nishūnen kinenshi [Two years of the Topaz Co-op: Commemorative publication]. Topaz, 1944. 146 pp. Mimeo.

   A brief summary of the Topaz Co-op.

943. 臼田葉子　　臼田天珉子遺句集・楡の落葉
Usuda Yōko (ed.). Usuda Tenjōshi ikushū: Nire no ochiba [Fallen elm leaves: Collection of verses left by Usuda Tenjōshi]. [Hillsboro]: Privately printed, 1957. 105 pp., photo, chronology.

   An anthology of verses by Usuda Masaaki (Tenjōshi, 1892-1955) divided into three sections. Part one reprints his haiku published in the Hototogisu; part two consists of miscellaneous verses; and part three, the longest section, contains his haiku composed during the war years from December, 1941 to October, 1945.

944. 湯木三岳　　米壽
Yuki Sangaku (pseud., ed.). Beiju [Eighty-eighth birthday celebration]. Amache, 1945. [22] pp., illus. Mimeo.

   A collection of haiku, senryu, tanka, and Chinese poems in honor of the 88th birthday of Nobe Riichirō by his friends at Amache. Includes a brief biography.

945. 前進
Zenshin [Forward]. no. 3, 5-8 (Mar., May-Aug. 1945). Monthly. Crystal City. Mimeo.

   A literary monthly published from January to August, 1945 at Crystal City.

3. SPECIAL PAPERS AND DOCUMENTS

946. ANDERSON PAPERS, 1944-1950. 1 box.

   Anderson, Hugh H. Member, the Friends of the American Way and the Pacific Coast Committee on American Principles and Fair Play. Advisor on cooperatives, Poston. Assisted Japanese at the time of internment and resettlement. A long-time resident of Pasadena. Correspondence, financial records, and other papers relating to the Friends of the American Way; and other correspondence, 1949-1950.

947. AUSTIN PAPERS, 1943-1945. 3 boxes and 2 oversize scrapbooks.

Austin, Verne (1894-   ). Lt. Col., USA Ret. Commander, 752nd Military Police Battalion, Tule Lake, California, 1943-1944. Copies of the official files, Headquarters, 752nd Military Police Battalion, October 26, 1943-October 10, 1945; copies of 145 dispensary records, January, 1944; copies of approximately 250 English letters written by "trouble-makers," December, 1943-May, 1944 and other papers; personal chronologies of events, September 16, 1943-November 5, 1943; two large scrapbooks of newspaper clippings, photos, and mementoes.

948. BARNHART PAPERS, 1942-1954. 7 boxes.

Barnhart, Edward N. Professor of Rhetoric, University of California, Berkeley. Bibliographer, Japanese American Evacuation and Resettlement Collection, University of California, Berkeley. War Relocation Authority documents and xeroxed copies of the office files of Wayne Collins, the ACLU attorney of Japanese internees from Peru.

949. CARR PAPERS, 1941-1962. 6 boxes and 5 oversize scrapbooks.

Carr, William C. Real estate agent, Pasadena. One of the founders, Pasadena Chapter, Pacific Coast Committee on American Principles and Fair Play and the Friends of the American Way. One-time Chairman of the latter. Assisted many Japanese at the time of internment and resettlement. A sizable collection of anti-Japanese propaganda literature published during World War II, publications and documents of the Friends of the American Way, the Pacific Coast Committee on American Principles and Fair Play, and other organizations; 5 large scrapbooks, and a large collection of War Relocation Authority reports and publications and other materials relating to internment.

950. DeFOREST PAPERS, 1942-1945. 6 folders and 1 scrapbook.

DeForest, Charlotte B. Miscellaneous documents and personal mementoes of the Manzanar Relocation Center of a former employee.

951. FURUYA PAPERS, 1942-1945. 1 scrapbook.

Furuya Shin'ichi (古谷愼一). Biography unknown. A scrapbook of sketches of the Santa Anita Assembly Center and Granada Relocation Center, transcripts of speeches, and other notes.

952. HIGA PAPERS, 1944-1964. 1 folder.
*

Higa, Thomas Taro (1916-   ). A Hawaii-born Kibei. Former member, 100th Infantry Battalion. Documents on his speech tour of the mainland from September 15 to December 10, 1944, sponsored by the Japanese American Citizens League, and other personal papers.

953. ISHIGO PAPERS, 1941-1956. 5 boxes, 2 oversize albums, and 1 oversize portfolio.

   Ishigo, Estelle (1899-   ). Artist. Caucasian and native of Oakland, California. Married, 1928, Arthur Shigeharu Ishigo (1902-1957), a Nisei. Accompanied him to Heart Mountain. Commissioned to sketch camp life by the War Relocation Authority. Original sketches and camp mementoes, postwar records of her life in the resettlement trailer camp at Lomita, California, autobiographical manuscript, and miscellaneous correspondence and papers.

954. JAPANESE AMERICAN EVACUATION AND RESETTLEMENT COLLECTION, Bancroft Library, University of California, Berkeley. 9 reels.

   Microfilm copies of selected documents: Reel no. 1: F 2.01, F 2.10; reel no. 2: F 2.11, F 2.15, F 2.18, F 2.20A; reel no. 3: F 2.20B, F 2.25, F 2.55, F 2.70, F 2.781, F 2.89; reel no. 4: F 2.92, F 3.25A, F 3.25B, F 3.27, F 3.28, F 3.31, F 3.34, F 3.37, F 3.64; reel no. 5: A 16.260; reel no. 6: A 16.213; reel no. 7: T 1.66, T 1.69; reel no. 8: A 16.13; reel no. 9: T 17.06, T 17.07.

955. McGOVERN PAPERS, 1942-1945. 8 boxes.

   McGovern, Melvin P. Biography unknown. Documents relating to the educational programs and student activities of the Merced Assembly Center and Granada Relocation Center. Includes War Relocation Authority reports, publications, and photos, and other camp reports and publications.

956. MORITA PAPERS, 1942-1944. 1 folder.

   Morita Jirō (森田次郎 , 1892-   ). Merchant, Pasadena. A native of Shizuoka Prefecture who arrived in 1909. Miscellaneous papers on his internment at Poston and his service as a Japanese language instructor, U.S. Military Intelligence Service Language School, Camp Savage, Minnesota.

XV. Published Photographic Albums

957. 赤堀最　　レモン画帖
   Akahori Masaru. Remon gachō [Lemon photo book]. Los Angeles: Remon Gachō-sha, 1923. [90] pp.

   An album of the author's family and friends with a humorous twist.

958. 同胞社　皇太子殿下御成年式記念・皇國臣民寫眞帖
   Dōhōsha. Kōtaishi Denka Goseinenshiki kinen: Kōkoku shinmin shashinchō [Commemoration of the majority of the Imperial Crown Prince: Photographic album of the subjects of Imperial Japan]. Seattle: Dōhōsha, 1919. [524] + 12 pp.

   An album of the Japanese in the Pacific Northwest.

959. Goto, Baron Y. Children of Gannen-mono: The first-year men. Honolulu:
 *   Bishop Museum Press, 1968. [15] pp.

   A photographic booklet of the descendants of the Hawaii gannen-mono.

960. 片山影雄　　米加出生日本兒童・寫眞ブック
   Katayama Kageo (comp.). Bei-Ka shussei Nihon jidō: Shashin bukku [American and Canadian-born Japanese children: Photographic book]. Seattle: Nichibei Hyōronsha, 1918 (2nd printing). [4] + 4 + 235 pp.

   An album of Nisei children in the Pacific Northwest and Canada.

961. 前田昭男　　渡布記念寫眞帖
   Maeda Teruo (comp.). To-Fu kinen shashinchō [Photographic album of the Hawaiian tour]. Los Angeles, [1934]. 20 pp.

   A photographic album of the Rafu Shōjo Kabuki Gekidan [Los Angeles Girls' Kabuki Troupe] which went on tour to Hawaii in 1934.

962. 松坂屋書店編纂部　　布哇日本人寫眞帖
 *   Matsusakaya Shoten Hensanbu. Hawai Nihonjin shashinchō [Photographic album of the Japanese in Hawaii]. Honolulu: Matsusakaya Shoten, 1934. 8 + 3 + 118 + 1 + directory 47 pp.

963. 日本人協賛會　　金門萬國大博記念
   Nihonjin Kyōsankai. Kinmon Bankoku Daihaku kinen ["Golden Gate International Exposition, 1939"]. San Francisco, 1939. 42 pp.

   A souvenir photographic booklet of the 1939 Golden Gate International Exposition.

181

964. Sansei Keiyukai. San Sei Kei Yu Kai Golden Anniversary, 1968. Bountiful, 1968. [69] pp.

    An English album of the Japanese from Shizuoka Prefecture in the Rocky Mountain region.

965. 笹井鹿之助   母國震災救濟事業記念寫眞帖
Sasai Shikanosuke, et al. (comps.). Bokoku shinsai kyūsai jigyō kinen shashinchō [Photographic album commemorating the Kanto earthquake relief work]. Los Angeles: Bokoku Shinsai Kyūsai Jigyō Kinen Shashinchō Hakkō-jo, 1923. [3] + 66 pp.

    An album of an emergency committee in Southern California established to render assistance to the victims of the 1923 Kanto earthquake.

966. 新世界朝日新聞社   同胞家庭及第二世大記念帖
Shin Sekai Asahi Shimbunsha. Dōhō katei oyobi dai-nisei daikinenchō ["Memorial book of Japanese families in U.S.A."]. San Francisco: Shin Sekai Asahi Shimbunsha, 1939. [526] pp.

    An album of family portraits.

967. 新世界新聞社   昭和グラフ
Shin Sekai Shimbunsha. Shōwa gurafu [The Showa graph]. San Francisco: Shin Sekai Shimbunsha, [1929]. 56 + photos 56 pp.

    A special album to commemorate the formal accession of the Showa Emperor. Includes biographical sketches.

968.* 品川末繼   中村福藏   布哇在留熊本縣人略歷寫眞帖
Shinagawa Suetsugu and Nakahara Fukuzō (comps.). Hawai zairyū Kumamoto Kenjin ryakureki shashinchō [Biographical sketches and photographic album of the Japanese from Kumamoto Prefecture in Hawaii]. Honolulu: Hawai Benrisha, 1927. [798] + 78 + 7 pp.

    A photographic Who's Who from Kumamoto Prefecture in Hawaii.

969. 白兼玄郎   中村鐵雄   サンオーキンバレー實業家之面影
Shirogane Genrō and Nakamura Tetsuo. San Ōkin Barē jitsugyōka no omokage [A photographic view of Japanese enterprises in the San Joaquin Valley]. Stockton: Jitsugyōka no Omokagesha, 1914. Photos 88 + text 48 pp.

    A photographic Who's Who in the San Joaquin Valley. Includes a brief history of the Japanese in this area.

970. 田中亮平   南加州同胞發展寫眞帖
Tanaka Akihira (comp.). Nan Kashū dōhō hatten shashinchō [Photographic album of the history of the Japanese in Southern California]. Los Angeles: Bunrindō Shoten, 1913. 4 + 248 pp., maps, plates.

    A photographic Who's Who in Southern California.

971.* 田中稠穗   布哇寫眞帖
Tanaka Chūho (comp.). Hawai shashinchō [Photographic album of Hawaii]. Honolulu: Tanaka Jimusho, 1911 (3rd printing). [100] pp.

    A photographic Who's Who in Hawaii.

972. 藤賀與一　　　　　日米關係寫眞史
Tōga Yoichi (comp.). Nichi-Bei kankei shashinshi [A photographic history of U.S.-Japan relations]. San Francisco: Zaibei Nihonjin Shiryō Hozonkai, 1941. 4 + 195 pp.

A photographic history of U.S.-Japan relations and the Japanese in America compiled to complement no. 275.

973. 　　　　　南加州日本人
[Unknown]. Nan Kashū Nihonjin [The Japanese of Southern California]. Los Angeles (?), 1919 (?). iv + text 10 + 117 pp. (imperfect copy).

A photographic Who's Who in Southern California to commemorate the formal accession of the Taisho Emperor.

974. 山下信太郎　　　　　在米靜岡縣人寫眞帖
* Yamashita Shintarō (comp.). Zai-Bei Shizuoka Kenjin shashinchō [Photographic album of the Japanese from Shizuoka Prefecture in America]. Tokyo: Kōmeisha, 1938. [166] pp.

A photographic Who's Who from Shizuoka Prefecture in Hawaii and the continental United States.

XVI.
Oral History Tapes

Note: These 307 taped interviews of Issei, Kibei, Nisei, and others were recorded by the late Joe Grant Masaoka and members of local chapters of the Japanese American Citizens League as part of the Japanese American Research Project from 1964 to 1969. The majority are in Japanese, many are group interviews, and a few have restrictions placed on them. (Unintelligible interviews have not been listed.) Since we do not know the Japanese characters for all the individual names, we have retained the interviewees' own romanization, and we have listed them in Western order without macrons. All the tapes are arranged by place of interview.

CALIFORNIA:

    San Francisco

975. Sanjiro Kawaguchi (1)
976. Shichinosuke Asano (2)
977. Frank M. Nonaka (3)
978. Yasuji Tsumori (4)
979. Tokinobu Mihara (5)
980. James Junichi Hikido (6)
      Thomas Toshiteru Doi
981. Yasuji Tsumori (7)
982. Karl Yoneda (8)
983. Masako Sumida (9)
984. Eizo Miyahara (10)
985.   "   (11)
986. Shichisaburo Hideshima (12)
987.   "   (13)
988. Dr. Kunisada Kiyasu (14)
      Kyonosuke Shigezumi
989. Suzie H. Arimoto (15)
      Kyonosuke Shigezumi
990. Iwao Shimizu (16)
      Eizo Miyahara
      Isaburo Kurita
      Motoo Hatani
      Takeshi Koga
      Kumesaburo Kosaka
      Motoji Kitano
991. Masao W. Satow (17).

Southern California

992.	John Fujio Aiso	(18)
993.	"	(19)
994.	Kuju Fukunaga	(20)
995.	"	(21)
996.	Ben Fukuzaki	(22)
997.	Masakazu Iwata	(23)
998.	"	(24)
999.	Jiro Kai	(25)
1000.	Charles Kamayatsu	(26)
1001.	"	(27)
1002.	"	(28)
1003.	Yutaka Katayama	(29)
1004.	Bert Yosaburo Kaneko Kameichi Kuida	(30)
1005.	Kiyo Komatsu	(31)
1006.	Yukitaro Kawasaki	(32)
1007.	Joe Koide	(33)
1008.	"	(34)
1009.	Saburo Kido	(35)
1010.	"	(36)
1011.	Saburo Kido Mike Masaoka	(37)
1012.	"	(38)
1013.	Choyei Kondo	(39)
1014.	"	(40)
1015.	"	(41)
1016.	"	(42)
1017.	Frank Kuwahara Shigematsu Takeyasu	(43)
1018.	Manki Matsumoto	(44)
1019.	"	(45)
1020.	"	(46)
1021.	"	(47)
1022.	"	(48)
1023.	"	(49)
1024.	"	(50)
1025.	"	(51)
1026.	Taeko Mitamura Masuo Mitamura	(52)
1027.	David Miyamoto	(53)
1028.	Toyo Miyatake Kiyotsugu Tsuchiya	(54)
1029.	Toyo Miyatake	(55)
1030.	Katsuma Mukaeda	(56)
1031.	Mrs. Ken Nakazawa	(57)
1032.	Kazuichi Jack Numamoto Teizo Yonai	(58)
1033.	Robert I. Okazaki	(59)
1034.	Kumakichi Sekiguchi	(60)
1035.	Shinkichiro Shima	(61)
1036.	Masumi Tajima	(62)
1037.	Margaret O'Brien Takahashi	(63)
1038.	James Matsuo Yokomizo	(64)
1039.	Rokuro Watanabe Seigo Murakami Ueto Matsuda Yasaji Kaku Arata Mizushima Tetsujiro Ishikawa	(65)
1040.	Evacuation Marriage Club	(66)
1041.	Toshiro Henry Shimanouchi	(67)
1042.	Daisuke Iwataki	(68)
1043.	Ben Masaru Akahori	(69)
1044.	"	(70)
1045.	"	(71)

1046.   "   (72)
1047.   "   (73)
1048.   "   (74)
1049. Ayaka Takahashi (75)
1050.   "   (76)
1051. Torajiro Sumi (77)
1052. Japanese Chamber of Commerce of
       Southern California (78)
1053.   "   (79)
1054. Kagoshima Prefectural Association of Southern California (80)
1055.   "   (81)
1056. Matsunosuke Oi (82)
1057. Dr. Yoriyuki Kikuchi (83)
       Miya Kikuchi
1058. Miya Kikuchi (84)
1059. Glenn Matsumoto (85)
  *   Congressman Spark Matsunaga
1060. George Kiyoshi Togasaki (86)

Other Locales

1061. Keiji Shiota (87)
1062. Yasutaro Takano (88)
1063. Rie Kanemoto (89)
       Tomokichi Tanaka
       Isuke Tanaka
       T. Hamataka
       Mr. & Mrs. S. Noburo
       Mr. & Mrs. K. Oku
       Mr. & Mrs. S. Okimura
1064.   "   (90)
1065. Ichiji Sugiyama (91)
1066. Fusakichi Dairiki (92)
       Soichi Nakatani
       Ben Suekichi Yamamoto
1067. Soichi Nakatani (93)
       Toyoji Inouye
1068. Toyoji Inouye (94)

       Tokio Ed Kadoya
       Masao Umeda
       Mojiro Hamakawa
1069. Masao Itano (95)
1070. Masataro & Ginji Mizutani (96)
       Nobujiro Nakamura
1071. Mr. & Mrs. Shosuke Nitta (97)
1072. Ken Kitasako (98)
1073. Hirojiro Nakamura (99)
       Hirokuni Fuchiwaki
1074. Mr. & Mrs. David Kainichi
       Kamitsuka (100)
       Shigechika Kobara
1075. Hitoshi Ikeda (101)
       Shizue Morita
       Mary Hoshizaki
       Yoshiko Kodama
1076. George Hoshizaki (102)
       Hatsuo Morita
1077. Masaji Eto (103)
       George T. & Kofuji Fukunaga
1078. Henry Yaemon Minami (104)
       Tom H. Kurokawa
       Rev. Arthur Yamabe
1079. Kotaro Hayashi (105)
       Kameo Furukawa
       Isamu Henmi
       Shiroichi Koyama
1080. Shigeru Yoshiwara (106)
       Masa Toyama
       Mrs. Yasu Kawamura
1081. Niisaburo Aihara (107)
1082. Setsugo Sakamoto (108)
       Gunzo Miyamoto
1083. Frank Urasaburo Kamiyama (109)
1084. Sally Slocum (110)
1085. Charles Nitta (111)
       Kiichi Nodohara
       Ruby Tomeo Nakae
       Shunsaku Yamasaki
       Ellen Kubo
       Masayuki "Hike" Yego
       Harry M. Kawakata

       Mike Kakiuchi
       Clifford Yamada
       Kay Takemoto

1086. Rev. Taro Goto (112)

1087. Jusuke Shingu (113)

1088. Unosuke Higashi (114)

1089. Michisuke James Suenaga (115)

1090.   " (116)

1091. Buntaro Nakamura (117)
       Kenjiro Yoshikawa

1092. Gohachi H. Kawano (118)

1093. Mrs. Haruo Kawaguchi (119)

1094.   " (120)

1095. Harry Momita (121)

1096. Kumachiyo Kamiji (122)

1097. Mrs. Hideo Katsumoto (123)

1098. Risuke Kawaoka (124)

1099. Mr. N. Hirooka (125).

1100. Mr. K. Tsujihara (126)

1101. Ushitada Masuoka (127)

1102. Waichi Matsumoto (128)

1103. Motoji Kitano (129)

1104. Tamaki Ninomiya (130)

1105. Maruo Fujii (131)

1106. Sango Fukushima (132)

1107. Rui Oishi (133)

1108. Iwasuke Rikimaru (134)

1109. Shizuma Takeshita (135)

1110. Wakako Adachi (136)
       Ichiro Endo

1111. Matsusaburo Nagata (137)

1112. Joseph Shigeo Aoki (138)

1113. Frank Ogawa (139)
       Heizo Oshima

1114. Hikoichi Tajima (140)

1115. Chiura Obata (141)

1116.   " (142)

1117.   " (143)

1118.   " (144)

1119. Toichi Domoto (145)
       Junichi Kami

1120. Toichi Domoto (146)
       Sam Sakai

1121. Junichi Kami (147)
       Henry Moriya Takahashi

1122. Rev. Gordon Chapman (148)

1123. Rev. Gordon Chapman (149)
       Motoji Kitano

1124. Kamezuchi Sakamoto (150)

1125. Mrs. Shinobu Matsuura (151)

1126. Suzie Tanaka Kreider (152)

1127. Thomas Shinichiro Oka (153)

1128. Tomiyo Uyeyama (154)

1129. Chisato Kawamoto (155)

1130. Harry N. Sato (156)

1131. Eisaburo Abe (157)
       Toshio Inouye
       Shotaro Otsubo

1132. Mine Shigematsu (158)
       Thomas Shinichiro Oka

1133. Eiichi Yamamoto (159)

1134. Ichiji Sugiyama (160)
       Soichi Nakatani

1135. Sidney Mashbir (161)

1136.   " (162)

1137.   " (163)

1138.   " (164)

1139. Col. Verne Austin (165)

1140. Rindge Shima (166)

1141. Mike M. Masaoka (167)

COLORADO:

1142. Phoebe Asano (168)
Mrs. Harry M. Otsuki
Rev. Hiram K. Kano

1143. Shinkichi Tokunaga (169)
Otsuji Kageyama
Inokichi Fukuda
Harry Ujifusa

1144. Zadankai, Tri-State Buddhist Church (170)

1145. Sojiro Yoritomo (171)
Fred Nobuichi Kawamura
Rev. Yoshitaka Tamai
Rev. Ryotetsu Kazumata

1146. Rev. Jonathan Fujita (172)
Dr. Frank Eizo Hayano

1147. Heijiro Nakano (173)

1148. Rev. Yoshitaka Tamai (174)
Rev. Ryotetsu Kazumata
Seishiro Nakamura

1149. Rev. Noboru Tsunoda (175)
Matajiro Watada
Katsuhei Sakaguchi
Tadashi Nakada
Seishiro Nakamura

1150. Some Kosuge (176)
George T. Fukuma
George Y. Inai
Roy M. Suehiro
Yuzo Honda
Misayo Mizoue

1151. Minoru Yasui (177)

1152.   "   (178)

HAWAII:

1153. Rev. Theodore Kamasuke Chinen (179)
Thomas S. Higa

1154. Thomas S. Higa (180)
Toshiyuki Hirabayashi
Barton H. Nagata

1155. Y. Baron Goto (181)
Adam A. Smyser
Gov. John A. Burns

1156. Koji Ariyoshi (182)

1157. Masaji Marumoto (183)
Masayuki Tokioka

1158. Katsuro Miho (184)
George J. Fukunaga

1159. Yutaka Doi (185)
Noboru Miyake
Harvey S. Kawakami

1160. Hiro Higuchi (186)
Mark Y. Murakami

1161. Yoneto Yamaguchi (187)
Mayor Shunichi Kimura
Nelson K. Doi

1162. Tsutomu Takeda (188)

1163. Donald Ayashi Tokunaga (189)
Thomas Seikichi Yagi
Daniel Takeru Shigeta

1164. Benjamin M. Tashiro (190)
Matsuno Yasui
Takeyuki Yoshizu

IDAHO:

1165. Kiyo Kasai (191)
Toshiko Abe
Mrs. Y. Murakami
Chuzaburo Kanomata
S. Wakamatsu
Mrs. Yori Endo
Mrs. H.Y. Kawamura
Mrs. S. Inashima
Mrs. S. Yokota
Mrs. M. Yamada

1166. Takemaru Hirahara (192)
Henry Hajime Fujii
Mrs. Roy Abe
Mrs. S. Kawai
John Arima
Takashi Koyama

1167. Sashichi S. Koyama (193)
E.A. Huntley
Henry Hajime Fujii
Mrs. Roy Abe
Mrs. S. Kawai
Takemaru Hirahara

1168. Richard Suenaga (194)

ILLINOIS:

1169. Natsuko Orita (195)
Bunji Takano

1170. Bunji Takano (196)
Tomejiro Shigetomi

1171. Tomejiro Shigetomi (197)
Mrs. Jingoro Ozaki
Kiyoshi Joichi
Kintaro Yogi

1172. Jingoro Ozaki (198)
Kiyoshi Joichi
Kintaro Yogi
Kenji Nakane
Ralph Kanzaki
Yutaka Kanemoto
Yukio Hashiguchi
Paul Shimokubo

1173. Dr. Newton K. Wesley (199)

NEBRASKA:

1174. Noriaki Okada (200)
Walter J. Allen, Jr.
Mr. & Mrs. Chozo Kumagai

1175. Earl Harano (201)
Toshiro Yamagida

1176. Kaz Tokichi (202)
Mike Watanabe
Jim Miyeno
Tom Arikawa

1177. Harry Watanabe (203)
Mrs. Ritta Mori
Kiyoko Watanabe
Cecil J. Ishii
Gladys S. Hirabayashi
Tom Arikawa
Jim Miyeno
Mike Watanabe

NEVADA:

1178. Moto Fukui (204)
Ida Fukui
Tom Oki
Leo Yamamoto
Mr. & Mrs. Mas Baba
Eunice Oshima
Mr. & Mrs. Fred Aoyama
Mr. & Mrs. Paul Nozu
Wilson Makabe

1179. Sonao Imagire (205)

1180. Chika Tsujimichi (206)

1181. Shizu Matsumoto (207)

1182. Kametaro Ishii (208)

1183. Janet Shigeko Kikushima (209)

1184. Yoshitaro Baba (210)

1185. Hatsutaro Chikami (211)

NEW YORK:

1186. Benjamin Kengo Takenaka (212)

1187. " (213)

1188. Edward J. Ennis (214)
Moonray Kojima

1189. Senzo Kuwayama (215)

1190. Yae Murata (216)

OHIO:

1191. Taichi Yatsu (217)
Satsuyo Omura

OREGON:

1192. Masami Asai (218)
Ray T. Yasui
Henry T. Kato
George Nakamura
Ray Sato

1193. Ray T. Yasui (219)

1194. Kozo Miyako (220)
Umata Matsushima

1195. George Tanezo Niiyama (221)
Roy Y. Yokota

1196. Newton Noboru Takashima (222)
Henry Kato

1197. Katsuharu Nakashima (223)
Tamaichi Yamada

1198. Tamaichi Yamada (224)

1199. James Keijiro Kida (225)
Henry Hitoshi Nakamura

1200. Seishichi Matsumoto (226)

      Masuko Kawasoe
      Mrs. Hatsui Uriu
      Mrs. Yuki Sato
      Frank Ogami
      Harry Kuramoto
      Harry H. Morikawa
      Kango Wada

1201. Kyuda Ouchida (227)
      Jack T. Ouchida

1202. Mrs. Haru Tsuji (228)
      Elmer Y. Nishimoto

1203. Mitsuo Nakata (229)

1204. Harry Kuramoto (230)
      Bob Uriu
      John Arima
      George Sugai
      Taka Akita
      Ben Tsukamaki
      Dr. George Iwasa
      George Iseri

1205. Teruo Tsuboi (231)

1206. Naoko Tsuboi (232)

1207. John A. Rademaker (233)
      Mitsuo Nakata
      Matthew M. Masuoka
      Henry D. Kato
      Ike Iwasaki

1208. Tamaichi Yamada (234)

1209.   "   (235)

1210. Sadaji Shiogi (236)

1211.   "   (237)

1212. Misao Yada (238)

1213.   "   (239)

1214. Katsuharu Nakashima (240)

1215.   "   (241)

1216. Ike Iwasaki (242)

PENNSYLVANIA:

1217. Satsuyo Kawano (243)

1218. John Nitta (244)
      William Marutani
      Tom Tamaki

TEXAS:

1219. Mr. & Mrs. Yonakichi Kagawa (245)
      Mrs. Watanabe
      Kyoko Arai

1220. Mrs. Wakei Sando (246)
      Hachiro Sawamura

1221. Paul & Mary Katsuro (247)
      Mannosuke Shiraishi

UTAH:

1222. Koe Hanaya (248)

1223. Koe Hanaya (249)
      Eijiro Kawamura
      Tadashi Nakata
      Matajiro Watada
      Katsuhei Sakaguchi
      Togo Nakano
      Lee Murata
      Rev. Yoshitaka Tamai

1224. Koe Hanaya (250)
      Chieko H. Ogawa
      Thomas Tomihei Ogawa
      Harry H. Kumagai

1225. Kame Toyota (251)

1226. Rupert & Josie Hachiya (252)
      Elna Miya
      Yukiko Kimura
      Alice Kasai

1227. Shigao Tokunaga (253)
      Sue Kaneko
      Chiyomatsu Shiozawa

1228. Harry M. Eda (254)

1229. Harry M. Eda (255)
      Roy R. Takada
      Charles S. Kawakami
      Yosh Amano
      Frank Tamagawa
      Mary Kawakami
      Shozo Niwa

1230. Mrs. Kuniko Terasawa (256)
      Terry Terumasa Adachi
      Alice Kasai
      Mitsuko Sasaki
      Naoki and Sakae Kobayashi

1231. Rev. Masanori Ohata (257)
      Roy Nakatani

Mr. & Mrs. T. Maeda
Gonai Yamaguchi
Kenzo Shiki
Mr. & Mrs. G. Yano
Shig Hamada
Tats Koga
Yorimoto Murakami
Saburoji Yoshimura
J.G. Miya
Toshio Kato
Mrs. Ise Kato
Mrs. Toriko Yei

1232. Jiro Mochizuki (258)
Daisuke Miyatake
Mataju Ushio
Bunzo Fujii

1233. Toru Shimizu (259)
Gin Namba
Mataju Ushio
Charles J. Umemura
Shigao Tokunaga

1234. Hatsue Esther Hirasawa (260)
Hiro Yasukochi

1235. Jiro Mochizuki (261)
Mr. & Mrs. Hinokichi Kawaguchi
Kamasaku Miyagishima

1236. Terumasa Y.K. Miyagishima (262)
H.Y. Enomoto
Naka Miya
Kumakichi Endow
Heijiro Shiozawa
Sadahiko Oda
Gozo Shimada
Shichizo Takahashi
Tami Akisada
Take Uchida
Tomoko Horton
Kazuko Monobe
Mrs. Robert C. Hancock

1237. Tosh Kano (263)

1238. Tosh Kano (264)
Zadankai, Japanese Church of
    Christ, Salt Lake City

WASHINGTON:

1239. Kazumi Mizote (265)
Takeshi Kubota

1240. Shigeru Osawa (266)
Tadashi Yamaguchi

1241. Genji Mihara (267)

Harry Sotaro Kawabe

1242. Dick Kanaya (268)
Rev. Emery E. Andrews

1243. Nobuko Suzuki (269)
Minoru Masuda
Shigeru Asawa
Ralph Y. Kono
Frank Hattori

1244. George Susumu Ota (270)

1245. Thomas T. Sakahara (271)

1246. Arthur Ichiro Somekawa (272)

1247. Harry Sotaro Kawabe (273)
Yoshito Fujii

1248. Shuichi Fukui (274)

1249. Thomas T. Sakahara (275)

1250. Seiichi Tamaki (276)

1251. Chuji Roy Takahashi (277)

1252. Naonobu Mizukami (278)

1253. Shikataro Nakagawara (279)

1254. Toraichi Seto (280)

1255. Gohachi Yoshida (281)

1256. Yasukichi Hamanishi (282)

1257. Goroku Kubo (283)

1258. Tsugio Yaguchi (284)

1259. Shintaro Takagi (285)

1260. Sam Kubata (286)

1261.   "   (287)

1262. Buheiji Hattori (288)

1263. Buehiji Hattori (289)
Mrs. Yoshinato

1264. Buheiji Hattori (290)

1265. Tadashi Yamaguchi (291)
Dick Kanaya

1266. Hatsugoro Toda (292)
Yoshito Fujii

1267. Masanori Sato (293)

1268. " (294)

1269. Mr. & Mrs. Tom Shioji Yamamoto (295)

1270. " (296)

1271. Kumaichi Horike (297)

1272. Harry S. Kawabe (298)

WASHINGTON, D.C.:

1273. Lillian Katsuyo Takeshita (299)
Miyo Nishio

1274. Dillon S. Myer (300)

1275. Francis Biddle (301)
Clarke H. Kawakami

1276. Roger Baldwin (302)

1277. Rear Adm. A.H. McCollum (303)
Congressman Spark Matsunaga

1278. Congressman Spark Matsunaga (304)

WYOMING:

1279. Tomizo Miyamoto (305)
Itsuki Hashimoto
Tatsuhei Tsuda
Johnny Kiyoshi Saiki

1280. Johnny Kiyoshi Saiki (306)
Tommy Tadayoshi Shito
James M. Kuga
Haruko Kobayashi
Minoru Yasui

1281. Hana Hayashi (307)
Mrs. Tsuta Kushibashi
Jusaburo Sakata
Toki Sakata
Gontaro Kubota
Kiyo Kubota

XVII. Dissertations and Theses

Note: The dissertations and theses listed below are arranged alphabetically without annotations.

1282. Abe, Steven K. "Nisei personality characteristics as measured by the
+   Edwards personal preference schedule and Minnesota multiphasic personality inventory." Ph.D. Dissertation, University of Utah, 1958.

1283. Akamatsu, Alfred S. "The function and type of program of a Japanese minority church in New York City." Ph.D. Dissertation, Columbia University,
+   1948.

1284. Aller, Curtis C. "The evolution of Hawaiian labor relations." Ph.D. Dissertation, Harvard University, 1958.
+*

1285. Bell, Mary S. "Naturalization procedures in California with special reference to Alameda County." M.A. Thesis, University of California, Berkeley,
+   1923.

1286. Bell, Reginald. "A study of the educational effects of segregation upon
+   Japanese children in American schools." Ph.D. Dissertation, Stanford University, 1932.

1287. Berkowitz, Madelon H. "Progressivism and the anti-Japanese agitation in
+   California." M.A. Thesis, University of California, Berkeley, 1966.

1288. Bratton, J. Wesley. "A study to determine the extent and nature of educa-
+   tional legislation obtained through the initiative and referendum in the United States with special application to the state of California." Ph.D. Dissertation, University of Southern California, 1951.

1289. Bridge, David A. "A study of the agencies which promote Americanization in the Los Angeles City Recreation District." M.A. Thesis, University of Southern California, 1920.
+

1290. Bristow, R.M. "English and native Japanese test score relationship to college grade point average for Japanese students." Ed.D. Dissertation, University of Southern California, 1966.
+

1291. Brown, Arthur J. "Means of promoting immigration to the Northwest and Washington to 1910." M.A. Thesis, University of Washington, 1940.
+

1292. Bunch, Ralph E. "The political orientation of Japanese Americans." Ph.D. Dissertation, University of Oregon, 1968.
+

1293. Carey, John J. "Progressives and the immigrants, 1885-1915." Ph.D. Dissertation, University of Connecticut, 1968.
+

1294. Carras, Mary. "Everett, Washington: A demographic and ecological analysis." M.A. Thesis, University of Washington, 1954.
+

1295. Caudill, William A. "Japanese American acculturation and personality." Ph.D. Dissertation, University of Chicago, 1950.
+

1296. Chansler, Horace F. "The assimilation of the Japanese in and around Stockton." M.A. Thesis, College of the Pacific, 1932.
+

1297. Chijiwa, Saikichi. "A social survey of the Japanese population in Palo Alto and Menlo Park." M.A. Thesis, Stanford University, 1933.
+

1298. Cho, Chang-Soo. "The correlates of cultural assimilation of two groups of Issei women." M.A. Thesis, University of Washington, 1953.
+

1299. Conroy, Francis H. "The Japanese expansion into Hawaii, 1868-1898." Ph.D. Dissertation, University of California, Berkeley, 1949.
+*

1300. Croft, Carma H. "Comparative scholastic achievements of Japanese-American students and Caucasian students of University of Utah for the academic year 1942-43." M.S. Thesis, University of Utah, 1944.
+

1301. Daniels, Roger. "The politics of prejudice; the anti-Japanese movement in California and the struggle for Japanese exclusion." Ph.D. Dissertation, University of California, Los Angeles, 1960.
+

1302. Darby, Harold E. "The general intelligence of American-born Japanese children in California as measured by the Leiter International Performance Scale." M.S. Thesis, University of Southern California, 1940.

1303. Doi, Helen N. "A study of the elementary grade children attending the Greek and the Japanese language schools." M.S. Thesis, University of Utah, 1954.

1304. Fowler, Ruth H. "Some aspects of public opinion concerning the Japanese in Santa Clara County." M.A. Thesis, Stanford University, 1934.

1305. Freeman, George H. "A comparative investigation of the school achievement and socio-economic background of the Japanese-American students and the white American students of Gardena High School." M.A. Thesis, University of Southern California, 1938.

1306. Fukuoka, Fumiko. "Mutual life and aid among the Japanese in Southern California with special reference to Los Angeles." M.A. Thesis, University of Southern California, 1937.

1307. Fukuoka, Hajime. "The lemon industry in Southern California." M.A. Thesis, University of Southern California, 1918.

1308. Fuller, Varden. "The supply of agricultural labor as a factor in the evaluation of farm organization in California." Ph.D. Dissertation, University of California, Berkeley, 1940.

1309. Gardner, Dorothy A. "Mental fatigue of Japanese children." M.A. Thesis, University of Denver, 1929.

1310. Garrity, Donald L. "Tacoma, Washington: A demographic and ecological analysis." M.A. Thesis, University of Washington, 1953.

1311. George, Robert C.L. "The Granada (Colorado) Relocation Center secondary school." M.A. Thesis, University of Colorado, 1944.

1312. Gibbons, Don C. "Spokane, Washington: A demographic and ecological analysis." M.A. Thesis, University of Washington, 1953.

1313. Glenn, Jana. "A study of the incomes and the money value of living of 44 Japanese families in Hawaii." M.S. Thesis, University of Chicago, 1938.

1314. Grodzins, Morton M. "Political aspects of the Japanese evacuation." Ph.D. Dissertation, University of California, Berkeley, 1945.

1315. Gruver, Rebecca B. "Japanese-American relations and the Japanese exclusion movement, 1900-1934." M.A. Thesis, University of California, Berkeley, 1956.

1316. Guiang, Marcelino C. "The Japanese immigration problem; a discussion of
 +   Japanese immigration into the United States, 1900-1907." M.A. Thesis,
      University of San Francisco, 1963.

1317. Hale, Robert M. "The United States and Japanese immigration." Ph.D.
 +   Dissertation, University of Chicago, 1945.

1318. Harada, Koichi G. "A survey of the Japanese language schools in Hawaii."
 +*   M.A. Thesis, University of Hawaii, 1934.

1319. Hata, Donald T. "'Undesirables': Unsavory elements among Japanese in
 +   America prior to 1893 and their influence on the first anti-Japanese
      movement in California." Ph.D. Dissertation, University of Southern
      California, 1970.

1320. Hayashida, Akiyoshi. "Japanese moral instruction as a factor in the Ameri-
 +*   canization of citizens of Japanese ancestry." M.A. Thesis, University
      of Hawaii, 1933.

1321. Hayes, Robert W. "A phonological study of the English speech of selected
 +*   Japanese speakers in Hawaii." M.A. Thesis, University of Hawaii, 1953.

1322. Hennings, Robert E. "James D. Phelan and the Wilson Progressives of Cali-
 +   fornia." Ph.D. Dissertation, University of California, Berkeley, 1961.

1323. Hertzler, Virginia B. "A sociometric study of Japanese students in a
 +   polyethnic high school." M.A. Thesis, University of Washington, 1949.

1324. Hertzog, Dorothy B. "The history of Japanese exclusion from the United
 +   States." M.A. Thesis, University of Southern California, 1931.

1325. Hirabayashi, Gordon K. "A sociometric study of University of Washington
 +   students of Japanese ancestry." M.A. Thesis, University of Washington,
      1948.

1326. Holliday, Margaret A. "Social relations between the Japanese and the Cali-
 +   fornians." M.A. Thesis, Columbia University, 1921.

1327. Horinouchi, Isao. "Educational values and preadaptation in the accultura-
 +   tion of Japanese Americans." M.A. Thesis, Sacramento State College,
      1967.

1328. Hunter, Louise H. "Buddhism in Hawaii: Its impact on a Yankee community."
 +*   Ph.D. Dissertation, University of Hawaii, 1966.

1329. Hyde, Helen I. "A comparison of the physical characteristics of American,
 +   Japanese, and Mexican school children." M.A. Thesis, University of
      Southern California, 1928.

1330. Iga, Mamoru. "Acculturation of Japanese population in Davis County, Utah."
+   Ph.D. Dissertation, University of Utah, 1955.

1331. Ikeda, Kiyoshi. "A comparative study of mental illness differences among
+*   the Okinawan and Naichi Japanese in Hawaii." M.A. Thesis, University
        of Hawaii, 1955.

1332. Ishikawa, Michiji. "The Japanese in California." M.A. Thesis, Columbia
+   University, 1928.

1333. Jackman, Norman R. "Collective protest in relocation centers." Ph.D.
+   Dissertation, University of California, Berkeley, 1955.

1334. Johnson, Florence B. "A comparative study of the basic music talents of
+*   three racial groups: Chinese, Japanese, and part Hawaiian." M.A.
        Thesis, University of Hawaii, 1933.

1335. Kaapu, Myrtle K. "A study of the influences of Japanese syntax and idiom
+*   upon the spoken and written English of a group of ninth grade pupils."
        M.A. Thesis, University of Hawaii, 1937.

1336. Kai, Gunki. "Economic status of the Japanese in California." M.A. Thesis,
+   Stanford University, 1922.

1337. Kallstedt, Frances E. "A consideration of some of our immigration poli-
+   cies in the light of the economic contribution of a group of prominent
        immigrants who have arrived in the United States since 1860." M.A.
        Thesis, University of California, 1927.

1338. Kanagawa, Wayne Y. "A study of old-age assistance recipients of Japanese
+*   ancestry under the Honolulu County, Department of Public Welfare, Terri-
        tory of Hawaii, January 1955." M.A. Thesis, University of Hawaii, 1955.

1339. Kasahara, Yoshiko. "The influx and exodus of migrants among the 47 Pre-
+   fectures in Japan, 1920-1935." Ph.D. Dissertation, University of
        Michigan, 1957.

1340. Kawasaki, Kenichi. "The Japanese community of East San Pedro, Terminal
        Island, California." M.A. Thesis, University of Southern California,
        1931.

1341. Kelley, Tim K. "The commercial fishery of Washington." Ph.D. Disserta-
+   tion, University of Washington, 1946.

1342. Kern, Ruth. "The political policy and activities of the American Legion,
+   1919-1925." M.A. Thesis, University of California, Berkeley, 1934.

1343. Kessler, James B. "The political factors in California's anti-alien land
+   legislation, 1912-1913." Ph.D. Dissertation, Stanford University, 1958.

1344. Kimura, Yukiko. "A comparative study of collective adjustment of the
+*   Issei, the first generation Japanese in Hawaii and in the mainland
         United States since Pearl Harbor." Ph.D. Dissertation, University of
         Chicago, 1952.

1345. Kimura, Yukiko. "A sociological analysis of types of social adjustment
+*   of alien Japanese in Hawaii since the war." M.A. Thesis, University of
         Hawaii, 1947.

1346. Kitamura, Samuel H. "An accentual study of the Japanese speech in Hawaii;
+*   lexical pitch patterns of selected Okinawan speakers." M.A. Thesis,
         University of Hawaii, 1959.

1347. Kono, Ayako. "Language as a factor in the achievement of American-born
+*   students of Japanese ancestry." M.A. Thesis, University of Hawaii, 1934.

1348. Kosaki, Mildred D. "The culture conflicts and guidance needs of Nisei
+*   adolescents." M.A. Thesis, University of Hawaii, 1949.

1349. Kuhler, Joyce B. "A history of agriculture in the Yakima Valley, Washing-
+   ton, from 1888-1900." M.A. Thesis, University of Washington, 1940.

1350. Kurokawa, Minako. "Occupational mobility among Japanese businessmen in
+   San Francisco." M.A. Thesis, University of California, Berkeley, 1962.

1351. La Violette, Forrest E. "Americans of Japanese ancestry: A study of
+   assimilation in the American community." Ph.D. Dissertation, University
         of Chicago, 1946.

1352. Leiter, Russell G. "A comparative study of the general intelligence of
+   Caucasian, Chinese and Japanese children as measured by the Leiter In-
         ternational Performance Scale." Ph.D. Dissertation, University of
         Southern California, 1938.

1353. Lentz, Katherine J. "Japanese American relations in Seattle." M.A.
+   Thesis, University of Washington, 1924.

1354. Lind, Andrew W. "Economic succession and racial invasion in Hawaii."
+*   Ph.D. Dissertation, University of Chicago, 1931.

1355. Linderfelt, Florence M. "A comparative study of the Rorschach protocols
+*   of Japanese and Caucasian college students." M.A. Thesis, University
         of Hawaii, 1949.

1356. Loosley, Allyn C. "Foreign born population of California, 1848-1920."
+   M.A. Thesis, University of California, Berkeley, 1928.

1357. Lum, Kalfred D. "The political influences of the Orientals in the 'Para-
+*   dise of the Pacific'." M.A. Thesis, Columbia University, 1923.

1358. McReynolds, George E. "American sentiment regarding Japan, 1924-1934."
   +   Ph.D. Dissertation, Clark University, 1937.

1359. Marshall, Emily L. "A study of the achievement of Chinese and Japanese
   +*   children in the public schools of Honolulu." M.A. Thesis, University
          of Hawaii, 1927.

1360. Masuoka, Jitsuichi. "Race attitudes of the Japanese people in Hawaii: A
   +*   study in social distance." M.A. Thesis, University of Hawaii, 1931.

1361. Masuoka, Jitsuichi. "The westernization of the Japanese family in Hawaii."
   +*   Ph.D. Dissertation, University of Iowa, 1940.

1362. Matson, Floyd W. "The anti-Japanese movement in California, 1890-1942."
          M.A. Thesis, University of California, Berkeley, 1953.

1363. Matsui, Shichiro. "Economic aspects of the Japanese situation in Califor-
   +   nia." M.A. Thesis, University of California, Berkeley, 1922.

1364. Maxwell, Edward J. "The McCarran-Walter Immigration and Naturalization
   +   Act of 1952." M.A. Thesis, Stanford University, 1962.

1365. Meredith, Gerald M. "Acculturation and personality among Japanese-American
   +*   college students in Hawaii." Ph.D. Dissertation, University of Hawaii,
          1969.

1366. Milnes, Harold P. "A history of the Japanese in California." M.A. Thesis,
   +   College of the Pacific, 1926.

1367. Misaki, Hisakichi. "The effect of language handicap on intelligence tests
   +   of Japanese children." M.A. Thesis, Stanford University, 1927.

1368. Miyamoto, Shichiro. "A study of the Japanese language ability of the
   +*   second and third generation Japanese children in a Honolulu language
          school." M.A. Thesis, University of Hawaii, 1937.

1369. Modell, John. "The Japanese of Los Angeles: A study in growth and accom-
   +   modation, 1900-1946." Ph.D. Dissertation, Columbia University, 1969.

1370. Montgomery, William L. "The Japanese controversy in California during
   +   the Roosevelt administration." M.A. Thesis, Columbia University, 1927.

1371. Nagata, Kiyoshi. "A statistical approach to the study of acculturation of
   +   an ethnic group based on communication-oriented variables: The case of
          Japanese Americans in Chicago." Ph.D. Dissertation, University of
          Illinois, 1969.

1372. Naka, Harry M. "The naturalization of the Japanese veterans of the
 +   American World War forces." M.A. Thesis, University of California,
       Berkeley, 1939.

1373. Naka, Kaizo. "Social and economic conditions among Japanese farmers in
 +   California." M.S. Thesis, University of California, Berkeley, 1913.

1374. Nakagaki, Masami. "A study of marriage and family relationships among three
 +   generations of Japanese-American family groups." M.A. Thesis, University
       of Southern California, 1964.

1375. Nepomuceno, Larry A. "Japanese restriction in California, 1900-1913."
 +   M.A. Thesis, University of California, Berkeley, 1939.

1376. Niesley, Margaret. "California and the anti-Japanese movement." M.A.
 +   Thesis, University of Southern California, 1931.

1377. Nishi, Midori. "Changing occupance of the Japanese in Los Angeles County,
       1940-1950." Ph.D. Dissertation, University of Washington, 1955.

1378. Nishi, Setsuko K. "Japanese American achievement in Chicago: A cultural
 +   response to degradation." Ph.D. Dissertation, University of Chicago,
       1963.

1379. Nishinoiri, John I. "Japanese farms in Washington." M.A. Thesis, University of Washington, 1926.

1380. Nishioka, Norton O. "Expatriation without emigration." M.A. Thesis,
 +   University of California, Berkeley, 1959.

1381. Nishiyama, Toshihiko P. "Primary relationships and academic achievement:
 +   A comparative study of American and Japanese youth." Ph.D. Dissertation,
       St. Louis University, 1965.

1382. Nodera, Isamu. "A survey of the vocational activities of the Japanese in
       the city of Los Angeles." M.A. Thesis, University of Southern California, 1937.

1383. Oberst, Alma E. "The policy of the San Francisco News on the evacuation
 +   and relocation of the Japanese during W.W. II." M.A. Thesis, University
       of California, Berkeley, 1964.

1384. Oka, Wilfred M. "A study of Japanese social institutions in Hawaii."
 +*   M.Ed. Thesis, Springfield College, 1935.

1385. Onishi, Katsumi. "A study of the attitudes of the Japanese in Hawaii
 +*   toward the Japanese language schools." M.A. Thesis, University of
       Hawaii, 1943.

1386. Opperman, David R. "The distribution of the Negroes, Indians, and Sino-
+   Japanese in the U.S. in 1950." Ph.D. Dissertation, University of
       Illinois, 1956.

1387. Ozaki, Norio. "A survey of interdenominational cooperation within each of
       three Japanese religions in Los Angeles: Shinto, Buddhism, and Christian-
       ity." M.A. Thesis, University of Southern California, 1941.

1388. Penrose, Eldon R. "California nativism: Organized opposition to the Japa-
+   nese, 1890-1913." M.A. Thesis, Sacramento State College, 1969.

1389. Perry, Neal C. "An investigation of certain aspects of the social, eco-
+   nomic, and educational status of second-generation Chinese and Japanese
       graduates of the high schools of Fresno, California." M.S. Thesis,
       University of Southern California, 1938.

1390. Probasco, Barbara. "Japanese exclusion proposals before the Congress of
+   the United States, 1890-1924." M.A. Thesis, Stanford University, 1929.

1391. Provido, Generoso P. "Oriental immigration from an American dependency."
+   M.A. Thesis, University of California, Berkeley, 1931.

1392. Pugh, Richard L. "Anti-Japanese sentiment in California, 1900-1924."
+   M.A. Thesis, Sacramento State College, 1967.

1393. Pursinger, Marvin G. "Oregon's Japanese in World War II, a history of
+   compulsory relocation." Ph.D. Dissertation, University of Southern
       California, 1961.

1394. Rademaker, John A. "The ecological position of the Japanese farmers in
       the state of Washington." Ph.D. Dissertation, University of Washington,
       1939.

1395. Rice, Richard B. "The Manzanar War Relocation Center." M.A. Thesis,
+   University of California, Berkeley, 1947.

1396. Richardson, John M. "A comparative study of Japanese and native American
+   white children." M.A. Thesis, University of Southern California, 1937.

1397. Robbins, Albert M. "Exclusionism as a factor in the relations of Japan
+   and the United States, 1913-1924." M.A. Thesis, University of Southern
       California, 1954.

1398. Ross, Robert H. "Social distance as it exists between first and second
+   generation Japanese in the city of Los Angeles and vicinity." M.A.
       Thesis, University of Southern California, 1939.

1399. Saito, Akira. "California press and anti-Japanese movement, 1905-1924."
\+   M.A. Thesis, University of California, Berkeley, 1968.

1400. Sakamaki, Shunzo. "A history of the Japanese press in Hawaii." M.A.
+*   Thesis, University of Hawaii, 1928.

1401. Samuels, Fred. "The effect of social mobility on social distance: Some
+*   changes in the race attitudes of Honolulu's Japanese." M.A. Thesis,
      University of Hawaii, 1963.

1402. Sasamori, Junzo. "Social life of Japanese in America." Ph.D. Dissertation,
      University of Denver, 1927.

1403. Schlicher, Reynold J. "Restriction of immigration into the United States
\+   since 1917." M.A. Thesis, University of Iowa, 1939.

1404. Scott, Alice J. "The Alien Land Law of 1913 and its relation to Japanese
\+   immigration." M.A. Thesis, Columbia University, 1929.

1405. Shikamura, Alice H. "The vocational intentions of second generation Japa-
\+   nese students in three California universities." M.A. Thesis, Stanford
      University, 1948.

1406. Smith, Mildred J. "Backgrounds, problems, and significant reactions of
\+   relocated Japanese American students." Ph.D. Dissertation, Syracuse
      University, 1949.

1407. Sowers, Lloyd E. "A comparative study of the reading ability of Mexican,
\+   Japanese, and American children." M.A. Thesis, University of Southern
      California, 1942.

1408. Speier, Matthew R. "Japanese-American Relocation Camp colonization and
\+   resistance to resettlement: A study in the social psychology of ethnic
      identity under stress." M.A. Thesis, University of California, Berke-
      ley, 1965.

1409. Staniford, Philip S. "Values of some Issei Japanese of Hanapepe Valley,
+*   Kauai." M.A. Thesis, University of Hawaii, 1961.

1410. Stemen, John R. "The diplomacy of the immigration issue: A study on
\+   Japanese-American relations, 1894-1941." M.A. Thesis, University of
      Indiana, 1960.

1411. Stier, Wilhelm R.F. "The attitude of the American press to Japan and the
\+   Japanese." M.A. Thesis, Columbia University, 1917.

1412. Stroup, Dorothy A. "The role of the Japanese American press in its com-
+   munity." M.A. Thesis, University of California, Berkeley, 1960.

1413. Svensrud, Marian. "Some factors concerning the assimilation of a selected
+   Japanese community." M.A. Thesis, University of Southern California,
        1931.

1414. Tajima, Paul J. "Japanese Buddhism in Hawaii: Its background, origin,
+*   and adaptation to local conditions." M.A. Thesis, University of Hawaii,
        1935.

1415. Takahashi, Kyojiro. "A social study of the Japanese Shinto and Buddhism
+   in Los Angeles." M.A. Thesis, University of Southern California, 1937.

1416. Tan, Lien-piao. "Racial problem in the American and Australian labor
+   movements as between peoples of European and Asiatic origin." M.A.
        Thesis, Columbia University, 1930.

1417. Tanaka, Tamiko. "The Japanese language school in relation to assimilation."
        M.A. Thesis, University of Southern California, 1933.

1418. Thompson, Richard A. "The 'Yellow Peril,' 1890-1924." Ph.D. Dissertation,
        University of Wisconsin, 1957.

1419. Thomson, Ruth H. "Events leading to the order to segregate Japanese
+   pupils in the San Francisco public schools." Ph.D. Dissertation, Stan-
        ford University, 1931.

1420. Toyama, Chotoku. "The Japanese community in Los Angeles." M.A. Thesis,
+   Columbia University, 1926.

1421. Tuthill, Gretchen L. "A study of the Japanese in the city of Los Angeles."
+   M.A. Thesis, University of Southern California, 1924.

1422. Uono, Kiyoshi. "The factors affecting the geographical aggregation and dis-
        persion of the Japanese residents in the city of Los Angeles." M.A. Thesis,
        University of Southern California, 1927.

1423. Uyeki, Eugene S. "Process and patterns of Nisei adjustment to Chicago."
        Ph.D. Dissertation, University of Chicago, 1953.

1424. Watanabe, Shinichi. "Diplomatic relations between the Hawaiian Kingdom
+*   and the Empire of Japan, 1860-1893." M.A. Thesis, University of Hawaii,
        1944.

1425. Wax, Rosalie H. "The development of authoritarianism; a comparison of the
+   Japanese-American Relocation Centers and Germany." Ph.D. Dissertation,
        University of Chicago, 1951.

1426. Weston, Rubin F. "The influence of racial assumptions on American impe-
+   rialism, 1893-1964." D.S.S. Dissertation, Syracuse University, 1964.

1427. Whitney, Helen E. "Care of homeless children of Japanese ancestry during
+   evacuation and relocation." M.S.W. Thesis, University of California,
        Berkeley, 1948.

1428. Wisend, William F. "The anti-Japanese movement in California." M.A.
+   Thesis, University of Southern California, 1931.

1429. Woodbury, Robert L. "William Kent: Progressive gadfly, 1864-1928."
        Ph.D. Dissertation, Yale University, 1967.

1430. Woolston, Katherine D. "Japanese standard of living in Seattle." M.A.
+   Thesis, University of Washington, 1927.

1431. Yamamoto, George K. "Social adjustment of Caucasian-Japanese marriages in
+*   Honolulu." M.A. Thesis, University of Hawaii, 1949.

1432. Yanagita, Yuki. "Familial, occupational, and social characteristics of
+   three generations of Japanese Americans." M.S. Thesis, University of
        Southern California, 1968.

1433. Young, Clarence K. "Rights of aliens in the U.S." Ph.D. Dissertation,
+   Princeton University, 1924.

1434. Young, Hobart N. "Some implications from the occupation situation of
+   American-born Japanese." M.A. Thesis, University of Southern California,
        1931.

1435. Yumiba, Carole K. "The educational program at Jerome, Arkansas, United
+   States War Relocation Center, 1942-1944." M.A. Thesis, University of
        California, Los Angeles, 1971.

1436. Zald, Mayer N. "Family patterns and 'authorianism' among some Japanese-
+*   American students." M.A. Thesis, University of Hawaii, 1955.

XVIII.
Miscellaneous

1437. 赤堀最　　帰化試験の虎の巻・「市民権の二十五課目」
Akahori Masaru (ed.). Kika shiken no tora no maki 'shiminken no nijūgo-kamoku' ["Twenty-five lessons in citizenship"]. Los Angeles: Town Crier, 1950 and 1952 (2nd edition). 44 pp.

  A citizenship manual to assist the Issei to pass their naturalization examination.

1438. 青柳郁太郎　　ブラジルに於ける日本人發展史・上巻
Aoyagi Ikutarō. Burajiru ni okeru Nihonjin hattenshi, jōkan [History of the Japanese in Brazil, part 1]. Tokyo: Burajiru ni Okeru Nihonjin Hattenshi Kankō Iinkai, 1941. 15 + 424 pp., photos, tables.

  A general history of Japanese emigration to Brazil and the economic achievements of Japanese immigrants from 1908 to 1939. Includes the role of Japanese steamship companies as the principal promoters of emigration and statistical data on Japanese agriculture.

1439. 阿世賀紫海　　北米大陸一周紀行
Azeka Shikai. Hoku-Bei tairiku isshū kikō [Travel account of a tour of America]. Fukuoka: Privately printed, 1952. 8 + 302 pp., photos, map.

  A travel account of a grand tour of America taken by the Issei author and his wife.

1440. ブラジル日系人実態調査委員会　　ブラジルの日本移民
Burajiru Nikkeijin Jittai Chōsa Iinkai. Burajiru no Nihon imin [The Japanese immigrant in Brazil]. v. 1, Shiryō-hen [Statistical tables], v. 2, Kijutsu-hen [Description]. Tokyo: Tōkyō Daigaku Shuppankai, 1964. v. 1, xxxix + 766 pp. and v. 2, [10] + 370 + errata [2] pp., tables, maps.

  A comprehensive, 2-volume statistical study of the Japanese in Brazil as of 1958. Volume one consists of detailed statistical tables in both English and Japanese, while volume two is a descriptive summary and digest of the former in Japanese.

1441. 長谷川新一郎　　墨國一覧
Hasegawa Shin'ichirō. Bokkoku ichiran ["Mexico"]. Hosono Kiyoshi, 1917. 5 + 7 + 12 + 288 + 31 pp., photos.

  A guide to Mexico published by an Issei resident of Los Angeles who views the country as a prospective place to which to emigrate because of the 1913 California Alien Land Law.

1442. 伊藤敬一　墨國を語る
Itō Keiichi. <u>Bokkoku wo kataru</u> [Stories of Mexico]. Tokyo: Itō Setsuo and Itō Jōji, 1956. 145 pp., photos.

    Personal recollections, originally published in the <u>Rafu Shimpō</u>, on the history of the Japanese in Mexico by an Issei who arrived in 1897 as a government student.

1443. 近藤長衛　日本の将来と民主主義
Kondō Chōyei. <u>Nihon no shōrai to minshushugi</u> [Democracy and the future of Japan]. Tokyo: Kyōbunkan, 1950. 182 pp.

    A political tract on the necessity of reconstructing a postwar democratic Japan by an Issei Christian.

1444. 松田英二　低き生活高き思念
Matsuda Eiji. <u>Hikuki seikatsu takaki shinen</u> [A short life, lofty ideals]. Tokyo: Dokuritsudō Shobō, 1937. 22 pp., photo.

    A biographical booklet on the life of Fuse Tsunematsu, a Japanese pioneer in Escuintla, Chiapas, Mexico.

1445. 村井政　米國市民讀本
Murai Kō. <u>Beikoku shimin tokuhon</u> ["U.S. citizenship reader"]. Denver: J.A.C.L., 1952. 35 pp.

    A citizenship pamphlet to assist the Issei to pass their naturalization examination.

1446. 永田稠　ブラジルに於ける日本人發展史・下巻
Nagata Shigeshi. <u>Burajiru ni okeru Nihonjin hattenshi, gekan</u> [History of the Japanese in Brazil, part 2]. Tokyo: Burajiru ni Okeru Nihonjin Hattenshi Kankōkai, 1953. [2] + 8 + 346 pp., photos.

    A sequel to no. 1438 which was originally published in 1942 but lost during the course of World War II. Republished in its original form in 1953 with an additional chapter and photographs. Concentrates upon the internal development of Japanese settlements, emphasizing the educational, religious, social, and economic institutions before World War II.

1447. 日米時事社　帰化手ほどき市民讀本
Nichibei Jijisha. <u>Kika tehodoki shimin tokuhon</u> [Citizenship reader: Introduction to naturalization]. San Francisco: Nichibei Jijisha, 1953. 47 pp.

    A citizenship pamphlet to assist the Issei to pass their naturalization examination.

1448. 日墨協會　日墨協會會報
Nichiboku Kyōkai. <u>Nichiboku Kyōkai kaihō</u> [Japan-Mexico Society bulletin]. no. 1, 2 (Apr. 30, 1916, Mar. 30, 1917). Irregular. Tokyo.

    The bulletin of the Japan-Mexico Society founded in October, 1924 to promote good relations between the two nations.

1449. 新里貢一　事變下の滿鮮を歩む
Niisato Kan'ichi. <u>Jihenka no Man-Sen wo ayumu</u> [Trip through Korea and

Manchuria after the Manchurian Incident]. Tokyo: Shimpōsha, 1938. 12 + 4 + 397 pp., photos. X.

Impressions of a trip to Korea and Manchuria taken in 1936 by a deaf-blind Issei Christian.

1450. 羅府歸化權獲得期成同盟　　記録
Rafu Kikaken Kakutoku Kisei Dōmei. "Kiroku" [Records]. MSS. 1 vol., 1947. Los Angeles.

The minutes of the Naturalization Committee of Los Angeles from February to April, 1947, an organization established in February, 1947 to secure naturalization rights for the Issei.

1451. 瀧 初太郎　　世界無比の親日国大寳庫メキシコ
Ryū Hatsutarō. Sekai muhi no shin-Nichikoku: Dai-hōkō Mekishiko [The world's most pro-Japan nation: The vast treasure house of Mexico]. Mexico City: Kōshinsha, 1927. 2 + 12 + 15 + 687 + 79 pp., photos, map.

A compendium on Mexico which includes a Who's Who and directory.

1452. 齊藤広志　　ブラジルの日本人
Saitō Hiroshi. Burajiru no Nihonjin [The Japanese of Brazil]. Tokyo: Maruzen, 1960. [4] + 3 + 326 + index 6 + [5] pp., photos, bibliog., glossary, tables.

A scholarly, sociological study of the geographical, occupational, and social mobility of the Japanese immigrants and their descendants in Brazil.

1453. 佐々木三一郎　　吾らは何を學ぶべきか
Sasaki San'ichirō. Warera wa nani wo manabu beki ka ["What should we study?"]. New York: Kagaku Shisō Fukyūsha, 1923. 35 pp.

A communist pamphlet.

1454. 佐藤傳　　晩香坡日本共立語學校沿革史
Satō Tsutae. Bankūba Nihon Kyōritsu Gogakkō enkakushi ["History of the Vancouver Japanese Language School"]. Vancouver: Bankūba Nihon Kyōritsu Gogakkō Ijikai, 1954. 18 + 3 + 524 pp., photos.

A history of the Vancouver Japanese Language School established in 1906.

1455. 柴田峠太郎　　生命一元論
Shibata Shuntarō. Seimei ichigenron ["The monism of life"]. San Francisco: Aoki Taiseidō, 1921. [1] + 2 + 225 pp.

A philosophical treatise on human evolution.

1456. 大陸日報社　　加奈陀同胞發展史 第二
Tairiku Nippōsha. Kanada dōhō hattenshi: Dai-ni [History of the Japanese in Canada: No. 2]. Vancouver: Tairiku Nippōsha, 1917. 91 pp., photos. M (imperfect copy).

An updated successor to Kanada dōhō hattenshi [History of the Japanese in Canada] published in 1909 by the Tairiku Nippō [The Continental Daily].

The JARP microfilm includes pp. 28-91 on the economic status of the Japanese in British Columbia, the exclusion movement, and the Japanese who fought in Europe during World War I.

1457. 大陸日報社　　加奈陀同胞發展史第三
Tairiku Nippōsha. Kanada dōhō hattenshi: Dai-san [History of the Japanese in Canada: No. 3]. Vancouver: Tairiku Nippōsha, 1924. 112 + app. 38 pp. M (imperfect copy).

An updated successor to above. The JARP microfilm includes pp. 51-112 and the appendix.

1458. 竹下トマス　　大和魂と星条旗
Takeshita, Thomas K. Yamato-damashii to Seijōki ["Yamato-damashii under the Stars and Stripes"]. Tokyo: Sanno Shobō, 1967. 293 pp., photos.

A history of the Japanese struggle to secure naturalization rights and indemnification for evacuation losses during the immediate postwar period. Includes a brief autobiography of the author who assisted Mike Masaoka in Washington. Edited by Saruya Kaname.

1459. 都地聖一　　日英對照市民權受驗早わかり
Toji Seiichi. Nichi-Ei taishō shiminken juken hayawakari ["Lessons in citizenship in Japanese and English"]. Los Angeles: Toji Seiichi, 1951. 84 pp.

An English-Japanese booklet of typical questions and answers in naturalization examinations.

1460. 富田謙一　　日本人の新發展地・南米事情
Tomita Ken'ichi. Nihonjin no shin hattenchi: Nan-Bei jijō [The new land for the Japanese: Facts about South America]. Tokyo: Jitsugyō no Nihonsha, 1920 (9th printing). [3] + 7 + 325 pp., map.

A journalistic survey of Mexico, Peru, Chile, Argentina, and Brazil. The author depicts these countries as ideal places to which the Japanese should emigrate to solve Japan's population problem. First published in 1915.

1461. 当舎勝次　　全墨日系人住所錄
Tōsha Katsuji. Zen-Boku Nikkeijin jūshoroku ["Directorio general de los Japoneses residentes en la Republica Mexicana y sus descendentes"]. Mexico City: Shimizu Yukio Shoten, 1955. 442 pp., photos.

A directory and Who's Who of the Japanese in Mexico.

1462. 山崎寧翁傳記編纂會　　足跡
Yamazaki Yasushi-ō Denki Hensankai. Ashiato [Imprints]. Tokyo: Yamazaki Yasushi-ō Denki Hensankai, 1942. 10 + 6 + 429 + 2 pp., photo, chronology.

A biography of Yamazaki Yasushi, the publisher of the Tairiku Nippō [The Continental Daily], the founder and head of the Japanese Association of Canada, and a long-time member of the Japanese community of Vancouver.

INDEX

Abe, Eisaburo, 187
Abe Isoo, 71
Abe, Mrs. Roy, 188
Abe Seizō, 153
Abe, Steven K., 193
Abe, Toshiko, 188
Abiko Kyūtarō, 49, 137, 138, 162, 163, 169
Abiko, Yasuo W., 163
Adachi, Terry Terumasa, 190
Adachi, Wakako, 187
Agricultural Union of Southern Colorado. See Nankaku Nōgyō Kumiai
Agriculture, 10, 24, 25, 28, 30, 35, 71–79 passim., 83–87 passim., 120, 133, 164–171 passim.; floriculture, 83, 84, 142. See also Texas Rice Colony
Aichi Prefectural Association, 81
Aidaho-shū Chūō Nihonjinkai, 119–120
Aidaho-shū Nihonjinkai Rengō Kyōgikai, 120
Aihara, Niisaburo, 186
Aino Shigematsu, 122
Aiso, John, 161, 185
Aizumi Hisaharu, 157
Ajiya, 47
Akabane Chūemon, 162
Akagi Teiji, 153
Akahori, Ben M. See Akahori Masaru
Akahori Kiku, 163
Akahori Masaru, 112, 116, 140, 163, 175, 181, 185, 186, 205
Akamatsu, Alfred S., 193
Akamatsu Hiroyoshi, 65
Akamine Seichirō, 42
Akana Seiichi, 60
Akihiro Shūkō, 42
Akisada, Tami, 191
Akita, Taka, 190
Akiya Ichirō, 124–125
Allen, Walter J., Jr., 189
Aller, Curtis C., 193
Amano Keitarō, 15
Amano Torasaburō, 42
Amano, Yosh, 190

American immigration history, 7, 52
American Legion, 27
Amerika, 46
Amerika Gahō, 141
Amerika Shimbun, 92, 132–133
Anahaimu Furī Mesojisuto Kyōkai, 153
Anderson, Hugh H., 178–179
Andrews, Emery E., 191
Aoki Hisa. See Yamamoto Asako
Aoki, Joseph Shigeo, 187
Aoyagi Ikutarō, 103, 205
Aoyama, Mr. & Mrs. Fred, 189
Apton, Frank, 37
Arai Kyōko, 153, 154, 190
Aratani Setsuo, 131
Aratani Ukitarō, 144
Ariga Chiyokichi, 154
Arikawa, Tom, 189
Arima, John, 188, 190
Arima Sumikiyo, 50
Ariyoshi, Koji, 188
Arizona Nihonjinkai, 50
Asai, Masami, 189
Asakawa Kan'ichi, 48
Asami Nobuo, 36
Asano, Phoebe, 188
Asano Shichinosuke, 136, 154, 184
Asawa, Shigeru, 191
Ashizawa Riichi, 163–164
Associated Sugar Beet Growers of Southern California. See Nanka Rengō Satōdaikon Kōsakusha Kumiai
Atsuto Kuwa'ichi, 104–105
Austin, Verne, 179, 188
Autobiographies and biographies, 9, 10, 153–162, 163–172 passim., 206, 208
Ayakawa Takeji, 50
Azeka Shikai, 205
Azumi Suimei, 140, 143

Baba, Mr. & Mrs. Mas, 189
Baba, Yoshitaro, 189
Bailey, Paul, 4
Bailey, Thomas A., 5

Bakurei Gakusō, 142
Bakurei Nihonjinkai, 120
Baldwin, Roger, 192
Ban Shinzaburō, 48, 49, 159
Barnhart, Edward N., 13 *n.*, 173, 179
Beifu Kenkyūkai, 96
Beikoku Gokyō, 93-94
Beikoku Jitsugyō Jihō, 133
Beikoku Kōyasan Betsuin Jihō, 94
Beikoku Nihongo Kenkyūkai, 108
Beikoku Sangyō Nippō, 133
Beikoku Seihokubu Renraku Nihonjinkai, 74, 118
Bell, Mary S., 193
Bell, Reginald, 8, 193
Berkeley Free Methodist Church, 90-91
Berkowitz, Madelon H., 193
Berry, Arthur D., 52
Biddle, Francis, 192
Blaine Memorial Methodist Church, 147
Boddy, Manchester E., 6
Bowles, Gilbert, 52
Bratton, J. Wesley, 193
Bridge, David A., 194
Bristow, R.M., 194
Brown, Arthur J., 194
Bryan, William Jennings, 60, 66
Buddhist Churches of America, 94, 147
Buell, Raymond L., 4, 5
Bunch, Ralph E., 194
Burajiru Nikkeijin Jittai Chōsa Iinkai, 205
Burns, John A., 188
Burns, Philips & Co., Ltd., 36
Businesses, 3, 35, 77, 83-87 *passim.*, 142-143, 164-171 *passim.*

California Flower Market, Inc., 142. See *also* Kashū Kaki Ichiba Kabushiki Kaisha
California Japanese Shoemakers League. See Kashū Nihonjin Kutsukō Dōmeikai
California White Spot Association, 27
Carey, John J., 194
Carr, William C., 179
Carras, Mary, 194
Cartoons, 112
Caudill, William A., 194
Central Japanese Agricultural Association of California. See Kashū Nihonjin Chūō Nōkai
Chansler, Horace F., 194
Chapman, Gordon, 187
Chiba Toyoji, 58
Chicago Japanese Congregational Church, 94, 95
Chijiwa, Saikichi, 194
Chikami, Hatsutaro, 189

Chinda Sutemi, 21, 162
Chinen, Theodore Kamasuke, 188
Chinese exclusion movement, 52-55 *passim.*, 57, 62, 66
Chinese in America, 6, 38
Chinese Six Companies, 38
Chino Tsuneji, 164
Cho, Chang-soo, 194
Chū-Hokka Hiroshima Kenjinkai Remmei Kyōkai, 147
Chūka Jihō, 133
Chūō Jihō, 133
Civic Unity Hostel, 85
Coletta, Paolo E., 5
Colusa Japanese Language School, 115
Colusa Memorial Society. See Korūsa Bosankai
Communiqué, 173
Conroy, Francis H. See Conroy, Hilary
Conroy, Hilary, 4, 9, 11, 194
Co-operative Farm Industry of Southern California, 161. See *also* Nanka Chūō Sangyō Kumiai
Cornell, John B., 10-11
Cortez Japanese Language School, 105
Croft, Carma H., 194
Crystal City Times, 173
Cummings, Orpha, 13 *n.*

Dai-Hiroshima-ken, 41-42
Dai Nihon Bummei Kyōkai, 69
Dairiki, Fusakichi, 186
Daniels, Roger, 4, 5, 10, 194
Darby, Harold E., 194-195
Davis, Merle, 52
DeForest, Charlotte B., 179
Denba Shimpō. See *Santō Jiji*
Denson Jihō, 173
Denson Tribune, 173
Desert Sentinel, 174
De Vos, George, 10
Dōhō, 133
Dōhōsha, 181
Doi, Helen N., 195
Doi, Nelson K., 188
Doi, Thomas Toshiteru, 184
Doi Uchizō, 133
Doi, Yutaka, 188
Domoto, Takanoshin, 9
Domoto, Toichi, 187
Downing, Ferne, 175

Ebara Soroku, 52
Ebihara Hachirō, 132
Ebihara Naoko, 126
Eckstein, Gustav, 9

Eda, Harry M., 190
Ekuni Jinzō, 147
Emigration: ideology of, 4, 36–49 *passim.*; origins and causes of, 8, 9, 19–49 *passim.*, 69–71, 168; Japanese government policy, 19–49 *passim.*, 74; emigration companies, 20–22, 33, 36, 37, 45; passport laws and regulations, 20, 32–34, 42, 45, 46; transmigration from Hawaii, 20, 22, 26, 32; to South America, 21, 22, 32, 33, 36–41 *passim.*, 70, 71, 205, 208; to other countries, 21, 22, 32, 33, 36, 37, 41, 70, 71; of *yobiyose*, 24, 30; education of emigrants, 38, 39, 41; journals, 46, 47
Endo, Ichiro, 187
Endō Kōshirō, 105
Endō Reiko, 96
Endo, Mrs. Yori, 188
Endow, Kumakichi, 191
Enko-shi Nihonjinkai. *See* Yuta-shū Nihonjinkai
Ennis, Edward J., 189
Enomoto, H.Y., 191
Enomoto Takeaki, 46
Esthus, Raymond A., 5
Eta, 10
Eto, Masaji, 186
Etō Tameji, 161
Evacuation Marriage Club, 185

Ferguson, Edwin E., 5
Fiction and literary essays, 124, 125, 175–178 *passim.*
First Japanese Congregational Church of San Diego, 90
Fishery, 84
Fisk University, 10
Five Pacific Coast Regional Committees and The Institute of Social and Religious Research, 154
Flowers, Montaville, 6
Fowler, Ruth H., 195
Freeman, George H., 195
Frick and Satow Case, 30
Fuchiwaki, Hirokuni, 186
Fujii, Bunzo, 191
Fujii, Henry Hajime, 188
Fujii Hidegorō, 74
Fujii, Maruo, 187
Fujii Sei, 83, 135, 140
Fujii Shin'ichi, 50
Fujii Shūji, 133
Fujii Yoshito, 164, 191
Fujimoto, Isao, 13 *n.*
Fujimura Nobuo, 69
Fujioka Shirō, 48, 50–51, 71, 118, 154, 161, 164
Fujioka, Teruo, 154
Fujishima Taisuke, 175
Fujita, Jonathan, 188
Fujita, Michinari, 10
Fukano Riichirō (Shun'u), 126
Fukkatsu, 94
Fukuda, Inokichi, 188
Fukuda Masako, 154
Fukuda Yoshiaki, 96, 154
Fukui, Ida, 189
Fukui Kenjinkai, 147. *See also* Fukui Prefectural Association
Fukui, Moto, 189
Fukui Prefectural Association, 81. *See also* Fukui Kenjinkai
Fukui, Shuichi, 191
Fukuinkai, 9, 42, 82, 92
Fukuma, George T., 188
Fukunaga, George J., 188
Fukunaga, George T., 186
Fukunaga, Kofuji, 186
Fukunaga, Kuju, 185
Fukunaga Torajirō, 74
Fukuoka, Fumiko, 195
Fukuoka, Hajime, 195
Fukuoka Prefectural Association, 80
Fukushima Kumazō, 88
Fukushima Overseas Association, 81
Fukushima Prefectural Association, 81
Fukushima, Sango, 187
Fukutomi Masatoshi, 136
Fukuzaki, Ben, 185
Fukuzawa Yukichi, 158
Fuller, Varden, 195
Fumikura Heisaburō, 92
Funagoshi Mitsunojō, 60
Furukawa Eiji, 79
Furukawa, Kameo, 186
Furuya Magojirō, 155
Furuya Shin'ichi, 179
Fuse Tsunematsu, 206

Gādenā no Tomo, 142
Gaimushō, 19, 36, 60
Gardena Valley Young Buddhist Association, 90
Gardner, Dorothy A., 195
Garrity, Donald L., 195
Garyū Gakujin, 60–61
Geibijin, 142
George, Robert C.L., 195
Gibbons, Don C., 195
Gila News Courier, 174
Girdner, Audrie, 3
Glenn, Jana, 195

Godaishū, 142
Golden Gate International Exposition, 1939, 181
Gospel Society. *See* Fukuinkai
Goto, Baron Y., 181, 188
Gotō Chinpei, 112
Gotō Takeo, 51
Goto, Taro, 187
Granada Pioneer, 174
Greater Japan Agricultural Society (North American branch), 84
Griswold, A. Whitney, 5
Grodzins, Morton M., 195
Gruver, Rebecca B., 195
Guiang, Marcelino C., 196
Guides to America, 42–46
Gulick, Sidney, 6, 7
Guranada Ginsha, 175

Hābā Nikkeijinkai, 147
Hachimonji Kumezō, 164
Hachiya, Josie, 190
Hachiya, Rupert, 190
Hagio Iwao (Imosaku), 126
Hairando Pāku Mesojisuto Kyōkai, 96
Hale, Robert M., 196
Hamada, Shig, 191
Hamakawa, Mojiro, 186
Hamanishi, Yasukichi, 191
Hamano Hideo, 70
Hamataka, T., 186
Hanasono Photo Studio, 147
Hanaya Koan, 164
Hanaya, Koe, 190
Hancock, Mrs. Robert C., 191
Hanihara Masao, 49, 64
Hara Katsurō, 66
Harada, Koichi G., 196
Harada Toyojirō, 51, 66
Harano, Earl, 189
Hasegawa Shin'ichirō, 66, 205
Hashiguchi, Yukio, 189
Hashimoto, Itsuki, 192
Hata, Donald T., 196
Hatani, Motoo, 184
Hatchmonji, K. *See* Hachimonji Kumezō
Hāto Maunten Bungei, 175–176
Hātosan Senchinerusha, 176
Hattori Ayao, 48
Hattori, Buheiji, 191
Hattori, Frank, 191
Hattori Takayuki, 176
Hawai Bukkyō Seinenkai, 96
Hawai Chū Gakkō, Hawai Kōtō Jogakkō Kōyūkai, 105
Hawai Hōchi, 133–134. *See also* Hawai Hōchisha
Hawai Hōchisha, 145
Hawai Kyōikukai, 105, 108, 109. *See also* Hawai Kyōikukai Hensanbu
Hawai Kyōikukai Hensanbu, 105
Hawai Nihonjin Iminshi Kankō Iinkai, 74
Hawai Shimpōsha, 145
Hawai Taimusu, 134. *See also* Hawai Taimususha; Nippu Jijisha
Hawai Taimususha, 145
Hawaii Education Association. *See* Hawai Kyōikukai; Hawai Kyōikukai Hensanbu
Hawaii Evangelical Association, 96
Hawaii Girls' School, 105
Hawaii High School, 105
Hawaii Y.B.A., 97
Hawaiian Bureau of Immigration, 36
Hayano, Frank Eizo, 188
Hayashi, Hana, 192
Hayashi Hisajirō, 37
Hayashi, Kotaro, 186
Hayashi Tomihei, 61
Hayashida, Akiyoshi, 196
Hayes, Robert W., 196
Heart Mountain Sentinel, 174
Henmi, Isamu, 186
Hennefrund, Helen E., 13 *n*.
Hennings, Robert E., 196
Hertzler, Virginia B., 196
Hertzog, Dorothy B., 196
Hibi, George M. *See* Hibi Matsusaburō
Hibi Matsusaburō, 164
Hidekawa Motohiko, 165
Hideshima Shichisaburō, 70, 184
Higa, Thomas S., 188
Higa, Thomas Taro, 179
Higashi, Unosuke, 187
Highland Park Methodist Church, 90, 101. *See also* Hairando Pāku Mesojisuto Kyōkai
Higuchi, Hiro, 188
Hikido, James Junichi, 184
Hilo Independent Girls' High School. *See* Hiro Dokuritsu Chū Jogakkō
Hioki Eki, 37
Hira Jihō, 174
Hirabayashi, Gladys S., 189
Hirabayashi, Gordon K., 196
Hirabayashi, Toshiyuki, 188
Hiraga Shigemasa, 136
Hirahara, Takemaru, 188
Hiramoto Mōdō, 66
Hiranuma Yoshirō, 51
Hirasawa, Hatsue Esther, 191
Hiro Dokuritsu Chū Jogakkō, 105
Hirohata, Paul T., 103

Hirooka, N., 187
Hirose Shūrei, 79–80
Hiroshima Kenjinkai, 147
Hiroshima Prefectural Association, 80, 81, 82, 142. See also Chū-Hokka Hiroshima Kenjinkai Remmei Kyōkai; Hiroshima Kenjinkai; Nanka Hiroshima Kenjinkai
Hiroshima-ken Kaigai Kyōkai, 41–42
Hiroshima-ken Naigai Jihō, 41
Hiroshima-ken Shokumin Kyōkai, 41
Hirota Tsunegorō, 80
Historiography, 10, 11, 11 n.
Hokka Kirisuto Kyōkai Dōmei, 88, 97
Hokka Kirkutokyō Dendōdan, 95
Hokka Kirisutokyōto Dōmei, 95
Hokka Nihongo Gakuen Kyōkai, 106
Hokka Nihonjinkai, 75
Hokubei Hōchi Shimbunsha, 151
Hokubei Hōchisha, 148
Hokubei Hyōron, 140–141, 142
Hokubei Jijisha, 145
Hokubei Mainichi Shimbunsha, 145, 148
Hokubei Mesojisuto. See *Beikoku Gokyō*
Hokubei Okinawa Kurabu, 148
Hokubei Senryū, 126
Hokubei Senryū Ginsha, 126
Hokubei Senryū Gosenkai, 126
Hokubei Shimpō, 134. See also Hokubei Shimpōsha
Hokubei Shimpōsha, 148
Hokubei Tairiku Seichō no Ie Renrakubu, 148
Hokushin, 134
Holliday, Margaret A., 196
Hompa Hongwanji, 97
Hompa Hongwanji Gakumubu, 112
Hompa Hongwanji Mission of Hawaii, 88, 89, 97, 114. See also Hompa Hongwanji; Hompa Hongwanji Gakumubu; Hongwanji Gakumubu
Honda Shinjirō (Kahō), 126
Honda, Yuzo, 188
Hongwanji Gakumubu, 109
Honjō Eijirō, 15
Honoruru Shimbun, 134
Horike, Kumaichi, 192
Horinouchi, Isao, 196
Horiuchi, Mas, 134
Hoshi Hajime, 136
Hoshimiya Sadayo, 165
Hoshimiya Tosuke, 165
Hoshizaki, George, 186
Hoshizaki, Mary, 186
Hosokawa, William K., 4
Hototogisu, 130
Hozaka Kamesaburō (Kiichi), 124
Hull, Eleanor, 9

Hunter, Louise H., 196
Huntley, E.A., 188
Hyde, Helen I., 196
Hyūga Terutake, 49

Ibuka Seiko, 97
Ichihashi, Yamato, 7, 8, 48
Ichikawa Nuisaburō (Dogū), 126
Ichioka, Yuji, 10, 11
Iesu no Tomo, 94
Iga, Mamoru, 197
Iijima Eitarō, 43
Iijima Kanjitsu, 97
Ike Hyakumatsu, 80
Ikeda, Hitoshi, 186
Ikeda Kandō, 113, 140–141, 142, 176
Ikeda, Kiyoshi, 197
Ikeda Nobumasa, 155
Ikemura Heitarō, 71
Imagire, Sonao, 189
Imamura Emyō, 51, 88, 89, 97
Imin Hogo Kyōkai, 45
Imin Mondai Kenkyūkai, 37, 69–70
Immigrant society: general studies of, 3, 4, 6, 7, 10; origins and development of, 9, 19–49 passim.; "undesirables" in, 19, 20; monetary remissions from, 24–26, 32; deaths in, 25, 32, 34; picture-brides of, 27, 29, 58; Consular registries of, 34, 35; population of, 35, 49; general histories of, 71–74; regional and local histories of, 74–79; histories by Prefectural origins of, 79–82. See also Emigration
Inabata Katsutarō, 51
Inada Shūnosuke, 48
Inahara Katsuji, 52, 58, 59, 61
Inai, George Y., 188
Inashima, Mrs. S., 188
Ino Masayoshi, 155
Inose Inosuke, 159
Inoue Kakugorō, 157–158
Inoue Kikuchi, 108
Inoue Masaji, 37
Inoue Masakatsu, 37
Inoue Tanefumi, 44
Inouye, Toshio, 187
Inouye, Toyoji, 186
Internment, 175–178; studies of, 3, 4; autobiographies of, 154, 160; personal papers of, 163–172 passim., 178–180; assembly center and camp newspapers, 173–175
Irie Toraji, 70
Iriye, Akira, 4, 5, 11
Irwin, Robert W., 36
Iseri, George, 190

Ishida Kumajirō, 43
Ishida, Sue, 168
Ishida Tenkai, 155
Ishigo, Arthur Shigeharu, 180
Ishigo, Estelle, 180
Ishii, Cecil J., 189
Ishii Itarō, 37–38
Ishii, Kametaro, 189
Ishii Kikutarō, 110
Ishikawa Kiyoshi, 98
Ishikawa, Michiji, 197
Ishikawa Misao, 144
Ishikawa, Tetsujiro, 185
Ishikawa Yasujirō, 52
Ishioka Hikokazu, 75
Ishizaki Senmatsu, 136
Ishizuka Iozō, 43
Isobe Hōsen, 89
Issei Dendōbu, 90
Itano, Masao, 186
Itō Banshō, 75, 98
Ito, Hiroshi, 10
Itō Kazuo, 75
Itō Keiichi, 206
Iwamoto Hideo, 59
Iwanaga Tomoki, 155
Iwasa, George, 190
Iwasaki, Ike, 190
Iwasaki Yasukichi, 165
Iwata, Masakazu, 10, 126, 185
Iwata Sakutarō, 72
Iwata Tatsue, 126
Iwataki, Daisuke, 185
Izutsu Shirō, 133

Jackman, Norman R., 197
JACL, 148. See also Japanese American Citizens League
JACL Reporter, 134
Japan, America, Hawaii Society. See Nihon Beifu Kyōkai
Japan American Society of Los Angeles, 167
Japan Herarudo, 134
Japan-Mexico Society, 206
Japan Society of Los Angeles, 167. See also Japan Society of Southern California
Japan Society of Southern California, 66
Japan Trader's Club of Los Angeles, 144
Japanese American Citizens League, 1, 4, 11, 134, 137, 166, 168, 184; miscellaneous records of, 111; Pocatello Chapter, records of, 111
Japanese American Courier, 134
Japanese American Evacuation and Resettlement Collection, 180
Japanese-American Fraternity of Los Angeles, 167
Japanese American League of Los Angeles, 167
Japanese-American News Corp. See *Hokubei Shimpō*
Japanese American Research Project, 1, 168, 184; history of, 11–13; survey schedules of, 155
Japanese Associations, 10, 21, 24, 28, 30–32, 71–79 *passim.*, 117, 118; publications of, 118, 119; records of, 119–123
Japanese Benevolent Society. See Kashū Nihonjin Jikeikai
Japanese Businessmen's Association of Los Angeles, 86, 142. See also Japanese Chamber of Commerce of Southern California; Nanka Nihonjin Shōgyō Kaigisho; Rafu Nihonjin Jitsugyō Kumiai
Japanese Chamber of Commerce of Southern California, 77, 86, 143, 144, 169. See also Nanka Nihonjin Shōgyō Kaigisho; Nanka Nikkeijin Shōgyō Kaigisho
Japanese Children's Home of Southern California, 114, 116. See also Nanka Shōnien
Japanese Church Federation of Southern California. See Nanka Dendōdan; Nanka Kirisutokyō Kyōkai Remmei
Japanese Community Council of Los Angeles, 148
Japanese exclusion movement, 19–68 *passim.*, English studies of, 4–7; opponents of, 6, 7, 26, 27, 31; 1924 Immigration Act, 7, 26–31, 60–65; alien land laws, 23–25, 28–30, 58–60, 164; Japanese language schools, 28, 29, 39, 145; Americanization, 31, 51, 54, 92. See also Immigrant society; Law; Second generation; United States-Japan relations
Japanese Farmers' Association of Turlock. See Tārakku Jitsugyōkai
Japanese Humane Society of Los Angeles County. See Rosuanzerusu-gun Nihonjin Jindōkai
Japanese in other countries, 25, 26, 43, 68, 206, 207, 208
Japanese Jewelers' Association of Los Angeles. See Rafu Tokeishō Kumiai
Japanese Language School Cooperative System, Inc. See Nihongo Gakuen Kyōdō Shisutemu
Japanese language schools, 71–79 *passim.*, 104–109, 115, 165, 207. See also Japanese exclusion movement; Second generation
Japanese Presbyterian Churches and Mission of the Pacific Coast, 101

Japanese Presbyterian Mission of Wintersburg, 90
Japanese Student Association of Los Angeles, 143
Japanese Student Bulletin, The, 94
Japanese Student Club, University of California, Berkeley, 142
Japanese Students' Christian Association in North America, The, 94, 148
Japanese Youth Association of Pocatello. See Pokatero Nihonjin Seinenkai
Jichikai Jihō, 174
Jikihara Toshihei, 128, 165
Jiryū, 124
Jitsugyō Geppō, 142
Jitsugyō no Hawai, 142, 146
Jitsugyō no Nihon, 48
Jitsugyō no Sekai. See *Mita Shōgyōkai*
Jiyū. See *Takoma Jihō*
Jōdo Shinshū, 96
Johnson, Florence, B., 197
Johnson, Hiram W., 52
Joichi, Kiyoshi, 189
Jones, Maldwyn, 7
Jordan Dōshikai, 170

Kaapu, Myrtle K., 197
Kadoya, Tokio Ed, 186
Kagawa Toyohiko, 94
Kagawa, Mr. & Mrs. Yonakichi, 190
Kageyama, Otsuji, 188
Kagiwada, Frank E. See Kagiwada Eiho
Kagiwada Eiho, 165
Kagiwada, Harry Y. See Kagiwada Yoshifusa
Kagiwada Yoshifusa, 165
Kagoshima Prefectural Association of Southern California, 186
Kai, Gunki, 197
Kai, Jiro, 185
Kai Shizuya, 98
Kaigai Ijū, 37
Kaigai Nikkeijin Renraku Kyōkai, 70
Kaihara Sakae, 80, 112
Kaikyūsen, 135
Kaji, Bruce, 137
Kakazu Hashiji, 155–156
Kakiuchi, Mike, 187
Kaku, Yasaji, 185
Kakudo, 124
Kakushū Jiji, 135, 151
Kallstedt, Frances E., 197
Kamada Eikichi, 52
Kamae Takashi, 175, 176
Kamayatsu, Charles, 185
Kami, Junichi, 187

Kamide Masataka, 156
Kamiji, Kumachiyo, 187
Kamikawa, Hikomatsu, 5, 38, 52
Kamitsuka, Mr. & Mrs. David Kainichi, 186
Kamiyama, Frank Urasaburo, 186
Kanagawa Prefectural Association, 82
Kanagawa, Wayne Y., 197
Kanai Shigeo, 52, 75
Kanashiki, 124
Kanaya, Dick, 191
Kanehara Setsu, 166. See also Nagata Setsuko
Kaneko, Bert Yosaburo. See Kaneko Yosaburō
Kaneko, Sue, 190
Kaneko Tetsugo, 136
Kaneko Yosaburō, 166, 185
Kanemoto, Rie, 186
Kanemoto, Yutaka, 189
Kaneshiro Takeo, 142, 156
Kano, Hiram K., 188
Kanō Hisanori, 154, 156
Kano, Tosh, 191
Kano, Toshiyuki, 166
Kanomata, Chuzaburo, 188
Kanzaki Kiichi, 61
Kanzaki, Ralph, 189
Kasahara, Yoshiko, 197
Kasai, Alice, 166, 190
Kasai, Henry Y. See Kasai Yoshihiko
Kasai Hiroshi, 156
Kasai Hiroshi-ō Yawa Kankō Iinkai, 156
Kasai Jūji, 166
Kasai Kenji, 166
Kasai, Kiyo, 188
Kasai Shigeharu, 52
Kasai Yoshihiko, 166
Kashitani Junrō, 156
Kashiwamura Kazusuke, 75
Kashū Kaki Ichiba Geppō, 142
Kashū Kaki Ichiba Kabushiki Kaisha, 83
Kashū Mainichi Shimbun, 135. See also Kashū Mainichi Shimbunsha
Kashū Mainichi Shimbunsha, 148
Kashū Nihonjin Chūō Nōkai, 83
Kashū Nihonjin Jikeikai, 115
Kashū Nihonjin Kutsukō Dōmeikai, 83
Kashū Nōsan Shūhō. See *Beikoku Sangyō Nippō*
Kataoka Guardianship Case, 30
Katayama Kageo, 143, 181
Katayama Sen, 43, 47, 48, 49, 169
Katayama, Yutaka, 185
Katō Bungo, 66
Kato, Henry, 189
Kato, Henry D., 190

Kato, Henry T., 189
Kato, Mrs. Ise, 191
Katō Jūshirō, 71–72
Katō Kisaburō, 70
Katō Shin'ichi, 72, 76
Kato, Toshio, 191
Katsumoto, Mrs. Hideo, 187
Katsuro, Mary, 190
Katsuro, Paul, 190
Kawabe, Harry S. See Kawabe, Harry Sotaro
Kawabe, Harry Sotaro, 166, 191, 192
Kawabe Sōtarō. See Kawabe, Harry Sotaro
Kawada Ken, 156
Kawaguchi, Mrs. Haruo, 187
Kawaguchi, Mr. & Mrs. Hinokichi, 191
Kawaguchi, Sanjiro, 184
Kawai, Mrs. S., 188
Kawai Yoshisada, 156
Kawakami, Charles S., 190
Kawakami, Clarke H., 167, 192
Kawakami, Harvey S., 188
Kawakami, Karl K. See Kawakami Kiyoshi
Kawakami Kiyoshi, 6, 7, 9, 48, 157, 167
Kawakami, Mary, 190
Kawakata, Harry M., 186
Kawamata Giichi, 98
Kawamoto, Chisato, 187
Kawamura, Eijiro, 190
Kawamura, Fred Nobuichi, 188
Kawamura, Mrs. H.Y., 188
Kawamura Masahei (Yūsen), 109, 167
Kawamura Tetsutarō, 44
Kawamura, Mrs. Yasu, 186
Kawano, Gohachi H., 187
Kawano, Satsuyo, 190
Kawaoka, Risuke, 187
Kawasaki, Kenichi, 197
Kawasaki Minotarō, 48
Kawasaki, Yukitaro, 185
Kawashima Isami, 66–67
Kawashimo Nihonjinkai, 120
Kawashimo Nōgyō Dōmeikai. See Kawashimo Nihonjinkai
Kawasoe, Masuko, 190
Kawazoe Zen'ichi, 75–76
Kayōkai, 126, 127
Kazahaya Katsu'ichi, 80
Kazumata, Ryotetsu, 188
Keieisei, 157
Kelley, Tim K., 197
Kemuyama Sentarō, 52
Kenmochi Sada'ichi, 135
Kern, Ruth, 197
Kessler, James B., 197
Kida, James Keijiro, 189
Kido, Saburo, 138, 185
Kigen Nisenroppyakunen Hōshuku Kaigai Dōhō Tōkyō Taikai Honbu, 70
Kikuchi Kenji, 157
Kikuchi, Miya S., 167, 186
Kikuchi, Yoriyuki, 186
Kikushima, Janet Shigeko, 189
Kimura Akira, 52–53
Kimura Ki, 177
Kimura, Shunichi, 188
Kimura Yoshigorō, 44, 134
Kimura, Yukiko, 190
Kimura, Yukiko, 198
Kinmon Nippō, 135
Kirisuto Kyōkai Shūhō, 176
Kishida Eizan, 98
Kita Reikichi, 67
Kitagawa Keijirō, 157
Kitamura, Samuel H., 198
Kitano, Harry L., 3, 13 n.
Kitano, Motoji, 184, 187
Kitasako, Ken, 186
Kitazawa Tetsuji, 98
Kitazawa Toranosuke, 44
Kiyama Yoshitaka, 112
Kiyasu, Kunisada, 184
Kiyohara Danzō, 167
Kobara, Shigechika, 186
Kobayashi, Haruko, 192
Kobayashi Masasuke, 53, 97, 155, 162
Kobayashi, Naoki, 190
Kobayashi, Sakae, 190
Kōbe Kōtō Shōgyō Gakkō Shōgyō Kenkyūjo, 15
Kōda Keisaburō, 70
Kōda Kisatsuchi, 57
Kodaira Naomichi, 98
Kodama Hosoe, 167
Kodama Kinsuke, 167
Kodama, Yoshiko, 186
Koga Gentarō, 167
Koga, Takeshi, 184
Koga, Tats, 191
Kōgen no Hoshi, 94
Koide Jō, 157, 185
Kojima, Masamori, 144
Kojima, Moonray, 189
Kojimoto Yūjirō, 157
Kojō Yutaka, 157–158
Kokumin no Tomo, 48
Kokumin Shimbun. See *Hokushin*
Kokusai Shokuryō Nōgyō Kyōkai, 83–84
Kokusaku Kenkyūkai, 67
Komatsu, Kiyo, 185
Kondo, Carl, 114
Kondō Chōyei, 98, 185, 206

Kondō Kikujirō, 106, 148
Kono, Ayako, 198
Kono, Charles Hio, 28
Kono, Ralph Y., 191
Konvitz, Milton R., 7
Kōriyama Tadashi (Sansen), 127
Kororado Shimbun, 135
Korūsa Bosankai, 115
Kosaka, Kumesaburo, 184
Kosaki, Mildred D., 198
Kōshijin, 159
Kosuge, Some, 188
Kotani Tokusui, 99
Koyama, Sashichi S., 188
Koyama, Shiroichi, 186
Koyama, Takashi, 188
Koyasan Buddhist Temple, 94, 148
Kreider, Suzie Tanaka, 187
Kubata, Sam, 191
Kubo, Ellen, 186
Kubo, Goroku, 191
Kubota, Gontaro, 192
Kubota Kenzō, 95
Kubota, Kiyo, 192
Kubota, Takeshi, 191
Kubota Tetsuo, 84
Kubushiro Naokatsu, 158
Kubushiro Ochimi, 158
Kuga, James M., 192
Kuida, Kameichi, 185
Kumagai, Mr. & Mrs. Chozo, 189
Kumagai, Harry H., 190
Kumamoto Overseas Association, 81
Kumiai Jihō, 135
Kunitsugu Shirō, 129
Kuramoto, Harry, 190
Kurita, Isaburo, 184
Kuroda Ken'ichi, 38
Kurokawa, Minako, 198
Kurokawa, Tom H., 186
Kuroki, Ben, 10, 161
Kurosawa, Kiyoko T., 9
Kushibashi, Mrs. Tsuta, 192
Kuwahara, Frank, 185
Kuwayama Senzō, 156, 189
Kuzuhara Sada'ichi, 101
Kyōdan, 94
Kyōgoku Itsuzō, 99
Kyōyū Jiji, 135–136

Laborers, 44, 75, 85, 164, 165. *See also* Agriculture; Emigration; Immigrant society
La Violette, Forrest E., 8, 198
Law: naturalization question, 55, 56, 59–61, 74, 146, 205–208; naturalization litigation, 28, 52; alien land law cases, 28, 30, 168; guardianship and other cases, 28, 30, 31. *See also* Japanese exclusion movement
League of Nations, 52, 54, 140
Lehman, Anthony L., 3
Leiter, Russell G., 198
Lentz, Katherine J., 198
Lerrigo, Marion Olive, 9
Light, Ivan H., 3
Lind, Andrew W., 198
Linderfelt, Florence M., 198
Loftis, Anne, 3
Loosley, Allyn C., 198
Los Angeles Examiner, 27
Los Angeles Free Methodist Church, 100
Los Angeles Japanese Baptist Church, 148
Los Angeles Methodist Episcopal Church, 94. *See also* Yuki Shōjirō; Rafu Nihonjin Mii Kyōkai
Los Angeles Nippon Institute. *See* Rafu Uwa-Machi Dai-Ni Gakuen
Lum, Kalfred D., 198
Lum, William W., 13 n.
Lutscher, Francois, 36
Lyman, Stanford M., 3

Maboroshi no Tsubasa, 94
Machida Tamotsu, 99
Maeda, Mr. and Mrs. T., 191
Maeda Teruo, 181
Magistretti, William, 14
Maguna, 124
Makabe, Wilson, 189
Makiki Seijō Kyōkai, 99
Makino Kinzaburō, 134, 158
Makino Kinzaburō Den Hensan Iinkai, 158
Makishima Tokuhisa, 70
Manchurian Incident, 67
Manzanar Free Press, 174
Marshall, Emily L., 199
Martin, Ralph G., 10
Marumoto, Masaji, 167–168, 188
Marutani, William, 190
Maruyama Senkyoku, 76
Marysville Japanese Language School, 107
Masaoka, Joe Grant, 12, 168
Masaoka, Mike, 111, 161, 185, 188, 208
Mashbir, Sidney, 187
Masuda, Minoru, 191
Masuoka, Jitsuichi, 199
Masuoka, Matthew M., 190
Masuoka, Ushitada, 187
Matson, Floyd W., 199
Matsubara Kazuo, 61
Matsuda Eiji, 206

Matsuda, Mitsugu, 14
Matsuda Motosuke, 151
Matsuda Shizuko, 158
Matsuda, Ueto, 185
Matsuda Umasaburō, 158
Matsuda Yoshiko, 127
Matsueda Yasuji, 53
Matsui, Haru, 9
Matsui, Shichiro, 199
Matsumoto Gennosuke (Rokuyō), 127
Matsumoto, Glenn, 186
Matsumoto Honkō, 141, 152, 176
Matsumoto Kazumitsu, 113
Matsumoto, Manki, 185
Matsumoto, Seishichi, 189
Matsumoto, Shizu, 189
Matsumoto Tomiko, 127
Matsumoto, Toru, 9
Matsumoto, Tsuyoshi, 168
Matsumoto, Waichi, 187
Matsunaga, Spark, 186, 192
Matsuo Shōichi, 73
Matsuoka Toshiya, 103
Matsusakaya Shoten Hensanbu, 181
Matsushima, Umata, 189
Matsushita Iwao, 99, 141
Matsuura, Mrs. Shinobu, 187
Maui Education Association. *See* Maui Kyōikukai
Maui Kyōikukai, 106
Maui Shimbun, 131, 136. *See also* Yasui Satosuke (Shōsō)
Maxwell, Edward J., 199
May, Ernest R., 11
McClatchy, V.S., 57
McCollum, A.H., 192
McGovern, Melvin P., 180
McGovney, Dudley O., 5
McKenzie, Roderick D., 7
McReynolds, George E., 5, 199
Mears, Eliot G., 7
Medals and citations, 34
Meiji Emigration Company, 22, 36–37
Mercedian, The, 174
Meredith, Gerald M., 199
Merisubiru Chihō Nihonjinkai, 76
Methodist Voice, The, 94
Mie Prefectural Association, 80–81
Mie-ken Kaigai Kyōkai, 80–81
Miematsu Yasuo (Jōnan), 127
Mihara, Genji, 191
Mihara Tokinobu, 168, 184
Miho, Katsuro, 188
Mikuriya Tadafumi, 168
Millis, Harry A., 6, 7
Milnes, Harold P., 199

Minami Engan Jihō, 136
Minami, Henry Yaemon, 186
Minami Ryō, 53
Minidoka Irrigator, The, 174
Misaki, Hisakichi, 199
Mita Shōgyōkai, 48
Mitamura, Masuo, 185
Mitamura, Taeko, 185
Mitoma Tōshichi, 158
Mitoma Yoshie, 158
Miura Sōgorō, 99
Miwa Haruie, 74
Miya, Elna, 190
Miya, J.G., 191
Miya, Naka, 191
Miyagi Prefectural Association of Southern California, 82. *See also* Nanka Miyagi Kenjinkai
Miyagishima, Kamasaku, 191
Miyagishima Nonkibō, 168
Miyagishima, Terumasa Y.K., 191
Miyahara, Eizo, 184
Miyakawa, T. Scott, 4, 12
Miyake, Noboru, 188
Miyake Yūjirō, 48
Miyako, Kozo, 189
Miyamoto, David, 185
Miyamoto, Frank S., 10, 11
Miyamoto, Gunzo, 186
Miyamoto, Shichiro, 199
Miyamoto, Tomizo, 192
Miyamura, Hiroshi, 161
Miyata Kazue, 138
Miyatake, Daisuke, 191
Miyatake, Toyo, 185
Miyeno, Jim, 189
Mizote, Kazumi, 191
Mizoue, Misayo, 188
Mizukami, Naonobu, 191
Mizushima, Arata, 185
Mizutani Bangaku, 81, 137
Mizutani, Ginji, 186
Mizutani, Masataro, 186
Mizutani Shōzō, 76
Mochizuki, Jiro, 191
Modell, John, 10, 199
Mohabe, 176
Momii Ikken, 113, 138
Momita, Harry, 187
Monobe, Kazuko, 191
Montgomery, William L., 199
Mori Keizō, 71
Mori, Mrs. Ritta, 189
Morikawa, Harry H., 190
Morishige Toshio, 103
Morita, Hatsuo, 186

Morita Jirō, 180
Morita Riichi (Gyokuto), 127
Morita, Shizue, 186
Morita, Tohru, 9
Moriyama Morito, 62
Moroi Rokurō, 38
Mukaeda Katsuma, 81, 185
Murai Kō, 84, 133
Murakami, Mark Y., 188
Murakami Noboru, 168
Murakami, Seigo, 185
Murakami, Mrs. Y., 188
Murakami, Yorimoto, 191
Murano Kōken, 89
Muraoka Suezō, 113
Murata, Lee, 190
Murata, Yae, 189
Mutō Sanji, 38
Myer, Dillon S., 3–4, 192

Nadeshiko, 103
Nagahara Hideaki (Shōson), 125
Nagai Eiko, 127
Nagai Gen, 127
Nagai Hajime, 135
Nagai Matsuzō, 72
Nagami Itoko, 128, 176–177
Nagata, Barton H., 188
Nagata, Kiyoshi, 199
Nagata, Matsusaburo, 187
Nagata Setsuko, 125, 166
Nagata Shigeshi, 38–39, 69–70, 206
Nagura Rakuyō, 113
Naigai Shimpō. See *Tobei Zasshi*
Naitō Keizō, 110
Naka, Harry M., 200
Naka, Kaizo, 200
Nakada, Tadashi, 188
Nakadegawa, Clifford T., 99
Nakadegawa Hatsuko, 99
Nakae, Ruby Tomeo, 186
Nakagaki, Masami, 200
Nakagawa Akiko, 158
Nakagawa Kakutarō, 138
Nakagawa Yoriaki, 113, 158
Nakagawa Zenkyō, 99
Nakagawara, Shikataro, 191
Nakahara Fukuzō, 182
Nakajima, H., 149
Nakamura Baifū, 128, 177
Nakamura, Buntaro, 187
Nakamura, George, 189
Nakamura, Henry Hitoshi, 189
Nakamura Junzō, 90
Nakamura Masatoshi, 81
Nakamura, Nobujiro, 186

Nakamura, Seishiro, 188
Nakamura Tetsuo, 182
Nakamura Tōkichi, 113
Nakane, Kenji, 189
Nakano, Heijiro, 188
Nakano, Togo, 190
Nakashima, Katsuharu, 189, 190
Nakashima Kurō, 62
Nakata, Mitsuo, 190
Nakata, Tadashi, 190
Nakatani, Roy, 190
Nakatani, Soichi, 186, 187
Nakayama Tenji, 109
Nakazawa, Mrs. Ken, 185
Nakazawa Tamaki, 53, 62
Namba, Gin, 191
Nan'eikai, 128
Nanigawa Shin, 39, 53
Nanka Bungei, 125
Nanka Chūō Nihonjinkai, 120
Nanka Chūō Sangyō Kumiai, 85. See also Takahashi Ayako
Nanka Dendōdan, 92
Nanka Fukui Kenjinkai, 81
Nanka Fukuin Jihō, 95
Nanka Fukuoka Kenjinkai, 149
Nanka Fukushima Kenjinkai, 149
Nanka Gakusō, 143
Nanka Hana Ichiba, 84
Nanka Hiroshima Kenjinkai, 149
Nanka Jihō, 136
Nanka Kirisutokyō Kyōkai Remmei, 95
Nanka Kumamoto Kenjinkai, 149
Nanka Kyōikukai, 106
Nanka Miyagi Kenjinkai, 115
Nanka Nagano Kenjinkai, 149
Nanka Nihongo Gakuen Kyōkai, 106
Nanka Nihonjin Kirisutokyō Kyōkai Remmei, 89
Nanka Nihonjin Shōgyō Kaigisho, 86. See also Japanese Chamber of Commerce of Southern California
Nanka Nihonjin Shōgyō Kaigisho Geppō. See *Shōgyō Kaigisho Geppō*
Nanka Nihonjin Shokuryōhinshō Kumiai, 86
Nanka Nikkeijin Shōgyō Kaigisho, 76–77, 149
Nanka Nisshō-dayori, 143
Nanka Okayama-kei Kurabu, 149
Nanka Paionia Kurabu, 149
Nanka Rengō Satōdaikon Kōsakusha Kumiai, 86
Nanka Saga Kenjinkai, 149
Nanka Sangyō Nippō. See *Beikoku Sangyō Nippō*

Nanka Shizuoka Kurabu, 149
Nanka Shōhō, 143
Nanka Shōnien, 113. See also Rosuanzerusugun Nihonjin Jindōkai
Nanka Teiengyō Remmei. See Gādenā no Tomo
Nanka Yamanashi Kenjinkai, 149
Nanka Yamanashi Kurabu, 150
Nankaku Nōgyō Kumiai, 86
Nankaku Nōgyōka Rengō Kyōgikai, 86
Nankaku Shūyōkai, 115
Narizawa Kinpei, 44, 113
Natsume Sōseki, 124, 125
Nepomuceno, Larry A., 200
Neu, Charles E., 5
New Japanese American News Co. See Shin Nichibei
Nichibei Hyōron, 143
Nichibei Jidai, 143
Nichibei Jihō, 136
Nichibei Jiji (Los Angeles), 136
Nichibei Jiji (San Francisco), 136. See also Nichibei Jijisha
Nichibei Jijisha, 146, 206
Nichibei Mainichi, 136–137
Nichibei Shimbun, 134, 137. See also Nichibei Shimbunsha
Nichibei Shimbunsha, 146, 150, 152
Nichibei Shūhō. See Nichibei Jihō
Nichiboku Kyōkai, 206
Niesley, Margaret, 200
Nihon Beifu Kyōkai, 103–104, 110
Nihon Imin Kyōkai, 39, 41
Nihon oyobi Nihonjin. See Nihonjin
Nihon Shingaku, 158
Nihongo Gakuen Kyōdō Shisutemu, 106
Nihongo Gakuen Hensan Iinkai, 109
Nihonjin, 48
Nihonjin Kyōsankai, 181
Nihonjin Rōdō Kyōkai. See Rōdō no Chikara
Nihonjin Yōrōin, 115
Niimura Eiichi, 169
Niimura Yasuhiko, 140
Niisato Kan'ichi, 104, 114, 158, 159, 206–207
Niiyama, George Tanezo, 189
Nikkei Shimin, The, 137
Nimura Yeichi. See Niimura Eiichi
Ninomiya, Tamaki, 187
Nippon to Amerika, 143
Nippon Yoshisa Emigration Company, 36
Nipponjinsha, 150
Nippu Jiji. See Hawai Taimusu
Nippu Jijisha, 146
Nisei Survey Committee, 110
Nishi, Midori, 200
Nishi Rafu Nikkeijin Kyōgikai, 150

Nishi, Setsuko K., 200
Nishimoto, Elmer Y., 190
Nishimura Masamoto, 99–100
Nishimura Yoshio (Kantaishi), 138, 169
Nishinoiri, John I., 200
Nishio, Miyo, 192
Nishioka, Norton O., 200
Nishioka Ryōichi, 169
Nishiyama, Toshihiko P., 200
Nitobe Inazō, 48
Nitta, Charles, 186
Nitta, John, 190
Nitta, Mr. & Mrs. Shosuke, 186
Niwa, Shozo, 190
Nixon, Lucille M., 128
Nobeoka Tsunetarō, 72
Noburo, Mr. & Mrs. S., 186
Noda Otojirō, 159
Nodera, Isamu, 200
Nodohara, Kiichi, 186
Noguchi, Ayako, 177
Nomura Kichisaburō, 161
Nonaka, Frank M., 184
Northern California Japanese Chamber of Commerce, 150
Northern California Japanese Language School Association. See Hokka Nihongo Gakuen Kyōkai
Norton, Tomoko, 191
Nō-Shōmushō Shōkōkyoku, 84
Nō-Shōmushō Suisankyoku, 84
Nozaki Reikai, 100
Nozu, Mr. & Mrs. Paul, 189
Numamoto, Kazuichi Jack, 185
N Y Bungei, 124–125
Nyūyōku Nichibei, 137

Obata Chiura, 169, 187
Oberst, Alma E., 200
O'Brien and Inouye Case, 30
Ochi Dōjun, 77
Oda, Sadahiko, 191
Official Journal, 95
Ōfu Inshi, 159
Ōfu Nippō, 132–133, 137. See also Ōfu Nippōsha
Ōfu Nippōsha, 146
Ogami, Frank, 190
Ogawa, Chieko H., 190
Ogawa, Dennis M., 4
Ogawa, Frank, 187
Ōgawa Jinjō Kōtō Shōgakkō, 39
Ogawa, Thomas Tomihei, 190
Ogden Central Japanese Farmers Association. See Okuden Chūō Nōkai
Ōhashi Kanzō, 77

Ohata, Masanori, 190
Oi Matsunosuke, 169, 186
Oi Tsunehide, 124
Oishi, George, 168
Oishi, H., 150
Oishi, Rui, 187
Oishi, Tom, 168
Oka Naoki, 81
Oka Satotada (Sōshi), 128
Oka, Seizo, 1, 92
Oka Shigeki, 132–133, 137, 169
Oka, Thomas Shinichiro, 187
Oka, Wilfred M., 200
Okada Isaburō, 134
Okada, Noriaki, 189
Okamoto Ichibei, 153
Okamoto Tsuyoshi, 53–54
Okamura Yoshiyuki, 141
Ōkawahira Takamitsu, 39–40
Okayama Prefectural Association, 80, 165
Okayama Women's Society, 80
Okazaki, Robert I., 185
Oki Kenji, 137
Oki, Tom, 189
Okimoto, Daniel I., 10
Okimura, Mr. & Mrs. S., 186
Ōkina Hisamitsu (Rokkei), 159
Ōku, Mr. & Mrs. K., 186
Okubo Shinjirō, 158
Okuda Heiji, 48
Okuden Chūō Nōgyō Kumiai. *See* Okuden Chūō Nōkai
Okuden Chūō Nōkai, 86, 87
Ōkuma Shigenobu, 48–49, 52, 54
Okumiya Takeyuki, 40
Okumura Takie, 54, 99, 100, 159
Ōkura Kihachirō, 48
Olin, Spencer C., Jr., 5
Ōmi Kurabu, 150
Omi Masahiro, 90–91, 97, 100
Omura, Satsuyo, 189
Onishi, Katsumi, 200
Opperman, David R., 201
Orita, Natsuko, 189
Ōsawa Eizō, 134, 139
Osawa, Shigeru, 191
Oshima, Eunice, 189
Oshima, Heizo, 187
Ōshima Kōsei, 62
Ota, George Susumu, 191
Ōtani Naofumi, 159
Otsubo, Shotaro, 187
Ōtsuka Shun'ichi, 139
Otsuki, Mrs. Harry M., 188
Ouchida, Jack T., 190
Ouchida, Kyuda, 190

Outpost, The, 177
Overseas Japanese Conference, 70, 71
Overseas Japanese Educational Association Foundation, 110
Ōwada Yakichi, 45
Ōyama Ujirō, 54–55, 62, 63, 106
Ozaki, Mrs. Jingoro, 189
Ozaki, Norio, 201
Ozawa, Fumio, 151
Ozawa Takao, 28
Ozawa Takeo, 143

Pacific Citizen, 1, 137
Pacific Japanese Methodist Episcopal Church, 93, 95
Pacific Japanese Provisional Annual Conference of the Methodist Church, 95
Packard, Mrs. Everett T., 169–170
Paionia, 174
Pajus, Jean, 6
Panama-Pacific Exposition, 1915, 23, 24, 56, 147
Park, Robert E., 9, 30, 154
Pasadena Nihonjin Yunion Kyōkai Shūhō, 95
Pasadena Union Presbyterian Church, 150
Penrose, Eldon R., 201
Perry, Neal C., 201
Petersen, William, 3
Poetry, 126–131, 175–178 *passim*.
Pokatero Nihonjin Aiyūkai. *See* Pokatero Nihonjin Seinenkai
Pokatero Nihonjin Seinenkai, 115
Pokatero Nihonjinkai, 120
Popii, 177
Popii no Kai, 177
Porterfield and Mizuno Case, 30
Posuton Bungei, 177
Probasco, Barbara, 201
Prohibition Society of Los Angeles. *See* Rafu Kinshukai
Provido, Generoso P., 201
Pugh, Richard L., 201
Pursinger, Marvin G., 10, 201

Rademaker, John A., 190, 201
Rafu Kikaken Kakutoku Kisei Dōmei, 207
Rafu Kinshukai, 116
Rafu Mesojisuto, 95
Rafu Mii Kyōkai Shūhō, 95
Rafu Nichibei, 137–138
Rafu Nihon Ryōjikan, 34, 35
Rafu Nihonjin Jitsugyō Kumiai, 87
Rafu Nihonjin Mii Kyōkai, 92–93, 95
Rafu Nihonjinkai, 120–121
Rafu Nikkeijin Hoteru Apāto Kumiai, 150

Rafu Nikkeijin Kyōgikai, 121
Rafu Shimpō, 51, 71, 138
Rafu Shōjo Kabuki Gekidan, 181
Rafu Tokeishō Kumiai, 87
Rafu Uwa-Machi Dai-Ni Gakuen, 107
Religion: Buddhism, 88–102 *passim.*; Christianity, 88–102 *passim.*; Seichō no Ie, 89, 148, 153; Konkōkyō, 96, 154
Relocation. See Internment
Remon Shisha, 128
Remonchō, 128
Rice, Richard B., 201
Richardson, John M., 201
Rikimaru, Iwasuke, 187
Rikkō, 47
Rikkō Sekai, 46
Rikkōkai, 40, 44, 46, 47
Robbins, Albert M., 201
Rōdō, 138
Rōdō no Chikara, 138
Rōdō Sekai. See *Tobei Zasshi*
Rōdō Shimbun, 172. See also *Kaikyūsen*
Rohwer Outpost, 174
Rohwer Relocator, 174
Rokkī Jihōsha, 77, 150
Rokkī Shimpō, 138
Ross, Robert H., 201
Rosuanzerusu, 143–144
Rosuanzerusu-gun Nihonjin Jindōkai, 116
Rosuanzerusu Nihon Bōeki Konwakai Kaishi, 144
Rōwa Jihō, 174, 177
Rōzubāgu Jihō, 174
Ryū Hatsutarō, 207

Saibara Kiyoaki, 83–84
Saibara Seitō, 9, 48, 83–84, 155. See also Texas Rice Colony
Saigusa Jisaburō, 76–77, 152
Saiki, Johnny Kiyoshi, 192
Sailor's Union of the Pacific, 55
Saito, Akira, 202
Saitō Hiroshi, 207
Saka Hisagorō, 77
Sakaguchi, Katsuhei, 188, 190
Sakahara, Thomas T., 191
Sakai, Sam, 187
Sakai Shizuo, 48
Sakamaki, Shunzo, 202
Sakamoto, James Y., 134
Sakamoto, Kamezuchi, 187
Sakamoto Kiju, 177
Sakamoto, Setsugo, 186
Sakamoto Tomio, 152
Sakata, Jusaburo, 192
Sakata, Toki, 192

Sakurai Guardianship Case, 30
Samuels, Fred, 202
San Fernando Valley Japanese American Community Center, 150
San Francisco Buddhist Church. See Sōkō Bukkyōkai
San Francisco Japanese Chamber of Commerce, 146
San Jose Buddhist Church, 91
San Pidoro Taimusu. See *Minami Engan Jihō*
Sanchūbu Nihonjinkai, 121–122
Sando, Mrs. Wakei, 190
Sansei Keiyukai, 182
Santa Anita Pacemaker, 175
Santa Fe Jihō, 175. See also Santa Fe Jihōsha
Santa Fe Jihōsha, 177
Santa Fe Kirisuto Kyōkai, 178
Santō Jiji, 138
Santō Nihonjinkai, 118
Saruya Kaname, 208
Sasai Shikanosuke, 182
Sasaki, Mitsuko, 190
Sasaki San'ichirō, 207
Sasaki Shūichi (Sasabune), 144, 159–160
Sasaki Suketsugu, 100
Sasaki Yaeko, 100
Sasamori Junzō, 161, 202
Sato, Harry N., 187
Satō Ichizō, 28
Satō Komakichi, 128
Sato, Masanori, 192
Sato, Ray, 189
Satō Tsutae, 107, 207
Satō Yasuji, 81
Sato, Mrs. Yuki, 190
Satow, Masao W., 185
Sauki Ijō, 178
Sawamura, Hachiro, 190
Scene, 144
Schlicher, Reynold J., 202
Scott, Alice J., 202
Seattle Buddhist Church, 91
Seattle Japanese Hotel & Apartment Association, 150
Seattle Japanese Methodist Church, 100. See also *Sha-shi Nihonjin Mii Kyōkai Shūhō*; Shiyatoru Nihonjin Mesojisuto Kyōkai
Second generation, 9, 10, 30, 31, 58, 103–111 *passim.*, 134; studies of, 8; problems of, 69, 103, 104, 114; education of, 96, 103, 110; dual nationality of, 104, 119. See also Japanese American Citizens League; Japanese language schools

Seibu Aidaho Nihonjinkai, 118
Seibu Aidaho-shū Nihonjinkai, 122
Seichō no Ie Honbu, 89
Seimei, 95
Sekiguchi, Kumakichi, 185
Sekiguchi Nobara, 40, 100, 101, 158, 160
Seno Manrō, 81–82
Senryū Tsubame, 128–129
Seto, Toraichi, 191
Shakai Bunko, 72–73
Shakai Seisaku Gakkai, 40
Shakaishugi. See *Tobei Zasshi*
Shakō Nihon Ryōjikan, 35, 65
Sha-shi Nihonjin Mii Kyōkai Shūhō, 95
Shiatoru Nikkeijinkai, 118–119
Shiba Teikichi, 67
Shibata Shuntarō, 207
Shibuya Kinkichi, 170
Shibuzawa Eiichi, 48, 63
Shiga Shigetaka, 40, 48
Shigaki Bujirō, 101, 160
Shigekawa Yoshimasa, 156
Shigematsu, Mine, 187
Shigeno Kinzuchi, 170
Shigeta, Daniel Takeru, 188
Shigetome Tomejirō, 170, 189
Shigezumi, Kyonosuke, 184
Shikamura, Alice H., 202
Shiki, Kenzo, 191
Shima, George. See Ushijima Kinji
Shima, Rindge, 188
Shima Shinkichirō, 129, 170, 185
Shimada, Gozo, 191
Shimada Gunkichi, 55
Shimada Shigeo, 101
Shimanouchi, Toshiro Henry, 185
Shimanuki Hyōdayū, 40, 44, 47, 48. See also Rikkōkai
Shiminken Kakutoku Kisei Dōshikai, 55
Shimizu, Iwao, 184
Shimizu Tōru, 170, 191
Shimizu Tsuruzaburō, 44
Shimojima Takeo, 125
Shimokubo, Paul, 189
Shimomura Hiroshi, 69
Shimoyama Eitarō, 129
Shin Nichibei, 138. See also Shin Nichibei Shimbunsha
Shin Nichibei Shimbunsha, 150–151
Shin Sekai, 151
Shin Sekai Asahi, 151
Shin Sekai Asahi Shimbun. See *Shin Sekai Shimbun*
Shin Sekai Asahi Shimbunsha, 182
Shin Sekai Nichinichi Shimbun. See *Shin Sekai Shimbun*
Shin Sekai Shimbun, 138–139. See also Shin Sekai; Shin Sekai Asahi; Shin Sekai Asahi Shimbunsha; Shin Sekai Shimbunsha
Shin Sekai Shimbunsha, 147, 152, 182
Shin Tenchi, 95
Shinagawa Suetsugu, 182
Shinano Kaigai Kyōkai, 70
Shin-Boku-shū Nissei Kyōkai, 122
Shingu, Jusuke, 187
Shinonome, 132
Shiogi, Sadaji, 190
Shiota, Keiji, 186
Shiozaki Keizō, 71
Shiozawa, Chiyomatsu, 190
Shiozawa, Heijiro, 191
Shiozawa Masatada, 55
Shiraishi Kiyoshi, 95
Shiraishi, Mannosuke, 190
Shirakawa Chōichirō, 160
Shirakawa Saku, 160
Shirogane Genrō, 182
Shishimoto Hachirō, 104
Shito, Tommy Tadayoshi, 192
Shiyatoru Nihonjin Mesojisuto Kyōkai, 91
Shiyatoru Tankakai, 129
Shōansei, 45
Shōgyō Jihō, 144. See also Shōgyō Jihōsha
Shōgyō Jihōsha, 147
Shōgyō Kaigisho Geppō, 144
Shokumin Jihō. See *Shokumin Kyōkai Hōkoku*
Shokumin Kyōkai, 46
Shokumin Kyōkai Hōkoku, 46–47
Slocum, Sally, 186
Smith, Frank H., 93
Smith, Mildred J., 202
Smith, Robert J., 10–11
Smith, William C., 8
Smyser, Adam A., 188
Socialists and communists, 10, 47, 71, 72–73, 85, 133, 134, 169, 172, 207
Société Anonyme le Nickle, 36
Soeda Juichi, 97
Soejima Hachirō, 134, 139
Soejima Michimasa, 55, 63, 67
Sōga Makoto, 129
Sōga Yasutarō (Keihō), 129, 141, 160
Sōkō Bijutsu Zakkashō Dōmeikai, 85
Sōkō Bukkyōkai, 91
Sōkō Jiji, 139
Sōkō Nihon Ryōjikan, 35
Sōkō Nihon Shimbun. See *Japan Herarudo*
Sōkō Shimbun. See *Sōkō Shimpō*
Sōkō Shimpō, 139
Sōkō Shūhō, 139
Sōkō Taimusu, 172

Somekawa, Arthur Ichiro, 191
Sone, Monica, 9
Southern California Educational Society. See Nanka Kyōikukai
Southern California Flower Market. See Nanka Hana Ichiba
Southern California Japanese Historical Society, 76
Southern California Japanese Language School Association, 105
Southern California Japanese Retail Grocers and Merchants' Association, 143
Southern Colorado Character Building Society. See Nankaku Shūyōkai
Sowers, Lloyd E., 202
Speier, Matthew R., 202
Spicer, Edward H., 3
Sports, 112, 113, 114
Staniford, Philip S., 202
Stearns, Marjorie R., 10
Steiner, Jesse F., 7
Stemen, John R., 202
Stier, Wilhelm R.F., 202
Strong, Edward K., 8
Stroup, Dorothy A., 203
Sturge, Ernest A., 101
Suehiro, Eiji, 101
Suehiro, Roy M., 188
Suehiro Shigeo, 48, 55, 56, 59, 64, 67
Suenaga, Michisuke James, 187
Suenaga, Richard, 189
Sugai, George, 190
Sugimachi Yaemitsu, 106, 109
Sugimoto, Etsu Inagaki, 9
Sugiyama, Ichiji, 186, 187
Sumi, Torajiro, 186
Sumida, Masako, 184
Survey of Race Relations, 30, 154
Suski, Peter M. See Susuki Sakae
Susuki Sakae, 160–161, 170
Sutanisurausu Nihonjinkai, 122
Sutō Kōtarō, 170
Sutōji Zenshū Kankōkai, 101
Suzuki Bansaburō, 152
Suzuki Bunji, 39
Suzuki Hansaburō, 56
Suzuki Kakuichirō (Mugen), 125
Suzuki, Nobuko, 191
Suzuki Rokuhiko, 78
Suzuki Saburō, 64
Suzuki Shichirō, 107
Svensrud, Marian, 203

Tachibana, 129
Tachibana Ginsha, 129–130

Tacoma Japanese Methodist Church. See Takoma Nihonjin Mesojisuto Kyōkai
Taguchi Kichimatsu, 171
Taiheiyō Engan Nihonjinkai Kyōgikai, 122
Taihoku Nippō, 139
Tairiku Nippōsha, 207–208
Taishū, 139
Taiyō, 48
Tajima, Hikoichi, 187
Tajima, Masumi, 185
Tajima, Paul J., 203
Takada, Roy R., 190
Takagi, Shintaro, 191. See also Takaki Shintarō
Takahashi Ayako, 161, 186
Takahashi Chinko, 96
Takahashi Chiyokichi, 171
Takahashi, Chuji Roy, 191
Takahashi, Henry Moriya, 187
Takahashi, Kyojiro, 203
Takahashi Kyōka, 130
Takahashi, Margaret O'Brien, 185
Takahashi Rien, 101–102
Takahashi Sakuei, 48, 49, 68
Takahashi, Shichizo, 191
Takahashi, Shizuko, 9
Takahashi Sozan, 124. See also Takahashi Kyōka
Takaki Shintarō, 79. See also Takagi, Shintaro
Takamine Jōkichi, 9, 48
Takano, Bunji, 189
Takano, Yasutaro, 186
Takashima, Newton Noboru, 189
Takeda Hisatarō, 137
Takeda Jun'ichi, 82
Takeda, Tsutomu, 188
Takehara Yasutami, 102
Takei Nekketsu, 78
Takekoshi Yosaburō, 49
Takemoto, Kay, 187
Takenaka, Benjamin Kengo, 189
Takeshita, Lillian Katsuyo, 192
Takeshita, Shizuma, 187
Takeshita, Thomas K., 208
Taketa, Henry, 9
Takeuchi Kōjirō, 78, 139
Takeuchi Kōsuke, 78
Takeyasu, Shigematsu, 185
Takoma Jihō, 139–140
Takoma Nihonjin Mesojisuto Kyōkai, 91
Takoma Nihonjinkai, 78, 122–123
Takoma Shūhō. See *Takoma Jihō*
Takoma Shūhōsha, 78–79
Tamagawa, Frank, 190
Tamai Yoshitaka, 110, 188, 190

Tamaki, Seiichi, 191
Tamaki, Tom, 190
Tamamoto Shūyō, 107
Tamano, 130
Tamura Heishi, 40–41
Tan, Lien-piao, 203
Tana, Tomoe, 128
Tanabe, Eiji, 114
Tanabe Sannojō, 107
Tanaka Akihira, 182
Tanaka Chūho, 182
Tanaka, Isuke, 186
Tanaka Masaharu (Shūrin), 159–160, 177
Tanaka Ryōryō, 125
Tanaka, Tamiko, 203
Tanaka, Togo, 144
Tanaka, Tomokichi, 186
Tanforan Totalizer, 175
Tārakku Fujinkai, 116
Tārakku Jitsugyōkai, 87
Tārakku Nihongo Gakuen, 107
Tārakku Shakō Kurabu, 116
Tashiro, Benjamin M., 188
Tekisasu Shisha, 178
Temmei, 95–96
tenBroek, Jacobus, 5
Tenjū Jihō, 175
Terakawa Hōkō, 89–90
Terasawa, Mrs. Kuniko, 190
Terrace and Nakatsuka Case, 30
Terui Heikichi, 28
Texas Rice Colony, 9, 22, 43, 48, 49, 68, 83–84, 85, 155
Thomas, Dorothy S., 10
Thompson, Richard A., 203
Thomson, James C., Jr., 11
Thomson, Ruth H., 203
Tobei Kyōkai, 43, 47
Tobei Shimpō, 47
Tobei Zasshi, 47
Toda, Hatsugoro, 191
Toda Shinzō, 152
Toda Shirō, 138
Tōga Yoichi, 73, 90, 102, 183
Togasaki, George Kiyoshi, 186
Tōgasaki Kikumatsu, 161
Togawa Akira, 130
Tōgō Minoru, 41, 64
Toji Seiichi, 208
Tokichi, Kaz, 189
Tokioka, Masayuki, 188
Tokunaga, Donald Ayashi, 188
Tokunaga, Shigao, 190, 191
Tokunaga, Shinkichi, 188
Tokushima Kenjinkai, 114, 116
Tokuyama Jitsutarō, 176

Tōkyō Keizai Zasshi, 48–49
Tōkyō Kōseisha, 42
Tomimoto Iwao, 82, 161
Tomita Gentarō, 45
Tomita Ken'ichi, 208
Tomo, 96
Tomori Mokuo, 79
Topāzu Jihō, 175
Topāzu Shōhi Kumiai, 178
Torai Jun'ichi, 73
Tōsha Katsuji, 208
Totsukuni Tankakai, 130
Tottori Kurabu, 151
Town Crier, 140, 151, 163
Toyama, Chotoku, 203
Tōyama Kyūzō, 156
Toyama, Masa, 186
Tōyama Tetsuo, 142
Tōyō Keizai Shimpō, 49
Toyota Hidemitsu, 28
Toyota Kame, 171, 190
Toyota Seitarō, 171
Tri-State Buddhist Church, 91–92
Tsubame Ginsha, 129
Tsuboi, Naoko, 190
Tsuboi, Teruo, 190
Tsuchiya, Kiyotsugu, 185
Tsuchiya Seiichi, 144
Tsuda, Tatsuhei, 192
Tsuda Yasaburō, 171
Tsuji, Mrs. Haru, 190
Tsujihara, K., 187
Tsujimichi, Chika, 189
Tsukamaki, Ben, 190
Tsumori, Yasuji, 184
Tsunashima Kakichi, 56–57
Tsuneishi Shisei, 130
Tsuneya Moriyuki, 41
Tsunoda, Noboru, 188
Tsunoda Ryūsaku, 102, 114
Tsurare-gun Nihonjinkai, 119
Tsurutani Jirōkichi, 161
Tsūshō Isan, 49
Tsuyuki Sōzō, 82
Tupper, Eleanor, 5
Turlock Farm Corporation, 87
Turlock Japanese Language School. *See* Tārakku Nihongo Gakuen
Turlock Women's Society. *See* Tārakku Fujinkai
Tuthill, Gretchen L., 203

Uchida Sadatsuchi, 41, 48
Uchida, Take, 191
Uehara Etsujirō, 39, 67
Uemura Tora, 73

Ujifusa, Harry, 188
Umeda, Masao, 186
Umemura, Charles J., 191. *See also* Umemura Jūzō
Umemura Jūzō, 114
United Farmers' Association of Southern Colorado. *See* Nankaku Nōgyōka Rengō Kyōgikai
United States Immigration Commission, 6, 9
United States-Japan relations, 19–68 *passim.*; English studies of, 5–7; historiography of, 11; Gentlemen's Agreement, 1907–1908, 21, 23, 24; treaties and conventions, 22–24, 30, 61, 67; Washington Conference on Arms Limitation, 1921–1922, 51, 53. *See also* Emigration; Japanese exclusion movement
United States Library of Congress, 13 *n.*
United States National Archives, 13 *n.*
United States War Relocation Authority, 13 *n.*
Uono, Kiyoshi, 203
Uriu, Bob, 190
Uriu, Mrs. Hatsui, 190
Ushijima Kinji, 48, 80, 155, 159
Ushio, Mataju, 191
Usuda Masaaki (Tenjōshi), 178
Usuda Yōko, 178
Utah Nippo, The, 151. See also *Yuta Nippō*
Uyehara, Cecil H., 14, 19
Uyeki, Eugene S., 203
Uyeyama, Tomiyo, 187

Vancouver Japanese Language School, 207
Versailles Peace Conference, 51, 52, 54

Wada, Kango, 190
Wada Seikai, 102
Wagatsuma, Hiroshi, 10
Wailuku Japanese Language School. *See* Wairuku Gakuen
Waipafu Gakuen Kōyūkai, 107
Waipahu Japanese Language School. *See* Waipafu Gakuen Kōyūkai
Wairuku Gakuen, 108
Wairuku Nihonjinkai, 123
Wakabayashi Heitarō, 57
Wakamatsu, S., 188
Wakatsuki Cabinet, 38
Wakayama-ken, 70–71
Wapato Japanese Methodist Church, 94
Wasa Rinko, 96
Washinton-fu Nihonjinkai, 123
Washizu Bunzō (Shakuma), 57
Wassonbiru Uesutobyū Chōrō Kyōkai, 91

Watada Matajirō, 91–92, 188, 190
Watanabe, Harry, 189
Watanabe Kanjirō, 45
Watanabe, Kiyoko, 189
Watanabe, Mike, 189
Watanabe Minojirō, 57
Watanabe, Rokuro, 185
Watanabe Shichirō, 79
Watanabe, Shinichi, 203
Watanabe Shirō, 45
Watanabe Sōsaburō, 94
Watanabe Tomo'ichi, 102
Watari Tokuji, 139
Watsonville Westview Presbyterian Church. *See* Wassonbiru Uesutobyū Chōrō Kyōkai
Wax, Rosalie, H., 203
Wesley, Newton K., 189
West Los Angeles Community Methodist Church, 92, 151
Weston, Rubin F., 204
Whitney, Helen E., 204
Wilson, Robert A., 12
Wisend, William F., 204
Wittke, Carl, 7
Women, 97, 105, 113, 116, 126, 127, 144. *See also* Immigrant society
Woodbury, Robert L., 204
Woodrow, Wilson, 66
Woolston, Katherine D., 204
World's Parliament of Religion, 89

Yada, Misao, 190
Yagi, Thomas Seikichi, 188
Yaguchi, Tsugio, 191
Yakima Indian Reservation, 28
Yakima Nihonjinkai, 79
Yamabe, Arthur, 186
Yamada Akiyoshi, 137
Yamada, Clifford, 187
Yamada Fudesaburō, 41
Yamada, Mrs. M., 188
Yamada Saburō, 67
Yamada Sakuji, 136
Yamada, Tamaichi, 189, 190
Yamada Tatsumi, 104
Yamagida, Toshiro, 189
Yamaguchi, Gonai, 191
Yamaguchi Tadashi, 171, 191
Yamaguchi, Yoneto, 188
Yamaki Akikazu, 57
Yamamoto Asako, 141, 161–162
Yamamoto, Ben Suekichi, 186
Yamamoto, Eiichi, 187
Yamamoto, George K., 204
Yamamoto Kumatarō, 42
Yamamoto, Leo, 189

Yamamoto Miono, 42
Yamamoto, Mr. & Mrs. Tom Shioji, 192
Yamamuro Buho, 162
Yamanaka Chūji, 57–58, 64
Yamanashi Prefectural Association, 79–80
Yamane Goichi, 45
Yamaoka Ototaka, 48, 79
Yamasaki, Shunsaku, 186
Yamashita Kihei, 171
Yamashita Shintarō, 183
Yamashita Sōen, 71, 104, 110, 114
Yamato. See *Hawai Taimusu*
Yamato Masao, 139
Yamato Shimbun. See *Hawai Taimusu*
Yamauchi, Chester M., 114
Yamazaki Yasushi, 208
Yamazaki Yasushi-ō Denki Hensankai, 208
Yanagita, Yuki, 204
Yano, Mr. & Mrs. G., 191
Yashima, Taro, 9
Yasuda Hakuhanshi, 130
Yasui Matsuno, 131, 171, 188
Yasui, Minoru, 188, 192
Yasui, Ray T., 189
Yasui Satosuke (Shōsō), 131, 136, 171
Yasukochi, Hiro, 191
Yatsu Riichirō, 82
Yatsu, Taichi, 189
Yego, Masayuki "Hike," 186
Yei, Toriko, 191
Yogi, Kintaro, 189
Yokohama Specie Bank, 24
Yokomizo, James Matsuo, 185
Yokota, Roy Y., 189
Yokota, Mrs. S., 188
Yokoyama Gennosuke, 162

Yonai, Teizo, 185
Yoneda, Karl, 1, 72, 184. See also Yoneda, Kāru
Yoneda, Kāru, 85, 172
Yoneda Minoru, 48, 58–60, 64, 65, 108
Yoritomo, Sojiro, 188
Yoshida, Gohachi, 191
Yoshida, Jim, 10
Yoshida, Yosaburo, 8
Yoshiike Hiroshi, 159
Yoshikawa, Kenjiro, 187
Yoshimura Daijirō, 45, 46, 85
Yoshimura, Saburoji, 191
Yoshiwara, Shigeru, 186
Yoshizu, Takeyuki, 188
Young, Clarence K., 204
Young, Hobart N., 204
Young Men's Buddhist Association of Honolulu. See Hawai Bukkyō Seinenkai
Yuki Sangaku, 178
Yuki Shōjirō, 92
Yumiba, Carole K., 204
Yūsa Keizō (Hanboku), 131
Yuta Nippō, 140. See also *Utah Nippo, The*
Yuta-shū Nihonjinkai, 123

Zaibei Fujin no Tomo, 144
Zaibei Fujin Shimpō, 97
Zaibei Nihonjin Rengō Kyōgikai, 119
Zaibei Nihonjinkai, 73–74, 119, 123
Zaibei Rōdō Shimbun, 172. See also *Kaikyūsen*
Zai-Shakō Nihon Ryōjikan. See Shakō Nihon Ryōjikan
Zald, Mayer N., 204
Zenshin, 178